Ideological Lunacy

Bernadette & Michael,

Stay RIGHT always!

Eric @ Tygrrr Express

Ideological Lunacy

A politically conservative and morally liberal Hebrew
alpha male watches crazed liberal swelled botoxed heads
explode trying to dislodge them from their (redacted).

eric aka the TYGRRRR EXPRESS

IDEOLOGICAL LUNACY
A POLITICALLY CONSERVATIVE AND MORALLY LIBERAL
HEBREW ALPHA MALE WATCHES CRAZED LIBERAL
SWELLED BOTOXED HEADS EXPLODE TRYING TO
DISLODGE THEM FROM THEIR (REDACTED).

iUniverse books may be ordered through booksellers or by contacting:

iUniverse
1663 Liberty Drive
Bloomington, IN 47403
www.iuniverse.com
1-800-Authors (1-800-288-4677)

ISBN: 978-1-4917-6339-1 (sc)
ISBN: 978-1-4917-6340-7 (hc)
ISBN: 978-1-4917-6338-4 (e)

Library of Congress Control Number: 2015905875

Print information available on the last page.

iUniverse rev. date: 5/20/2015

Eric is the brilliance (God bless declining standards) behind *The Tygrrrr Express*, the 2007 Bloggers Choice Award for Most Passionate Fan Base.

He is also the author of the political books *Ideological Bigotry, Ideological Violence, Ideological Idiocy* and the religious book *Jewish Lunacy*.

The Tygrrrr Express has been published in the *Washington Times, Jewish Journal, RealClearPolitics Online, Commentary Magazine Online*, and on the Web sites of Hugh Hewitt, Mark Steyn, and Andrew Breitbart's *Big Hollywood*.

A sought after public speaker, he has addressed many chapters of the College Republicans, Young Republicans, Republican Jewish Coalition, and the most powerful people on Earth, the ladies of the Republican Women's Federated.

A radio host since 1992, his radio beginning was a sophomoric hard rock music program entitled *Hard as a Rock*. Maturation eventually settled in (some disagree), and serious radio interviews with top politicos and other notables ensued. On the flip side of the microphone, *The Tygrrrr Express* has been a radio guest of Sean Hannity, Hugh Hewitt, Dennis Miller, Armstrong Williams and many others.

Interviews with many notable politicians and candidates ensued.

Honors and privileges include sleeping for an entire week in a sports bar with full access to the beverages and pizza, in addition to meeting many hot Republican Jewish brunettes.

Often referred to as a typical white person, *The Tygrrrr Express* aspires to be the editor of the yet to be created *Average Non-descript Caucasoid Monthly*.

About: *The Tygrrrr Express* is me. I am Brooklyn born, Strong Island raised, and currently living the good life in Los Angeles.

I am a former stockbrokerage and oil professional. While Wall Street is forever in my blood, I left it in 2009 for the full-time speaking circuit.

I like politics, the National Football League, '80s hard rock music, stocks, and red meat. Speaking and writing is a shameless ploy to get what I really want, to impregnate a Republican Jewish brunette. A ceremony will occur several months beforehand since my parents are NRA members.

The only political issue more important than killing taxes is killing terrorists. I do not sing "Kumbaya" with Islamofascists or leftists. Scorched earth is my approach, with the grace and subtlety of a battering ram. The events of 9/11 fuel my emotions every day. Civilization must defeat barbarism. My generation is up to the challenge. We will win the War on Terror, because we are Americans.

eric aka *The Tygrrrr Express*

To Borah Van Dormolen, the toughest Republican woman I ever met. She taught me that when a GOP lady calls you at an odd hour, it is because she can. When my telephone rang at 4:00 a.m. and I saw the number, I immediately picked up and said, "Yes ma'am!" She replied, "Good. You're learning."

Borah, you were the best. R.I.P.

Warning: This book was written between April of 2010 and April of 2015. Luckily nothing happened during that time to alter perceptions about anything. For the sake of keeping the material fresh, references to President Franklin Delano Roosevelt were removed. It is my hope the Democrat Party will follow my example and offer some fresh ideas of their own. When told of my request, liberal operatives responded, "Why start now?"

Contents

Chapter 0: A Crazed From the Get-go Foreword

My first three books discussed my beliefs without offering a window into my personal life. That trend will continue since beliefs matter more. Far too many people confuse taking selfies and celebrating their being with actually doing something. I am just a guy. I put on my pants one leg at a time when not walking around town pantsless. One day I will be less than a footnote to history. God willing my ideas and beliefs will make a much bigger impact.

Private. That sums up my family. They have so many questions about me that they cannot begin to ask about you. I would ask about you but I have a ton of questions about me as well. Too much free time once had me waking up screaming that I was French. Some guy was chasing me as I yelled, "I don't want to wear a beret. Leave me alone. I am American." No nightmare since has been as awful. Without love and laughter, there is no life. If I can get a stiff person to lighten up and smile, mission accomplished. Getting an imbecile to think is a bonus.

In *Ideological Bigotry* I explained why the left hates the right. We exist and breathe air. Think about how Palesimians feel about Jews. That is the liberal pathology that fosters their attitude toward conservatives. Liberals put all conservatives into one of two categories, evil or stupid. *Ideological Violence* and *Ideological Idiocy* detailed the two ways the left uses ideological bigotry to try and dehumanize us.

Ideological Lunacy is what happens to the left when their worst plans inevitably fail. The world is on fire. Islamofascists are trying to spread a worldwide caliphate. Terrorists are running wild. There is global financial instability. Conservatives are busy trying to save the world from domestic and foreign threats. Liberals led by rich white leftists are worried about temperature changes in a world God created and the name of a football team. Issues they pretend to care about are forgotten once they are elected.

Liberals care about nonsense. They spread nonsense by governing badly. Then they lash out at normal Americans for rejecting their nonsense and calling them out on their arrogance. Never introspective, always making excuses, and consistently screaming their righteousness, liberals deep down know they need detox. From pointy-headed witless academics to celebrity bimbos, *Ideological Lunacy* calls out the craziest people in society and attempts to teach them how to act normal. Whether your favorite charity is Burn the Forests or Molotov Mocktails for Metrosexuals, the political spectrum has space for you. Have some dead cow and some sugar-flavored carbonation and enjoy this book. For the perpetually angry left, this is an intervention.

Welcome to *Ideological Lunacy*. Welcome to *The Tygrrrr Express*.

eric

Chapter 1: Ideological Lunacy

Sane people look at what matters in this world and try to come up with practical solutions to problems. Crazy people take an issue only they care about and try to force the rest of the world to care. American liberals truly went off the deep end of a pool that contained no water. The water was most likely not there because some flaky California liberal wanted to conserve it for the Delta Smelt.

After hitting their collective heads, they blamed President George W. Bush, Sarah Palin, Rush Limbaugh and *Fox News* for not passing legislation that banned going off the deep end. The left then decided that the only solution was to ban all swimming pools to protect the children.

This is far from an exaggeration. Some public schools banned freeze tag and kickball for promoting something that offended somebody, somewhere.

The issue is not that the left fails at virtually everything. What matters is that they never learn. They then attack the majority of people who do understand the simplest things in life.

Ideological lunacy is their guide. The conservative response is to call it out, offer practical solutions, and have a ton of fun along the way.

Leftists, Islamofascists, and perpetual outrage

Most people wake up, go to work, come home, spend time with their families, and quietly live their lives. They keep on keeping on, earn what they keep and appreciate life. Two groups of people live in a perpetual state of rage. Inflicting misery on others is how they derive happiness. This is the world of leftists and Islamofascists.

Whenever these thin-skinned groups are criticized, the inevitable charges come through. The critics are racists, sexists, bigots, homophobes, infidels, blasphemers, and other epithets that lost their meaning years ago.

When those epithets fail, critics are labeled biased. I am an opinion columnist. Of course I am biased. I'm also right. Leftists and Islamofascists cannot get through a day without savaging the rest of the world.

With Islamofascists, any criticism of their God or religion is a capital offense. Judaism has thrived for thousands of years by being self-critical, sometimes overly so. Radical Islam disallows any criticism. Radical Islam leads to violent and short-term victories when weak-kneed Western jellyfish enablers allow it. Radical Islam proves destructive in the long run. Israel has made spectacular advances in law, medicine, and technology while many Arab Muslim nations are held hostage by Islamofascists who remain mired in seventh century barbarism.

This is how Islamofascists are able to take an American ambassador and murder him in cold blood. This is how Islamofascists can burn down American embassies and consulates. This is how they can rape, beat, stone, and hack off heads without the slightest moral concerns. Their behavior is justified because they are offended. Leftists feed into this psychotic behavior by blaming Western culture. Most people never saw the movie that supposedly sparked Benghazi but heard from somebody they do not know in real life that it was offensive.

Could it possibly be that the Islamofascists were offended to begin with? Did enablers simply guess reasons why until they found something fitting their predetermined narrative? Islamofascists are offended. They wake up angry. So do leftists. Water is wet. It is a given.

Anybody insulting demigod Barack Obama or his supporters is a blasphemer who must be destroyed. The veracity of the critical statements is irrelevant. Merely uttering them is a capital offense. Vigorous debate that could strengthen critics and defenders alike is discarded. Intellectually rigorous thought is tossed aside in favor of rigid, inflexible, unbending leftist groupthink.

Media liberals are more upset by critics blaming failed Obama policies for the death of an American ambassador than they are about the actual death of the American ambassador. They are more upset by Mitt Romney implying liberal Obama voters are parasites than the fact that many liberal Obama voters actually are parasites.

Liberals yell at me for pointing out Obama's policies have resulted in colossal failure. They should be angry with Obama for actually enacting the failure. Liberals are angry at me for pointing out that Sandra Fluke is a drain on society who demands free stuff at my expense. They should be angry with her for demanding it.

They are angry with me when I point out that Chicago public schoolteachers are useless individuals failing to help young children. They should be angry at what actually happens to the children.

Shooting the messenger cannot work forever, because the Internet has created an explosion of messengers. When leftist Occupy Wall Street protesters or Hamas and Hezbollah terrorists resort to violence, evidence can surface instantaneously. When tea partiers are accused of violence, a lack of visual evidence anywhere also speaks volumes.

Leftists and Islamofascists thrive because other ideologies do not resort to their tactics. They can spread chaos knowing others will act in an orderly manner.

Normal people get it wrong when they try to apply social norms and standards to those who lack any boundaries. Most cultures and ideologies see dissenters as human beings in a world filled with differing ways of existing. Leftists and Islamofascists do not allow, respect, or tolerate dissent. Those refusing to worship the leftist or Islamofascist supreme leader face everything from ostracism and ridicule to murder.

Leftists and Islamofascists are bullies. The only thing bullies understand is force.

With leftists, point out that everything they believe in has failed. The end of the Chicago teachers' strike meant students could return to being condemned to a life of misery unless they are lucky enough to get shot or stabbed in school early on. Chicago teachers who truly care about their students should quit so the school folds and the children enter charter schools.

Shame the various activists in the leftist coalition. The environmental and animal rights movements are riddled with fraud and would rather lash out than fix themselves. They want to clean the world but cannot clean their own houses. Leftists are slowly killing civilization through terrible schools, anti-business policies, worship of trees and animals at the expense of human beings, and government handouts from birth until death that rob humans of their last shred of dignity.

Islamofascists at least act with efficiency, quickly murdering anyone who gets in the way. The solution for them is much simpler. They must be obliterated from Earth. That is done through the use of munitions.

American society need not determine the root causes of why leftists and Islamofascists are outraged. We must not surrender faster than we can giggle about the French resistance.

French satirists posted cartoons of Mohammed. Islamofascists screamed and then murdered the satirists. The French left acted like themselves and entered full groveling apology mode.

Leftist and Islamofascist outrage is permanent. They are incapable of introspection and unwilling to moderate their anger. Shining a light on them does not work. The only hope for light for the rest of us is by defeating them.

What conservatives and liberals care about

Conservatives fight for what matters. Liberals focus on nonsense. The evidence is unmistakable.

Conservatives: Prepared to do whatever it takes to eradicate radical Islam.

Liberals: Prepared to do whatever it takes to eradicate Walmart.

Conservatives: Willing to intervene to stop terror in Iraq, Iran and Syria.

Liberals: Willing to intervene to change the Washington Redskins name.

Conservatives: Worried that the real global economy is collapsing and determined to help put human beings back to work.

Liberals: Worried that human workers cause climate change and determined to lay off as many workers as it takes to save a few trees based on junk science and fraud.

Conservatives: Understand that businesses cannot hire people and workers cannot find work when government policies depress hiring.

Liberals: Want to spend billions to build windmills paid for by a decreasing number of taxpayers.

Conservatives: Determined to stop Iran from building nuclear bombs and blowing up the world.

Liberals: Determined to stop Israelis from building houses on their own land.

Conservatives: See religious zealotry in the Muslim Brotherhood taking non-Muslims and murdering them.

Liberals: See religious zealotry in socially conservative Christians taking non-Christians and preaching love thy neighbor.

Conservatives: Try to help farmers till their land and get their water so the entire country can eat.

Liberals: Try to protect snail darters while farms fold and people starve.

Conservatives: Passionate about developing energy sources like oil that actually work.

Liberals: Passionate about freeing enslaved Americans from work so they can become hopelessly dependent on government.

Conservatives: Dedicated to increasing entrepreneurship, the gateway to job growth and financial freedom.

Liberals: Dedicated to increasing unions and the minimum wage, which produces nothing and hurts growth.

Conservatives: Want healthcare to be a choice between a patient and their physician.

Liberals: Want a government takeover of the healthcare system, reducing the quality and leading to rationing.

Conservatives: Encourage religious liberty from government.

Liberals: Encourage drug use.

Conservatives: See social disorder and societal threats coming from problems in the inner cities of Detroit and Chicago.

Liberals: See social disorder and societal threats coming from the Koch Brothers hiring people and paying them decent wages.

Conservatives: Reduce crime by spreading the ancient ethos of biblical respect for God, country, and neighbor.

Liberals: Remove bibles from hotel rooms for fear the book may jump out of the desk and force someone to read it.

Conservatives: Preserve the integrity of elections.

Liberals: Legalize mass numbers of illegal immigrants and reducing felonies to misdemeanors to increase the number of people voting for Democrats. Block attempts to remove dead people and other illegal voters from the rolls by calling it bigotry.

Conservatives: Want more free speech for everyone and vigorous discussions of issues.

Liberals: Want speech regulated to suppress non-liberal opinions. This includes regulating print, radio, television, and Internet communications through the Fairness Doctrine, net neutrality by the FCC, and the IRS targeting people engaging in their right to public assembly.

Conservatives: Worry about people struggling to feed families and put gasoline in their cars.

Liberals: Worry what name to use when their ideas fail. Progressives became liberals and then back to progressives trying to put a new name on failure.

Conservatives: Determined to stand up to al-Qaeda.

Liberals: Determined to suck up to France.

The conservative coalition: Individuals who unite on a coherent philosophy of cutting taxes and reducing spending to increase economic growth. They want to aggressively kill terrorists. A stronger economy and safer world benefits everybody. Conservatives want to be left alone to live their lives and allow people who disagree with them to live those alternate lives as well.

The liberal coalition: A disparate group of activists who want to change virtually everything despite most people not caring about liberal priorities. Most liberal obsessions reduce growth and contribute nothing to national security. Liberal activists have to force their agenda on everybody else by stifling dissenting opinions. Most liberal groups including abortion, gay rights and animal rights activists have issues that appeal directly to very narrow slices of the population. Liberals tend to lash out at people who disagree with them and even at anybody neutral trying to live quietly. This leads to liberals committing physical and verbal violence in the name of the greater good.

Why liberals resort to violence

Seattle, Colorado, Wisconsin, Michigan, Missouri and New York are a few of many areas where liberal mobs frequently descended into violence and chaos. Occupy Wall Street, pro-marijuana advocates (who are supposed to be mellow) and anti-WTO protesters led mob scenes that were anything but peaceful. In New York City and Ferguson, Missouri, phony slogans like, "Hands up, don't shoot"[1] led to more social disorder. Lansing union thugs celebrated 12/12/12 by abusing Michigan hot dog vendor Clinton Tarver for selling food to conservatives.[2] These occurrences all have a common thread that is anything but coincidental. The violent perpetrators were all leftists.

The myth is that both sides do it. Despite right-wing statistical aberrations, most American violence emanates from the left. The very leftists calling for civility are the ones spreading the most hate.

If one combed thousands of hours of Sean Hannity or Bill O'Reilly speeches, researchers would struggle to find one example of true hatred. Finding leftist hatred takes seconds. Look up Keith Olbermann, Ed Schultz, E.J. Dionne, Paul Krugman, Al Sharpton and many others.[3]

Liberals claim moral equivalence to stifle truthful analysis. This promotes laziness. Conservatives are virtually blameless. The left owns and exacerbates verbally and physically violent conflict because they want, need and love violent conflict. This is due to their emotional wiring and the situation on the ground.

Conservatives generally want policy discussions because we disagree with liberals. Liberals need gutter politics because they despise conservatives personally. There are two explanations for this, one warm-blooded and one cold-blooded.

The warm-blooded explanation is God. There are more religious conservatives than liberals and more secular liberals than conservatives. Belief in a higher power telling you to love your neighbor, feed the poor, house the hungry, and live honorably increases the chances of people doing that. Secularists falsely believe religious people are a threat.

This explanation is flawed because crossover exists. Atheists and agnostics can live nobly. Religious hypocrites exist. The warm-blooded theory feels good but the cold-blooded theory works better.

Conservatives want impersonal politics for a calculating reason. We lose at personalized politics. Always. This is a center-right country. We do fine discussing policy. Most Americans want lower taxes, more freedom and liberty, and limited regulation. The welfare state is unpopular. Hand-ups are preferred to handouts.

Criminals and terrorists are the bad guys, law enforcement the good guys. The rights of victims should trump the rights of villains. Americans support capital punishment. Bill Clinton won the White House by talking tough on crime, supporting welfare reform and capital punishment, and preaching tax cuts. Barack Obama ran as a centrist, hiding his liberalism. Moderate supporters liked him personally, but did not necessarily agree with him on issues.

The left loses most policy debates, leading them to engage in the politics of personal destruction. Many liberals see conservatives as inhuman, so demonizing them as stupid or evil is inbounds. Saul Alinsky's *Rules for Radicals* teaches leftists to polarize and personalize.[4]

How can people improve society using such behavioral guidelines? Liberals cannot credibly say everyone should tone it down when their electoral survival depends on ripping conservatives and their loved ones to shreds.

Policy is impersonal. Personal polarization divides people, the antithesis of unity. The left does this because it often works. Like any bully, they then get more emboldened. Why debate policy when you can call somebody a racist, sexist, Nazi, Fascist, homophobic pig wanting dead seniors and starving children?

Liberal Alec Baldwin once said he wanted to take the late conservative Henry Hyde and "stone him to death."[5]

There were zero attacks on Obama's lovely children, yet routine cheap shots were taken at the Palin children including Down syndrome baby Trig.[6]

I was even drawn into controversy by liberals desperate to harm Sarah Palin. I was one of several speakers at an event featuring Palin on September 3, 2011 in Indianola, Iowa.

My exact unedited remarks were the same ones I had said at many conservative gatherings to sustained applause.

"Liberals should love Sarah Palin. She has a beautiful, adorable special needs child that she takes care of while balancing everything else. Liberals should worship Sarah Palin and adopt her as one of their own because liberals are an entire ideology of special needs children. Every word out of their mouths is 'gimme, gimme, I need, I want, I deserve, I'm entitled.' No, you don't. When you're two years old it's mildly adorable. When you're sixty-two like Hillary Clinton, Barbara Boxer and the Pelosiraptor, it's intolerable."

The Indianola crowd cheered wildly. The video is there for all to see. I ad-libbed one more line. "Unlike Trig, they're not lovable."

A 22-year old *CNN* neophyte trying to imitate a reporter opened the leftist floodgates. Dan Merica neglected to mention in his column that he used to work for Democrat Senator Harry Reid and *NPR*. The former *National Palestinian Radio* worker took delight in going after a Jewish conservative with the inflammatory headline, "Comedian tells 'special needs' joke at Palin event."[7]

The left went crazy as I spent three days in a bunker wondering if my speaking career was finished. I will always be grateful to Sarah Palin for having the courage to not condemn my remarks despite intense liberal media pressure to do so. Any honest person would know I was calling out the Palin-haters and not the Palin family. Dan Merica knew this. He did not care.

Liberals demanded an apology. On September 6, 2011, I responded to the mob in the appropriate manner.

"I was wrong. I apologize. I should never have compared liberals to special needs children. Liberals are nothing like special needs children. Special needs children have value."

Conservatives cheered even louder and my speaking career grew. When I got Merica on the telephone, he got scared, mumbled something in a panic, and hung up. Bullies are cowards. He will not be a problem anymore. He brought a knife to a gunfight. I brought a verbal bazooka.

Conservatives must not engage in unilateral disarmament or wait around hoping that good liberals will stand up and criticize the bad ones. There can be no negotiation with the Dan Mericas of the world.

If leftists would stop hating, conservatives would love policy discussions. Liberals can prove this theory wrong through leading by example. Stop calling conservatives the various "ists" over policy disagreements. Stop attacking individual conservatives unless evidence of crossing the line exists. When conservatives cross the line, other conservatives stand up. Right is right, wrong is wrong, and we know the difference. The challenge to liberals is twofold.

Do not attack a single conservative ever again on a personal level unless they say or do something beyond the pale. Campaign rhetoric from decades ago does not provide justification. Otherwise, the song, "We Will Rock You"[8] would be a death threat. Without specific examples, knock it off and stick to policy.

The second challenge for liberals is to stop whitewashing their own behavior. Do what conservatives have done for decades. Renounce any and all political violence without excuses or equivocations. Outside of defending human life, renounce violence as wrong.

If somebody kicks animals or invalids, exacting justice may involve violence. Be honest about whether you are defending goodness or being an aggressor bully. Liberals have beaten wheelchair-bound conservatives and conservative minorities at tea parties.[9] Conservative equivalents are non-existent.

Declaring violence unhelpful is insufficient. Violence will be lessened when counterproductive but still used whenever effective.

This is why conservatives have their cars keyed and their lawn signs stolen. It is also why liberals try to run over conservatives with their cars.[10] Statistical aberrations aside, calculating all these crimes would reveal the leftist tilt.

We on the right do not hate the left. We see opposition. They see enemies. When the left gives up all verbal and physical violence, they will be surprised how peaceful conservatives are. Sadly, this potential love-fest will never happen.

The left needs warfare to win. The ends justify their destructive means. The only solution for conservatives is full throttled self-defense.

This desired leftist war ends when liberals surrender and conclude they cannot win using warfare. Only then will they come to the table and dialogue. As long as violence works for them, they will keep burning the entire village while wondering why there is ruin all around them.

Inauguration 2013: Obama saved the world, but nobody knows how

An old joke says God created the world in six days and spent the seventh say wondering how he did it. President Barack Obama reached godlike status for saving the world, yet his worshippers still cannot articulate what he actually did or how he did it.

On January 21st, 2013, Obama celebrated his second inauguration. Based on his behavior, it was day 1,461 of his first inauguration. His entire life is a celebration of himself.

He somehow finds the will to take time out from relaxing to publicly self-praise before returning to accomplishing nothing. His entire second-term excuse for an agenda involved forward, fairness, and a balanced approach. These regurgitated platitudes constituted his 2013 State of the Useless address.

Obama desires a national conversation provided that only people agreeing with him speak. A real constructive dialogue would occur if everyone took an inaugural oath requiring conversations be policy-based. The last two decades has seen liberals demand everything they say be taken at face value simply because they said so. True dialogue about hard issues deserves serious, honest analysis.

No policy creates a measurable immediate effect. There is a lag time. President Obama allegedly saved America from the next Great Depression. He somehow saved the auto industry, a major economic cog. How? What specific policies did he enact that had anything to do with healing the American economy? Can anyone name the policies?

Treasury Secretary Hank Paulson created the $787 billion Troubled Assets Relief Package to save the financial sector. President George W. Bush signed TARP into law on October 3, 2008, one month before anyone knew whether Barack Obama or John McCain would succeed Bush as President.[11] Obama created his own $1.3 trillion dollar stimulus package that made it through his Democrat Congress. Obama publicly admitted that it did not do what he said it would.[12]

Timelines are non-partisan. Even somebody as glorious as Obama cannot solve problems before taking office or get credit for being the only man in history to enact policies without a lag time. The economy rebounded from the depths during his tenure, but before he could have possibly contributed anything positive or negative.

Since recoiling from the brink, the economy then stagnated for the next six years of his presidency with no relief in sight. This is more than enough time to scrutinize his policies. If things were as bad as initially described, then the rebound should have been significantly better. Reaganomics sharply reversed the Carter economy. The policies were supply-side tax cuts. President Obama enacted healthcare and environmental policies. The former increased the debt while the latter made no positive economic contribution.[13] Automobile companies that refused Obama bailout money are healthier than their competitors.[14]

If the narrative of Obama saving the world is going to be rammed down American throats, it is perfectly reasonable to inquire how he did this. If the narrative is true, every leader on Earth should learn from him. What did he do? Would it have happened without him? If not, then he is the one indispensable man the world truly has been waiting for. More likely, his significance is vastly overstated.

Platitudes, slogans, and talking points are not policies. Cleaning up his predecessor's mess is nonsense unless one can state exactly what policies caused the mess to begin with. Tax cuts in 2001 and 2003 have nothing to do with the financial crisis of 2008 in the same way that Clintonomics does not deserve credit for the 1990s dot-com economy or blame for the 2000 crash.

If liberals cannot name a single successful Obama economic policy, then maybe it is possible he never had one. Maybe his supporters despise his predecessor so much that they do not care what Obama does. They love Obama for merely being.

This is great for liberal partisans but Obamanomics offers nothing positive from a policy standpoint.

This is why Obama Inaugurations and his other speeches are a hollow celebration of failed nothingness beyond liberal self-regard. Liberals need this illusion to tide themselves over during the self-worship gap between the *Golden Globes* and *Oscars*.

Democrats: Just a bunch of old, white Christians

Former Vermont Governor and 2004 presidential screamer Howard Dean said that he hates everything Republicans stand for.[15] He derided the GOP as nothing but a white, male Christian party.[16] Ironically, one place to find only lily-white male Christians is Howard Dean's Vermont.

It is the Democrat Party and their geriatric representatives that need facelifts. The GOP is younger and far more diverse. Democrats have a partially black president, but once Obama is dragged kicking and screaming from the stage, Democrat multiculturalism goes with him. The Democrat Party includes women as minorities despite 55 percent of the country being female. This is the big inclusion illusion designed to paper over an old, white party.

Republicans have Hispanic Governors Brian Sandoval of Nevada and Susanna Martinez of New Mexico and Indian Governors Nikki Haley of South Carolina and Bobby Jindal of Louisiana. All of them are fairly young. Democrat Governors include California's elderly Jerry Brown.

Republican Senators include Tim Scott of South Carolina, who is black, and Florida's Marco Rubio and Texas's Ted Cruz, both Latino. They are all fairly young. Democrat Senators Barbara Boxer and Dianne Feinstein of California are white. Feinstein is an octogenarian and Boxer is almost there. Massachusetts Senator Elizabeth Warren lied when she listed herself as a Native American in a directory of law professors. Claiming to be 1/16th Cherokee Indian allowed her to take advantage of affirmative action benefits. Her evidence of minority status was her high cheekbones, which is about as plausible (and frankly, racist) as somebody claiming Jewish status based on a bulbous nose or black status based on a plump posterior. Warren's offensive stereotyping does not alter her status as an angry grumpy old Caucasoid.

The Republican House leadership features the Republican "Young Guns." This included proud Jew Eric Cantor of Virginia until late 2014. The Democrat House Leadership consists of old white people in Nancy Pelosi of California and Steny Hoyer of Maryland.

Republican 2016 presidential candidates include the previously mentioned Ted Cruz and Marco Rubio. Even top white contenders, including New Jersey Governor Chris Christie and Kentucky Senator Rand Paul, are fairly young. Democrat 2016 presidential candidates include Hillary Clinton, Maryland Governor Martin O'Malley, and Vice President Joe Biden of Delaware, all old white Christians.

Since liberals want to place everybody into groups, two more categories include gay people and the disabled.

Republicans had an openly gay Jewish 2012 presidential candidate in Fred Karger. The asterisk in the polls was still more than what the Democrats offered. Ken Mehlman, a gay Jewish man (Mehlman came out after he left the position, but it was a wide open secret among GOP power brokers), led the Republican National Committee. Michael Steele of Maryland, a black man, followed. Angry whites Howard Dean and Florida's Debbie Wasserman Schultz (Wasserman Schultz is technically Jewish, but often votes against Israel when the Obama White House commands her to do so) represented the Democrat National Committee.

Republicans have had two partially disabled presidential candidates in recent elections. War heroes Bob Dole of Kansas and John McCain of Arizona both had virtually no use of one arm. Democrats have not had a handicapped presidential candidate.

Black Mia Love and Jewish Lee Zeldin began their GOP House careers in 2015.

Liberal Democrats can blather on about diversity and multiculturalism, but they distrust minorities to reach the hierarchy. Rich, old white liberals lament the downtrodden but would never let them near their own homes. The diverse Democrat Party offers Ivory Soap pure white and even the lily-whitest who are whiter than that.

For those who want to be led by people of all races and ethnicities with actual ideas and strong character, look to the conservative ideology and the Republican Party.

Democrat Rule 2009-2011: What did they do?

Democrats demanded action in 2014. President Obama declared 2014 to be a year of action. The slogan Americans kept hearing was, "We can't wait."

What were they doing from January of 2009 through January of 2011?

The 2008 elections gave Democrats total and complete control. They had Obama in the White House, Nancy Pelosi as Speaker of the House, and Harry Reid presiding over a filibuster-proof Senate with sixty votes. Democrats could have enacted any laws they wanted. Republicans had zero power to stop them.

Democrats could have tackled inequality instead of passing a failed stimulus package. They could have raised the minimum wage. While gun control may have faced some red state Democrat defections, virtually every other plank in the liberal agenda was ripe for expansion. Cap and trade legislation was doable. High-speed rail could have been built. They could have invested in education before Americans discovered that was code for spending one trillion dollars on top down pre-school for children. Enacting a comprehensive immigration bill was feasible long before voters realized it was a cynical ploy to gain millions more voters for Democrats.

Democrats focused solely on nationalizing healthcare rather than governing. Income inequality and the war on women were campaign slogans, not legislative proposals. Democrats pretend to cherish these issues only when Republicans win or are about to win elections. When Republicans win the White House, newspapers write about the homeless. They never exist during liberal administrations.

Democrats insist they had to clean up the financial crisis but cannot name any actual legislation they passed that fixed the problem. They rolled the dice that the Affordable Care Act would succeed and make liberals heroes for a generation in the same way the New Deal and Civil Rights legislation did generations earlier.

When Democrats lost a political skirmish within the rules, they arbitrarily changed the rules. When Ted Kennedy's death led to Scott Brown being the 41st Republican Senator, Democrats got around the filibuster by just declaring an earlier bill deemed as passed.[17] Democrats cheated because the ends justified the means.

Obama could have emulated President Bill Clinton's triangulation strategy after the 1994 Republican midterm triumph. Clinton fought House Speaker Newt Gingrich on some issues and worked with him on others. A bipartisan budget deal coupled with an Internet revolution led to a phenomenal economy that allowed everybody to get partial credit.[18] Clinton easily won reelection and continued working with a Republican Congress.

Obama tried the scorched earth approach while claiming Republicans refused to work with him. It got him reelected, but at a heavy price. He had no working relationships. Some Republicans were able to work with Democrats only when Obama was out of the room and relegated to the sideline.

Democrats talk about climate change. Why talk rather than act? Obama said he had a pen and a telephone. Democrats refused to turn their pipe dreams into law because they know they are trying to sell an ideology the American voters never wanted and still do not want.

America is a center-right republic, not a European-style social democracy. Americans will tolerate less job stability and security for more individual freedom and opportunities to acquire wealth. Liberalism requires restricting individualism.

Americans are not right-wingers or left-wingers, but the conservative philosophy of wanting to be left alone is the heart of Americanism. For Democrats to be allowed to do big things, they have to be able to handle little things like fixing potholes, helping farmers, cleaning the streets after snowstorms, and letting mom and pop shops operate without bureaucracy. This often proves beyond their abilities as they gaze off into the future with grandiose visions of utopia where trains take us everywhere and trees are our hobby.

In January of 2015 the Senate gavel was ripped from Harry Reid's cold arthritic hands. Nothing Democrats bleat or bluster about going forward changes their deliberate impotence from 2009 through 2011.

Hopefully Republicans have learned from their mistakes. There is no time to waste, and the Obama liberals wasted everybody's time just like they did when Jimmy Carter and Bill Clinton helped Democrats briefly control everything. Then conservative Republicans took over and things finally got done.

The five demigods who tell liberals what to think

Whenever conservatives explain ideas to liberals, the inevitable tart replies come back in spades. Conservatives are incapable of thought. Every conservative is told what to say by Rush Limbaugh and funded by the Koch Brothers. While this is idiocy, American liberals have never been guilty of differentiating smugness from knowledge.

What if conservatives acted like liberals? We could declare that liberals spouting idiocy about everything from climate change to the war on women were robots with liberal microchips planted in their posteriors.

Conservatives constantly hear about a Republican civil war, as if that is a bad thing. Paleocons fight Neocons. Supply-siders debate flat tax and fair tax advocates on how to stimulate growth. *The Wall Street Journal* and *National Review* disagree on illegal immigration. Social conservatives and libertarians sharply diverge on abortion and gay rights. These passionate exchanges of ideas make conservatism vibrant. Nobody is censored.

Liberals claim to love diversity, but they drum anybody out of the Democrat Party if total obedience to liberalism fails to occur. Former Senator Joe Lieberman's ninety-two percent liberal voting record was insufficient. Liberals go out of their way to silence discussion, from mandatory unionizing to having conservative commentators like Dinesh D'Souza indicted. Who is in control? Not bystander Obama.

Five people tell liberals what to think, say, believe and feel. From chanting meaningless slogans to righteous indignation over the mythical income inequality gap, large segments of the liberal populace are captured by these five individuals.

1. George Soros — He is global liberalism now that Senator Ted Kennedy has departed to an alcohol-filled bubble bath in the sky. Soros funds every major leftist outfit. His tentacles reach David Brock's *Media Matters, Moveon.org*, and of course Valerie Jarrett and David Axelrod. A convicted felon insider trader, Soros made his money destroying currencies and leaving millions of people in poverty.[19] He also regaled his delight in helping send his fellow Jews to the gas chambers during the Holocaust.[20] Leftists love him for his obsession with legalizing all drugs and his anti-war stance.

2. Thomas Friedman — This *New York Jayson Blair Times (NYJBT)* writer is lightly regarded by many of his colleagues.[21] Liberals still treat his words on the Middle East as if they came down from on high. His expertise consists of having lived overseas and eaten foreign food. A demigod in the liberal

Jewish community, they gush over his columns advocating Israeli surrender and national suicide. "Thomas Friedman said" is the eleventh commandment in liberal circles. Conservatives see Friedman as the overrated and frequently wrong columnist he is. Liberals define this as being an intellectual.

3. Paul Krugman — Writing for *The NYJBT* is how to win a Nobel Prize in economics for the economic theory of hating President George W. Bush. Krugman and his beard later switched to hating Sarah Palin. He does occasionally write about things within six degrees of economics, but like Friedman, Krugman is an intellectual. He is virtually always wrong. The former Enron advisor predicted the Obama stimulus would succeed.[22] When it failed he claimed it was not large enough, since one trillion dollars is chump change. Now he insists that $90 trillion in unfunded liabilities is a non-issue. If only America were more like Europe, everything would be fine. He types and liberals rush to Twitter without correcting the errors. Leftists see recycled Krugman columns akin to fact-checking.

4. Jon Stewart — He is a hero to all who confuse smugness and nastiness with comedy. Stewart makes his living selectively editing videos of people he dislikes for maximum humiliation. Imagine if Sarah Palin said, "We should eat healthier. We need to be a good influence on our children." Stewart would splice the tape so Palin's comment would read, "We should eat children." When not manipulating videos, he is dropping expletives on conservatives for disagreeing with him. He is a leftist's dream, a Jew who made his living telling anti-Jewish jokes on the comedy circuit.[23] Millennials consider him hip and cool as they grow up with matching inflated egos and zero meaningful accomplishments. The metrosexual Stewart is the last thing American boys should ever become.

5. Katy Perry — She has forty million Twitter followers. She strutted around in 2012 wearing skin-tight dresses with Obama slogans on them. This walking billboard is inspiring an entire generation of Millennials to strive to become bimbos spouting gibberish. When not offending virtually every segment of society by her tasteless actions in her music videos, she is offering stupidity on current political issues.[24] Forget that her commentaries lack any depth. The truly dangerous part is how many kids look up to and listen to her.

Soros represents the dangerous liberals. Friedman speaks to the naive ones. Krugman handles the angry ones. Stewart speaks for the insufferable, weak, pompous passive-aggressive ones. Perry handles the dumb ones. These five people control the automatons. All five are rich and white, since rich whites run liberalism. They are not subjected to the rules and regulations they advocate that strangle the rest of us. They are the five demigods leading the heartless religion of liberalism.

Supreme Court votes unanimously to ban metrosexual marriage

In a unanimous decision, the U.S. Supreme Court voted to ban metrosexual marriage. Swing vote Justice Anthony Kennedy declared that every man has to pick a side, gay or straight, and stick with it.

Homosexual marriage sparked fierce debate. Metrosexuals, also known as she-males and beta males, are virtually universally hated.[25] Real men are alpha males and retrosexuals.[26] Alphas have shown utter hostility to feminized men who constantly tuck their shirts in, know nothing about football (skating is not a sport), wear their pink Cardigan sweaters draped ever so perfectly around their pencil necks, and cry on cue.

The gay and lesbian movement also seems to hate metrosexuals for projecting an inaccurate stereotype of the LGBT movement as feminized. Gays are tired of getting blamed for metrosexual behavior.

Justice Ruth Bader Ginsburg pointed out that while some straight women keep metrosexual friends around for arm candy, they would never sleep with wussies. Justice Antonin Scalia was more caustic, telling these "prissy, sissy candy-asses to man up and grow a pair." Another case before the High Court will test the constitutionality of dragging metrosexuals to reeducation camps such as sports bars to be reprogrammed into full-fledged males. Retrosexuals plan to celebrate a victory in that case by burning copies of *Beaches*[27] and *Steel Magnolias*[28] while forcing metrosexuals to either watch Sylvester Stallone or Bruce Willis movies or have *Fried Green Tomatoes*[29] shoved down beta male throats.

While homosexuality has become more widespread, metrosexuality is on the decline. Outside of tea houses, bridge clubs, and Democrat presidential campaigns, metrosexuals are in hiding. Some metrosexuals have even been caught wearing old sneakers and jeans to keep up appearances. Bill Clinton is the only Democrat presidential nominee in the last 30 years not to be afflicted with the sissy virus.

While all nine justices agreed that no woman in her right mind would want to marry these momma's boys, a ban was the only way to discourage them from procreating and creating a whole new generation of girly-boys.

The justices also by a narrow 5-4 margin declared that existing metrosexual marriages would remain valid. Chief Justice John Roberts opined that, "President Barack Obama will still be allowed to have his wife Michelle tell him what to do on a daily basis. Why any man would want that henpecked lifestyle is not for this court to decide." Secretary of State John Kerry expressed relief at this provision while preparing to go windsurfing with Biff and Muffy in matching earth tone sweaters made from a combination of actual earth dirt and hemp.

Ron Paul supporters and other Libertarians said they would not oppose the court decision provided everyone involved could have legalized marijuana.

Pro and anti-gay marriage advocates returned to fighting, both relieved that metrosexuals refusing to fight about anything were no longer clogging up the courts with their terrible personalities and dreadfully snobby fashion sense.

SCOTUS to decide if gay couples can have abortions

In a Supreme Court shocker, the High Court agreed to hear the politically charged case of whether gay couples should be allowed to have abortions.

Liberal activists demanding abortion equality insist that Roe vs. Wade applies to homosexual couples as well as heterosexual couples. The Equal Protection Clause in the Fourteenth Amendment means that it would be a civil rights violation if gay couples were banned from having abortions.

A spokesperson from the Gay and Lesbian Defamation League made it clear that gay marriage is just the beginning. Gays have the right to have children or get rid of potential children if they become an inconvenience. Pro-family advocates publicly expressed exasperation. The Family Research Bureau insisted that gay couples could adopt but not produce natural children.

The GLDL called the FRB's comments, "bigoted," "hateful," and "intolerant." The FRB offered to donate free biology books to all schoolchildren in neighborhoods with a large gay populace.

The FRB pointed out that since gays cannot conceive children, aborting them would be tougher. The GLDL responded by referring to the FRB as a bunch of "bible-thumping zealots trying to legislate morality."

Liberal Justice Ruth Bader Ginsburg said she would consult French law before determining whether the ACLU-GLDL case has merit. She would also speak to some French protesters to solicit their opinions. Conservative activists pointed out that since there may not be any heterosexual people left in France, it would be best to stick to America and its Constitution.

Transsexuals and transgendered individuals filed a friend of the court brief demanding that the court stand up for hermaphrodite abortion rights and bi-solo termination equality.

The NYJBT immediately produced a study showing that men and women were the same. "The science is settled," read the headline. To deny homosexuals the right to abortions is part of the white male heterosexist power structure.

President Obama declined to comment until he could obtain polling information from the American people telling him what to believe. Vice President Biden had plenty to say on the matter, but he was tackled, bound and gagged by Secret Service agents charged with saving Obama's life. Biden was then warned he would be droned if he opened his mouth on the volatile subject.

Not all leftists support the homosexual abortion fight. The Perpetually Outraged Against Everything Group issued a statement calling the gay termination movement a distraction. The Code Pink offshoot POAEG stated that the Supreme Court should focus on more pressing matters including illegal Israeli settlements in Palestine causing climate change.

Spokespeople for the Supreme Court had no comment. Privately some of the justices wanted to join conservatives in spraying liberal protesters with fire hoses.

SCOTUS *declares gay couples boring*

In a 5-4 ruling that a slice of the American electorate cared about, the United States Supreme Court declared gay couples boring. In a ruling where they decided not to decide, the SCOTUS lamented that Americans had nothing better to do on a summer Wednesday than watch their decision not to deliberate key issues. While Justice Ruth Bader Ginsburg declared gay people "fabulous," an angry Justice Antonin Scalia wrote a scathing dissent telling court gawkers to "Get off the court's lawn and get jobs."

The Supreme Court struck down the Defense of Marriage Act, signed by marriage expert Bill Clinton. Striking down DOMA makes gay couples eligible for the same tax hikes and bad healthcare as their heterosexual counterparts.

SCOTUS rejected attempts to restore California's Proposition 8 banning gay marriage due to a lack of standing. Justice Roberts exclaimed, "You Californians created this mess. You fix it. We don't have time to deal with your foul-ups. It is not the judiciary's responsibility to save you from your own legislators. When the next earthquake makes you part of Russia, Vladimir Putin can handle it."

When asked how he felt about the decision, elated *South Park* resident Big Gay Al replied, "I'm super! Thanks for asking!"[30]

President Obama, who was for gay marriage before he was against it before he was for it again, insisted on holding a press conference to talk about it. He praised the court's decision while lamenting that it distracted from his other historic, unprecedented, and totally ignored speeches about nuclear weapons, climate change, and illegal immigration. He blamed Republicans for claiming that gays cause illegal immigration and climate change, insisting that straight people did as well.

While Obama was not providing Americans with tax relief or silence relief from his speeches, news of the SCOTUS decision allowed Americans one day of relief from hearing about Jodi Arias, Trayvon Martin, George Zimmerman, and Kim Kardashian and Kanye West's baby North West.

SCOTUS also left unresolved whether gay divorce lawyers had to wait until after the marriages became legal to start chasing wedding limousines and handing out business cards. The High Court refused to hear a case brought by Jesse Jackson and Al Sharpton demanding reparations for gay black couples. The SCOTUS declared both men were a day late. Racial issues were reserved for Tuesdays, gay issues on Wednesdays, and religious issues for Thursdays.

Meanwhile, the rest of the world continued to burn as most Americans engaged in a collective shoulder shrug.

Chapter 2: Jewish Ideological Lunacy

Trying to find a rational explanation for the irrational is a waste of time. Some things do not make sense. Among the incomprehensible things in life are reggae music, speeches by boxing promoter Don King, the platypus (thank you Robin Williams),[31] and Jews voting for liberal Democrats.

The reason why liberal Jews consistently love people who hate them and hate people who love them is easy enough to explain. The tougher part is dragging them to their come to Moses moment. The ones who insist on demonizing conservatives deserve as little mercy as any other bigots.

Jews, Obama, Hillary, 2016, DLFs, and DJLFs

Barack Obama kicked Israel in the teeth by demanding that they return to their 1967 borders.[32] His many liberal water carriers tried to explain why he did not say what he actually said, and that we should not take his words literally.

Israeli Prime Minister Benjamin Netanyahu gave Mr. Obama a cold dose of reality before Congress and AIPAC.[33] Republicans applauded him out of solidarity while the liberals sought cover.

The question that gets asked is whether liberal Jews will abandon Obama, Hillary, and rest of the Democrats.

As a Jewish Republican, I can emphatically say that the answer is…no way.

Give liberal Jews a simple task and watch them offer tortured non-answers. Rank abortion, global warming, gay marriage and Israel in terms of importance.

(Hint: I typed them in order of liberal Jewish importance. Notice I refer to them as liberal Jews and not Jewish liberals. Again, order matters.)

Liberal Jews insist that they care about Israel. That is not the question. The question is how much. Force liberal Jews to rank issues and they will make excuses not to do so when Israel is thrown in the mix. Understanding liberal Jews is very simple. They stick to liberals because they believe liberals share their values. What are those Jewish values?

When liberal Jewish women say that a Democrat is pro-Israel, what they really mean is that the Democrat is pro-choice on abortion. Liberal Jewish men see liberals as pro-Israel because of support for cap and trade. Both genders see Democrats as Pro-Israel because they support gay marriage. Jews blindly support Democrats, liberals and progressives, so they assume that blind support is mutual.

Rather than confront Democrats who dislike them, liberal Jews simply rationalize that the offender really is on their side. This is no different from battered housewives making excuses for their abusive husbands.

Obama and Hillary may not be anti-Israel, but one cannot be pro-Palestinian and pro-Israel. Liberal Jews clearly grasp that one cannot be pro-choice and pro-life. On abortion, environmentalism and gay rights, they demand one hundred percent purity. The slightest restriction is disqualification. With Israel everything becomes morally relative and nuanced, which is code for nothingness.

Despite rabid anti-Semitism in America from many leftists, liberal Jews overlook this for their greater good. Pro-Israel Republicans are dismissed as radical Christian zealots wanting to convert Jews and create a Christian theocracy to bring about the Rapture. This idiocy is spouted because liberal Jews know that social issues trump Israel. Saying they care about lots of things allows them to hide.

Pro-Israel Democrats exist, as do intelligent liberals. Those who make excuses for everything Barack Obama and Hillary Clinton say and do fear questioning them because it would mean questioning themselves. These weak-minded Stockholm syndrome Jews cannot accept the shock to the system.

The Holocaust was a shock to the system. People saw true evil while the world did nothing. 9/11 was another system shock. Many formerly liberal Jews moved to the right because they saw the world had changed. Many others simply doubled down and made excuses.

Many Jewish liberals are too fragile to handle any further shocks to their systems. Ostrich imitations make the problems go away so that everything turns out fine. Democrats will stand up for them because there is no way they would betray loyalty and shove useless allies under the bus.

Jews have been bullied throughout history. Aligning with liberals allows Jews to be the bullies rather than the victims. Leftist anti-Semitism is ignored because bashing Republicans makes Jews feel socially accepted. This desperate desire to be liked by those with no use for them is pathological.

A *TYGRRRR EXPRESS* acronym to forever enter the American lexicon describes liberals who engage in willful blindness rather than confront reality. They are now and forever known as DLFs, which stands for "dumb liberal (redacted)." The Jewish apologists are one viral strain of DLFs known as DJLFs, "dumb Jewish liberal (redacted)."

DLFs think religion relates to global warming and that Jesus and Moses spent their time worrying about carbon dioxide emissions. For DJLFs, Israel has to matter to DLFs. If Israel is just another issue, then Israel is a non-issue.

DJLFs cannot understand that although DLFs share their rabid passion about abortion, gay marriage, and environmentalism, the similarities end there. That is why they are only DLFs and not DJLFs. The DLFs know what they are. The DJLFs live in denial. Denial is not a river in Egypt, but all of Israel would be part of Egypt if the DLFs had their way.

DJLFs consider Republican Jews to be puppets of the Christian evangelicals, but it is DJLFs being treated like marionettes. DLFs see DJLFs as useful idiots. When they stop being useful, Piggy in *Lord of the Flies*[34] is how it ends.

DLFs supported Samantha Power and every other anti-Israel Obama administration miscreant. They know what Reverend Jeremiah is about. They don't care because they don't need to make excuses. DJLFs make excuses because they are more afraid of being pre-Israel than pro-Israel. DJLFs will be pre-Israel Jews if they break away from the DLFs, a people without a country.

What is to be done with DJLFs?

We force them to stop making excuses and answer the question I originally asked. Rank abortion, global warming, gay marriage, and Israel. Then look in the mirror.

Religious Christians are not using Republican Jews. Secular DLFs are using the DJLFs. Republican Jews and Christians are friends through thick and thin. Secular DLFs are foes.

The cure for DJLFs requires getting Dr. Benjamin Carson to come out of retirement and perform a procedure not covered by Obamacare. Cranial-gluteal extraction surgery cures all DLFs including DJLFs. DJLFs must ask themselves if this even matters. If it does, there is hope. If not, they forever remain DJLFs.

Ideological Bigotry Part XXVI–Debbie Does Denny's and Eminem Returns

I was once verbally assaulted by hotel employees when I attending a function where a liberal congressman was speaking. I had a valid invitation. On another occasion a five-minute cab ride felt like a hostage situation. I have had women scream at me for feeling a certain way without them asking me or knowing how I felt. In the Jewish community, this ideological bigotry is especially noxious.

When Osama bin Laden was being hunted, liberal Jewish women wanted to know his stance on abortion before determining if he was a bad guy. They were curious if the car he drove to greet his suicide bomber employees was a hybrid. When he spoke about drinking the blood of dead Americans and Jews, they wanted to ensure it was from a biodegradable cup.

One Jewish function ended with several people going to the local Denny's within walking distance of my home. "Debbie" sat at my table. She was pushing forty and struggling financially, working as a part-time nanny. The conversation was light, breezy, and harmless until she asked what I did for a living. I used to avoid answering that question because of unprovoked personal attacks. Republican Jews are the new gays in the closet out of fear.

I have since come out as a proud Jewish Republican. When asked what I do, I say I am a speaker. If asked, I mention that some of my speaking is political. I also make it clear that I like everybody and do not let that affect my friendships.

Many liberals have political litmus tests for friendships. My constant obsession with ending ideological bigotry, especially in the Jewish community, has led me to be much less patient with people exhibiting it.

Ideological bigotry is not codified like racial or ethnic bigotry. Since it does not factor into hate crimes penalties, it must be less important. Saying that serious hatred would already be illegal is a pathetic rationalization.

At Denny's, Debbie proudly claimed she was a socialist. I was still friendly but she then offered up the usual tired litany of insults. She insisted that, "Republicans don't care about people" and offered up pure charm with, "I can't stand Republicans."

I said she shouldn't label a whole group of people, especially since I was one. She made it clear that while I may personally not be bad, most of them are.

I had a decision to make. I could let it go, but if this were racial or ethnic bigotry I would be criticized for staying silent. Why should anti-Republican bigotry be tolerated?

I unloaded, calling her a bigot and giving a liberal a taste of her own medicine. The difference was she spewed real bigotry, not the fictional stuff the left invents.

I told her she hated Republicans because she failed at life. I worked my behind off to be successful. I was not going to have a failed human being tell me I was a bad person for refusing to redistribute my success to her pathetic failed existence.

She claimed to have been reduced to tears over this, but cry me a river of crocodile tears. Spare me the ideological passive-aggressive game disguised as a reverse gender gap. Liberals love to put conservatives on defense by calling us mean and insensitive. Liberal women and conservative men adds the irrelevant gender component. These women should just act like guys (with breasts), (wo)man up, and grow a (figurative) pair. It is the crybabies, not the system. Conservatives are tired of liberals throwing punches and then getting hysterical when we fight back.

Debbie then pretended she did not mean what she said. What I wanted from her was a promise not to say such things again. Apologizing to me and then saying the same bad things to others is phony, even by liberal standards. She refused my request and stated I had no right to limit her speech. Like a typical leftist, she was unaware that plenty of speech is restricted, such as hate speech. It was time to play hardball.

I had a mailing list of 10,000+ people. I was going to make her the next famous poster child for liberal bigotry gone wild. She threatened to sue me, as if she could afford a lawyer. Liberal lawyers doing pro bono work do not care about white Jewish liberal women unwilling to shut up. Other oppressed groups are far more sympathetic.

I decided to seek advice from the Real Slim Shady. What would rapper Eminem say in this situation? Eminem knows how to handle nasty women who criticize his success.

In "Without me," Eminem explained the emptiness of Debbie's threat. I called her ridiculous bluff and accelerated my fury while maintaining a great beat.

"Get ready 'cause this sh*t's about to get heavy. I just settled all my lawsuits, f*ck you Debbie!"[35]

I became a heat-seeking missile because I have had enough. I light myself on fire so others can continue being nice. Jumping on the grenade is a valuable public service. Replace the word Republican with gay or black and then liberals understand. Why not let others handle this? Philosopher Eminem again has the answers.

"This looks like a job for me. So everybody else just follow me."[36]

I am really good at taking wretched human beings and ripping them to shreds. I wish otherwise. My hands are daggers and my words are stilettos. I will retire this character trait when other conservatives stand up for themselves.

Debbie finally relented at 2:00 a.m after about three hours of battering. She promised not to defame or defile me in any way. I promised not to use her last name when telling her story. Several years later I am still living my life. She is still complaining and blaming Republicans in her pointless existence.

While Debbie does Denny's, I reach for the snack bowl and enjoy free Eminems. I did not start this conflict, but I sure finished it. The Debbies of the world will crawl back to their leftist holes when faced with a fusillade of superior verbal firepower.

"Get ready, 'cause this sh*t's about to get heavy. This looks like a job for me. So everybody else just follow me."

You're welcome.

Chapter 3: Domestic Policy Lunacy

Whether the issue is education, climate change, healthcare, gun control or illegal immigration, two domestic policy truisms exist. Liberals have a very different approach from conservatives. Conservatives believe in ideas that actually work. Liberals have Ivy League professors with advanced degrees in writing postulates. The faculty toddler room is Pontification Nation. Liberal elitists lounge around the lounge thinking about their next grand future failed idea. Conservatives actually do things because over the course of their lives they have done things.

It is time to draw a big red X on the foreheads of the theoreticians and let the adults get to work. Here are plenty of fun conservative solutions to solve the most vexing problems liberals created the last time they escaped from their playpens.

A gun control compromise for everyone

Let's all come together and unite on gun control.

When a pot smoking reader of the Communist Manifesto shot Congresswoman Gabrielle Giffords, President Obama did not ban left-wing books or in any way enforce drug laws. The Choom Gang[37] slacker did not want to alienate drug users.

Offering more gun control legislation is harmless for Obama since most gun owners did not vote for him. He never cared about moderate Democrats losing their jobs. He really has taken "To thine own self be true"[38] to stratospheric levels.

I am a staunch Second Amendment supporter, but it is High Noon time for a gun control compromise that will make conservatives happy and liberals less miserable than usual.

Since liberals favor gun control and conservatives are against it, just take away all guns from liberals. That way, if there is ever a conflict like the 2000 election that cannot be resolved peacefully, the right will win because we will have all the guns.

This could lead to fantastic policy developments.

Liberals favor higher taxes and conservatives favor lower taxes. If the left likes socialism and wealth redistribution so much, take away the money from the left and give it to the right. If they try to stop us, remember the first bullet point. We will have all the guns and the bullets.

KinderGarden of Eden author Evan Sayet brilliantly points out that certain reasonable gun restrictions should exist. "Nobody should own a gun if they have a criminal record, a psychiatric record, or a Barbra Streisand record."[39]

Even conservatives opposing all gun control should be nervous about the idea of liberals owning guns. Would you want violent SEIU or *Moveon.org* protesters owning guns? Should Wisconsin protesters screaming about Hitler and Khadafi running their government have guns? These governors need extra security, but not because of elderly tea party ladies in wheelchairs with knitting apparel.

Would you want Jeremiah Wright owning guns? His church upstairs is already a few pews short of a full congregation. Should Ward Churchill own guns? Mental derangement is common among liberal professors but the firearms industry should have standards.

Should liberal politicos own guns? Many lefties are one violent outburst away from their own heads exploding. With nuclear explosions and meltdowns a serious threat, those wanting to keep firearms away from nuclear reactors should not let Elizabeth Warren, Howard Dean or Debbie Wasserman Schultz own guns. Andy Weiner and Barney Frank already got in trouble for discharging their guns inappropriately. For this same reason leftist singer George Michael and his ilk should not pack heat if they are already in heat.[40]

The Supreme Court successfully and barely blocked Al Gore from stealing the George W. Bush presidency because those threatening death to the court's conservatives were unable to carry out their desires.

The only thing saving American society from total breakdown is the fact that violent leftists remain in the horse and buggy stage with regards to weapons. AFL-CIO thugs throwing rocks and wielding billy clubs like in the good old mob days can be subdued with fire hoses. Even tear gas would be ineffective if leftists had guns.

Conservatives brought guns to tea party rallies but kept them at their waists. They were responsible. Irresponsible people violate the law through illegal strikes, handing out fake medical sick notes, or vandalizing government buildings. It is perfectly fair to keep guns away from petty criminals to prevent bigger crimes.

Anybody in a street fight knows that the sword actually is mightier than the pen. Outside of the *Jayson Blair Times*, this is common knowledge.

Ban liberals from owning guns. They don't need them, can't be trusted with them, and as with most other issues, have no understanding of them or the Constitution that allows the rest of us to have them.

Amnesty: The ultimate illegal immigration compromise

They gather by the thousands, disrespect American culture, openly defy American laws, and drag down this great nation. They are American liberals.

President Obama is flooding the country with illegal immigrants and plying them with free services that are not really free solely to increase the number of Democrat votes. If third-world people risking life and limb coming to America are stuffed into internment camps and left to die, that is the cost of doing business with leftists. The ends justify the means.

Obama liberals want to permanently break the GOP. If the country suffers, that is not his problem. Liberals stay silent rather than put country over party. Besides, it is not the first time Obama got innocent Mexicans and others killed to advance his liberal political agenda. The Fast and Furious scandal[41] unfolded the exact same way.

Compromise is elusive given the toxic political environment. We could send all illegal immigrants to Detroit or Chicago, but that would be considered cruel and unusual punishment under the Eighth Amendment. Giving children the death penalty is not a wise political strategy. If anything, airlifting children out of those cities would be an act of compassion.

A better solution is the illegal immigration compromise that should take place once conservatives are back in charge. Conservatives should take a page out of Al Gore's playbook. Gore favors carbon offsets. America should start doing people offsets.

Amnesty is the solution. For every illegal immigrant given amnesty in America, deport one white liberal activist. Deport radical feminists, radical vegans, anti-gun zealots, and community organizers. They can then organize the drug cartels in Honduras and get them to give up their guns while they are at it.

As an extra inducement, fifty lucky amnestied illegal immigrants should be given $100,000 jobs in the California legislature and United States California Congressional delegation. In exchange, America can deport Jerry Brown, Dianne Feinstein, Barbara Boxer, Nancy Pelosi, and every other liberal basket case. Replacing them with Mexicans would increase diversity, a just and good liberal agenda item.

Given how self-loathing many guilty white liberals are, this program is perfect. By deporting only white people, conservatives would avoid charges of racism. The deported white liberals should be men. The Hispanics and Latinos granted citizenship should be women. This ends the phony war on women while making

America a more physically appealing nation. Latinas are far more beautiful than bald white guys.

Liberals keep saying that illegal immigrants are not the ones harming America. They are right for once. Mexicans, Central Americans and South Americans did not mess up California. White liberal legislators born and bred in San Francisco and other cities America cannot sell off destroyed the once Golden State.

Latinos work hard. They do tough jobs white liberals refuse to do. Without Hispanics, McDonalds would close its doors. Mexicans sneak into America to work hard. White upper-middle class college girls protest all day, demand free contraception and get degrees in lesbian vegan grievance studies. Who benefits America more?

Immigration strengthens America. American-born spoiled brats spitting on this country and blaming it for all of the world's evils do not. Those deriding Mexicans and South Americans as unskilled labor should observe Millennials. Young Obamabots are not brimming with useful skills or an admirable work ethic. Mexicans would probably not be texting or updating their social media platforms in the middle of a job interview.

Make America stronger. We need more people from Mexico, Honduras, and El Salvador and fewer people from San Francisco, the Upper Westside of Manhattan, Malibu and Hollywood. America deserves people who risk their lives to enter America rather than people born into privilege who never stopped complaining about America.

(Mexico is resisting this plan. The Mexican government has threatened that if we try to give them our liberals, they will immediately start building a border fence. They love Mexico too much to turn it into Mexifrisco. Delicate negotiations will fail, but bribery in the form of United States Treasury dollars should seal the deal. Pesos for Pelosiraptors may be our last hope.)

Every bad idea and useless policy proposal emanates from rich white liberals. Illegal immigrants care about feeding their families, not climate change. Bring in the illegal Hispanics. Deport the white liberals. Get America back to work. Support the Great Illegal Immigration Compromise. We can do this.

What if a climate scientist fell in the forest?

If a climate scientist falls in the forest, is anybody, anywhere affected?

That burning question is the heart of a new strategy designed by a leftist writer unfamiliar with the concept of leverage. A column written for *MSNBC* expressed frustration at the lack of action on climate change. Like scientology and breakdancing, climate change became a sensation for a precious few. Most of the world found the topic and its supporters boring.

The column lamented the inability of climate change supporters to forcibly make seven billion people care about some bizarre concept of environmental Armageddon. Expensive gatherings at luxury European hotels failed to produce any meaningful political progress. While opinion is divided on the issue itself, this proposed *MSNBC* solution has the power to unify us all.

"So at this point it's absurd to keep asking the scientific community to churn out more reports. In fact, it might almost be more useful if they went on strike: until you pay attention to what we've already told you, we won't be telling you more."[42]

Go on strike? Quit? Refuse to preach?

This threat if carried out may still not advance climate change. However, it probably will lead to an increase in another religion that actually involves God. Getting climate scientists and other liberals to cease their noise pollution is what most conservatives pray for every night.

If climate scientists went on strike, what would be the downside? Very rarely does somebody inadvertently do such a spectacular job of making the opposing side's case.

"They've done their job. (And they've done it for free – working on these endless IPCC reports is a volunteer job)."[43]

Volunteer job? Finally, a liberal admits that these climatologists have been wasting their time as well as ours. They poured blood, sweat and tears into an unpaid job and found out nobody cares. The proper thing for these over-age interns to do is to give up and go do something meaningful that the world can care about.

MSNBC seems to miss the point of how a strike works. People who provide value strike because they believe they are indispensable. They have what their employer desperately needs.

The climatologists worked for free churning out reports that were ignored. Once something provided is utterly useless, it is by definition no longer a good or service. Commerce requires value.

Climate scientists going on strike would be like the French going on strike. How would anybody tell? Not since *Married With Children's* Peggy Bundy threatened her husband Al with a strike has a refusal to do anything been so celebrated.[44]

MSNBC is late to the party. Satire magazine *The Onion* wrote a 1999 piece entitled, "Nation's Experts Give Up." *MSNBC* could learn from *The Onion's* brilliant bluff.

"Citing years of frustration over their advice being misunderstood, misrepresented or simply ignored, America's foremost experts in every field collectively tendered their resignation Monday."

"Since you don't seem to care about things you don't understand, screw you. We quit."

"Because the experts' advice was barely followed, the mass resignation is expected to have little impact on the lives of most Americans."[45]

Striking climatologists would quickly learn what *The Onion* wickedly figured out in the last century.

This is bigger than one leftist columnist, one failed television network, or even a few failed liberal politicians. This is about an entire ideology that still confuses power with authority. Power is the ability to force people to do things. Saddam Hussein had power. Vladimir Putin has power. Authority is the moral respect that causes people to willingly follow a person. Liberals occasionally amass power in America but never try to gain the authority to govern in a center-right nation.

Calling climate change skeptics stupid or evil is a lousy selling point. Trying to force Americans with better things to do to drop everything and obsess over nonsense is a losing strategy. It hurts the left to hear this, but more Americans would care if leftist issues mattered. The masses are not imbeciles. They are bright enough to see the elites as condescending bookworms with lousy people skills.

Leftist climatologists will never strike. Like many liberals, they love the sound of their own voices. They remain convinced that forcing their world vision on everybody leads to a public grateful for being browbeaten into submission. The left never accepts the system shock that comes with leaving and having nobody follow or care in the slightest.

The science is settled. Leftist climatologists and their *MSNBC* apologists are boring, wrong, and irrelevant in the court of public opinion. An increase in glossy reports with slick PowerPoint slides will not make these gasbags any less insufferable.

That is what is truly beyond dispute. All the kicking, screaming, stomping and threatening to stop providing what most people never asked for will have zero effect on the lives of normal people. Even if climate change obsessives refuse to quit speaking, conservatives can be happy knowing most of the world long ago quit listening. When enough people repeatedly refuse to accept a message, it becomes apparent that the messengers have nothing of value to say.

At long last, some green jobs

Maybe Barack Obama was right all along. It took him several years, but he finally helped improve America. All that was necessary was redefining improvement.

It started in a California field where Pedro toiled. He insists that he immigrated here legally, but this is not an immigration discussion. Pedro with his sore back works fourteen hours every day picking lettuce.

Far away in Arkansas is a guy named Clem trying to catch frogs. His friend offered him one dollar for every frog he caught. The collected frogs were then involved in some elaborate sorority party mattress prank. The screams from the coeds were hilarious.

In a wealthy Connecticut enclave, high school student Dave just began his new job at a juice bar making smoothies. He can make broccoli, cauliflower, and asparagus smoothies for those more concerned with health than flavor. Everything tastes good when put in a blender except for everything he blends.

A terrible New York traffic jam occurred when a traffic light malfunctioned. Due to a glitch, this one Manhattan light stayed red. The crisis was averted when a panicked Mayor Bloomberg brought Sam in to fix the problem. Sam showed up with his construction belt around his waist and a ladder. Sam replaced the malfunctioning red light and pushed a button. The new red light started blinking and then turned yellow. Moments later all systems were go.

A bored North Dakota college student bought marijuana from a rising young entrepreneur doing brisk campus business. The commerce was a victory for both students. The seller of the cannabis had spending money for the weekend. The buyer earned the pleasure of rolling the pot up into a cigarette, smoking it, and then giggling while demanding munchies.

Between the California lettuce-picker, Arkansas frog catcher, Connecticut smoothie maker, New York light fixer, and the North Dakota drug dealer, one thing is crystal clear. Barack Obama is the greatest political leader in the history of civilization. His supporters are right. He is Jesus, Moses, and Gandhi all rolled into one emblem of perfection.

It took weeks to find these five workers all across America, but lettuce, frogs, broccoli smoothies, lights telling drivers to go, and marijuana all share the same beautiful quality.

They are all varying shades of green. Obama is the king of green jobs. Let us all bow down before the leader of the new green economy. Green collar jobs are real. Green is the new…well…green, perhaps.

Next week in Florida, Obama meets with twelve-year-old Bobby. He was just hired for ten dollars per week to mow lawns. That makes six green jobs, or as the Obama campaign proudly reported, a twenty percent increase.

President Obama's historical Fairness Initiative

President Obama delivered a groundbreaking speech on the best way to instill fairness in America. While this came less than 24 hours after his speech at the Democrat National Convention in Charlotte, North Carolina, he felt it was necessary to say a bit more. As part of C-SPAN's *Road to the White House*[46] coverage, his remarks are now rebroadcast in their thrilling entirety.

Good evening. As you all know, yesterday I accepted the 2012 Democratic nomination for President. Things went so well in 2008 that we decided to do it again. Vice President Joe Biden would like to thank everyone who skipped the NFL season opener this week to watch his convention speech. The game was fantastic, and Joe tells me his speech was quite good as well. I guess we'll all just have to take his word for it.

Four days ago on Labor Day, I opened the Democratic Convention by unveiling my new Sincerity Initiative. Normally the President does not speak on all four nights of the convention, but you all understood that since the event was about me, I had to do it. While it is unprecedented to give another speech the day after in prime time, think of it as getting five convention nights for the price of four. It was important that the taxpayers and high-priced lobbyists get their money's worth.

Tonight I am unveiling a new, historical, and unprecedented program that shall forever be known as the Fairness Initiative. As you all know, it is imperative that fairness be restored to this country at all costs. For those who were told life is unfair, it no longer has to be that way.

Some of you have expressed concerns. Forcing the National Basketball Association to have a height cap at five foot ten would allow the vertically challenged to make the team, but perhaps with a lower quality product. Demanding that the Miss America Pageant only accept contestants over 300 pounds would restore the dignity of the proportionally challenged, but possibly lead to reduced ratings if not caloric intake. Any organization will be allowed to request a waiver from my Fairness Initiative. Waivers will be granted based on total obedience to the rest of my agenda. This policy worked well with healthcare, hence the continuity.

Leaders must lead by example. That is why they are called leaders, and their examples are called examples. Therefore, in an attempt to spread the wealth around and insure fairness, I will be making an unprecedented Election 2012 campaign donation.

It was brought to my attention that I have one billion dollars in the bank. George Clooney and the rest of Hollywood have filled my coffers to the brim. To the family of the homeless man that Mr. Clooney's motorcade ran over quickly so as not to be late for the fundraiser, apologies have been sent out. Compassion comes at a price.

Anyway, it seems that my opponent Mitt Romney is a less wealthy plutocrat than we originally thought. Whether it was the economy I inherited or rich Republicans on Wall Street failing to do their jobs, Governor Romney is down to his last 100 million dollars of campaign money. In the interest of fairness, I will be donating 450 million dollars to the 2012 Romney campaign.

It is unfair that in America some candidates like me have so much and some candidates like him have so little. Maybe he has a higher burn rate, but this should not have anything to do with fossil fuels. In the new green economy, there should be enough green for everybody. I was going to have Ben Bernanke just print 900 million dollars and give it to Mr. Romney so we would both have one billion, but I did not want inflation to eat away at the value of my campaign war chest. That is what fiscal responsibility is all about.

Mr. Romney and I will both have 550 million dollars to start. On the first day of every month, I will continue to transfer money toward his effort to defeat me in an effort to keep the playing field level. One week before the election, a final transfer of funds will take place.

Some on the left are worried that Republican and conservative Super PACs will raise additional money. The left need not worry. George Soros is prepared to use his expertise of campaign finance law necessary for the greater good of electing me. Chicago Mayor Rahm Emanuel knows where all of the bodies are buried, and he will make sure they vote as well.

This wealth transfer is the right thing to do. This is a teachable moment and a great example of us all coming together. Virtually every platitude uttered in the last four years can be enhanced with this donation.

People have accused me of not putting my money where my mouth is. Well now I am putting it where Mr. Romney's trousers are. That may seem awkward, but I am never awkward. The money will go into his wallet. Now that my commitment to economic justice is complete, my next step will be demanding that the media cover both Governor Romney and myself with equal fairness. The media has already covered me so they can spend the rest of the campaign focusing on him. Mechanisms to enforce this exist but most people agree that my merely saying such things is praiseworthy.

Thank you and good evening.

This has been C-SPAN's *Road to the White House* coverage. Next week we will cover President Obama as he visits a homeless shelter filled with former green economy employees. The shelter used to be where solar panels were made until it was shut down for failing to produce a single worthwhile unit of any product. Mr. Obama's visit will showcase Mr. Romney's lack of empathy for the new green economy homeless movement.

PRESIDENT OBAMA DISAVOWS OBAMACARE ADVISERS JONATHAN GRUBER AND BILL COSBY

As part of C-SPAN's *Road to the White House* series, we covered President Obama's most recent press conference since MIT Professor Jonathan Gruber revealed inconvenient truths about the Affordable Care Act. President Obama has given several thousand speeches since the United States Supreme Court decision was handed down two years ago. Ratings for C-SPAN have never been higher. Frustrated news viewers know that local news is even more boring than we are. C-SPAN will not be covering Gruber's testimony before a House subcommittee due to its expected graphic, violent content. Rather than watch Election 2016 coverage, here we present President Obama explaining why a tax is not really a tax.

Good afternoon. Tomorrow I will be speaking about immigration. The next day I will be speaking about climate change. The day after I will speak about whatever topic comes to mind that I know you all agree with me on. We have to cherish these precious moments before my term ends. Today's discussion will focus on healthcare.

As you all know, the non-partisan Supreme Court upheld my signature piece of legislation, the Affordable Care Act. It was the right thing to do, and Justice John Roberts knows this as well. I instructed SEIU representatives to help his family find their pets, who went missing in the days before that decision. I worked hard to make sure they were returned safe and sound in the same way I tracked down and killed Osama bin Laden.

As you all know, I headed the Harvard Law Review. Most people do not realize the significance of this, but this is not about me, even though I did head the Harvard Law Review. This is about the American people being told that the healthcare mandate constitutes a tax. Although it is a penalty and not a tax, reasonable minds disagree. However, there is nothing reasonable about the Republicans who insist on calling a tax a tax.

The good news is that the days of gridlock are over. I have crafted a compromise that should satisfy everybody who cares about this country and disappoint only those who don't. From now on, the penalty assessed will no longer be referred to as a fee, penalty, or tax. It is now and forever known as a "garbleschnizzle." This stems from the Latin word "garble," involving undecipherable language, and "schnizzle," which derives its roots from the German word "schnitzel." As you know, politics is sausage making.

I did not consult with MIT professor Jonathan Gruber. If I had, I would have called it a Gruberschnizzle. As any reasonable person can see, a garbleschnizzle does not contain his name in the title. When he attacked the "stupidity of the American voter,"[47] I was so angry that I could barely contain my emotions. As everyone knows, I am an emotional person who frequently emotes, not a cold, analytical professorial-type lacking human empathy. My auricles and ventricles have not been replaced with old defective Intel Pentium chips. I overflowed with emotion when discussing the cycle of violence between Israelis and Palestinians. Anyway, back to healthcare.

While I barely know Jonathan Gruber, I did consult with various celebrities from some of my most recent fundraisers. Rapper Snoop Dogg heard the idea and exclaimed, "Foshizzle garbleschnizzle," and we decided to go ahead with it. Now this term is not to be confused with other words such as garbleschazzle and garbleschnuzzle. Those are separate terms we will be applying to other pieces of legislation as we see fit.

There are rumors circulating that we then ran the idea by Bill Cosby, who replied, "Schizemflop, flazzmajazz, flizzmflazzm."[48] Given that Mr. Cosby is facing serious allegations of wrongdoing, it is important for people to understand that I have never personally met him. This is in keeping with his insistence that he never met me when I faced my bevy of scandals from Benghazi to Fast and Furious to IRS abuses. Unless Mr. Cosby is exonerated, it is important that the media know that I have never had a meeting with him, Gruber or Mary Landrieu. I have barely heard of her. Somebody may have mentioned her name once in connection with something involving somebody needing a life preserver and not getting one. Apparently my predecessor George W. Bush left her to sink during Hurricane Katrina.

We tried to get Reverend Jesse Jackson to make a healthcare word that rhymed but he was incomprehensible to us all. Even Snoop and Coz could not understand him and they speak fluent Blingflazzlish.

Before making this garbleschnizzle executive decision, I instructed Vice President Joe Biden to reread his Dr. Seuss books to make sure that the term was not already being used. We also consulted with comedian Rich Hall and instructed him to come up with some new Sniglets[49] in case we run out of multi-syllabic words.

This will help the healing begin, since House Minority Leader Nancy Pelosi and Attorney General Eric Holder have discovered that in some communities, referring to this as a tax might be racially and culturally insensitive.

Lastly, I want to address those who criticized the selling of BFD t-shirts in celebration of the momentous court ruling agreeing with me.[50] BFD stands for Big Falliptigon Deal. As you know, Falliptigons are the offspring of Deceptagons and Velociraptors, just less well known.

Let me leave you with slogans to end the discussion, since this subject bothers me by forcing me to interact with the American people I deeply love and respect. The time for talk is over. The time for talk about anything is over. We had our debate. I won. We must move forward, onward, upward, and even to the Ninth Ward. While some people claimed that my policies were on the ballot in 2014, I was not. What matters is that the real electorate voted for me in 2012.

Although other candidates will be running for president in 2016, the election will be a referendum on my policies. While this is not about me, fairness requires that the record be set straight. I am the most qualified person to do this. Therefore, my address to the American people about things I know they care about from climate change to investing in education will continue taking place every day.

To those Republicans who stand in the way of making progress for the American people, I think I speak for Joe Biden and everybody else when I say, "Go Falliptigon yourself." New t-shirts with GFY will be on sale later this week. Thank you.

This concludes C-SPAN's *Road to the White House* coverage. Next up we will have coverage of President Obama reading to schoolchildren from a newly discovered, Common Core approved Dr. Seuss knockoff book entitled, "President Obama and the Affordable Care Act." Until next time, lavorkivus, presidentalanus.

Obamacare: If you like your president you can keep him

As President Obama remains accused of broken promises, an interesting irony is developing. Every meaningful comment regarding Obamacare can be applied to Obama himself. The policy represents the heart of Obama's beliefs. He takes criticism of his policies personally because he and his policies are inseparable.

If his policies succeeded, it would be a personal validation of everything Obama. Therefore, failed policies are only the surface. Obama's very core is on the line.

Take the policy promise, replace it with the person, and observe the results.

"If you like your doctor, you can keep your doctor. If you like your plan, you can keep it."[51]

If you like your president, you can keep him. Except you cannot. Many Americans who liked George W. Bush were saddened to see their president and his plan replaced with an inferior model. Bush gave us protection from threats to our health such as radical Islam. Obama chose to replace effective treatment with dialogue and understanding.

"We have to pass the bill to find out what is in it."[52]

We had to elect Barack Obama to find out who and what he was. Questions about his beliefs were dismissed as partisanship, allowing Americans to invest in a completely blank slate of hope and change.

Obamacare is working.

These people think Obama is successful. After all, catastrophic failure is now known as moving in the right direction. Endless foul-ups are slow, steady progress.

Obamacare is settled law and constitutional.

So is Obama. Legally he is in charge. That does not mean he is moral, ethical, competent or wise. Winning an election reflects an ability to campaign, not govern.

Just because the website failed does not mean Obamacare itself failed. Just because Obamacare failed does not mean Obama himself failed. Just because Obama failed does not mean liberalism itself failed.

Actually, yes it does. Dissenters are free to name a single big-government program that has ever worked as intended and fulfilled its promises. At this point liberals pick other failed programs and declare them successes because they say so.

Obama supposedly had no idea that the website was incredibly flawed.

Liberal voters had no idea that Obama was incredibly flawed. Millennials chanted "Yes, we can" but never told anybody or understood what they actually can do. Beneath those chants was a man who apparently cannot. Cannot what? Not much of anything, apparently.

Obamacare was in its early stages. Glitches happen with new product rollouts.

Obama had glitches in 2009 when his stimulus package failed. Six years of being in charge did not fix a single meaningful glitch. Glitches worsened, sometimes resulting in Americans being murdered. Benghazi? Fast and Furious? Dead bodies? Just glitches.

Obamacare was meant to fail and be replaced with a true single-payer program.

Obama was meant to fail and be replaced with a conservative Republican president like Ronald Reagan. The results are in. Reagan conservatism succeeded. His rising tide lifted all boats. Obama liberalism crashed and burned.

To reduce the number of failed programs, reject the failed people promoting these programs and the failed ideology that keeps churning out these failed people.

Obamacare settled law? Try enforcing it

Liberals desperate to preserve the Affordable Care Act did what they frequently do when their beliefs are about to collapse. They declare matters settled to stifle debate and end conversations.[53] From climate change to healthcare, their prize projects are settled simply because they say so.

Liberals should heed the words of former Democrat President Andrew "Old Hickory" Jackson. In the 1830s, the Marshall Supreme Court ruled against Jackson on a matter involving gold found on an Indian reservation. The issue was supposedly settled until it was not. Jackson made his declaration public and emphatic (The quote is also attributed to Horace Greeley).

"John Marshall has made his decision; now let him enforce it."[54]

President Obama took those words to an art form. When Obama dislikes laws, he simply disobeys them. He substitutes his own moral conscience for black letter law, discounting others with different moral beliefs.

Illegal immigration, DOMA, Obamacare and New Black Panthers intimidating white voters are examples of Obama's selective enforcement or non-enforcement of laws.

Obama tried to subject Americans to a law that a majority never wanted. The ACA was passed using barely legal legislative machinations in a raw naked political power play. The law has been besieged by unworkable assumptions, flawed methodology, unsafe privacy protections and dreadful technological glitches.

It is time to turn the tables. Hardball begets hardball. Obama passed his precious law. Let him try enforcing it.

The only thing holding Obamacare together is the mandate. Obamacare orders Americans to purchase health insurance. What if enough people refuse to comply?

While Obama has access to predator drones, nuclear weapons and the greatest military in the world, even *The NYJBT* and *MSNBC* would pause if those were his enforcement mechanisms. His first layer of enforcement is the Internal Revenue Service. He already used the IRS to target Americans attempting to prevent the law's passage.

IRS agents carry pencils, not guns or drones. They send threatening letters on non-recyclable paper, which can be discarded. Even if Obama hired every member of Organizing For Action to work in the IRS collections department, they could not visit every person refusing to comply.

The penalty for refusing to purchase insurance is a fine. Failure to pay the fine leads to increased levies, which can also be ignored. The IRS could make unscheduled visits, but attorneys are ready to do pro bono work blocking enforcement actions.

The next step would be for Obama to send law enforcement officials to arrest individuals refusing to pay the fines and levies. Imagine the nightly news. The same Obama administration refusing to round up illegal immigrants would be rounding up American citizens. Doomsday scenarios about government storm troopers kicking down doors and Americans defending themselves with their Second Amendment rights are non-starters. This is not the Whiskey Rebellion.

Government abuses have already created a backlash. IRS and DoJ officials are subjects in a myriad of congressional investigations. The government has power, but true enforcement comes from moral authority. This requires an almost universal level of voluntary citizen compliance. Unless Obama liberals are evil or crazy enough to send soldiers to arrest every conservative in America (not yet), Obamacare has zero enforcement powers. A more likely scenario would be Congress defunding any agency that harasses Americans. If Obamacare cannot be defunded, enforcers can certainly have their budgets stripped bare.

Even if people were arrested, Americans are still entitled to a trial by a jury of their peers. One juror can hang a case. When half the country is upset, finding one out of twelve to acquit is easy. Not one person will be convicted for refusing to purchase insurance.

The 2014 elections rendered Obama powerless to impose his will. Lame ducks are called that for a reason. There is not enough time for Obama to send out threatening letters, much less conduct any meaningful follow-through. He is left to giving angry speeches, which turns off independent voters. Democ-rats are jumping from his sinking ship since all politics remains local.

The only thing settled is that Obamacare is dead. Ineptitude and corruption had it staggering around weakened. Deliberate civil disobedience through non-compliance will be the stake through its heart.

Obama liberals substituted their own beliefs for codified law. Now they will get more than a lesson in how the legal system works. In this healthcare fight they deserve a heaping taste of their own medicine. The community organizer can be out-organized. Obama's predecessor understood enforcement. His catchphrase is the only thing left to say to Obama. "Bring 'em on."[55]

Chapter 4: Islamofascist Foreign Policy Lunacy

Suicide bombers are crazy. Only nutcases would deliberately subject themselves to a painful death. Only the truly craziest people would consider a reward for that death to be seventy-two women having no idea what to do sexually.

Islamofascist terrorist leaders are very rational. The world is a chessboard they wish to dominate. They know Democrats have not had a serious leader willing to fight evil in almost fifty years.

Never send a liberal to do a man's job. In both cases the results are deadly. The difference is conservatives wage war against radical Islamofascists and kill bad guys. Liberals get their own people killed leading from behind[56] in half-hearted overseas contingency operations[57] to combat workplace violence.[58]

Put the children to bed and let the adults keep us safe.

Challah Akbar!

Whenever anyone shows that Islamofascists act violent, Islamofascists respond by acting violent. We draw Mohammed. Islamifascists respond with death threats.

Pamela Geller should have Mexicans draw the Prophet on Cinco de Muhammado. This adds to diversity and multiculturalism because #Jihadistlivesmatter.

Anybody who thinks Pamela Geller provoked Islamofascists has already been beheaded, is dead from the neck up, and has their severed head up their hide.

A woman in a short skirt in a bad neighborhood at night is not asking to be raped. Pamela Geller is not asking to be beheaded. Liberal feminists remain confused.

Is a woman who mouths off to her man "asking for it?" If not, liberal feminists must defend Pamela Geller, not tell her metaphorically to "shut up b*tch."

Liberal feminists believe that violence against women is wrong unless the aggressor is a liberal or a Muslim or the victim is a conservative. The war on conservative women continues.

Islamofascists kill those mocking their religion. They are almost as intolerant as climate changers & feminists.

When Islamofascists come for leftists, conservatives will not be there to speak up. Liberals with a suicide wish may be too dumb to save.

It is long past time for me to decree anti-Islamofascist fatwas.

Fatwa: Any Islamofascist caught eating Jewish bread before washing their hands and saying a Jewish prayer shall be stoned to death. **Challah Akbar!**

Fatwa: On the Jewish Sabbath, any Islamofascist not in synagogue learning Chasidis is violating the Lubavitche Rebbe's teachings and must be killed. **Shabbos Akbar!**

Fatwa: Woman-beating patriarchical Islamofascist cowards shall from now on celebrate Mother's Day or get a stick to their behinds. **Mama Akbar!**

Fatwa: Islamofascists who call Jews descendants of apes and pigs shall immediately be put to death for insulting the Prophets of Abraham, Isaac and Jacob. **Hashem Akbar!**

Fatwa: Sharia law is now illegal. Any man caught practicing Islamofascist law shall be locked in a room with Elizabeth Warren. She will lecture about equality and read the *Vagina Monologues* while naked. Thus it is decreed! **Feminism Akbar!**

Fatwa: Climate change skeptics shall be pelted with vegetables by a nearly naked, hemp loinclothed screaming Al Gore. **Gaea Akbar!**

Fatwa: Anyone criticizing or drawing a picture of President Barack Obama shall be forced to watch MSNBC's screaming pantsless Chris Matthews. **Obama Akbar!**

(A fatwa that anyone criticizing President Obama be subjected to IRS targeting was issued by Eric Holder in January of 2009. **Obama Akbar!**)

Fatwa: When Cinco de Mayo falls on Taco Tuesday, Americans must use Halal approved Pico de Gallo. **Taco (ak)Bar!**

Fatwa: Sesame Street and all kids programs since 1979 are Zionist propaganda. To dance your cares away insults the Prophet's law. **Fraggle Rockbar!**

Fatwa: All Islamofascists shall be forced to sit through a political convention's platform committee meeting. The ACLU has vowed to sue, citing the Geneva Convention's ban on torture. Islamofascists begged for mercy and asked if they could sit on Rules or Resolutions Committees instead. Democrat delegates said they have no rules and resolve nothing. Islamofascists were caught yelling a battle cry that sounded like **"Quorom!"**

A fatwa on Pamela Geller was mistakenly issued on Sarah Michelle Gellar. Islamofascists apologized and said they support slaying Zionist vampires. **Buffy Akbar!**

Ross & Monica Geller were declared part of the Zionist conspiracy since David Schwimmer is Jewish. Chandler Bing will be spared until Matthew Perry can be identified. Other *Friends* can survive as long as they are not Friends of the IDF.

Islamofascists plotting to blow up Hawaii killed each other instead when a fight broke out over whether to yell **"Aloha Akbar"** or **"Mahalo Akbar."**

When told neither phrase made sense, Islamofascists pointed out that nothing they say or do makes sense.

On Lag B'Omer, Jews light bonfires. Islamofascists got excited until learning that the fires are contained, buildings are not torched, and no infidels are thrown in the fire.

Fatwa: If Islamofascists want to start a new Jewish tradition, some Jews would be happy to celebrate Lag B'Omer by burning Islamofascist headquarters and tossing Islamofascists into the bonfires. **Lag B'Omer Akbar!**

Issuing Fatwas is tiring.

Fatwa: A sleepy Supreme Islamofascist leader, after consulting with the even more domineering Mchelle Obama, decreed a FLOTUS-approved multicultural lunchtime and naptime. **Fiesta Siesta Akbar!**

President Obama's post-Armageddon press conference

Today C-SPAN joins President Obama live in the Rose Garden. This will be his first live press conference since the total obliteration of Israel three weeks ago on New Year's Eve of 2015. One day before that on December 30th, Iran announced that it had successfully developed nuclear bombs. The next day they eliminated Israel off the map just before the clock struck 2016. Two weeks ago, Iran launched successful nuclear attacks on New York City, Pittsburgh, Philadelphia, Boston, and Hartford. The death toll currently stands at about one hundred million people, or about one-third of the American population. These are President Obama's final remarks before tomorrow's State of the Union. The Iowa caucus and New Hampshire primary soon follow.

My fellow Americans:

These last few weeks have been challenging. America has been attacked, but we are as resilient as ever. As you know, I was elected to end wars. My predecessor launched a faulty war in Iraq rather than deal with the threat of Iran. Our military was strained from wars in Afghanistan and Iraq. Our military were further pushed to the brink due to sequester budget cuts that decimated our intelligence gathering capabilities. The results of those reckless actions led to a more dangerous world.

As most of you know, Israel no longer exists. The first nuclear bomb Iran detonated eradicated the Jewish state. I am deeply upset about this. Nobody is madder about this than me. When we find the killers who did this, they will be brought to justice. The murderers who took innocent lives will be held responsible. I am outraged that more was not done to prevent this attack. I have ordered Attorney General Eric Holder to investigate who failed to prevent these attacks. I will hold people accountable.

A couple of weeks ago, an act of overseas aggression led to the deaths of millions of Americans. While the motive for the acts is not clear, let me be perfectly clear. Any nation that attacks America will face severe consequences. A nuclear attack violates accepted 21st century societal norms and international law. The killers murdered American citizens, but they did not murder the American spirit. They did not harm the American government. Washington, DC is still standing. Unless Republicans and tea party activists shut down the government, Social Security and welfare checks will go out on time. Except for our Ambassador to Israel, all diplomats are safe. Millionaires and billionaires on Wall Street were killed, but the United Nations building was miraculously spared.

Let me be crystal clear. Nobody is more upset about the murder of one hundred million Americans than me. I am profoundly angry and offended by this. The killers will face justice. We will lead an investigation and hold the killers responsible. I will hold whoever failed to prevent these attacks personally accountable. Steps will be taken to make sure that an attack like this never happens again. I will be working with the international community to pass a resolution authorizing further sanctions against Iran. These will be the toughest sanctions against Iran in American history. First Lady Michelle Obama's Twitter hashtag campaign #warisnottheanswer has one million likes on Facebook. That is a social media record response to this kind of tragedy.

What matters most is that we do not let these attacks destroy our values. We are better than that. Iran is a rich nation with a civilization dating back to ancient Persia. The people of Iran belong to many different religions. They are a diverse, multicultural people. They are your neighbors.

Before the attacks, America was on the slow road to recovery from the 2008 financial crisis and the mountain of debt piled up in the years preceding my inauguration. We must not let these attacks slow that momentum. We must continue to provide healthcare for those who need it, invest in education, and grow our economy in an environmentally friendly way through alternative energy. I am not happy about the price of gasoline spiking to over $20 per gallon since the attacks. Nobody is angrier over this than me. However, we cannot drill our way out of this mess and we cannot cut our way to prosperity.

Although the Iowa caucus is around the corner, we cannot let partisan politics interfere with the hard work of governing. Too many on the other side have been playing politics when we should be coming together and finding solutions to prevent future overseas contingencies and other acts of workplace violence.

I will be discussing these issues tomorrow during my State of the Union address and during my weekly radio address. The time for talk is over. The time to act is now. I urge Congress to get to work and bring me their ideas. I am open to ideas from everybody provided they do not compromise America's values and my values.

America's remaining allies know they can always count on America to lead the way to a brighter future. Together we will move forward to end the war on women, combat climate change, expand opportunities for minorities, pass immigration reform and continue on the path to peace. This is the right thing to do. God bless you, and God bless America.

This concludes C-SPAN's coverage of President Obama's post-Armageddon speech. Join us tomorrow for live coverage of his State of the Union address.

Next week we cover his vacation at Martha's Vineyard, which was not damaged in the nuclear attacks. We then follow him to Pittsburgh. While Vice President Biden meets with bombing survivors, President Obama will be holding a rally for Hillary Clinton with the United Steelworkers Union before heading to George Clooney's Los Angeles homes for Democrat fundraisers.

Half-naked picture of Muhammad with a goat

Screw Islamofascists. It is time to show a picture of a half-naked Muhammad and a goat.

If *The Tygrrrr Express* burns and I get beheaded, the war of civilization vs. barbarism will claim another casualty.

Muhammad was once special, but today this former warrior could not beat up most people. He is a shell of what he was. He's 1,400 years old. He probably has bursitis at that age. Muhammad would fight his own battles himself and not need Islamofascists to do his dirty work if he was really that tough.

Deal with it, George Clooney. *The Men Who Stare at Goats* is more than a bad movie nobody watched.[59] It is now the published image concluding this column.

Perhaps I am not being offensive enough, but it is hard to show a picture of Muhammad when I have no idea what he looks like. If I did, I would post it. I do know that he looked like a human and not a bear. Therefore, the creators of *South Park* did not offend anybody.[60] Perhaps Islamofascists may wish to stop calling Jews apes and pigs.

South Park mocks all religions brilliantly. One episode poked fun at the Jewish holiday of Purim.[61] Creators Trey Parker and Matt Stone showed that Catholicism's leader is a bunny rabbit. The large, long hat the Pontiff wears fits perfectly over rabbit ears.[62]

Catholic League President Bill Donohue retaliated by murdering 3,000 New Yorkers on 9/11. Never mind. That was Khalid Sheikh Mohammed, not to be confused with his Catholic cousin Khalid Sheik John Paul.

Matt Parker and Trey Stone do not attack religions. They attack people who abuse religion for nefarious purposes. After the Purim episode, a Chasidic devotee of the Lubavitcher Rebbe strapping a suicide belt around his waist.

Never mind again. That was another Mohammedan.

The Virgin Mary has been covered in fertilizer. A cross was hung in a jar of something that resembles but is definitely not Apple cider.

Christians protest. They try to cut off funding. ACLU and other brain-dead liberals claim censorship by confusing free speech with government-subsidized speech from confiscated taxpayer dollars.

The left will never admit the truth. It is acceptable to ridicule Jews and Christians because they do not retaliate with genocidal rage. The canard about peaceful Muslims is irrelevant. There are one billion Muslims. Ninety-nine point nine percent of Muslims are peaceful, which means the remaining one million are bloodthirsty Islamofascist savages.

Rather than try to kill these million, the left gives them undeserved cover. Most people know it is wrong to lump decent Muslims in with the murderers. By making excuses for the murderers, it is the left heinously lumping the murderers in with the decent ones. Refusing to mention radical Islam allows the Islamofascists to hide behind the cloak of the moderate Muslims. By refusing to separate Islamofascists from the ninety-nine point nine percent of good Muslims, leftists are actually harming the very moderate Muslims they claim to want to help. Call it blasphemy. Islamofascists kill people who criticize them. There is no word on whether Islamofascists wish to kill leftists for refusing to criticize them. It sounds convoluted, but genocidal barbarians are not the most logical creatures. Neither are their emotion-driven enablers.

When Muslim cartoons showed Mohammed to be violent, what was the response from radical Muslims?

Islam's violent strain has the advantage because Judaism and Christianity do not come even close on the violence scale. Islamofascists are calculating that this equation will not change. Like children using Common Core textbooks, the Islamofascists calculate wrong. One of two things is going to happen.

Either Christians will surrender as they did in Europistan, or they will fight back with equal if not greater brutality. The Crusades Part II will be even bloodier.

Jihadism is a cancer that can only be eradicated through forceful self-defense. Islamofascists are sodomizing innocent civilians with baseball bats. What if this behavior were done back to them and then they were fed to the goats they use as spouses? Would they finally understand they have gone too far? Who outside of leftists could object to defending themselves and the world from Islamofascists? The normal world including ninety-nine point nine percent of sane Muslims want Islamofascist terrorism stopped.

I will not be part of the Caliphate. I don't need to be sensitive or understanding. Tolerant liberals can go live in areas controlled by radical Islam. ACLU human rights advocates will beg for Christians and Jews as leaders once they are deported to live under savage butcherers.

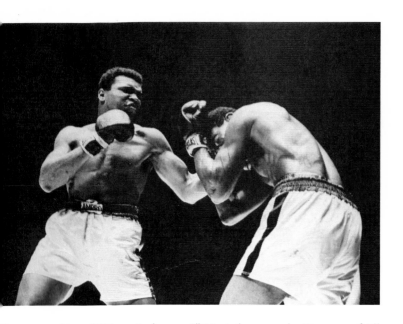

f you are asking, "Where is the goat?" He *is* the goat, the Greatest of All
Ie repeatedly said so himself. Anybody who thinks Muslim Muhammad
ceful never saw the violence Ali inflicted on Joe Frazier in the Thrilla
ila.[63]

Until then, *South Park* needs to keep doing exact
versions of the Danish cartoons must be printed eve
to stop crucifying peaceful Christians and coddling

What if Jews and Christians acted like Islamofa:
Islamofascist calls Jews apes or pigs, should Israel shou
on their country and obliterate them all? After all, isi
those who insult the children of Abraham? The next
should Christians go into random Muslim neighl
infidels, and shoot first and ask questions never?

No. The goal is to stop the bad guys, and only the ba
dialogue does not work with Islamofascists. The only
defense. Stopping terrorism does not breed more terro
by definition is the antonym of addition. The liberal
that could just be from cowering under the bed. Th
Republicans. How brave of them.

Radical Muslims who practice a b@stardized form of M
to slaughter the Jews they label apes and pigs. They are n
the thousands in 2015 all across the world. Islamofascists
Theo Van Gogh supporters can draw cartoons of the ca
publish those cartoons. Until then, enjoy the half-nak
and the goat.

Sc
Ti
w
ir

Radical Islamofascists Murder Innocent Teddy Bears

Many on the left care more about trees and animals than human beings. Ironically, the 9/11 terrorists murdered trees and bunny rabbits.

It seems the terrorists have crossed a line so heinous that even leftist ostriches will have to remove their heads from…well, let's call it sand. Algerian hackers committed a chilling story of animal barbarism.

"Geographically mixed-up Algerian hackers made themselves look rather silly by defacing the website of an English stately home instead of Belvoir Fortress in Israel, their intended target. Belvoir Castle, a Royalist stronghold during the English Civil War, by contrast, is best known these days as the host of an annual teddy bears' picnic."[64]

This is an outrage. For decades kids have been singing, "That's where the teddy bears have their picnic."[65]

No more. These terrorists hacked a teddy bear website. They might as well have hacked off the heads of these young cubs.

It is one thing to shout about death to America and death to Israel. Plenty of imbeciles in this world hate Americans and Jews. Nobody should hate teddy bears. You can't hate Winnie the Pooh. How dare anybody attack Paddington! The Berenstein Bears brought joy to so many children. Terrorists looked at the Care Bears and decided that they did not care!

Islamofascists hate cute little bears. They don't care about caring or sharing. They even prefer swearing. Islamofascists are animals. Teddy bears are animals too, but nicer.

Live teddy bears are not the only ones in danger. Bloodthirsty Islamofascists even hate stuffed teddy bears. Terrorists hate you, your children, and the stuffed animals you bought them as birthday and holiday presents.

Like true terrorists, they even kill their own. Some politically correct toy company probably created Burka Bear for young Islamic children. Did the terrorists bother to think that some of the bears at this teddy bear picnic might have been Muslims?

No, of course not. In an attempt to hack Jewish and American bears, cubs just getting through Ramadan became collateral damage.

So who is to blame for all of this?

Barack Obama. It is as obvious as the cute little button nose on a teddy bear's face.

(For the uninitiated, that is as cute as it gets.)

President Obama is from Chicago. The sports teams in Chicago are the Cubs and the Bears.

(Obama claims to root for the White Sox, but that is to court white voters. If he rooted for the Black Sox he would be accused of kowtowing to Reverend Wright. Rooting for the Red Sox would bring up more communism charges. Rumor has it Van Jones went a Reds game.)

(Some Colts slaughtered the Bears in the Super Bowl, but George W. Bush was in charge at that time. Maybe everything is his fault after all.)

Terrorists are murdering teddy bears while our president does nothing. Mr. Obama never prevented this attack on bears because of partisan politics. Former Republican House Speaker Dennis Hastert was from Chicago and resembled a teddy bear. Republican Teddy Roosevelt was the original Teddy Bear President. If these were liberal animals, Mr. Obama would save them (provided it helped his poll numbers).

Additionally, Barack Obama hates Wall Street because he cannot snap his fingers and make stocks rise. Who fights him? The bears.

Not since self-loathing Stephen Colbert (ironically pronounced Col-Bear, yet he hates bears) attacked these adorable critters on his show has such a sweet adorable group of animals been so threatened while the world watched as helplessly as a United Nations Bear Committee.

If more teddy bears get murdered by Islamofascists on Mr. Obama's watch, he will not be able to blame his predecessor. The clock is ticking. Liberals, wake up already. It was one thing when Islamofascists murdered people. Now they are after warm fuzzy critters. This will make children cry.

The Secret Service had better watch Sasha and Malia Obama closely. Rumor has it they own teddy bears, and terrorists will stop at nothing to hurt those stuffed Cubs. Additionally, if Obama can fix the Chicago Cubs, he will be as superhuman as even he thinks he is.

Radical Islamofascists condemn hearings into radical Islamofascists

In a stunning turn of events, radical Islamofascists and their supporters condemned congressional hearings into radical Islamofascists and their supporters.

New York Republican Congressman Peter King insulted the decency of every warm fuzzy terrorist enabler by having the unmitigated gall to ask about a hole in the ground where towers in Manhattan once stood. Congressman King held hearings on the radicalization of young American Muslims. This selective prosecution occurred because the people profiled did it. Liberals protested because water is wet.

Liberals are normally obsessed with getting to the root causes of crime. This is code for excusing illegal behavior by minorities belonging to politically correct groups with protected statuses.

When radical Islamofascists are the guilty parties, liberals stop spouting about root causes. The liberal straw-man (forgive me, straw-person) argument is that targeting radical Islamofascists insults peaceful Muslims. This same train of thoughtlessness whitewashes (forgive me, multicolor washes) the disproportionate share of modern black crime to centuries of white racism.

This is not about targeting entire cultures or civilizations. It's about finding the bad guys whoever they may be and wherever they are.

The minute it becomes time to hold hearings on cannibals, Congress can start interviewing young white males from middle-class backgrounds in Iowa and Nebraska. Is every single Caucasian in Middle America a cannibal? No. Are too many cannibals young, middle class Caucasians with moms in the Parent Teachers Association? Yes. Midwestern PTA moms do not riot over this. They want to know if Hannibal Lecter is living in their homes before the next family dinner becomes a grisly affair.

Before the Obama administration turned the Global War on Terror into the earthly disappointment over inconveniences, the goal was to find and capture all those who promote, harbor, or finance terrorists.

Those who marched in the streets against Congressman King were the standard collection of politically correct sensitivity weepers who most likely swapped their peace pipes with crack pipes before leaving the house. There is no cure for these misguided souls. They cannot be reasoned with or deprogrammed. The only solution is to talk over them. Getting to the truth is more important than the feelings of those who only feel and never think.

When a black church burns to the ground and the charred remains of a burnt cross are found on the property, can intelligent people at least admit that there is a good chance that white people did it? Can we acknowledge that those who commit racial or ethnic crimes target people of other races and ethnicities? This is more than logical. It is definitional.

If the people who flew the planes into the towers happened to be green Belgian Dwarves wearing one red shoe, we would profile green Belgian Dwarves wearing one red shoe and anybody else fitting part of that description, including Tom Hanks.[66] It just so happens that very few Belgians are found ranting about jihad and infidels while yelling, "Allahu Akbar" and blowing innocent people to bits.

Once is an accident. Twice is a coincidence. Thrice is a trend. Four times is a problem. Many times is a way of life.

Focusing on tea party violence is useless because their rate of actual violence is zero. For those who went to public schools, that is less than once. Harping about Timothy McVeigh allows statistical aberrations to trump the norm. He was an outlier. Remove him from the data and a fascinating pattern emerges.

Most terrorists are radicalized young Muslim men with few career prospects and even fewer romantic options.

Burning the Curren in protest

For those who have strange hobbies such as golf or burning the Koran, it may be time for new recreational activities. Golf is boring. Koran burning causes problems.

Burning anybody's holy book is bigotry. Yet all religions are not created equal. Christians write protest letters. Jews pray for peace. Buddhists meditate. Even environmentalists occasionally react to being aggrieved in a calm, peaceful manner.

The most violent peace activists do not reach the level of bloodthirsty insanity of warm, furry Islamofascists.

Burning the Koran angers Islamofascists, but they have little credibility. Puppies anger Islamofascists. Everything angers Islamofascists.

Liberals coddle Islamofascists in the name of diversity, multiculturalism, and other discredited ideas. This has caused normal Americans to develop an affliction known as Islamofascist Sympathy Fatigue.

Those with ISF understand that burning inanimate objects is not akin to burning people. Flushing a book down a toilet (an event reported by *Newsweek* that never happened)[67] is not the same as hacking off heads and limbs. Even one madman killing sixteen individuals is not analogous to an entire virulent strain of a religion that flew airplanes into the Twin Towers and murdered 3,000 Americans.

For those spoiling for a fight with Islamofascists without descending to their level, some old-fashioned mocking is in order. It is time to burn copies of the Curren.

Some people choose to burn the Koran. Others choose to burn the Quran, since Islamofascists now want everything spelled with a Q to confuse people. Jihadists are not the best and brightest. Forget the Koran, Quran, or rock group Korn. Do not burn CDs of Korn or any other music group since pirated music is the greatest threat to the world except for climate change. If you think Eric Holder has better things to do than harass people trying to enjoy music, ask the folks at Gibson Guitar. The best way to teach Islamofascists a lesson is for everybody to start burning pictures of 1980s South African tennis star Kevin Curren.

The annual global Curren burning will take place on July 22, the anniversary of his highest ATP ranking (#5 in 1985).[68] Curren was chosen because he had a history of being a troublemaker on the court who constantly disrespected the game.

(Actually, he was fairly non-controversial.)

His pronouncements on political issues frequently landed him in hot water.

(There is no record of him discussing anything in his tennis press conferences outside of tennis.)

At no time did he express support for the Prophet Muhammad. Therefore, like the other six billion infidels on this planet, his image must be burned as a blasphemer.

Only an apology from Curren for failing to address controversies he had nothing to do with will satisfy the wrath of those calling for the burning. That and an apology for losing the 1985 Men's Wimbledon Final should suffice. He did not win the women's final either for reasons he has never explained.

In addition to Curren, anything within a slight phonetic resemblance will also be considered evil and worthy of destruction.

All infidels are immediately instructed to burn images of Corona Beer, the Long Island town of Coram, New York (terrible place), and all copies of the Steve Winwood song "Kyrie." *Current TV* was exempt due to its solidarity with Islamofascists, so its death was coincidental. All Curren supporters must cease and desist.

Anyone with images of Curren drinking a Corona shall immediately burn these images or be subjected to lashes faster than one can cry out for the god of *L'Oreal*.

If all of these actions against Curren fail to calm the Islamofascists, then there will be only one other viable solution. Rather than burn images of the Curren, it may be necessary just to kill the Islamofascists themselves. The ACLU may complain, but they are such sissies that they would probably declare Curren-burning a hate crime and a new virulent strain of anti-immigrant tenniphobia.

Were Nigerian schoolgirls kidnapped by Jews from Boca Raton?

There is nothing funny about Boko Haram Islamofascists kidnapping, sexually mutilating and murdering Nigerian schoolgirls. There is plenty of warped amusement in the pathetic responses to their acts of evil. Expect the same uselessness from the West as in July of 2013, when Boko Haram first began lynching young Nigerians.

First Lady Michelle Obama took to Twitter with the meaningless hashtag #bringbackourgirls.[70] President Obama and Secretary of State John Kerry perfected the liberal foreign policy doctrine of tough inaction. Words such as unacceptable are thrown around even though the United States through its impotence accepts whatever happens. Evil flourishes when good people do nothing, and United States liberals are fully prepared to do nothing. A better hashtag would be #bringbackbaracksballs, although that assumes he as a liberal ever had them.

Boko Haram are not Sikhs, Zoroastrians, or Christians. For all Obama knows, Nigerian schoolgirls were abducted by an evil sect of Jewish killers called Boca Raton. Obama can check every golf course in Florida, and probably has. He will not find the Islamic abductors or their captives.

Does anybody think anyone in the Obama administration had anything but meaningless words to offer? Was anybody delusional enough to think that America's feminism champion Hillary Clinton would do anything to help? The woman burning with entitlement to be President does not want to talk about Boko Haram or anything else that reminds the world of her failure in combating radical Islam. Hillary is more worried about her husband Bubba's harem back in Arkansas. If a few girls die, "What difference at this point does it make?"[69]

Does anybody think the National Organization for Women or any other pseudo-feminists could rescue these girls? Unless it involves Republicans and contraception, there is no war on women for them. Leftist women make up the heart of the Democrat coalition, and they will not demand that a Democrat leader do something. Liberals might react if Boko Haram were shown leaving a large carbon footprint. Even if Obama tried to act, he would not know how. See every other Obama foreign policy debacle for the evidence.

The kidnappings happened right before tax day, which explains liberals being confused. When told about hostage takers, Obama administration liberals said they knew all about and were closely monitoring tea party rallies for fiscal restraint.

All the sophomoric pep rallies and hashtags will not make a bit of difference to anybody valuing substance over style. Lighting candles is not a rescue mission.

If it was Obama's children, their father might actually do something. Other people's children receive platitudes followed by decisive inertia and smart meaningful impotence.

The murder of children is a tragedy. The unwillingness and inability to prevent it from repeatedly happening is a global disgrace. This is what happens when leftist plutocrats convince themselves that the biggest global threat is climate change and not radical Islam. Islamofascists kidnapped and murdered children in the forest, and American leaders neither heard nor made a meaningful sound.

Healing through humor amidst the Boston heartbreak

The Boston Marathon bombing and similar events lead Americans to take an appropriate holiday from comedy. In the wake of sorrow, people soon enough become desperate to feel good again and crack smiles. Our choices as Americans are to laugh or cry. While there are only tears for the families of the victims, the healing process eventually has to begin. Humor is part of that. To say it is too soon to talk about something is subjective.

In the wake of 9/11, after taking a few days off, David Letterman returned and was masterful.[71] The rest of the comedians soon returned. Saturday Night Live asked if it was ok to be funny. New York Mayor Rudy Giuliani smiled and asked, "Why start now?"[72] Gilbert Gottfried had the joke of all jokes to ease the tension. In junior high school he had an al-Qaeda nickname. "I was known as 'Nevah been laidin.'"[73]

With a deep internal sense of sadness and anger, here are some streams of consciousness that will hopefully make somebody, somewhere crack a smile.

"The next time the media or anybody else criticizes law enforcement for being deliberate, ask yourself how long it takes to find your car in a mall parking lot." (Inspired by Anthony Clark)[74]

"America got Noriega to surrender by blaring rock music. Couldn't we have just played Barbra Streisand records to make terrorists surrender? Or is that torture under the Geneva Convention?"

"The media should stop calling the two Marathon bombers 'lone wolves.' There's no such thing."

"Imagine an honest reporter. 'We have no information, but let's demand a press conference so law enforcement can refuse to comment because they have no information. We can then report that badly.'"

"The media reported the Boston Marathon bombing responsibly, fairly, and accurately, according to unverified media reports."

"Every time a crazy person goes bonkers like this Boston bomber, neighbors are like, 'He was a good kid. We are so surprised.' Just once can't one neighbor be like, 'Oh yeah, we knew he was going to snap. He was nuts.' They can't all be good kids. It is doubtful this kid was in the Glee Club or the yearbook group. One reason we are in such trouble is nobody wants to say any kid is bad. 'I'm just a soul whose intentions are good, oh lord please don't let me be misunderstood.'"[75]

"College students are innovative but not very sensitive. Huddled around televisions after the bombings, a new drinking game had them doing shots every time the media said the word. They spent Saturday night grieving in clubs by drinking while rapper Lil Jon sang his hit song 'Shots.'"[76]

"All this talk about suspect number one and suspect number two was getting confusing. Hollywood producers identified number two as the guy who tried to kill Mike Myers in the first *Austin Powers* movie."[77]

"The FBI has to be cautious, but not the media. Reporters apparently read Dr. Seuss books before covering the press conferences. The packages the suspects were carrying were referred to as Thing 1 and Thing 2."

"The search for Thing 1 and Thing 2 took a rough turn when innocent happy individuals in red jumpsuits with wild hair were detained. They were released and are back in Whoville, now known as Whattheheckville."

"One man was detained by police, told to get naked, and handcuffed. It turned out to be a college fraternity party and that man was no police officer."

"The reason many people feel safe in Los Angeles is because terrorists look at the city of Angels and think one of two things:

1) Leave them alone. They'll destroy it themselves.

2) There's nothing left to do. They already destroyed it themselves."

"When asked when things would get back to normal, Boston residents said it would take time. Los Angeles residents admitted to not knowing the meaning of the word."

"Is it coincidental that politicians are being mailed suspicious packages around the same time that Anthony Weiner contemplates running for New York City Mayor?"

"Some people are against the use of predator drones on American citizens on American soil. The Marathon Bomber was found in a boat. We should have let him take the boat a few feet over some water. Then he would not be on soil."

"Even Ron Paul and the Libertarians are willing to compromise on drones. It should be perfectly acceptable to use drones on American citizens on American soil if the target is the *Academy Awards* or the White House Correspondents' Dinner."

"When President Obama announced he was sending in drones, John Kerry stood up and said, "Finally, a job I'm qualified for.""

"Detroit and Chicago will remain on lockdown until the threat is lifted. This has nothing to do with the Boston Marathon bomber and everything to do with everyday life in Detroit and Chicago."

"Those searching for Islamofascist bombers should check local university faculty lounges. Provosts as we speak may be offering them tenure."

"After several media errors, they overcompensated. When told there was a suspect in custody, they prayed and said nobody knew if it was the right suspect or just any suspect. Meanwhile, their reporting remained suspect."

"President Obama cautioned Americans not to rush to judgment in the wake of these terrorist attacks. After seeing videos of the suspects, he blamed the video and had the filmmaker arrested."

May God bless us all, and may silver linings among the black clouds come sooner rather than later.

Secretary of State John Kerry: The perfect choice

One day after outgoing Secretary of State Hillary Clinton defensively screeched about murdered Americans in Benghazi, her successor testified on the Hill.

More handsome than Lurch and more Brahmin than Senator Rufus Choate,[78] Massachusetts Senator John Kerry settled in for a lovefest with his colleagues.

The closest thing to sparks at the Kerry hearing came when Lady Dianne Feinstein of California may have winked at him. The married Feinstein claimed that she was falling asleep, less a reflection of her octogenarian status than the utterly boring nature of congressional hearings not involving Hillary Clinton.

When the dust settled, Kerry was the one Obama nominee who breezed to confirmation. Easy confirmation was more proper than Kerry's since abandoned Genghis Khan accent.[79] While virtually every other Obama appointee is disastrous, Kerry is totally the right choice for Secretary of State in an Obama administration. Kerry is the greatest choice in the history of the State Department. Conservatives baffled by this assertion need to relax and look deeper. Kerry is perfect.

John Kerry is useless and not respected. He spouts gasbaggery as others pretend to listen to him. The world laughs at him because they know he is an order-taker. He spends his entire life chatting with other insincere individuals accomplishing absolutely nothing. This is the entire point of diplomacy.

At the State Department, inconsequential grandstanding is the posturing equivalent of gold. Kerry is a total success. He is the man who never mattered who aspired to run a department that doesn't matter in an entire organization that doesn't matter. He even looks French, which matters to people everywhere who never mattered.

The Swift Boat Veterans for Truth did not oppose Kerry because everyone knows the State job is not the Secretary of Defense job. Turtle Bay is exactly like Foggy Bottom, except with responsibilities. This is why a woman totally lacking in accomplishments such as Hillary Clinton can run State. Those who saw her as a hard worker overstated the significant of flying on the taxpayers' dime to Syria to ask murderer Bashar Assad if he prefers teacakes or scones. Kerry lectured Islamofascists on climate change. He educated suicide bombers on how to use Chevy Volts to blow themselves up without leaving the carbon footprint of oil-based rocket launchers.

Dr. Condoleeza Rice wanted the Defense job and was forced to settle for State. This is what makes Kerry so amusing. His entire life dream since his crib days playing with platinum Legos was to be a plutocrat. This man is so condescendingly aristocratic that even senators had little use for him. When one is too boring for the work of the Senate, few appealing vocational opportunities abound.

Kerry could be Ambassador to a fictional nation like East Gasbagistan or France. His only other option was to run a State Department engaging in fiction with every nation including our own.

Let his Royal Heinous of Haughtiness John Forbes Kerry have his Tiramisu chocolate digestive and eat it too, with cherry-topped crumpets. When he meets with the Queen of England, endless amusement can be had when a servant interrupts them. Greeted with, "Your Majesty," both heads would turn and reply.

The State Department exists to undermine the Defense Department and also the President in Republican administrations. Apologizing for the United States and condemning Israel periodically are just bonuses to please the global left.

Let John Forbes Global Test Sensitive War Rufus Choate Kerry enjoy his international sandbox.

Remember, it is only the State Department. What difference at this point does it make?

Global genocide through American environmentalism

Environmental extremists are responsible for more than shutting down businesses. They also contribute to global genocide.

Islamofascists threaten to blow up the world to bring about a cataclysm and hasten the return of the twelfth Imam. The world has far too many people believing in a virulent religious strain of Islamofascism that causes irrational behavior.

Unfortunately, so does America. The American cult is liberalism. The most toxic strain is radical environmentalism, and it threatens the world with genocide.

This is not, to use a favorite liberal word, nuanced. Some things truly are that black and white. The black part is black gold. The cliché about the golden rule is that he who has the gold makes the rules. Black gold is more powerful. Those who control the oil control the world.

Supply and demand works. America has the supply. By flooding the world market with oil and oil derivatives, America could crash the price of oil faster than George Soros destroying a third-world currency.

Vladimir Putin is finished as a world threat once the price of oil collapses. When his economy crumbles, his ability to back Syria and Iran is over. Destroying the price of oil wrecks Iran and takes Syria tumbling down with it.

Who could possibly want to prevent America from triumphing over genocidal madmen and their apocalyptic visions?

Liberal climate change zealots would. They demand submission to Gaea's will with the fervor of those willing to destroy everything in the name of Allah.

Greeniacs spent years blocking the Keystone Pipeline and drilling in ANWR in Alaska and off of the California coast. Liberals insisted that even though Solyndra and every other alternative energy project failed, America should still give alternative technologies a chance. These same hypocrites used the BP oil spill as an excuse to ban all oil drilling. The only proactive drilling is on private land out of the clutches of President Obama and his anti-oil EPA.

When a drunk driver kills a person, banning cars is not the answer. Yet crippling the one industry that allows America to triumph over enemies bent on ending the American way of life is somehow an appropriate response for those who just hate oil because they hate oil.

Collapsing the price of oil collapses America's enemies. Supporting high oil prices supports America's enemies. Anybody who tries to restrict attempts to bring down the price of oil has blood all over their hands.

Those who blather on about climate change and other alternative energy nonsense can join Duck Dodgers in the 24 1/2th century. People are being murdered right now.

Sanctions are worthless, especially when initiated by governments too weak to enforce them. Bombing a nation with nuclear weapons is not possible.

Oil is the solution. America has it. We must drill everywhere as if our lives depend on it. America's enemies do.

Rioting and protests from Egypt to Los Angeles

Western democracies and republics are absolutely the best way to live. In 2011, the Arab Spring saw riots break out throughout the Middle East. Although the first spark occurred in Tunisia, the first big domino was Egypt.

I was somewhat unfazed by the Egyptian riots. I live in Los Angeles. Between Downtown Los Angeles, Detroit, Chicago, and Philadelphia, rioting is not new. The level of rage and violence in the Middle East should not surprise Americans. It happens in America all the time. It is called community organizing. The organizations behind the riots are the Obama White House, *Moveon.org*, Al Sharpton's National Action Network, and labor unions.

The Egyptian rioters were mostly young people. Some things are universal. Young people riot every week at UCLA. Usually they are protesting for the right to cut class and stand in the streets holding signs and protesting. Those who found looting in Egypt proof of uncivilized baboonery should remember the 1992 Los Angeles riots. There was plenty of looting.

Beneath the similarities, there were major differences between the Egyptian riots and similar behavior among the young American leftists.

The Egyptians stood for something. They fought for an actual cause. In Egypt, the rioting was to escape legitimate persecution. The Los Angeles riots were about obtaining VCRs and television sets.

In Egypt, citizens fought for the rule of law. They wanted to stop having people beaten, jailed, and murdered without a fair trial. In Los Angeles, people rioted because they disliked a legal verdict in a fair trial. They broke the law in anger over a jury following the law. This pattern repeated in Ferguson, Missouri. A jury declined to indict an innocent man, so the angry liberal mob rioted.

In Egypt people can be murdered for practicing certain religions. The people want religious freedom. At UCLA, privileged white dilettantes go on hunger strikes to get subsidized degrees in anti-white privilege dilettante studies.

Egypt fought to create a new social fabric where all people can participate. They fought for individual rights. On college campuses rioting is meant to destroy the social fabric and replace it with shared collective misery.

Egyptians fought for the right to be treated like human beings and creatures of God. American college students yell in the street that God is dead while fighting to the death to protect trees and bunny rabbits.

Leftist misery groups from *Moveon.org* to liberal arts college dregs of society need to look at Egypt to see what really matters.

Cairo became ground zero in the next wave of human freedom. They are still fighting for the earth's noblest cause, the right to pursue liberty unshackled. Egyptians are not worried about trans fats in school lunches or global warming. They are not chanting, "Meat is murder" or other utter nonsense.

The next time college students complain about an oppressive paternalistic American society suppressing their freedoms, American choppers should airlift them and drop them off in Egypt for a few days. Being forced to shave and put on shoes, socks and a clean shirt before entering a restaurant is not tyranny. Being forced to show up to class on time and learn a useful employable skill is not oppression. The next time *Moveon.org* wails about George W. Bush and stolen elections, they should be sent to the Middle East to protest and see what happens.

The solution is simple. Leftist agitators need to try standing for something for once in their useless lives. Have beliefs that matter. Do something worthwhile. Stop complaining about shrubbery, minnows, and fast food joints serving hamburgers and potatoes. Stop screaming about justice and peace in a nation with the world's best justice system that is internally at peace. Care about something real like the people of Egypt. Demand that the Arab world move toward democracy now. Spread liberty and freedom, which directly spreads peace.

A democratic Middle East brings stability to places wracked by rage and lunacy. Then we can deal with the remaining crazed hot spots at American universities.

One day we will take back the campuses and return learning and education in place of activism about nothing. First we must defeat the despots, whether they shatter lives under brutal Middle East dictators or shatter windows in the name of peace under labor unions, college students and community organizers.

The UN Sends Khadafi to bed without supper

The useless bastion of worthlessness, anti-Americanism and anti-Semitism known as the United Nations decided to stop doing nothing and start looking busy.

Libyan strongman Moammar Khadafi was killing his own people in order to maintain his weakening grip on power. Khadafi spoke in a tone as incoherent and crazy as Howard Dean and Elizabeth Warren, although Khadafi is less organized.

The United Nations has meetings to decide whether to look like they have the ability and inclination to prevent genocide anywhere. Given the U.N.'s track record from Rwanda to Bosnia, it is unsurprising that Khadafi took fourteen-year-old-Libyan boys and subjected them to forced sixtieth trimester abortions. What would the U.N. do to stop atrocities, something?

President Obama took a brave stand by curling up in a fetal position and sticking to the community organizing he knows. Despite no Wisconsin Republicans using guns to pass their bills, Obama declared them guilty of an assault on people.[80] Regarding real assaults by Khadafi against his own citizens, Obama called the situation unacceptable. This is code for a voluntary reflexive muscle gesture known as shoulder shrugging.

Those determined to declare Mr. Obama right about everything spouted drivel about a tough stand endangering Americans in Libya. What the heck are Americans doing in Libya? Was Cancun out of hotel rooms? If Khadafi even dared to start firing on Americans, even Barack Obama would retaliate to avoid Jimmy Carter's impotence in an election year.

Obama represents individual inertia. The U.N. is an entire club of eunuchs who long ago failed to have their medical practitioners transplant a pair on to their decrepit (redacted).

In an attempt to get Khadafi Duck to stop using tactics that only Saddam Hussein or a Chicago Mayor could love, the U.N decided to send Khadafi to bed without supper. The U.N. then compromised and gave him supper but not dessert. To show flexibility, the decision was made to give him dessert but not read him a bedtime story. To avoid appearances of cruelty, Khadafi was offered a bedtime story but not a kiss on the forehead (blecchhh) goodnight.

The U.N. does not do things. It discusses things. It discussed kicking Libya off of the Human Rights Council. That persuaded Khadafi to stop murdering his own people, if by persuaded one means had no effect whatsoever. The U.N.

needed several weeks to discuss possibly having a vote on a meaningless gesture. Then the Obama administration working (back when working was defined as actually doing things) in conjunction with the U.N. decided to issue sanctions against Libya.

Sanctions? Nobody was sure if these were the tough sanctions, sanctions with bite, meaningful sanctions, or sanctions that send a message. Obama was either crystal clear, perfectly clear, or absolutely clear.

One part of sanctions was freezing Khadafi's accounts. Freezing his accounts was like American politicians freezing spending. We could freeze the accounts that we knew about. There was no way he could have other secret slush funds like Yasser Arafat or past New Jersey governors. He had plenty of money. All we did was freeze money earmarked for the very Libyan people the U.N. never feigned interest in.

We restricted Khadafi's air travel. We banned him from leaving Libya even though the whole crux of the problem was his refusal to leave Libya.

(My dad sent me to my room when I was a kid. It had no effect. When he came in and physically carried the television set out of my room, my grades improved rapidly. Taking a child's television is the parental equivalent of nuclear carpet-bombing.)

Libya has some poor areas, but Khadafi lived in a good neighborhood. Imagine if U.N. diplomats were banned from leaving their five-star Manhattan hotels. Where would they go, the Bronx?

Pretend that the U.N. actually cares about innocent people being slaughtered by megalomaniacal dictators. Assume that Khadafi and his dwindling but ruthless band of supporters were not, to quote Zell Miller, using spitballs.[81] Take it on faith that they are using real adult guns that fire real bullets.

Gun control advocates should notice what distinguishes America. When bad guys break into Texas and Idaho homes, it often ends up bad for the bad guys, who are by definition…say it with me…bad.

If the hypothetical goal is to prevent mass slaughter, could somebody in the civilized world figure out a way to get real guns with real bullets to people being unjustly murdered?

When sending in American troops is not the best option, either get weapons to the innocent victims or do nothing. If doing nothing is the objective, at least admit it. Babbling about sanctions is meaningless prattle only a State

Department bureaucrat could love. They need to defog their glasses at Foggy Bottom just once.

Until then, it is comforting that the U.N. decided to rethink their approach and stop being so aggressive. They kissed Khadafi on his forehead but would not pull his pants down and (redacted) him. Actually they did that as well, but some things are so disgusting that only people as filthy and vile as U.N. diplomats would even publicly discuss it.

Chapter 5: Palesimian Lunacy

There is no such thing as a Palestinian. They are as fictional as unicorns and Snuffalupagus. I gave up regular cola for diet a few years back so I am not going to pour sugar on their behavior. Their wretched, awful, miserable lot in life occurs because their leaders never listen and never learn. These leaders have all the tolerance of an American liberal after hearing somebody disagrees with them.

For those who say it is wrong to blame them all, I blame their leaders. They chose their leaders. They made bad choices. Those who disagree can write their own book defending the indefensible.

In the same way most Arab Muslims are not radical Islamofascist terrorists, it is necessary to distinguish between the Palestinian people and the Palesimians of Hamas, Hezbollah, and the PLO. Those blurring the lines would probably commit the ultimate sin of confusing a Cetiosaurus with a Ceratosaurus. That is as ignorant as confusing a Lavulkavus with a Levenkalus. The madness would never end.

Like every other group of basket cases, the Palesimian problem has plenty of solutions. Until then, step up to the Middle East circus and enjoy the show.

Israelis and Palestinians finally agree to waste everyone's time

A few years after both sides agreed to sit down and accomplish nothing, Israelis and Palestinians finally hammered out a broad agreement in principle to hold talks and waste everyone's time.

Hillary Clinton proudly announced that Benjamin Netanyahu and Mahmoud Abbas would sit down and talk about unresolved issues that will remain unresolved. Barack Obama played a major role in accomplishing nothing and then claiming that the problems existed during his predecessor's administration.

The Palesimians took Israeli concessions from past negotiations and declared that a new starting point. Israelis spoke about cautious optimism knowing that most people think Israelis are full of garbage when they speak about cautious optimism.

Palesimians spoke about a refugee problem and a Gaza humanitarian crisis that never existed. Palesimians offered a deal where Israel abolishes its own right to exist and relocates every Jew to wherever Helen Thomas wanted them to go.[82] Israeli diplomats replied that negotiations are complex but that the talks were productive.

Abbas claimed to have done everything he could do to stop Hamas and Hezbollah. This is true if everything is defined as nothing. Meaningless words with zero actions backing them up united Obama and Abbas in a warm embrace rivaled only by the hot smoochie shared by Hillary and Suha Arafat.[83]

The *NYJBT* waxed poetic about keeping an open mind while rockets rained down on Israel and Palesimian homicide bombers terrorize innocent Israelis engaging in bizarre activities such as walking and breathing. Hillary Clinton offered meaningless blather because that is what the Secretary of State does in general and Hillary does in particular.

160-year-old Shimon Peres offered heartfelt sentiments in fractured Heblish. Palesimians condemned his remarks publicly while privately admitting they had no idea what he said. His incomprehensible comments united Israeli and Palesimian teenagers. They still giggle when he discusses the p*ss process.

George Mitchell explained that he brought peace between the Catholics and Protestants in Northern Ireland. The Irish Republican Army helped matters by developing hobbies other than blowing stuff up. The Palesimians remained obtuse.

Platitudes such as hope, change, and "Yes, we can," were replaced with "Are you f*cking kidding me?"

Just because the Palesimians violated every single agreement they ever made does not mean they will do so again. Actually it does. One hundred percent failure is a good indicator.

There is good news. When Israelis inevitably surrender in negotiations due to American bullying, Palesimians inevitably reject the deal, wage more war, and then beg for peace when Israel fires back with ferocity. Until that time, lovers of wasted time should celebrate the end of the futility hiatus and the return of pointless conversations.

Obama should return to his 2007 borders

It is time for Israel to compromise and engage in a land swap that everybody can live with. As a Neocon and staunch Israel supporter, this proposal will finally solve some major lingering problems.

Since Barack Obama wants Israel to return to their 1967 borders, he needs to lead by example by returning to his 2007 borders.

He was doing just fine as a community organizer turned inconsequential politician from Illinois. In 2009 he won a political war and captured far more land than he was prepared to manage. Pressure is coming at him from all sides. He needs to give up some territory to others in order to focus on his core land. He should hand the White House to the GOP promptly. Republicans deserve right of return.

In exchange for returning to his 2007 borders, Republicans will promise to recognize his right to exist. By right to exist, we mean he will be able to sit quietly and not make any more speeches.

Even many Democrats privately wish that his teleprompters would get blown up with all the passion of the Palestinian homicide bombers that he only tacitly condemns.

Americans are tired of watching warring parties fight over disputed land. For the sake of peace in the American political process, Mr. Obama can make the painful concessions necessary. If he is willing to give up land for peace, it will show how magnanimous he is. Some will consider him a sucker for making such a deal, but at least his Nobel Peace Prize would finally be worth more than a romantic evening with Helen Thomas.

Obama is a humanitarian committed to human rights, not counting the hundreds of people shot in the Middle East on a daily basis as he turns a blind eye.

To reward Obama's hard work, Jimmy Carter can help build him a new house in Illinois. To keep faithful to Obama's socialist ideals, the house will be the exact average shape and size of every house in Illinois. To ensure the house is not better than average, union labor will build it. The builders will be hired based on diversity quotas and many other metrics. Experience building homes will not be a factor.

Mr. Obama's return to Illinois could be inevitable unless he succeeds in finally eliminating that awful Constitution and its charter of negative liberties. Obama has to leave his job in 2017 at the latest. This gives him a head start. If he tries to instill martial law and seek a third term he will be dead in a week at the hands of Hillary Clinton. She is Lady Macbeth except less ethical, which means Obama will need a new house.

In honor of his half-@ssed approach to everything, a halfway house can be built next door to his house. That house will hold Palesimian fictional refugees.

Netanyahu should embrace this plan. It leaves Obama with a small plot of land only nine miles wide, or approximately the size of Obama's ego.

In Israel, they call it partition. In Congress they call it redistricting and gerrymandering. For Obama, it can be called social justice. Those who love to yell about justice and peace can finally see justice done and peace accomplished.

Obama promised to unite Americans. Returning to his 2007 borders would do exactly that. Taking Hillary, Kerry and the rest of his failures with him could unite the world.

The John Kerry Doctrine: Perpendicular diplomacy

A decade after losing the presidential race, John Forbes Kerry finally achieved his dream of failing on the world stage. President Obama's Secretary of State was hired to browbeat the Jewish state into a culturally suicidal peace deal. Kerry had to obey Obama's only rule: Do not embarrass the boss. Obama does not have time to lead the world, raise his two children, and babysit Vice President Joe Biden. Kerry was never expected to be successful, but he was expected to be competent.

Competence at the State Department means speaking in platitudes, bromides and meanderings while avoiding any loaded words that could be translated from Foggy Bottomspeak into English. Kerry failed to obey the memo about Obfuscation Nation and paid the price.

The ultra-patrician lily-white Christian Kerry played to anti-Semites everywhere when he called Israel an apartheid state.[84] Israel is the furthest thing from an apartheid state, which is why Arabs would rather live in Israel than in any other Arab nation. Islamofascists living in Arab Muslim nations do not segregate minority groups. They just kill them.

If one wants to see an apartheid state, visit John Wellington Winthrop Chartwell Rufus Choate Kerry's Massachusetts. The only diversity in Kerry's posh boarding school was the different shades of gray on his elbow patches.

Kerry is Obama's dutifully obedient lapdog tasked with carrying out the liberal foreign policy doctrine of perpendicular diplomacy. The strategy failed with Vladimir Putin in Russia, Bashar Assad in Syria, and everywhere it has ever been tried. The key is confusing groveling with strength.

The only time perpendicular diplomacy ever has a chance of success is when the person used to bending over and prostrating themselves finds a weaker target that will bend over further and prostrate more.

Israel makes the perfect target for leftists used to being globally ridiculed by everybody not in academia. Bullying Israel works because there are no domestic consequences. Kerry-style liberals may have invented perpendicular diplomacy, but liberal Jews perfected it. Liberal Jews standing up to Kerry, Obama or Hillary is about as likely as any Democrat leaders standing up to Putin. Kerry and Obama have the occasional steel spine, but only when prostrating liberal Jews get lodged and wedged up theirs so tight that it uncomfortably forces the perpendicular to bend upright.

There are two ways to avoid perpendicular diplomacy. The first way goes above Obama and Kerry's pay grade. It involves them doing what non-academics would describe as something. President George W. Bush overthrew the Taliban in Afghanistan and Saddam Hussein in Iraq. The strategy worked until liberal perpendicular diplomacy lost most of those gains.

The second way is something that even bumblers Obama and Kerry could possibly develop as a capability. The doctrine of getting out of the way works. Those who cannot make things better should admit uselessness and do no harm.

George W. Bush was labeled an interventionist, but he got out of Israel's way and gave Israeli Prime Minister Ariel Sharon a free hand to root out Palesimian terrorism. Sharon crushed Arafat and reduced the violence. That and only that brought Palesimians to the peace table.

Kerry was hell-bent on forcing a peace process on parties mainly to counter the image of Kerry as useless and irrelevant. Trying to force a deal to remove a perception of weakness only enhances that perception. Kerry had no leverage, so he threatened to offer a final deal and tell the parties to take it or leave it. They left it and Kerry blistered the parties before doing nothing.

Kerry did manage to unite the Israelis and Palesimians. Both sides looked at each other and asked, "Why is Kerry here? Did you invite him? Tell him to leave. Is he with your side of the family? How do we get him out of here? Tell him they are serving brie cheese in Paris and he will be on the next plane."

Kerry and Obama perfectly analyzed the liberal American Jewish community's never-ending sniveling quest to be liked. This made them the perfect patsies for perpendicular diplomacy. What Kerry and Obama failed to grasp is that Israelis do not take their orders from Americans living comfortably on Boca Raton golf courses or Upper Westside Manhattan Trump Tower Condominiums.

Israelis are made of battle-hardened steel. They know they cannot be war-weary until the other side stops trying to wipe them off the face of the earth.

If Little Satan Israel goes down, Great Satan America is the next target. Then the Islamofascist dream of an Islamic Caliphate can finally be achieved.

A Caliphate with no Westerners would be an apartheid state. Anybody standing upright can grasp this. Kerry, Obama, and the perpendicular diplomacy crowd never will.

How to speak like a Palesimian apologist

To understand Palesimians, it is necessary to dispense with politically correct nonsensical platitudes. Here are some phrases with the appropriate translation.

"Not everybody who criticizes Israel is an anti-Semite."

Translation: Many people use criticism of Zionists as a fig leaf to hide anti-Semitism.

"I do not hate Jews. I hate Zionists."

Translation: You're an anti-Semite.

"Not all Arab Muslims are terrorists."

Translation: Virtually all modern terrorists claim to be acting in the name of Islam. Does what we say matter? If they say they are Muslims, how do we counter that? Peaceful Muslims countering the argument would make a major difference. As of now, far too few peaceful Muslims are standing up and making the distinction. This allows the radical Muslim argument to triumph.

"Some Palestinians truly want peace. They want to be free."

Translation: Freedom is something people fight and die for. Americans did it in 1776. Many Arabs did it during the Arab Spring in Egypt and Libya. Uprisings failed in Iran, Syria and China but at least the people tried. At no time have the Palesimians ever fought for their own freedom.

"The poor, suffering Palestinians…"

Translation: Poverty does not cause crime or terrorism.

"Not all Palestinians are Hamas or Hezbollah."

Translation: An overwhelming majority of Palesimians in Gaza voted for Hamas.[85] White Southern support for the Ku lux Klan never reached levels that high.

"Palestinians did not vote for terror. Hamas builds schools and roads."

Translation: The KKK also built civil institutions. Saddam Hussein wrote poetry and Adolf Hitler was a painter. Anyone who finances, shelters, harbors or supports terrorists in any way is every bit as much a terrorist as those actually planting the bombs or launching the rockets.

"Cycle of violence…"

Translation: There is no moral equivalence between terrorists trying to murder a neighboring people and those other people trying to defend themselves from being murdered.

"Disproportionate use of force…"

Translation: In recent years a football game saw one team humiliate the other side 58-0.[86] The losing team could have gone to the United Nations and claimed that the winners should have stopped at 10-0. The additional touchdowns were not necessary. The winning coach could have been brought up on human rights abuses. He was not Jewish, so the matter was dropped.

"The international community…"

Translation: The international community is worthless.

"Humiliating checkpoints and blockades…"

Translation: Palesimian terrorist groups including Hamas keep trying to murder Israelis. The restrictions are necessary to save Israeli lives.

"Refugees and right of return…"

Translation: These fictional terms are used by Palesimians seeking to destroy Israel. They consider one hundred percent of their people refugees with right of return to a place they never lived.

Two questions all Palesimian apologists must answer

Most Americans find the Palesimian position indefensible. Yet pockets of support for Palesimians are still found among college university professors and in Hollywood.

Since Hollywood celebrities and university professors rarely have their opinions challenged, it is easy for them to remain in their protective cocoons. Once these people have their beliefs questioned, it is easy to make their arguments crumble.

Any individual anywhere in this world who supports the Palesimians over the Israelis must be confronted with two basic questions. Due to the seriousness of the discussion, the Palesimians will be referred to as Palestinians for this topic only.

The first question is historical. Who is the father (or mother) of the Palestinian people?

The first human male was Adam. From his rib came Eve, the first human female. The first Jew was Abraham, son of Terah and father of Isaac. The first Christian was Jesus Christ. The first Muslim was Muhammad.

These people existed. There is no dispute. Muslims take pride in memorizing the birth of their religion in 622 A.D.

Who was the first Palestinian? When and where was that person born?

Nobody can answer this question. Yasser Arafat became the leader of the Palestinian Liberation Organization in 1970 (some sources say late 1969), but he was Egyptian by birth.[87] He was only the third PLO leader, since that organization began in 1964.[88]

Which Jew stole the land and which Palestinian did the Jew steal it from? How can any indigenous people struggling for their place in history fail to recite with certitude what that history even is or when it occurred?

George Washington was the Father of his country, the United States of America. He led a war against the British in 1776. Lord Cornwallis led the defeated army who lost the land. In 1789 Washington became the first President of the United States.

What battle saw the Palestinians lose their land? Who led the losing army? If they were displaced, who displaced them? What was the name of the victorious Jewish general?

The reason Palestinians cannot answer questions about their history is because this history is nonexistent. A band of rebel fighters were kicked out of Egypt and Jordan for trying to overthrow those governments. Jordan massacred thousands of them in one day in 1970.[89] Arabs killed other Arabs. The Arabs who fled then tried to take over Israel because it was the one area of the region where they would not be indiscriminately murdered. Rather than accept the role of gracious guests, the rebels tried to seize the land of a Jewish people who had a multi-thousand year documented history.

The second question about the Palestinians is geographical. They claim their land is being occupied. Exactly what land is being occupied?

The Gaza Strip is not occupied. Since 2005, there have been precisely zero Jews living in Gaza.[90] The West Bank could be an answer, but evidence points against this. In 2000, Arafat was offered all of Gaza and ninety-seven percent of the West Bank as part of a peace deal.[91] He turned the deal down because that still would not have ended what he considered the occupation.

Palestinians have made it clear that Jerusalem is the capital of their Palestine. At anti-Israel marches they chant, "From the river to the sea, Palestine will be free."[92] From the river to the sea encompasses all of the land. The Arabs have for decades talked about driving the Jews into the sea. This Palestinian goal is completely consistent with Arabs before them.

There are no Palestinians. Until Palesimian apologists can answer the two questions of where and when Palesimians came from and what land is occupied, the Palesimian position will remain indefensible

Chapter 6: Media Entertainment Lunacy

Not every person in the entertainment industry is a terrible human being. They are not all doing cocaine. Drugs are expensive and some Hollywood people cannot afford them. Some Hollywood celebrities fail to commit adultery. Plenty of them are too self-centered to get married. They do not all spout political opinions. Some of them get fired before expressing dissenting opinions.

If these charges sound unfair, try sitting through an *Academy Awards* ceremony as a conservative. It is like asking Orthodox Jews to attend an *Al Jazeera* telethon.

Hollywood is 15 minutes East of my home. My car only travels West.

Some people will just ignore Hollywood. My attitude is that the worst of the worst must be called out. Academics are worse than regular liberals, and Hollywood celebrities are even worse than academics. Somebody has to tell the truth about people who lie for a living to themselves, their business partners, their faux loved ones, and the society at large that Hollywood keeps corroding.

Drugged Out, Whored Out Screw-ups Admire Each Other–Academy Awards Report

At the *Academy Awards*, the Oscar for best insignificant narcissist goes to… some insignificant narcissistic. Nobody should care.

While Iraqis were voting in elections that vindicated President George W. Bush, media imbeciles focused on gaudy outfits, red carpets, and ever-pious millionaires pretending they cared about ordinary Americans. They were too busy bashing Sarah Palin to comment on the John Edwards sex tape. Perhaps some of them are on the tape. It could have won best documentary.

Watching the *Oscars* is not necessary to know that several leftist parasites on society will ridicule conservatives. Hollywood considers it edgy to regurgitate stale jokes in front of a sycophantic idiotic audience.

Only John Kerry could gush about the heart and soul of America in a building filled with people who have neither.[93] The *Oscars* are even more leftist, boring and long-winded than Obama and Kerry speeches, although it is close.

Some say it is unfair to indict every person in Hollywood. As with Palestinians and liberals, why blame the twenty percent of entertainment industry people not drenched in toxicity? After all, eighty percent is not a majority. Oh, wait. Never mind.

The industry is disgusting because left-wing politics long ago replaced quality.

All Academy voters should be required to sign an oath that they watched every movie they voted on. Anyone caught paying others to watch the movies and report back to them should have their voting privileges permanently revoked.

The *Oscars* are boring, predictable, and disgusting. Voters have a formula for what they like.

One way to get nominated is to play a homosexual activist. The activist must be the hero. A bonus comes if the actor is a left-wing activist. I would like to see the real Sean Penn movie. A conservative actor would play him and make sure to show the scenes where he engages in domestic violence against his wife and assaults cameramen.[94] For dramatic effect he can be shown praising Alec Baldwin while a tape runs of Baldwin verbally abusing his daughter.[95] I personally thought *Milk*[96] was a movie about lactation. The same people who praised the *Vagina Monologues*[97] as groundbreaking must have thought that a movie about breast milk would be courageous.

Another way to get nominated is to play somebody dying from a politically correct disease. AIDS is a good choice. Cancer is not. Many homosexuals and drug users get AIDS. To really stir the emotional pot, the person has to suffer discrimination from an evil corporation, vile Republican, or both. The exception to the cancer rule would be the Elizabeth Edwards life story. She would be cast as the innocent victim rather than a woman who put her ego and quest for power over the nation and her family's health.

Another option is to play a mentally slow or handicapable person. They are politically correct. Overcoming physical or mental illness does fine provided that the story tilts leftward. Anti-war activists injured in battle make great Oscar nominees.

When the Academy runs out of generic movies of leftist heroes, the next option is to find evil conservative villains. The lead actor should have a hostile attitude in real life toward Republicans. Anything attacking Republicans works. *Frost-Nixon* takes place three years after Nixon resigns in disgrace. Talk about kicking Checkers' owner while he is down. Listening to a conservative bellow, "I told you I didn't want to take any questions on Watergate!"[98] makes Academy voters feel tingly in their undies.

The last step is to ignore the movie altogether and find somebody who died tragically and way too young.

The 2008 *Batman* movie was politically conservative, an Academy non-starter. The Academy snobs would never deign to let a comic book movie win where it counts. *Batman: The Dark Knight*[99] was a stunningly brilliant movie that should have given Oscar nominations to Morgan Freeman (Lucius), Michael Caine (Alfred the Butler), Christian Bale (Batman), and especially Aaron Eckhart (Harvey Two-Face) and Gary Oldman (Commissioner Gordon). Michael Caine was praised in the past by the Academy, but that was for playing the lead role in a movie that pushed pro-choice activism on abortion. The movie was marketed as a sweet tale about children in an orphanage, but the agenda was clear.

Heath Ledger did deserve a nomination. He was excellent as well, although not as brilliant as Oldman or Eckhart. Ledger got the nomination because he died too young, and tragically.[100] The Academy proudly admits to such biases.

Heath Ledger killed himself, either accidentally or by suicide. That should not have any impact on the voters. Factoring in his death cheapens his nomination. Had he lived, he would have been worthy anyway.

Whether Janis Joplin, Jimmy Hendrix, Curt Cobain, or Heath Ledger, untimely avoidable deaths should have no bearing on *Emmys*, *Grammys*, or *Oscars*. Those deaths are not tragedies. Children dying of cancer and young American soldiers dying in war are tragedies. Rich celebrity addicts and abusers are not tragic figures.

When all else fails, foreign love stories are the secret to Academy glory. Anything foreign appeals to the Academy.

Whether Asians crouching about tigers and dragons[101] or Indians falling in love,[102] foreign lovers are all the rage. Votes probably thought *Slumdog Millionaire* was about poor people with cute puppies. An evil GOP landlord forced them to live in low-income housing and killed their dog.

If there is no love story, political activists are a global sensation. One year it is Irish revolutionaries, the next year Tibet. Odds for a nomination increase as fewer and fewer people care about the issue and watch the movie.

The worst of the *Oscars* is the self-congratulatory leftist blather. In very tough economic times, the Academy tries to scale things down. They then congratulate themselves on how spectacular they are at scaling things down.

Those truly caring about self-indulgent spoiled Academy brats can just walk outside. There will be celebrities bent over just enough to treasure their own aromas. If you still cannot see them, follow the trail of cocaine powder.

(Monique is exempt from criticism. She can say anything political whenever she wants. She is one plus-size bag of sexy.)

The best part of the *Oscars* is the ending. When the curtain falls the industry gets back to its day job of putting out left-wing crap and calling it art.

Expendables Alpha Male Friday

September 14, 2010 was a great day in American history that should forever be known as Testosterone Alpha Male Friday. On that day, *The Expendables*[103] arrived.

Thank the heavens and Sylvester Stallone for this movie. Sometimes alpha males go to watch movie bad-@sses just blow (redacted) up. This was Stallone at his coolest since *Judge Dredd* and *Over the Top*.

(Great scene 1 from *Judge Dredd*: [Stallone] "It's impossible! The evidence has been falsified! I never broke the law! I am the law!"[104]

Great scene 2 from *Judge Dredd*: [Bad guy Armand Assante after killing his political rivals] "Now who says politics is boring?"[105]

Over the Top had the best tough guy character name in Lincoln Hawk. Truckers slapping each other in the face to get pumped up before arm wrestling[106] is as good as it gets.)

In *The Expendables*, Stallone, Jason Statham, Bruce Willis, Arnold Schwarzenegger, Jet Li, Mickey Rourke, and Dolph Lundgren (As much fun to say as he is to watch) all exacerbate or reduce problems through carnage. While this movie was apolitical, liberal sissies were nowhere to be found. Nobody sang "Kumbaya."[107]

When watching *The Expendables*, the lads and I pictured the bad guys as Hamas and Hezbollah Palesimians and Ariel Sharon burning down their Gaza hideouts. It was a beautiful prequel to Rosh Hashanah later that night.

The Expendables 2[108] saw Stallone and his crew take down more bad guys, but not the mullahs in Iran.

While *The Expendables* could take down Palesimian terrorists, imagine how great life could be if the few Hollywood stars who are not completely worthless took down the rest of Hollywood.

Not since Ken Wahl of *Wiseguy*[109] played a guy named Boomer in *The Taking of Beverly Hills*[110] has an opportunity to wreak glorious havoc on the worst elements of American culture been so tantalizingly close.

The Expendables should invade an area even more corrupt and dangerous than the Middle East or South America. They should launch an attack from New York and take down New Jersey. They could have started with the *Jersey Shore*[111] cast. If Mike "The Situation" Sorrentino thinks he is a tough guy Guido, let him contend with Stallone. Lundgren is tough enough to beat the daylights out of Snooki(e) and force her to spell her own nickname right. *Jersey Shore* exited our lives in 2012 when *MTV* did the dirty work before *The Expendables* could. Network executives are among the most soulless mercenaries on the planet, but this was a mercy killing.

Once the *Jersey Shore* cast was eliminated, Jet Li could singlehandedly kickbox the tar out of the *Real Housewives of New Jersey*[112]. Given New Jersey's strict gun control laws, it has been impossible to give these ladies all guns and let them duel at ten paces. Therefore, Li's karate moves would be needed to eviscerate the worst garbage from the Garbage State. Then *The Expendables* can capture Jon Corzine and make him tell them where the missing MF Global billion dollars went.[113]

Governor Chris Christie can join the team if he passes the initiation test that Schwarzenegger did not, taking down the teachers' unions for good. Mayor Rudy Giuliani took down the mafia, but that pales in comparison to the teachers' unions. Governor Scott Walker can join whenever he wants.

California's Governor Schwarzenegger failed to crack down on crime, as Paris Hilton and Lindsay Lohan remained free during his term. He could redeem himself by taking down every celebrity to the left of Jon Voight.

Kiefer Sutherland as Jack Bauer[114] was not in the movie, but no movie is perfect. While Guns N' Roses was in the soundtrack (Schwarzenegger is a fan), not one of the characters smashed any Barbra Streisand or Cheryl Crow records. Again, no movie is perfect.

For those who attacked the movie as simplistic, jingoistic chest thumping, I summon Jack Nicholson's Colonel Nathan R. Jessup. You're d@mn right is is![115] We are all expendable. Yet for one hour and forty minutes, the complexities of life were boiled down to simple principles that Neocons understand and everyone else should.

Take the bad guys, blow (redacted) up, and shove the American flag up their hides until they go to the toilet red, white, and blue. Then pull their trousers down, and either hang the American flag from their (redacted) or take a cattle prod and brand a tattoo of Uncle Sam on their hides.

To paraphrase a famous NFL quarterback after a Super Bowl loss, we need to take the bad guys and **hand them their hides on a platter and make sure the tray is bent.**[117]

In *The Expendables 3*,[118] United Nations diplomats were not blown to kingdom come. For the last time, no movie is perfect. Other than that, for a brief window of time, the wussification of America was suspended.

Testosterone overload from alpha movies get men ready to wrestle live bulls. Then again, animal rights activists would complain. Instead, with all due respect to Chick-fil-A, every American man on Testosterone Alpha Male Friday should eat a dead cow after violently hitting a bottle of blood until it pours all over the steak. Those unwilling to use actual blood should use ketchup. It tastes better.

Don't worry about the alpha male crash after the high. In 2012, *Batman: The Dark Knight Rises*[118] saw the Caped Crusader beat the daylights out of Occupy Wall Street thugs to get the party started.

Long live Republican actors and all conservatives in Hollywood. They are true warriors. Long live *The Expendables*! All hail Testosterone Alpha Male Friday!

Hollywood shocker! Ellen Page publicly comes out as Canadian

Days after football player Michael Sam[119] admitted to being black with two first names and no last name, a young actress rocked Hollywood with a bombshell announcement. 26-year-old Ellen Page told the world that she is a proud Canadian.[120]

Rumors had been swirling for years that Page was North American but not a United States American. Page was born in Halifax, Nova Scotia, a city not in any of the Continental fifty states. Page was not only born in Canada, but raised there as well.

Page made it clear that she wants to be loved and accepted despite not bleeding red, white and blue. Tensions between America and Canada have been high ever since Canada won the 1992 and 1993 World Series and the 1993 Stanley Cup after some dreadful officiating. Canada's victory over the United States in the 2002 Olympic Hockey Gold Medal game did not help matters, especially since that game was on American soil at Salt Lake City, Utah.

Although Page's Canadian heritage was an open secret, Twitter rumors were buzzing over her online pictures. Even by Caucasian standards, Americans tend to only be eggshell or cream compared to lily-white Canadians.

Page insisted she was part of English Canada and was absolutely not French Canadian. Normal Canadians tend to find French people as annoying as normal Americans do. Despite being Canadian, Page protested that she was not boring. Thrice in her life she was less than exceedingly and unfailingly polite.

Page would not commit to trying out for the NFL Draft. While the NFL allows Canadian players to obtain American work visas, Page has never shown much skill passing, running, blocking or tackling. A spokesperson for Boys, Ladies, and Non-Descripts, BLAND, said that Canadians deserve every bit as much love as their Canadian-lite brethren in Wisconsin, Minnesota, Michigan and North Dakota. Toronto people may not officially be from Buffalo, but they could blend in with them, especially during tough winter snowstorms.

Page was emphatic that her coming out as Canadian was not a ploy to get American men to stop hitting on her. She did not comment on whether the movie *Canadian Bacon*[121] and the *South Park* song *Blame Canada*[122] were cheated out of Academy Awards due to Hollywood anti-Canadian nativism.

Page is said to be resting comfortably after her exhausting announcement. Hollywood producers and directors vowed to respect Page's geographical diversity provided Page is a leftist. Page cited her environmental activism,

Burma fundraising, and pro-choice abortion position. She was then flooded with more scripts.

TMZ could not confirm or deny rumors that her courage inspired Bob Seger to start crooning, "There I go, turn the Page"[123] for the first time. While Seger wrote the song fourteen years before Page was born, he is from Michigan, which is almost Canada.

In a side note, Page is gay, and once filmed a movie with Martha Gay, who is not. She may or may not like the music of the late Marvin Gaye, who definitely was not.

Suicide Bomber Helen Thomas finally blows herself up

Arab anti-Semite Helen Thomas was finally knocked off her perch to make room for some younger bats. The old bat had to go.

She said that the Jews of Israel should "Get out of Palestine,"[124] a fictional nation. She suggested that the Jews should all move to Poland, Germany, and America. She laughed as she said it, but she was deadly serious.

Shockingly, even some liberal Jews showed a tad of gumption (This is not the same as standing up to Obama, but it is something). Other moderate Democrats leveled Ms. Thomas. Ed Koch and Lanny Davis deserve particular praise for their immediate principled stands (Robert Gibbs was more circumspect, but better than usual). Conservative Republican Jews naturally understood the situation.

Thomas wanted her life narrative to be that of a terrific journalist. Nonsense. She was always terrible. She just never got called on it. When asked why she was liberal, she responded, "What else would I be?"[125]

Whether the topic was health care, environmental legislation or sports, Helen Thomas had an anti-Israel question to ask. The late Tony Snow once properly told her that she was advocating "The Hezbollah view."[126] Bernie Goldberg astutely noted that her views were expressed in the exact same manner as Iranian President Armageddonijad.[127] Former George W. Bush White House press secretary Dana Perino handled her perfectly. When Thomas would ask one of her insane questions, Perino would calmly say, "Now Helen…" so that the public record would reflect who asked the question.[128]

Let's not sugarcoat her retirement. Hearst fired Thomas. *The New York Post* headline should have read, "Helen gets the hearse from the Hearst," or, "The Truth Hearsts." Her firing was the best media comeuppance since Gunga Dan Rather and Mary Mapes got Monster Mashed for trying to help rig the 2004 election.[129] Their demises were an enjoyable self-inflicted graveyard smash.[130]

Thomas was not a senile old biddy. She was lucid when she spouted her bile. She was not a Nazi or murderer of Jews, but a parallel to her situation would be a 90-year-old SS Guard caught by Simon Wiesenthal. They should absolutely stand trial rather than get sympathy for escaping decades longer than deserved.

Some on the left offered the tired cliché about how we should all move on after her firing. Liberals love prematurely ending discussions. The firing does not end the matter. The issue now is ensuring that this horrible incident defines her legacy.

The days when liberals get to rewrite history and define their own legacies are over.

Dan Rather was the guy who relied on fake but accurate memos, dragging down *CBS News* from Edward R. Murrow and Walter "The most trusted man in America" Cronkite to the lowly Katie Couric.

Thomas does not get cover even though she covered every President since Abraham Lincoln and got her start by sleeping in the Lincoln Bedroom with Honest Abe himself.

Her comments about Jews…not Israel, but all Jews… expressed exactly who and what she was her entire career. The liberal White House press corps tolerated an anti-Semite because she was liberal. Liberal Jews kept quiet because she was liberal.

She was a verbal suicide bomber. We should be grateful she finally pulled the belt around her vest and blew herself up. I never want to know if she has the seventy-two virgins or is the seventy-two virgins. Less disturbing than Thomas receiving seventy-two bin Ladens is Osama bin Laden burning underground with seventy-two Helen Thomases. An Islamofascist was removed from the White House press corps.

Time will tell if her corpse is hired by *NPR*, *MSNBC*, or some other engine of hate. Perhaps *The Huffington Post* or *Daily Kos* will create a shrine for her decomposed rot. If liberals can have dead people vote, they can have them write. *The NYJBT* has been writing fake columns for years.

Did Thomas deserve to be euthanized? Her career certainly did. Now it is time to let sleeping anti-Semitic dogs lie, but not in print or video. Bad riddance.

Beck Restores Courage - Stewart restores cowardice

On August 28th, 2010, Glenn Beck held his Restoring Honor rally in DC.[131] Thousands of people came, hugged, laughed, cried, and left the streets cleaner than they were before the rally began. Many people said that their lives were changed for the better after attending that rally.

In his smug, never-ending quest to ridicule people of faith, Jon Stewart and his fellow secular barely humanist bullies held the Rally to Restoring Sanity and/ or Fear.[132] Part of restoring sanity involved a poetry reading by Islamofascist terrorist supporter Yusuf (Cat Stevens) Islam.[133] Saddam Hussein wrote poetry in prison but was hung before he could open any fan mail or party invites Stewart may have sent.

Beck wants to save the world. Stewart takes cheap shots and denigrates those he differs with. Beck lifts people up. Stewart tears them down. Beck benefits from bringing people together. Stewart benefits from ripping people apart. Beck loathes conflict and remains a reluctant warrior. Stewart loves conflict because it increases his ratings. Beck's rally encouraged people to love their neighbors. Stewart's rally attacked people for loving God and expressing religious pride and faith.

Beck then held his Restoring Courage rally on August 24th, 2011 in Israel.[134] He wanted people of faith to come together and stand with the one true democracy in the Middle East and the beacon of worldwide religious freedom and tolerance.

Stewart needs to mock this to satiate his oversized bile duct. Therefore, let the mother mocker be mocked. Although he failed to do it in 2011, Stewart must begin an annual tradition only his ilk could love.

In dishonor of Jon Stewart, he should hold the Restoring Cowardice rally. It is time that the truly gutless all get together and celebrate cowardice and ridicule those who believe in courage.

The list of speakers could represent every left-leaning wing of the Demagogic Party.

Rather than honor our troops, Bill Clinton could give a speech on why dodging the draft is patriotic. Hillary Clinton could kiss Suha Arafat all over again, although this time with more feeling and passion. John Kerry could throw ribbons, medals and anything else he wants to devalue into the crowd.[135] They could party like its 1969. Anthony Weiner could repeatedly yell and deny attending the rally to reporters standing right in front of him at the rally.

The rally must be held on Friday night so it conflicts with the Jewish Sabbath. Stewart can unite Palesimians and secular Jews in name only. Religion is so 2008.

College students could speak about why being spiritual is cool. Spiritual is code for saying, "Don't dare call me religious but don't call me Godless either. I believe in nothing but spiritual sounds hip."

All French people would be invited to the rally unless they are caught admiring America in any way. The French can speak about having the courage to make peace with rather than fight German warmongers. Metrosexuals could speak about the twenty-first century beta male. Letting women make every decision is new-agey. They can explain why standing up for a man's rights leads to conflict while surrendering is peaceful.

Since arm wrestling is cruel and barbaric, the attendees would compete in (sad) sack races. The first one to lose three times wins the contest. Everybody would finish last so everybody would win. George W. Bush, Sarah Palin, and Michele Bachmann could all be burned in effigy while the crowd sings John Lennon's "Give peace a chance."[136]

Stewart could speak about freedom, liberty and unity in a slang black dialect and call Herman Cain an illiterate baboon.[137] Stewart could then smirk and correct himself by claiming Cain is a semi-literate baboon. This would be followed by leaving empty (Godfather's) Pizza boxes on the grass while singing songs about conservative racism. The NAACP would refuse to condemn the remarks in the spirit of cowardice.

The crowd would be ninety-nine percent upper-middle class whites. The NAACP would be told that their invitations were lost in the mail. Hillary would tell them to go back to the "plantation, and you know what I'm talking about."[138]

In the name of tolerance and inclusion, Palesimian suicide bombers would air their grievances. Stewart would nod approvingly as they excoriated Israel, Ariel Sharon, Benjamin Netanyahu, and George W. Bush for killing many of them before they had a chance to do it to themselves. The suicide bombers would threaten to kill Stewart. He would identify with their frustration and share their loathing of Bibi and Dubya.

The French would join in the America-bashing as Stewart declared that we finally reached Sophistication Nation. Keeping with the event's theme, Barack

Obama would say he empathized with those in attendance but also understood why others would disagree.

Those who find restoring courage passé (Every speaker must use at least one French word in their remarks) must attend Jon Stewart's Restoring Cowardice Rally.

Somebody has to represent the dregs of society. It may as well be the King Dreg himself.

Gun owners demand right to conceal Jim Carrey

After Jim Carrey attacked the Second Amendment in a childish video, gun owners demanded a right to conceal Jim Carrey. The Supreme Court refused to hear the case, claiming that the *In Living Color*[139] and *Ace Ventura, Pet Detective*[140] actor had pretty much concealed himself over the last decade due to low quality work. Performing on YouTube honored his recent straight-to-video movie tradition. Cooler heads prevailed by pointing out why Mr. Carrey mocked the late Charlton Heston and rural America in an anti-gun video.[141]

Carrey turned fifty in 2012. Despite desperate attempts to rebrand himself as a serious actor, he will forever be "Fire Marshall Bill"[142] and the man who yelled, "Somebody stop me!"[143] Now time is stopping him, and there is only thing for post-menopausal Hollywood former stars and starlets to do.

To revive his flagging career, Carrey needs to go on a serious drug binge. Then he needs to go into rehab, recover and be hailed as a hero. Drug binges come in two different forms.

Option one is illegal drugs. Carrey is too old to be trying cocaine and heroine for the first time. Besides, President Obama used cocaine.[144] Like every issue he touches, Obama rendered drugs boring. Everybody does it now. Addiction recovery is dull.

Option two is the drug of mindless liberalism. For Matt Damon, there is anti-fracking.[145] Radical environmentalism is a popular tool for Hollywood tools. Others choose animal rights. Chaining oneself to trees is normal in Hollywood. Carrey opted for an anti-gun position. Among the phony, pious, angry left, that is all the liberal rage these days.

Being an elitist, coastal snob sniffing his own backside gave Carrey his last, best shot of finding an acting role to make people forget *The Cable Guy*.[146] Carrey is now on the casting couch. Female casting directors would prefer the fifty-year-old Carrey stay fully clothed while prostrating himself. He needs to prostitute himself but lacks the waxed body of *Deuce Bigalow*.[147] Spouting mindless liberal nonsense attacking Middle America is all he has left.

This strategy will fail because dopey college kids already have Jon Stewart. They lack the attention span to appreciate more than one nightly arrogant leftist snob. Carrey is no longer hip, edgy, controversial or ironic. If he were any more irrelevant he would be *The View* without Joy Behar, also known as *The View*.[148]

Carrey wanted to be outrageous and conservatives to be outraged. Instead he became the one death knell for an aging comedian: boring. Conceal and carry has outlived the idea of concealing Carrey. He has already faded into the shadows. The rebuttal video mocking Carrey for talking out of his hide was funnier.[149]

Carrey fans should not despair. There is still time for him to smoke crack, go on a rampage gun owners would never dream of, and enter rehab to begin his comeback. He can then play a liberal shooting victim and win an Academy Award for a movie nobody saw. This can be followed with an endless cycle of more Oscar parties, cocaine, rehab stints and liberal awards. For faded Canadian Hollywood leftists, it beats sitting in a rocking chair away from the most addictive drug of the spotlight.

Chapter 7: Financial Lunacy

Do not let liberals anywhere near money. They think spending is investing and real investing is greed. Profits should be capped and taxes should be raised. Tax revenues are used to expand government as it becomes more bureaucratic and less responsive to the people. To let liberals anywhere near the wallets of productive people is economic suicide. People who never attended medical school will not be performing open-heart surgeries. It is arrogance for people with no business experience to try and lecture businesses on how to conduct business. Businesses are indispensable. Governments are not. Never send a government bureaucrat to do a businessman's job. Anything business can do, government can and has done worse. 2008 brought a financial crisis. 2009 brought the government cure, which worked as well as draining blood from President Abraham Lincoln after he was shot. The liberal response to the financial crisis was worse than the crisis itself. It brought the world financial lunacy.

If a government shuts down in the forest...

If a government shuts down in the forest and nobody is around to see or hear it, have any of our lives been impacted?

If a government shuts down at midnight and Debbie Wasserman Schultz predicts the death of 70,000 seniors, how many minutes have to go by before this becomes another leftist prediction fiction?[150] If heaven forbid a tornado hits at 12:03am and kills a thousand people, is Wasserman Schultz now a Jewish prophet?

If only non-essential services are shut down, why should people care? If these services are non-essential, why do we have them? Why is government doing them? Shouldn't it spend more time on something essential like national security or fixing the economy?

Given that President Obama is fairly non-essential to most people, should he officially shut his presidency down and resign? He does not need to be President to play golf. Many retired Floridians play golf. They do almost as little else as he does.

Democrats controlled everything in 2010 and did not pass a budget. Should they be docked pay? Would Obama be willing to reduce the deficit by $400,000 by making his presidential pay merit based?

Is Obama violating the Eighth Amendment on cruel and unusual punishment by going to sleep early and keeping Harry Reid up all night? The exhausted Reid did a fantastic job as the lead character in *Weekend at Bernie's*[151] despite being less lively.

If the parks are temporarily closed, will liberals take time to pick up the signs and other trash they left there from their last Earth Day celebration? Will all parks be shut down? What about Bert Parks? Is his corpse allowed to sing at the *Miss America Pageant*?[152] What about Bernard Parks? What about Rosa Parks? If buses are shut down, will Republicans be accused of racism against her children?

What do Snooki and Lady Gaga think of the government shutdown? Barbara Walters and the other imbeciles on *The View* are dying to know. If Timothy Leary could tell people to, "Turn on, tune in, drop out,"[153] should the new slogan for politicians be, "Shut down, sit down, and shut up?"

Why would tax refunds be delayed but not tax payments? Why should people be forced to send in tax returns that will just sit idly by? Will bread companies unable to get business loans become matzo companies just in time for Passover?

If so, is this proof of the worldwide Jewish conspiracy, business adaptability, or both?

Would Obama's time be better spent trying to shut down Islamofascist governments rather than our own? Will Obama follow the tradition of JFK and Bill Clinton and use spring break to sample the interns?

Given that progressives run the government, how will Flo from Progressive Insurance be affected? Will this benefit animal rights activists supporting the Geico Gekko? Will the Progresso soup company go Regresso? Is the Geico Gekko related to Gordon Gekko? Would this prove greed is good and Wall Street Republicans are to blame for everything since the inception of time?[154]

Given that Hollywood worships Obama, shouldn't they shut down as well in solidarity? Isn't it time for another writers' strike anyway?

Like a government shutdown, wouldn't the impasse be as impactful as striking French workers? How can Wisconsin union workers strike? Doesn't a strike imply that at some point work was done? Can people go on strike from doing nothing?

Will you care? Will I care? WILL I AM? Should, "Let's get it started"[155] now become "Let's get it stopped?"

In reference to these musings, the answer is yes. In honor of the government, I am now shutting down this train of thought. Like Obama, the impact of my negligence will be negligible. Unlike Obama, I know and admit it.

Gas speculators, gas prices, and gasbags

Wind-powered press conferences aside, President Obama is not an energy expert. The price of gasoline topped more than $4 per gallon in many places across the nation as oil skyrocketed to more than $112 per barrel.

Obama's path to reelection involved creating another conservative bogeyman to demonize. He chose oil speculators. Attacking speculators is as boring as blaming George W. Bush, Dick Cheney, the Koch Brothers and Shell Oil. Obama might as well blame Buddy Ebsen. Jed Clampett and the rest of the *Beverly Hillbillies* made their money in oil.[156] This may explain why Obama frequently brings Los Angeles traffic to a standstill as thousands of cars idle away petrodollars. Somebody get *Barnaby Jones*[157] to investigate.

Those wanting to blame speculators should buy a dictionary and look in the mirror.

Somewhere in a nursing home there is a ninety-year-old grandmother with a mutual fund containing a few shares of stock in some oil company she bought back when the Charleston was the latest craze. Have this speculator arrested now.

Speculators play both sides of all markets and phony politicians only complain when the market refuses to cooperate with the public. When speculators drive the stock market higher, there is happiness. When speculators drive it down, there are calls for investigations. Commodities provide the reverse reaction. When oil skyrocketed to $147 a barrel in 2007, people screamed bloody murder. When it crashed down to $33 a barrel, nobody blamed speculators. When silver and gold hit all-time highs, nobody screamed at speculators.

To all the crybabies and the president desperate to appease them: The laws of supply and demand cannot be repealed or declared unconstitutional.

In Obama's mind, getting everybody off of oil and toward a green economy is noble.

Supporters find this laudable. Critics find it impractical. What is ludicrous is for a man to deliberately try to destroy the oil industry while wondering why this would affect prices.

There are so many ways to bring down the price of oil, from domestic drilling to turning Iran into a 50,000 hole golf course and seizing their oil. Kick their @ss and take their gas.

Obama telegraphed that his policies would lead to higher oil prices. Sensible gamblers played oil to the upside. The gamblers did not create the trend. They jumped on the bandwagon. Anybody criticizing this investment strategy should deliberately try to defy trends and see how they enjoy losing money.

Politicians are often irrational. Markets in the long run are as rational as can be.

Obama is wrong to blame those engaging in sensible actions when his own senseless actions led to the problem in the first place. Risk-takers built this nation. One obtuse politician cannot subvert centuries of global tradition and commerce. Obama is the problem. Speculators are the solution.

As people continue to bet on oil prices, stock prices, and presidential prospects, Obama liberals will continue to stew over what they cannot regulate, manipulate, or obfuscate. Freedom existed long before leftist anti-capitalists and will exist long after many more socialist models are discredited. Based on historical trends, that is a very safe bet to play to the upside whether Obama likes it or not. The one other thing Obama can do to help reduce oil prices for a very long time is to stop being himself.

Do any liberals pay taxes?

Much of the Democrat Party consists of beggars demanding tax credits for taxes they don't pay. The rest consists of guilty white uber-wealthy leftists demanding that the rich pay their fare share, which they then don't pay.

Do any liberals pay taxes?

Bill and Hillary Clinton had Whitewater. James B. McDougal had to explain to Hillary that she could not take tax deductions for interest on mortgages when she was not the one paying the interest.[158] John Kerry docked his Massachusetts yacht in Rhode Island to save $500,000.[159] Tom Daschle was going to run the entire health care industry in America despite not being able to keep track of his own financial oversights.[160] Kathleen Sebelius somehow obtained her job despite having the same mistake in her background.[161] Claire McCaskill was a prosecutor who built her career on ethics reform while apparently lacking any in her own career.[162] Charles Rangel was in charge of writing the entire tax code while flouting it.[163] Timothy Geithner was in charge of the entire economy, yet the man famous for understanding complex Goldman Sachs derivatives could not grasp TurboTax.[164] If Joe Biden truly believes that paying taxes is patriotic, is he saying that the entire Democrat Party is unpatriotic?[165]

General Electric made fourteen billion dollars in profits one year and paid zero taxes. GE CEO Jeffrey Immelt became a left-wing Obama shill. He took Jack Welch's global powerhouse and destroyed shareholder wealth by turning the productive company into a green company. He embraced radical environmentalism over corporate profits. Ironically, Immelt had no problem doing business with Iran, which hates environmental laws almost as much as they hate synagogues and churches.

Immelt turned over *MSNBC* and *NBC* to Obama and made those networks worship at his altar. One anchor had a tingling thrill up his leg hearing Obama.[166] Anchors at both Obama networks lost ratings. Value was destroyed for politics.

Obama returned the favor. GE got its tax breaks and Immelt became a top Obama economic adviser even though Obama did not attend adviser meetings. Immelt could now justify earning twice his normal pay because he had twice as many jobs he could ignore without consequences.

Imagine if George W. Bush had appointed the head of Enron to a top cabinet post. Leftist heads would explode and burn out faster than GE light fluorescent bulbs. The left actually did accuse George W. Bush of an Enron connection because they were both from Texas. Any day now Howard Dean could be arrested for eating Ben and Jerry's ice cream since they are both in Vermont and share a liberal ideology.

GE gives Obama favorable media coverage and embraces his agenda and Obama gives them tax breaks and promotes Immelt. The liberals who spend their lives howling about obscene profits had nothing to say.

The next time liberals talk about raising taxes on the rich, just remember that they really mean taxing Republicans and conservatives. Those seem to be the only people paying taxes anyway.

My 5-point tax reform compromise plan

Every April 15ᵗʰ, liberals rob productive Americans blind and give the money to liberal deadbeats in exchange for votes. Obama takes this to an art form. In 2012 he bashed the very tax cuts he extended four months earlier. Then on the campaign trail he bragged that he cut taxes.

Obama's ideal budget is a near one hundred percent cut in the defense budget while raising taxes on the wealthy to a bracket also nearing one hundred percent. His billionaire liberal friends and other Friends of Barry still continue to get special breaks. Obama is simply trying to cripple conservative Republicans financially and give the money to liberal Democrats. This is the Chicago way.

Rather than allow more liberal financial malpractice, it is time for a simplified tax plan. Every politician should follow five steps.

1. Shut up. Every politician should have their mouth duct taped except for Congressman Paul Ryan. They should be banned from television in the same way sports broadcasters no longer cover drunken fans who strip naked and run onto the field. As an adult, Ryan can speak. The other 534 kids and the First Toddler-in-Chief should be quiet since political children should be seen and not heard.

2. Cut taxes. America needs drastic tax cuts that would dwarf the Bush tax cuts. Slash taxes drastically. Reduce the capital gains tax to zero for anybody with less than $100,000 in stock. The 1980 Reagan and 2000 Bush supply-side tax cuts worked perfectly. Slash corporate and personal income tax rates. Slash harder than Freddie Krueger. Slash like a Guns N' Roses guitar god. Slash like former quarterback Kordell Stewart. Slash, baby slash (Liberals reading that sentence will insist I am advocating that we slash babies. I am not. Babies should not be blamed for their liberal parents).

3. Cut spending. Forget Obama and his scalpel. Use the mother of all machetes. Roll back all programs to 2000 levels. Democrats want to erase the very memory of George W. Bush. Let's return to the halcyon Clinton days. Every domestic program can start at 2000 levels. It is still the same century. Democrats are the candidates on the political version of *The Biggest Loser*.[167] They are bloated two-ton slobs. Dropping to 3,995 pounds will not avoid death. Liberals use fat-free dressing as budgetary window dressing. It is time for budgetary stomach stapling.

Defense can be on the table, but not before every single entitlement program is rolled back. People fifty-five and over will be exempt because promises to them must be kept. Those under fifty-five have at least a decade to prepare for reality. End all luxury items. Kill *NPR* and *PBS*. Shoot Elmo and Big Bird and serve them as school lunchmeat. All luxuries must either be financed by private citizens or eliminated forever. Only necessities should survive. Obama's pay should be merit-based and incentive-laden. If he does well, he can make more than $400,000. At his current ability rate, he owes the treasury a few billion dollars. Paying him nothing would have to suffice.

Liberals will call my proposal extreme and draconian. Just don't call it mean-spirited. Mean-spirited is liberals lying to the American people. Liberals truly believe we can spend on diamonds while earning minimum wage. Extreme draconian measures are needed to combat this spending lunacy. Welcome to austerity.

4. Sit down. This completes the sandwich of silence started in step one. The bread of silence in steps one and four covers the meat of steps two and three. Politicians have done nothing to slow rates of growth, much less cut anything. People who accomplish nothing should say even less. No more speeches. Let deeds be the words.

5. Resign. People who have never spent a day of their lives in the private sector are running it into the ground and celebrating the road to ruin. In 2007 Democrats seized Congress and wrecked the brilliant Bush economy. One by one, sanctimonious liberals tried to pass miserable policies while exempting themselves from the very catastrophic and completely intended consequences. They praised higher taxation while not paying taxes themselves. If these failed people really cared about America, they would get jobs in corporate America to give them an understanding of what real workers do.

Shut up. Cut taxes. Cut spending. Sit down. Resign. If this is not enough, one more point can and should be done in the name of compromise. It is the reversal of Obamanomics. Tax people based on ideology, not wealth. Obama already does this. It is time to shift the money back from the takers to the makers, from the parasites to the producers. Conservatives can call this seizing of assets an investment.

Liberals should be banned from investing. Real investing means taking risks with one's own earned money. Buying stocks and real property are investments. Oil companies and drug companies doing research and technology are investing. Crippling businesses is not investment. Phony environmental crackpot theories are not investment. Supporting the further decay of already failed public schools is not investment. Wrecking healthcare is not investment. Liberals cannot invest because they do not believe in real investments in people. They loathe the investor class. They are the union beggar class, where stealing is investing and producing is greed.

Enact my five-point plan. Otherwise, let children today know that liberal baby boomers were selfish spoiled brats until the very end of the country they inherited but killed off before it could be bequeathed.

S&P downgrades Obama presidency to junk status

In a move that shocked President Obama and everybody else dedicated to obliviousness, Standard and Poor's downgraded the Obama presidency to junk status.[168] In an effort to soften the blow, the spelling was changed to junque. At least Obama's decisions were the cream of the cr@p. His dazed leftist supporters were left to argue whether to say that the downgrade did not matter, or that it did but it was everybody else's fault.

Obama argued that Standard and Poor's was wrong with the same passion that a young boy in 1980 argued that his teacher was wrong in handing out a bad grade.

When my…ahem, I mean this anonymous young boy's…father was brought this argument, the response was, "You're not God. You don't get to decide this. That is why the teacher is the teacher and you are the student."

The message took several hours to get through that boy's thick skull. This was amateur stubbornness compared to the man who after a half-century of life still argues his own righteousness.

Obama drones attacked S&P for failing to see the 2008 crash. This is nonsensical. S&P initially refused to downgrade inferior securities, contributing to a crash. They then took steps to avoid making the same mistake. What should they do, wait for another crash so they can get blamed again for inaction? Who does Barack Obama think is running S&P, Barney Frank? Most voters will not blame a ratings agency for doing its job honestly. Unable to fix the problem and mollify S&P, Obama supporters had to rapidly comprise a list of others to blame.

Congressional Republicans were out of power when the worst spending took place.

Sarah Palin never held federal office. George W. Bush left office in 2008, allowing Barack Obama to inherit an AAA rating. The Koch Brothers and Grover Norquist committed the high crime of participating in the political process and advancing causes they believe in such as reducing spending. *Fox News* and Rush Limbaugh were in the private sector. Obama's spending sprees concerned ratings agencies before the tea party movement ever existed. The tea party was the response and antidote to reckless spending, not the cause of it.

S&P has to say that nobody in particular is to blame because criticizing a man with the IRS and predator drones at his disposal is not good for business.

The vindictive and petulant Obama would happily put S&P out of business (hopefully with the IRS and not drones) to save himself.

S&P wanted a budget deal with $4 trillion in real spending cuts mainly from entitlements. Obama agreed to a deal that contained nowhere near the required four trillion overall and zero real cuts in entitlements. The tea party opposed the deal and S&P issued the downgrade because the deal did not go far enough. The left blamed the tea party for a bad deal that the tea party opposed. This is lunacy, even by liberal standards.

The week before the deal was signed, tea party attendees were called hostage takers and terrorists. Americans were told that a deal had to be reached to avert a shutdown and protect our credit rating. A deal was signed that left the tea party out in the cold. Our credit rating was downgraded anyway.

Only in Obamaworld could a bad deal rejected by creditors be blamed on the very people who opposed and voted against it because they knew creditors would reject it. No wonder Barack Obama has been downgraded to junque status.

What else does one do with a man who speaks like an unqualified calculus professor but flunks remedial mathematics and accounting 101? This is the man who wants to control education!

The downgrade has absolutely nothing to do with the Iraq and Afghanistan wars or the Bush tax cuts. It has everything to do with entitlements. The left wants to expand entitlements. They raise taxes not to balance the budget, but to fund even more entitlement spending. The people who destroyed healthcare now want free education for everybody.

The left kicked and declared S&P executives either unqualified dolts or malicious liars (after taking polls to see which strategy works better) in the pockets of nefarious anti-Obama forces. They truly believe that we should invest more money in education, environmental extremism, government-run healthcare, and high-speed rail.

Conservatives understand that we already spend more on education than anybody else with utterly miserable results. The Chevy Volt may be the worst car in the history of automobiles. Obamacare destroyed our credit rating. It is the largest entitlement program in American history and entitlements are strangling the American economy. Conservatives are not interested in Buck Rodgers fantasies when austerity is needed. Obama is too old to be playing with trains. Somebody needs to replace his toy trains and eco-cars with sleek Matchbox cars.

Obama is the problem. He is an anti-business, anti-growth, spendaholic who embraces destructive policies with all the enthusiasm of a Hollywood celebrity freebasing cocaine off of their fellow liberal elitist celebrity's buttocks. It is time for detox. Obama quit cocaine, marijuana and (allegedly) cigarettes. Now his addictive personality needs to get rid of the spending habit.

The tea party tried to cut up his credit cards not because they hate him but because they love the America that was given to them by their parents and grandparents.

Conservatives criticize liberal spending not because Obama is black but because his binges leave us financially black and blue.

S&P staged an intervention in an attempt to prevent worldwide catastrophe.

America was downgraded on Barack Obama's watch after he had been in office nearly three years. The only solution is for Barack Obama and his junque status presidency to be downgraded one notch further to that of private citizen. He can spend his remaining days in a straitjacket locked in a white-walled rubber room with Al Gore, John Kerry, Paul Krugman, Joan Walsh, and every other failed elitist advocating the destruction of a once AAA nation built by ordinary people who spent within their means.

Obama is a predator drone that missed its target. His financial practices, priorities and policies are predatory toward real workers doing real jobs. He drones on and hopes boring people to death will create economic revival. Every candle he lights burns down a part of our house. The sanctity and honor that is the full faith and credit of the United States of America is dead. Now and forever, that is the Obama legacy. That is leftist carnage and decay we can believe in.

Maxine Waters begs tea party: Please visit my district

Los Angeles Congresswoman Maxine Waters begged tea party members to visit her district in a forceful plea that was roundly misunderstood. Maxine Waters emphatically told tea partyers to, "Go straight to hell."[169]

Pundits across the political spectrum wrongly declared this an insult. The lovely and gracious Waters wants tea partyers as close to her as possible. The reason why her message got lost in the fog is because most people do not know what her constituents have known for years.

Her district *is* hell. There is rampant crime and spiraling unemployment. Street vendors have to pay Waters money to obtain permits to sell hopelessness. When Obama said he would slow the rise of the oceans, even she knew he did not mean salvation for her district.

During her tenure her district has gotten worse, which says a lot. She represents the angry, enraged welfare class quite well given that she has never held a real job. She was on welfare and then got rich exploiting her constituents. The House Ethics Committee investigated her financial improprieties. She is so politically toxic that Obama will not bring his campaign bus or presidential motorcade anywhere near her area. He also does not want to get carjacked.

With Obama boycotting her district for his personal safety, her only hope to improve the local economy is to reach out to tea partyers with disposable income. She wants them to engage in transfer payments to her constituents. Unlike most of the free services they get, these transfer payments would result in tea partyers getting goods and services of value.

She told tea partyers not only to go to hell but that she would "help them get there." She meant that she would personally drive them to her part of the city. Not since Morgan Freeman drove Miss Daisy has somebody been so desperate to lug people around.[170]

She needs the commerce. Her reaching out is heroic. Her district is only ten percent white, with thirty-four percent black and forty-seven percent Hispanic. Many tea party people are Caucasoids. She is inviting them due to her deep commitment to diversity. I applaud that she not only allows white people to visit bad neighborhoods in Los Angeles, but that she actively invites them into her warm heart and land.

The tea party should accept her offer to visit hell with a mass entrance into the heart of her Southern California danger zone. Those coming from other states can stop off at the Nevada border to buy bullet-proof vests and flak jackets before visiting the land of failure where never still Waters run shallow. Tea partyers lack Secret Service protection or private security. Hollywood celebrities with their private bodyguards do not travel East of Beverly Hills. Tea partyers, be wary. Like Colonel Khadafi, Congressman Waters has loyal constituents. Some of them are not too kind to strangers visiting their part of the city.

In the interest of the liberal subjectively defined standard of civility, everybody please thank Waters for having the courage to put aside partisan politics and reach out to the heartland. Maybe they will give up their happy lives in functional Middle America to visit the burning cauldron of failure of Maxinistan, Los Angeles.

For those currently vacationing in Martha's Vineyard, Downtown Los Angeles is not for you. Only the truly special among us are worthy of entering the not-so-pearly gates of hell that is the Waters District.

The tea party makes no promise about visiting Maxine's Inferno, but the invitation is still appreciated. All we ask in return is that when Waters flees her own district either due to indictment or a simple desire for a better (meaning any) quality of life, that she not come to our district.

The corrupt gay union conspiracy

Gay marriage caused the oceans to rise and commerce to crash. *FoxNews.com* may not want to have had New York and North Dakota news stories on top of one another. The headline, "State legalizes gay marriage" preceded, "Floodwaters breach dike." On a cellphone it makes for hilariously insensitive reading when deliberately taken out of context. Deliberately combining a pair of seemingly disparate issues allowed me to uncover a conspiracy involving big government, big labor, and homosexual marriage.

Boeing decided to build a plant in South Carolina.[171] They currently build planes in Seattle, known for rain, grunge, coffee snobs, computer geeks and leftists gone wild. Fires set during the World Trade Organization meetings are how Seattle liberals settle labor disputes.[172] Boeing is a business. Shockingly enough, businesses are more comfortable in cities and states where they are welcomed rather than burned in effigy.

The real story is buried down so deep that nobody else but me could see it.

Seattle is a liberal city. South Carolina is a conservative state. This all comes down to gay unions.

Boeing did not want its planes made in a city where gay marriage would become law. For planes to fly straight, they have to be made by straight people. South Carolina is the Bible Belt. Their opposition to gay marriage makes them qualified to build planes. Look at the evidence. Ninety percent of Americans are heterosexual. Getting corroboration from the parties involved has been difficult since nobody has been willing to go on the record.

When Boeing was contacted, their spokesperson replied, "Are you out of your mind? What does gay marriage have to with manufacturing?" When the Seattle labor representatives were contacted, they replied, "We want good jobs at good wages. Social issues have nothing to do with this. You are insane." Both sides were in complete public agreement, which meant only one thing. This is the mother of all cover-ups. How dare Boeing move from an inevitable right-to-marry state to a state that bans gay unions! This is just an attempt to get around gay union rules. Boeing's B-29 plane is called the *Enola Gay* (Not to be confused with Ebola Gay).[173]

Wall Street offered further evidence. Governor Andrew Cuomo signed a law allowing gay marriage. The stock market reacted violently.

Actually, the market totally shrugged. Yet at some point the stock market will gyrate more wildly than college students on spring break. Based on statistics, ten percent of the students will be gay. They will be hooking up. While they are frolicking on the beach, they will be neglecting their responsibilities such as school and work (The ninety percent of straight students acting the exact same way will be excluded from the analysis as outliers).

This proves that gay unions lead to lower productivity in the workplace. Texas does not allow gay marriage. Texas has seen a massive increase in jobs. Businesses therefore are deliberately moving to states that ban gay unions. Exasperated gay rights advocates insist that the issue is labor unions, not gay unions. This is code for attacking heterosexual couples, since only they can create a situation that results in labor. Like many work stoppages, these labor situations last about nine months.

Labor unions claim that they just want to adopt new rules, but obviously this is code for gay adoption. For those still unconvinced, some gay activists chanted at a pride parade, "We're here. We're queer. It's 2011. Let us build the 7-8-7!" Because of background noise, it is conceivable that the protesters were fighting for boinking and not Boeing. Spread-eagled may have no correlation to building planes or flying.

Some would say I am divorced from reality, but that is also code for the next new industry to make millions of dollars off of recent legislation. Gay divorce lawyers are coming to a theatre near you. This will lead to more questions. If gay divorce lawyers force their clients to split their property, how do they decide who gets the condo in Seattle and who gets the house in South Carolina? The loser may never get to build an airplane. Such is life when companies try to evade gay union laws.

Chapter 8: Sexual Lunacy

Sex scandals have existed ever since Eve flashed her goods and manipulated Adam. Women with a different analysis can write their own books. Eve was obviously a liberal. She took the apple without paying for it. Some sex scandals are amusing. Wealthy liberals driving drunk over a bridge and getting their lover killed are less funny. Like Adam and Eve, Ted Kennedy was never one to take responsibility for biting the wrong apple bottom. Sexual lunacy crosses party lines up to a point.

Republicans pay the price for their misdeeds. For Democrats, sex is politics. Whether on the House floor or the Oval Office floor, liberals are screwing somebody. At their worst they are screwing 300 million people simultaneously. In 2015 Oregon appointed the first openly bisexual governor in American history. This is not news. She is a typical liberal Democrat, willing to equally screw men and women by raising taxes.

Does Anthony Weiner loathe Jewish women?

Apparently the Weiner dog does not like his kosher. Anthony Weiner added a creative layer to an already bizarre sex scandal. The appendage named after his surname became the front line for jokes, some of which were below the belt.

What people remember about Weiner is that he resigned in disgrace after being exposed sending naked pictures of himself to women other than his wife. He also had X-rated conversations with women.[174] The combative liberal was hardly a sympathetic figure, but he may not have done anything illegal. Unless he used his government office to send the pictures, the only thing he is guilty of is bad taste. Weiner may be the only public official to get brought down by a sex scandal without having any sex.

The story behind the story was even crazier. Weiner got caught making vile and defamatory comments toward Jewish women. If he were not Jewish, the comments could be considered anti-Semitic rather than just self-loathing.

Weiner married a non-Jewish woman. His reasons are his business. The problem is that too many Jewish men intermarry or date outside of the faith because of a negative and totally untrue stereotype about Jewish women.

The knock on Jewesses is that they are prudes. This is as totally fallacious as Congressman Weiner. One of Weiner's fantasy paramours was a forty-year-old Las Vegas Jewess. When she offered to perform oral sex on him, he expressed shock that a Jewish woman would do this.[175]

What planet is Weiner living on? Has he never heard of Monica Lewinsky?

I hate having to be the champion of feminists everywhere, but this unfair stereotyping of Jewish women must stop.

I learned the hard way. During my freshman year at American Jewish University, the lads and I drove to Mount Saint Mary's for a taste of Catholicism. Convinced that Jewish women were ice princesses, we went toward the hotter and warmer girls.

I quickly realized that women deflecting our advances, Jewish or otherwise, were not the problem. We were. Many women are intolerant. They demand guys earn a living, shave, wear clean shirts, have those shirts buttoned, and focus on having conversations. This intolerance is known in female circles as standards. Men do not suffer this affliction, so we do not grasp it.

The reason why many Jewish women eschew certain acts is not because they lack sexual desires. They just don't want to give their bodies to jack@sses. They respect themselves and demand that respect from men. Acts of imbecilic behavior in ascending order include inappropriate language, leaving the lid down or the seat up, and infidelity.

Many Jewish women are shocked that men with brains and careers exist. I would let Weiner read my diary about the many fine Jewish women I have known, but I did not write one.

Sex is biological, not theological. There is not one single sex act that non-Jewish women perform that Jewish women as a group are against. The People of the Book do not practice female circumcision. Jewish and non-Jewish women are equally capable of experiencing and giving physical pleasure. From alleged personal experiences, I am appalled at Weiner.

Jews are already practicing self-immolation and cultural suicide. The last thing we need is some leftist Jew married to a Muslim woman offering the world inaccurate stereotypes about Jewish women. Judaism encourages sex provided the couple is married. Jewish sex inside a happy Jewish marriage leads to Jewish children. Children don't grow on trees. Al Gore isn't Jewish.

The only thing to say about Jewish women is what Teri Hatcher said to Jerry Seinfeld in one of the best episodes of that show. She was talking about her breasts that Elaine thought were surgically enhanced. "They are real and they are spectacular."[176]

Oh my lord, yes they are. This can also be said for every aspect of the daughters of Sarah, Rebecca, Leah, and Rachel. Liberal Jewish women who voted for Weiner for decades hopefully realized that he is not their champion. Maybe the NOW will finally for once speak up and prove they care about women.

6,000 years of beautiful religious traditions mandate that I choose lusting over loathing when it comes to my own people. Jewish women really are the best. Andy Weiner's refusal to marry one does not hurt the religion. It allows them to meet somebody better, which helps the religion.

Ways to make the Anthony Weiner ethics hearings even more interesting

If anything could make sex more boring than sleeping with a NOW member, it would have to be a congressional ethics hearing about sex. An Anthony Weiner ethics hearing would have patched over the start of a rough summer before the return of football and *Desperate Housewives*.[177] It still would have been best to tamp down expectations. Powerful bald white guys discussing sex is not sexy. Weiner resigned so the hearings unfortunately never happened. There was a way to make the hearings more fun. Instead of Congress, reality television stars and other celebrities could have asked Weiner their questions.

American Idol[178] judges past and present and *Celebrity Apprentice*[179] candidates could have chimed in before every other inconsequential celebrity helped the hearings descend into madness.

With that, here are the digitally enhanced Anthony Weiner hearings in high definition and yet still low quality.

Simon Cowell: You obviously looked like a fool with your pants on the ground. Was your hat on sideways?[180] If you did not wear a hat, I hope the Center for Disease Control was contacted because your performance makes me sick.

Jennifer Lopez: What could possibly have made you think that people want to see your front side as much as my backside? You may act like one, but I'm real.[181]

Steven Tyler (singing): When it comes to making love I ain't no hype, because I practice on a peach most every night…Excuse my position, but it ain't missionary…[182]

Anthony Weiner: What is your question Mr. Tyler?

Steven Tyler: Ayayayayayayay.

Anthony Weiner: Well, when you put it that way.

Randy Jackson: Dog, you acted like a dog, dog, I can't believe you would dog us like that dog. You are not a cool cat. You dig, dog?

Anthony Weiner: I'm not sure I do.

Randy Jackson: Dog, I'm telling you dog.

Ellen DeGeneres: Do you favor gay marriage?

Anthony Weiner: Absolutely.

Ellen DeGeneres: I have no further questions. You are obviously innocent.

Trace Adkins: Do you like a woman with a Honky Tonk Badonkadonk?[183]

Piers Morgan: *Fox News* is killing *CNN*. *Hannity* is thrashing me. Will you appear on my show to help boost the ratings?

Anthony Weiner: Yes.

Piers Morgan: No further questions, I am satisfied.

Joan Rivers: Can we talk?

Anthony Weiner: About what?

Joan Rivers: I don't care, I have been saying that since the Civil War. Did you side with the Union or the Confederacy?

Anthony Weiner: I was not alive then, but I would have supported the Union. I am against slavery.

Joan Rivers: Well then you shouldn't have gotten married. Just kidding darling, I love you. My daughter Melissa is single. You should meet her. I will send you her picture. What is your email address? Are you on Facebook?

Gary Busey: Do you know where I can score some drugs and hookers? You are Eliot Spitzer, right?

Anthony Weiner: No, I am Anthony Weiner.

Gary Busey: Pleased to meet you, I'm Gary Busey.

Anthony Weiner: Yes, I know.

Gary Busey: Did you use protection, because helmet laws suck.

Meatloaf: So help me God I will rip your throat out if you say one more word!

Anthony Weiner: Meatloaf, I…

Meatloaf: Not you Congressman, Gary Busey.

Donald Trump: You are a total psycho.

Meatloaf: That's not nice Mr. Trump.

Donald Trump: Not you Meatloaf, Congressman Weiner. Anthony, you're a psycho. I may have you on the next season of *Celebrity Apprentice*.

Anthony Weiner: I don't think that's…

Donald Trump: Anthony, you're fired.

Anthony Weiner: I don't work for you.

Donald Trump: Right, because I fired you.

Anthony Weiner: I answer to the voters.

Donald Trump: I vote in New York, you're fired. Hey Jimmy Fallon and John Rich, sing it to him.

Jimmy Fallon and John Rich (singing): You're fired, you're fired, you son of a b*tch, you're fired. Take your rolling suitcase out the door.[184]

Then other Hollywood celebrities would have their say simply because they refuse to go away.

Lady Gaga: Congressman (singing)…I've had a little bit too much.

Anthony Weiner: Of what?

Lady Gaga: Wish I could shut my playboy mouth.

Anthony Weiner: Tell me about it.

Lady Gaga: How did I turn my shirt inside out?

Anthony Weiner: I have no idea. I am unfamiliar with you.

Lady Gaga: Stop calling, stop calling, I don't want to talk any more.[185]

Anthony Weiner: I never called you and I certainly did not use a government phone to do it. This is a disaster. I am ruined.

Lady Gaga: It'll be ok. Just dance.[186]

Justin Bieber: That pic you sent me was kind of gross.

Anthony Weiner: Oh come on! I'm not gay!

Lady Gaga: What do you have against gay people? You're intolerant!

Anthony Weiner: I support gay people!

Justin Bieber: Oh wait, that was a pic of some other Congressman. They all like me. It's kind of creepy.

Joy Behar: I hate Sarah Palin.

Anthony Weiner: I agree.

Joy Behar: You are obviously the victim of a right-wing smear machine. Sarah Palin is dumb and evil.

Star Jones: I will have my say.

Donald Trump: No Star, I already fired you.

Anthony Weiner: This is not your hearing.

Donald Trump: Pipe down psycho, you're fired.

Anthony Weiner: You people are nuts.

Donald Trump: Zip it Weiner. You're fired.

Rosie O'Donnell: I hate you Donald. Anthony, what is your stance on gay rights?

Anthony Weiner: I already answered that. Ask Ellen.

Rosie O'Donnell: Do I look like Ellen?

Donald Trump: No, you're hideous…and you're fired.

Jon Stewart: I shill for Anthony because we are personal friends but I have to pretend I am not a hack. Speaking of hacked, isn't Andrew Breitbart evil for hacking into your Twitter account?[187]

Anthony Weiner: Well, actually…

Jon Stewart: I know, he is a bad guy.

Anthony Weiner: I set myself up for blackmail.

Jon Stewart: Breitbart is blackmailing you? That b@stard!

Stephen Colbert: I'm Bill O'Reilly.

Anthony Weiner: Actually you're not sir.

Stephen Colbert: You're a liar! You lie about everything. I am Bill O'Reilly. You're a pinhead. See, who else but O'Reilly would say that? I have testified before Congress you know.

Anthony Weiner: I am not sure O'Reilly ever did.

Stephen Colbert: How dare you criticize Papa Bear! I can have you waterboarded.

Anthony Weiner: Actually, that is not the case sir.

Stephen Colbert: Who do you think you are you insolent young snip, John Stewart?

David Letterman: Earlier somebody said nuts. Oh my, we're having some fun now.

Anthony Weiner: Mr. Letterman, you just threw a pen at me and nearly poked out my eye.

David Letterman: I was aiming for the cameraman. Weiner, you really are an embarrassment with all this sex stuff with young women.

Jay Leno: Talk about the pot calling the kettle black.

Joy Behar: The term is African-American you racist.

Anthony Weiner: This is insane. Don't you people have any questions for me? Why is Sarah Palin here?

Tina Fey: I'm not Sarah Palin. I just look like her.

Anthony Weiner: Not funny.

Tina Fey: Hey, don't attack *Saturday Night Live* just because you're in trouble. I can't bring back Bill Murray and Chevy Chase you know.

Anthony Weiner: I didn't mean…

Tina Fey: Do you think it's easy writing for a show that hasn't been funny since bell-bottoms? You try writing Jerry Ford jokes.

Anthony Weiner: For the love of Peter…

Tina Fey: Leave your Peter out of this. That's how you got in trouble to begin with. See how tough my job is?

Oprah Winfrey: We all have to leave some time. Want to be on my *O Network* Congressman? Do you like the O?

David Letterman: He sure does. What a lying hypocrite.

Oprah Winfrey: I'll get my boyfriend Attorney General Steadman Graham to handle this.[188] Baby's got your back.

David Letterman: Baby got back indeed. I love Oprah and her back. Enough about phony Congressmen playing grab-@ss. I like saying grab-@ss.

Anthony Weiner: Does anybody have any questions for me about the reason why we are here?

Brett Baier: Brett Baier, *Fox News.* I have a...

Anthony Weiner: You're not a real network. I need somebody unbiased.

Chris Matthews: Chris Matthews from *MSNBC.* I get a thrill up my leg when Obama speaks. Do you?

Anthony Weiner: I'm not gay sir.

Chris Matthews: Can I kiss your boo-boo and make it better?

Anthony Weiner: Can anyone ask me a real question? Heck, I would settle for Bill O'Reilly at this point.

Stephen Colbert: Congressman, isn't it true...

Anthony Weiner: Not you, the real Bill O'Reilly.

Stephen Colbert: How dare you.

Eminem: Forget the real Bill O'Reilly. I'm the Real Slim Shady. So get ready, because this sh*t's about to get heavy.

Randy Jackson: Dog, I'm digging the surprise cameo dog. Any other dogs in the house, dog?

Snoop Dogg: Fo'shizzle my nizzle, Weinersizzle.

David Letterman: He said Weinersizzle. It's a party...in his pants!

Anthony Weiner: Enough already! This is worse than *C-SPAN*! I did it. I'm guilty. I broke the rules. I'll pay the consequences. Just end this already. Take me to jail, but take me away from this.

Chris Matthews: I'll visit every week for conjugal visits my liberal buddy. I loved the pictures.

Jon Stewart: Just like the ratings in my time slot, I'll take seconds and thirds.

This concludes the only way to make the work of Congress better and worse simultaneously.

The NOW/Anthony Weiner Summer Trouserthon

Every man in America who ever took a picture of his own (redacted) should mail the pictures to the National Organization for Women. They love that stuff. If it bothered them, they would have commented about Anthony Weiner. Guys, give the NOW what they want.

If women can do SlutWalk[189] marches, then men need to do something in the name of gender equality. June 21 is the Summer Equinox. Men should get a head start. Every June 20, men shall host the all-day **annual Male Summer Trouserthon**.

All men are ordered to drop trou in front of NOW members until they criticize liberal sexual predators and start defending conservative female victims. Men should not drop their trousers until they receive confirmation that the women are in the NOW. All other women must be treated with respect. Those unwilling to drop trou should send the NOW discount coupons for hot dogs.

All hail **Trouserthon**!

There will be fun for the entire family, unless the family consists of NOW members. They do not know how to have fun. The official Trouserthon mascot will be the NOW ostrich. Every time we show a picture of a liberal behaving badly, the mascot will run around aimlessly and then stick his head in the sand. There will be comedians performing at Trouserthon as well.

"The problem with women is their standards. They have them. My hope is that ninety percent of men act worse so I can be one of the best with less effort. They should not act so badly that women give up on all of us. Maintaining a delicate balance is hard work."

"Maybe Anthony Weiner was smart to take pics. I have been trying to prove for years that I fathered Elizabeth Hurley's baby and nobody believes me. I wish I had the proof. I would pay child support for eighteen years just for bragging rights."

"The real Anthony Weiner scandal is that he did not get to have sex with anyone. Even Deuce Bigalow had sex with one of them! One hundred years from now teenage boys will learn about Weiner and feel better about their own lives. Somebody stamp a scarlet L on this loser's forehead."

There will be poetry readings for sensitive sissy beta males. It will still be alpha male poetry. "As I kissed her lips sweet as molasses, she wiggled her hips and broke my glasses."

The official Trouserthon movie will be *Old School*.[190] A costume contest will give prizes to those most resembling Will Ferrell, Vince Vaughn, and Luke "The Godfather" Wilson. Those wanting to play in the Jell-O wrestling ring must be young nubile females or resemble Joseph "Blue" Pulaski.

There will be musical interludes. To quote Humpty Hump of Digital Underground, "I don't go nowhere without my Jim hat. 'Cause if I'm rapping as if she's clapping then I'm strapping 'cause I'm smarter than that."[191] The Divinyls will offer wisdom by crooning, "I don't want anybody else, 'cause when I think about you I touch myself."[192] I personally don't touch myself because I don't know where I've been. Anthony Weiner does not have that problem.

For those of you who grew up (or never did) in the 1980s, break out your jams.[193] Mine have red, yellow, blue, green and black fishies on them. Fishies are just as manly as duckies. There will be waterslides and plenty of food. Naturally there will be Weiner on a stick among other yummy noshables. Trouserthon is a combination carnival, circus and bazaar, not to be confused with a bizarre. That would be Anthony Weiner.

There will be parlor games similar to those at Six Flags. One can throw beanbags at bottles with pictures of Congressman Weiner, John Edwards, Bob Filner, Dominique Strauss-Khan, Eliot Spitzer, Bill Clinton, and Ted Kennedy on them. Only men that the NOW gives a free pass to will be featured. Those actually criticized for their misdeeds will be spared.

Old School clips will appear on the big screen followed by the "Frank the Tank" drinking contest. The winner gets a Matchbox or Hot Wheels replica of the Ted Kennedy mobile that drove off the Chappaquiddick Bridge as the NOW stayed silent.[194] The toy car will even have a pantsless action figurine shaped like the late Senator Kennedy.

Trouserthon is on. Let's party until there are consequences, which according to the NOW reaction toward liberals is never.

Kim Kardashian's bare bottom can save the world

The world remains on fire as ISIS, Boko Haram and other radical Islamofascist groups murder innocent citizens across the globe. Ebola threatens to engulf West Africa and lead to a worldwide pandemic. Food prices are skyrocketing and fuel prices are still higher than they were in January of 2009. With everything going on in the world, there was still time for one woman with a knack for publicity and a stunning posterior to stop the Internet world in its slack-jawed tracks.

Kim Kardashian became famous through a sex tape that revealed her to be a woman of numerous curves. In blunter terms, she has a spectacular backside. Kardashian shook her moneymaker for the cameras and made millions. Those mocking her lacked the luxury of laughing their posteriors all the way to the bank.

Kardashian was always beautiful but never important. Pop culture has long been a barren wasteland containing far too many useless individuals dumbing down society with their mindless prattling and hollow lives. Then Kardashian decided to break the Internet by posing naked for the cover of *Paper Magazine*.[195] She bared her luscious apple bottom to the world and started a debate on whether her behavior was appropriate.

Those who liked the pictures consisted of many men with pulses and many women content with a gorgeous woman showing her beauty loudly and proudly. Those who disliked the pictures included many jealous women and the emasculated men afraid of those women. Emasculated men terrified of their own women took great pains to feign indignity at the pictures. A third category consisted of people irritated that Kim Kardashian is ever a topic of discussion.

With matters of life and death at home and abroad, this theory posits that pop culture should never be mentioned for any reason. This usually accurate train of thought deserves an exception. Kim Kardashian accidentally now has the power to be relevant to American society and even very useful.

Radical Islamofascists seek to establish a global Caliphate. Their greatest wish is to destroy Great Satan America. They hate us because we are free, but they hate us even more because that freedom causes us to enjoy decadence. Erotic pictures of American women are one of the very reasons Islamofascists cite for trying to export Sharia Law to the world.

Islamofascists are trying to force their values down Western throats. What better way to counter Islamofascist violence than by beating them at their own goal?

American airplanes should drop millions of leaflets containing the naked Kim Kardashian pictures on every Islamofascist nation. Those finding this idea trivial fail to understand the power of lust. Western culture has frequently promoted lust to advance American interests. Our military has won wars, but our secular indulgences have won over people everywhere despite those determined to deny this.

1960s America was locked in a struggle with the U.S.S.R. for world control. Even while the Cold War was raging, Soviet citizens were paying top dollar for black market staples of American culture. Blue jeans and *Beatles* tapes were highly sought after prizes in the Russian empire.[196] While the *Beatles* were British, it was their star status in the United States that made the rest of the world want their merchandise at all costs. As for blue jeans, no article of clothing is more quintessentially American.

The Romanian overthrow of dictator Nicolae Ceausescu in 1989 involved a major American influence. Romanians citizens fell in love with the American prime time drama *Dallas,*[197] starring the late Larry Hagman as dastardly villain J.R. Ewing. Hagman himself even noted the show's role in showing off America's opulence to the Communist world. Romanians saw the lust, wealth and power and wanted it for themselves.[198] World leaders castigating America secretly watched *Dallas* and its copycats *Dynasty*[199] and *Falcon Crest,*[200] along with the *Dallas* spinoff *Knots Landing.*[201]

Rabbi Shmuley Boteach is the author of *Kosher Sex,*[202] a template for couples to strengthen their own marriages, Boteach has explained that lust is too powerful an emotion to be ignored. If General David Petraeus, one of the most disciplined men on Earth, could fall prey to temptation, then repressed Islamofascists trying to deny their own desires are ripe targets.

Osama bin Laden cited hatred of the American way of life as a justification for the September 11 attacks that murdered nearly 3,000 Americans. Many of the nineteen Saudi hijackers spent the night before the attacks gambling in casinos and cavorting with prostitutes. Men angry with American women provocatively parading around enjoyed those women very much. When bin Laden was killed, American Navy SEALs discovered his private stash of pornographic magazines.[203]

Inflicting repeated cultural images on a populace affects behavior. Homosexuality was once scandalous. Now gays live openly and most people shrug. This change was due to a relentless marketing and media campaign offering a specific point of view. The same goal can be accomplished everywhere.

It would be much tougher for Islamofascist hardliners to keep their young men indoctrinated when these barely adult-aged boys are salivating over pictures of Kim Kardashian's hindquarters.

Many Americans dislike overt displays of sexualized images because of the corrupting influence it has on the American people. Try as they might deny it, Muslims have the same internal desires. Sexuality and eroticism are not a unique American phenomenon. Adam and Eve confronted desire long before religion ever existed. Humanity was founded on lust and its consequences.

Kim Kardashian's exposed bottom should be sent everywhere in the Muslim world. Dictators can try and block the pictures and censor the Internet. That will make contraband copies more powerful than blue jeans were five decades ago. Islamofascists know that America's hyper-sexualized culture is a threat to the rigidity of radical Islam. They hate and fear it because they secretly love it.

America can truly spread its own global influence by dropping images of Kim Kardashian's rear end from the sky in all its perfectly picturesque posterior glory. Islamofascist boys can chant, "Death to America" while trying to kill each other for the right to view the images. Societies that turn inward inevitably collapse. That would be the best finale worth watching since *Dallas*.

Shocker! French Socialist Plutocrat Acts Like Himself

Dominique Strauss-Kahn was more than just the socialist head of the International Monetary Fund and a candidate for President of France. He was a villain so perfect that Republicans and conservatives could have spent years trying to create him without success. For those disgusted with leftism, Strauss-Kahn was manna from heaven.

Part of his compassion for weaker members of society was enhanced by sexually assaulting one in a New York hotel.[204] Being a leftist meant a free pass. The whole point of being a leftist is to exploit people in the name of compassion. American liberals Bill Clinton and Ted Kennedy made it their platforms. As long as men are pro-choice on abortion, they can abuse as many women as they like for as long as they like. What would the NOW say or do, something?

Here is the opening statement that any good leftist defense attorney would prepare:

"My client did not sexually assault that hotel worker. This is a right-wing smear campaign brought about by Neocons Sarkozy and Bush with help from the Zionists. My client was naked and running down the halls of the hotel because he was the victim. Neocons broke into his room and subjected him to coercive interrogation methods. Torture is always wrong, whether in the illegal Iraq War or here. He was running to escape his captors. The woman who found him reminded him of one of his captors. He tried to defend himself from her advances. She then tried to escape, which is proof of her trying to assault him.

My client has suffered enough. He is a man named Dominique. This led to him getting beaten up over the years by people thinking he is gay. He has always supported gay rights, and will not let the anti-gay right-wing fringe bigots win.

My client has a long history of support for women's rights. He is pro-choice on abortion and will not stand by and let people like Sarah Palin send women into back alleys. Convicting Mr. Kahn means supporting illegal American imperialist wars to benefit moneylenders, freemasons, gypsies, and Zionist aggressors. Palin is dumb, Bush is evil, and Wall Street bankers will not get to frame Mr. Kahn so they can get their greedy hands on the IMF the way they let Paul Wolfowitz run the World Bank."

Strauss-Kahn is French and socialist. His behavior was expected. Even if twelve liberals in Manhattan or Paris convicted this man who splendidly represents their values, the punishment needs to fit the crime. Jail is not the answer.

Dominique Strauss-Kahn is now perfectly qualified to be the Secretary General of the United Nations. He has executive experience at an organization that consistently fails to do right. His European bailouts are the epitome of making excuses for bad decisions. Who better to make sure Syria and Iran finally get to run wild with impunity? Hating America and Israel is very important for this job. He is a French socialist, so let's give him the benefit of the doubt and assume he does.

United Nations peacekeepers are great at raping innocent third world women they are supposed to be protecting. Who better to run the U.N. than an expert in abusing innocent women? Who better to pretend to care about the powerless than a man representing an ideology that allows powerful billionaires to spread misery to the masses in the name of compassion?

Let's not get bogged down with distractions such as right and wrong, treating women as people, and the rule of law. The ends justify the means. Anybody who either dislikes conservatives, Jews or both should be allowed an occasional violent felonious assault. The man is European, and they are so refined and sophisticated. We need men like him to stand up to American slobs who eat hot dogs and prefer sports to opera.

It is high time we stop harassing leftist plutocrats for acting like themselves. Stay classy, France. Stay compassionate, liberals. Keep up that sophisticated, caring stuff you do so well between centuries of indifference.

Chapter 9: Sports Lunacy

Professional sports are the major driver separating alpha males from their vile feminized beta cousins. Real men like football. Metrosexuals think that figure skating is a sport. Sports are violent in the great tradition of ancient Rome. They are tests of bravery and courage. Conservatives like sports, or what liberals call sport.

John Kerry referred to Lambeau Field as Lambert Field.[205] Al Gore confused Michael Jordan and Michael Jackson.[206] They cannot help it. They have the defective recessive beta gene. Sports separates the men from the boys. It separates the conservatives from the liberals. The most fun political sport is watching liberal politicians pretend they have ever watched or played a sport in their life other than windsurfing or hopscotch.

Barack Obama: Skeet-shooting beta male

President Obama should use his self-given enhanced absolute powers to drop a predator drone on the White House photographer. Photos of Obama attempting to skeet shoot, do pushups, and throw a football have become hilarious Internet fodder.[207]

The Obama White House is the most transparent administration in history, so their claim that the pictures were not photoshopped should be taken at face value. They wouldn't lie. We don't even know whether Obama knows how Photoshop works.

In the big scheme of things, the pictures are silly. From a psychological standpoint they provide an amusing window into Obama's id.

Obama said to his political director in 2008, "I think that I'm a better speechwriter than my speechwriters. I know more about policies on any particular issue than my policy directors. And I'll tell you right now that I'm a better political director than my political director."[208]

Obama's lack of humility is misdirected. It would be one thing if he were trying to impress women. Most men in the bar clumsily regale ladies with stories of how they killed a grizzly bear with their bare hands. Deep down every guy wants to be "The most interesting man in the world" Dos Equis guy.[209] Obama believes he is more fascinating than that. "I killed bin Laden. Stay thirsty my friends." In Obamaworld the Pajamaboy President even has a better beard.

The problem with Obama is his trying to impress other guys. Between bowling a thirty-seven and living with a woman who bans him from smoking and eating hot dogs, Obama is the man who no man should ever be.[210] It may kill him inside, but the evidence is clear. Obama is a metrosexual. Skeet shooting? Doing pushups? Throwing a football? Who does he think he is, Vladimir Putin? Next he will be hunting tigers, riding horses bare-chested, and driving NASCAR. He'll be standing next to Dale Earnhardt Jr. while incorrectly stuffing Skoal Bandit chaw in his mouth.

Obama thinks you can talk your way to being an alpha male. He is of the male gender but he is not a guy. He is certainly not a regular guy or a guy's guy. This is not totally his fault. Real men have been in decline since 1967. That was when Phil Donahue began a television show dedicated to convincing beta males that they were adequate as human beings. Donahue had his hindquarters kicked every night by wife Marlo Thomas. Dragging every other man down to his beta male level would render him less inadequate by comparison.

Barack Obama is not the boss of his house. His wife and his mother-in-law would slap him six ways to Sunday if he upset them. Obama's predator drone kills of al-Qaeda terrorists will not change the fact that Obama sometimes acts like a sissy prissy wussie throwing a hissy. To accuse him of acting like a woman would be sexist and unfair to the many strong American women who like men with a pair. Obama is a metrosexual beta male, and no amount of pictures to the contrary will undo the evidence. When he threw that baseball on live national television, he was wearing mom jeans. He even admitted that he stopped wearing them because his wife threw them out.[211] For different reasons than Ted Kennedy, Obama does not wear any pants. You can't be the leader of the free world when you are only the sixth most powerful person in your own household.

He can protest that he is athletic. He shot two for twenty-two in basketball.[212] He was zero for five in the football toss. Governor Chris Christie had to win him a stuffed animal at the Jersey Shore.[213] Obama is a liberal feminized she-male in the tradition of Gore, Kerry and Dukakis. The only alpha male in the entire Democrat Party is Bill Clinton, who shot a duck to win votes.[214] Maybe Obama can have Bubba redistribute a portion of his manliness so that Obama can have his fair share. Maybe a local Chicago drug dealer or former Choom Gang member can help Obama score some beta-blockers.

Obama keeps claiming he is a regular guy, not some elitist snob hanging out with Wellington, Winthrop, Chartwell, Biff and Muffy. He can claim that he didn't serve up plates full of carrots and celery sticks at his Super Bowl party while pretending to understand "sport." His memoir was about his realization that he fit in nowhere. Now he knows that beta males are not and never will be cool. Not even a photo of him shooting a football while doing Jack Palance one-armed pushups[215] on top of a moving Indy 500 car will change that. Real men are retrosexuals, and President Obama should never pretend to know what that means.

ISIS threatens to destroy everything except golf courses

ISIS butchers are taking no prisoners but also taking no chances. While they would love to reign terror down on American infidels, mosques are off limits. Churches and synagogues are fair game for fire-bombings. Most importantly, golf courses are not to be touched.

The ban on blowing up golf courses was established at a contentious ISIS board meeting. Tempers flared from the start due to lunch being served late. It was noted with irony that in a room filled with Islamofascists carrying swords, not one of them knew a good Halal butcher. The secretary in charge of lunch was tossed in a wood chipper.

After rounding up some local infidels and chowing down on sandwiches of Jewish and Christian breast meat smeared with Dijon mustard, the assembled ISIS bigwigs got down to business. The main concern was that damaging a major golf course would be the one thing that might arouse the normally passionless President Obama.

There were dissenting voices against the ban. Worrying about collateral damage is something Israelis do. ISIS should not be linked to any Israeli policy.

One board member pointed out that Obama is a metrosexual, selfie-taking Pajamaboy who would never have the guts to retaliate against them. A Pakistani board member pointed out that Obama did kill Osama bin Laden.

To that another angrily retorted, "Yeah, and John Kerry served in Vietnam. Who cares? Obama was curled up like an armadillo while the only man with any cojones overruled Obama's timidity and ordered the operation to go forward. That man is no longer with the administration, although he is on a book tour running for president in 2016."

The parliamentarian observed on a point of order that Hillary Clinton is female, which led to confusion and more debate. Further argument ensued over whether the j in cojones is silent and why Obama mispronounces Pakistan and keeps saying ISIL instead of ISIS.

The board finally decided that even somebody with less emotion than the love child of Al Gore and an IBM computer must care about something, somewhere. After a brief skirmish about IBM no longer making computers, they agreed that golf courses would be spared.

The next issue facing the board was whether ISIS should kill golfers when they are not on the course. Confusion reigned when the Scottish board member asked why they should spare the gophers, since gophers destroy golf courses.

An English board member screamed at his Scottish colleague, "The golfers, you bloody Haggistani! Not the gophers! Spare all the *golfers*!"

A motion passed to destroy all copies of the Zionist conspiracy movie *Caddyshack*.[216] *Happy Gilmore*[217] would be burned since Adam Sandler was part of the Zionist conspiracy. Kevin Costner's *Tin Cup*[218] could be spared since it was the least watched movie not involving an anti-Muslim filmmaker's YouTube video.[219]

Miniature golf courses were to be spared since Obama is rumored to spend time there after throwing temper tantrums and needing a timeout. The board concluded that the eighteenth hole with the clown should live on since Americans hate and fear those clowns. The Scottish board member's suggestion that ISIS soldiers wear clown suits to strike greater terror into America was promptly voted down, and he was unceremoniously dumped in the wood chipper.

The only unanimous vote came when the remaining board members agreed that the video of Robin Williams talking about Scotsmen and golf was the funniest video alive not involving a Zionist beheading.[220]

The conversation returned to whether golfers could be killed as long as they were not on the courses. Tiger Woods was deemed off limits. Any harm coming to Woods could trigger another boring Obama speech followed by an impartial investigation led by Attorney General Eric Holder. The board did not want to deal with Al Sharpton, who they all agreed was a crazy man who incited riots and murder.

If Woods were accidentally harmed, a confession letter would have to be placed at his side with a signature either implicating George W. Bush, Sarah Palin or some person named *Fox News* or talk radio.

After munching on imitation bacon-flavored chips, the board issued several fatwas after consulting their thesauruses to find out what a fatwa was.

In addition to golf courses, Ivy League universities, Hollywood studios, and any other areas with significant pockets of sympathy for Islamofascists will be spared. *MSNBC* and *NYJBT* personnel are to be protected at all costs. Liberals who look the most French will be temporarily spared provided they are not Jewish.

The most heated debate centered on what to do with gays. Some board members insisted that no gay people ever existed. Others claimed that the Prophet's fatwa ordering the killing of all gays was successful. A few board members worried that if gays exist, an attack on them could anger Obama if he was one. The younger members of the group explained to their elders that Obama is a metrosexual, not a homosexual. He is straight, just not very manly. Conversely, they explained that Hillary Clinton is also straight and female, just not a lady or feminine.

The ISIS board issued their fatwa. They decided to kill anyone openly gay, but that a "Don't ask, don't tell" policy could be implemented. Any American who insists he is straight will be killed for just being American instead.

A CIA operative who infiltrated the meeting tried to report to Obama, but was told the boss was busy on the golf course and did not want to be disturbed. The operative was referred to Islamofascist denier, video pusher, and communications svengali Ben Rhodes. Rhodes explained that Obama is aware of the situation because he is aware of everything. Obama and Kerry both expressed disappoint that ISIS continues to disrespect 21st century global cultural norms.

If ISIS kills Americans, Obama will express extreme disappointment and vow to immediately appoint a committee to contemplate a course of tough ineffectiveness. The CIA operative killed himself out of frustration, bringing the number of Obama employee suicides to a number the administration refuses to disclose. Hard drives containing the emails with the exact figures have been destroyed.

The final debate involved what to do with the leftists who had been coddling Islamofascists for years. ISIS determined that Lenin's useful idiots were no longer useful.[221] ISIS freedom fighters could flip a coin or spin a Dreidel to determine the fate of each leftist. Climate change advocates could be slaughtered because even ISIS found their whiny voices an annoying distraction from anything that anyone, anywhere cares about.

After the meeting ended, ISIS returned to work and set up security cameras using stolen NSA technology to spy on Obama and the rest of us. Upon determining that Obama was busy golfing again, ISIS prepared to kill everybody outside of the ten-mile radius of his eighteen-hole mulligan-fest.

Chapter 10: Hysterical Feminist Lunacy

Liberal feminists have a habit of treating any criticism of them as an attack on all women. These same hypocrites are the most vicious abusers of conservative women. The issue is ideological, not gender-based. Conservative Republican women are fantastic. Liberal women are as noxious as the liberal pseudo-men. Commenting about real men in the Democrat Party is unnecessary since there are none.

A clear message needs to be sent to Hillary Clinton, Elizabeth Warren, Sandra Fluke, Wendy Davis, Barbara Boxer, Debbie Wasserman Schultz and every other miscreant disguised as a champion of women. Take your fake feminism and your phony war on women and shut the Fluke up.

Dear Rush Limbaugh, Sandra Fluke should pay for my (redacted)

I apologize to both Rush Limbaugh and Sandra Fluke. My apology to Rush is because I have now switched sides. I now realize that Rush was wrong and Fluke was right. For those living either under a rock or in Vermont (same thing), Sandra Fluke is a thirty-something leftist activist posing as an ordinary woman. Like a typical liberal, she wants free stuff, in this case free contraception. What she really wants is to have recreational sex at taxpayer expense.

This has absolutely nothing to do with women's health issues. The war on women is in the Islamofascist Middle East. The religion angle is totally peripheral. While some religious people oppose contraception on principle, I am not one of them. Liberals should use contraception. Anything preventing more liberals from being created is fantastic. Forget gender. For the feminists who ranted and raved about men having Viagra or other E.D. treatments subsidized, even feminists are right from time to time. If men want to play, they should pay for it themselves. This is not even about attraction. Sandra Fluke has united gay and straight men. None of them want to date her. Her best hope was an emasculated beta-male (she found one). A guy without a pair means no possibility for sex or need for birth control.

This is about economics. Do what you want with your life. Just don't interfere with my right to live my life. That is why I opposed Sandra Fluke. I was wrong.

When I thought about the situation in a state of deep contemplation (more navel gazing), it became apparent that there is a serious health issue at stake. The government must intervene. Like most people, it took me personally walking in their moccasins to appreciate what others were going through. It is high time that America covers my mental, emotional, physical, and spiritual health needs.

This revelation came to me when a hypothetical individual who looked and acted like me was walking down Kuhio Avenue in Waikiki, Honolulu, Hawaii. I remember this hypothetical memory so vividly like it actually happened. It could have happened, so treat it as real despite possibly being fictional. A nubile twenty-year-old approached my fictional resemblance and asked if I wanted to have a good time. For a certain donation, anything I wanted was the offering. 1930s comedian Henny Youngman faced the same business proposition. He handed the woman money and said, "Wash my car and paint my house."[222] The Hawaii woman was probably not skilled or equipped enough to handle such tasks, and I did not live in Hawaii.

Very few things give me a good time. She was not willing to cook me a steak or give me football tickets. The imaginary me was confused over what she was offering from a transactional standpoint. We both pondered this riddle for a while, at which point an idea sprung. Imaginary me was a stressed-out business executive. She was a masseuse. Perhaps she could provide me with physical therapy for therapeutic purposes. My imaginary self called my CPA. After questioning why I called him at 5:00 a.m., he angrily refused to let massage be written off as a business expense.

The government must pay for this stress relieving physical and mental health need. Taxpayers must cover this form of birth control although it is a mystery to me how something as innocent as a massage by a nubile twenty-year-old could possibly be connected to sex. She said it was possible. Men accept anything hot women say at face and body value. Beyond the massage itself, so many extra expenses are involved with physical, emotional, mental, and spiritual healing.

My dry-cleaning bill must be subsidized. What if fictional me leaves his jeans on and they get stained? That could lead to discomfort and ridicule if others notice. The government should also provide tax-deductible laundry credits for cleaning my unmentionables or foot the cost of buying new ones if no laundry facility is nearby. Free tissues and other sundries must be given so dream me can clean up afterward.

Other expenses are vital to such relaxing experiences. Candles are essential whether they just stay on the table or are used in any wax rituals. Those opposed to wax rituals are culturally insensitive and insulting to the deeply held religious and spiritual beliefs of others. Anti-wax bigots need sensitivity classes. The government should cover the cost of the candles.

Music is vital. Free Barry White and Marvin Gaye CDs must be distributed. Sexual healing is important. Laws exist that currently prevent this medically necessary relaxation session from taking place outside in public areas. Lodging is required to insure privacy. Subsidized housing keeps the masseuse from passing on lodging costs to the consumer.

Good mental and physical health requires American subsidies. Otherwise we will have a frustrated populace, leading to higher crime and violence. Most men go only a few days without physical therapy from hot women before wanting to kill people.

Call girls save lives. More importantly, they spread happiness. Think of how many people in this world never smile. Look at Islamofascists and feminists. It's obvious why. Nobody will offer them therapy and they cannot afford to pay to play.

In the spirit of compassion, it is time that the government sponsor programs to help foster better health through repeated stress release. Since this works better in warm weather climates, the government should also take care of the airplane tickets as well (Like people go to the Bahamas for any other reason. They have golf in Florida).

Mr. Limbaugh, I can no longer sit idly by in my uncomfortably unclean jeans while you go on a moralizing tirade against a woman simply trying to become happy. Apologizing to Ms. Fluke is insufficient. You need to apologize to all men forced to pay for our own gallivanting on our own dime. How dare you spread a message of personal responsibility! You intolerant religious zealot! I may one day forgive you, because that is the type of guy I am.

Ms. Fluke, I apologize to you for not realizing that you were just trying to create a better world where we could all be deliriously, delightfully, and deliciously hedonistic for the sake of hedonism itself. If you were any more Roman you would wear a toga and chant about Caesar.

That reminds me. Spring break in South Beach, Miami, is around the corner. My toga should be back from the dry cleaners. I had them use extra stain guard. It was expensive, but who cares? The government will pay for it with Limbaugh's money.

The twenty-year-old Latina (I believe in diversity and multiculturalism and now apologize for calling it garbage. This was one wise Latina woman) masseuse who catered to the fellow who was a dead ringer for me is an American hero. We were in such good moods afterward that we went shopping, which provided even more stimulation to a local economy that has yet to overheat. We paid for the merchandise ourselves since the government check had yet to arrive.

My needs matter, but like any hero I am only one man. It is time for me to lead alpha males to their destiny and beta males out of purgatory. In addition to the necessary candles and mood music, the government must cover one more male physical health need. If the women look and act like Sandra Fluke, lots of hard alcohol will be necessary. For the sake of healing, the government must provide liquid courage credits as part of any college tuition package. The booze should come in a cheap brown paper bag that can be used to place over the woman's head if she looks and sounds like Sandra Fluke.

In 2015 I will lead the annual Million Frat-Boy March on college campuses across America. The discrimination must stop. #FratBoysLivesMatter

DiFi, PTSD, and PMS: Should radical feminists own guns?

Anti-gun Senator Dianne Feinstein is continuing her crusade to export another failed California idea. She has pushed gun control since Thomas Jefferson appointed her to the Senate. Feinstein wants law enforcement personnel to have more access to guns than private citizens. Given how successful this has worked in peaceful havens such as North Korea and Chicago, the pushback is understandable.

More absurd than removing guns from citizens is Feinstein's zeal to remove them from our military veterans. Feinstein believes that posttraumatic stress disorder (PTSD) makes gun-owning veterans a risk.[223] Senator Feinstein never served in the military, so perhaps insulting every veteran by stereotyping them as mentally ill and unstable comes out of ignorance and not malice. Feinstein called the NRA "venal,"[224] so she likely is that dangerous combination of ignorant and malicious.

Let's turn the tables and use language that Feinstein and other liberals can understand. Replace veteran men with feminist women and PTSD with PMS.

Feminists should not own guns because of pre-menstrual syndrome. Women suffering PMS are bonkers enough as it is. Let's paint every angry broad with a broad brush (Any minute now feminists will try to ban the phrase broad brush as sexist). Women are too crazy, hysterical, and irrational to be allowed anywhere near a firearm. Post-menopausal women are just as dangerous.

If the National Organization for Women had guns, one bad PMS episode could lead to a violent march on Washington resulting in dead men scattered around the city (as opposed to the normal weekly violence there). Many veterans are perfectly healthy people without PTSD. Not all women suffer from uncontrollable PMS rage or other emotional imbalances.

Feminists will scream the sexism card, because that is what feminists do. They will say it is wrong to demean an entire group of people just because normal fluctuations negatively affect some women to greater degrees than others. For once, the feminists would be correct. It is wrong to demean an entire group of people, DiFi. The few veterans with varying degrees of PTSD are able to do the same thing that PMS women do. They take medicine and consult with professionals.

To take away the rights of every veteran just because a small slice of them are troubled is wrong. Just because both California Senators are female and imbeciles does not mean we ban Republican women from running for office. If

Feinstein wants to spend her senile years throwing an anti-Second Amendment temper-tantrum, that is her First Amendment right. My First Amendment right allows me to tell her to put a sock in it and stop insulting our military veterans. She can spout her idiocy because of their bravery.

Cathy–Farewell and Good Riddance

Barack Obama and Katy Perry have a friendly rivalry to be the most vapid person in America. For shallowness in sheer quantity, they are the most hollow. For quality of lunacy, a woman who recently departed the scene wins the queen of shallow award. After three decades of babbling and complaining about nonsense, this all-too-real work of fiction finally left us and took her neuroses with her.

Cartoonist Cathy Guisewite lives on, but her cartoon character *Cathy* is finally gone.[225] Men everywhere should high five over this.

I have never met Cathy Guisewite. Her comic strip was apolitical, and certainly not mean. She could very well be a lovely human being.

Yet *Cathy* represented everything wrong with women. If one were to take every negative quality about women and somehow combine them into one gigantic disastrous train wreck, *Cathy* was it.

(Men have plenty of bad qualities. We just don't brag about them in print. Some men [not me, I am civilized] belch in public. That is terrible manners.)

Cathy was neurotic, obsessed over her weight and inability to get her boyfriend to marry her. Then he married her and loved her just the way she was. She responded by remaining as obsessive and compulsive as ever. Many times poor Irving wondered what he did wrong and why she was upset for no reason.

For those who want to save hundreds of thousands of dollars on therapy bills, let me explain the genders. Men are literal creatures. To understand us, take our words at face value. Comedian Chris Rock phrases it in a tactless manner. "Men want three things…food…sex…silence…feed me, f*ck me, and shut the f*ck up."[226]

I will be more tactful (for once). I am a simple guy, the doll with the string in the back. You pull the string and I say three or four things. "I'm hungry." "I'm thirsty." "I'm sleepy." "I want to watch the ballgame (It says one other thing but again I am trying to be tactful here)." If I am upset because my team lost, it does not mean I think the woman in my life is fat or ugly. It really does mean I get way too worked up over football. Guys take this stuff hard.

Picture a conversation between couples across the globe.

Woman: How do I look in this outfit?

Man: (I am never going to get out of this conversation alive) You look beautiful (a sincere answer).

Woman: What does that mean?

Man (Oh lord, my evening is about to get ruined.) It means you look beautiful.

(This is followed by questions that make a presidential press conference after a scandal look like a walk in the park. The man gets in trouble, wondering how a compliment could go so wrong.)

Some guys abuse women physically, sexually, and psychologically. These men should be locked in cages where guys like myself can beat the daylights out of them while yelling, "Stop messing it up for the rest of us!" Men actually try to hide their flaws. If they don't, they should.

Cathy does not represent all women but she does represent too many of them. *Cathy* celebrates women as insecurity-driven lunatics. She even bought a dog as a replacement for the baby that would never come. I felt for the dog.

If I go bald, I could sell my family for Rogaine or be sane and accept what life offers. When I gained a few pounds I did what people should do in that situation. I bought bigger clothing.

Cathy took pride in her neuroses. This had many women looking at *Cathy* and thinking, "I can relate, girlfriend." Driving everybody around you crazy because of neuroses is not something to be proud of. *Cathy* cannot and should not ever be accepted as the norm for female behavior. If it is, the war between the sexes will become Armageddon. Ironically, the women will be mad when we try to fight and also when we try to surrender.

Life is about decisions, and most decision matrices have right and wrong decisions. In *Cathy*'s world, every decision Irving made was wrong. If "A" and "not A" are both wrong, is it no wonder that the world's Irvings beat their heads against the wall?

Some will claim I am playing the role of Dan Quayle criticizing *Murphy Brown* (He was right, Candace Bergen was smug),[227] but *Cathy* cannot be just fictional and also resonate. Too many women today are nuts. Part of it is the 1970s feminist mistake that told women men were unnecessary. While many feminist disciples became spinsters, the original flaming feminist leaders happily settled into marriage. They also married upward. There is no sin in finding security in wealthy men, but the hypocrisy was typical outraged activist behavior.

(A deeper irony was that *Cathy* was no feminist. The feminists probably hated her for caring what others thought.)

Men and women need each other. We are better off when we communicate with each other in a normal manner. This involves listening. Yet listening and being tolerant does not mean accepting lunacy. I am a totally different guy from your father, brother or ex-boyfriend. The fact that another guy with a goatee and glasses made you feel bad ten years ago does not mean I will.

Thankfully I have been one of the lucky ones. My grandparents were happy. My parents are happy. I am a basically happy single guy. I cannot look at *Cathy* and see anything from her bizarre behavior that makes for healthy relationships. Dysfunctional lunacy and constant hassles do not have to be the norm. As one of my male friends who married a normal (Yes, they do exist) woman once said, "I like coming home to her." My parents have a refrigerator magnet that says, "Happiness is being married to your best friend." It helps that my mom is not crazy.

For the Milli Vanillionth time, there are plenty of things men can improve. This certainly includes me. If women want a good head start on improving, be the anti-*Cathy*. Observe her and do the opposite.

Cathy was good-hearted, never a (fictional) malicious woman. She was just crazy. She should have been locked up years ago or given enough sedatives to calm her down. After 34 years, women deserve better role models. Between a neurotic weight-obsessed lunatic and a model stick figure anorexic's dream, there is a middle ground. A great example would be *Sally Forth*.[228]

Sally is a wife, mother, and ardent feminist. Yet her husband is not an emasculated pansy (although he does understandably hide from her on the really bad days). *Sally* is not a ranting, raving momzilla. *Sally* is a great portrayal of a moderate feminist, proud to be female, assertive, and pleasant.

Goodbye, *Cathy*. Do not let the door hit your rumpus on the way out. As for your rumpus, I have no comment whatsoever. I don't make any comments where there are only wrong answers that will take years off my life while allowing me to catch your contagious insanity.

As a friend of mine (who happened to be black) said to me a decade ago, "The differences between black and white are nothing compared to the differences between men and women. As long as you are a man, there is a chance I can understand you."

May gender relations somehow get better before everyone is miserable and all hope for happiness is extinguished. It starts by celebrating healthy minds and quarantining the damaged ones far away from dating and marriage pools. Screwed up people almost never get better. They only drag healthy people down. *Cathy* was not funny. She was destructive. Goodbye, *Cathy*. Farewell and good riddance.

How Debbie Wasserman Schultz really feels about Scott Walker

Speaking at a Milwaukee roundtable event, Florida Congresswoman and Democrat National Committee Chairbeast Debbie Wasserman Schultz went for broke. She has a history of nasty comments about Republicans, but on this day she crossed the line from regular crazy to radical feminist lunacy.

Scott Walker has given women the back of his hand. I know that is stark. I know that is direct. But that is reality. What Republican tea party extremists like Scott Walker are doing is they are grabbing us by the hair and pulling us back. It is not going to happen on our watch.[229]

Sanity will not happen on her watch. Given how absurd her comments were, an equally absurd explanation might be warranted. Maybe Wasserman Schultz finds Scott Walker attractive and is having fantasies about him. Perhaps this uptight woman is just attracted to a man she considers a he-man. She would not be the first Jewish person to lust after forbidden Christian fruit.

Since Democrats like to dance around the grey even when the issue is clearly black and white, maybe Wasserman Schultz read *Fifty Shades of Grey*[230] and lost control. The story's erotic theme is coloring her thoughts. Since Wasserman Schultz never explicitly stated how Walker was supposedly hitting women, it could have been an erotic, masochistic assault or a playful tap to her bottom. Is her violent behavior pure political passion or sexual repression unleashed? Unless Wasserman Schultz clarifies her remarks, we're left to speculate about what lusty thoughts are going on underneath her fifty shades of grey hair dyed blonde.

Speculating about the dark recesses of her mind deserves, like the crude slurs of Wasserman Schultz, to be banished to the darkest parts of Crackpotistan. My theory is no less lunacy's love child than her comments about Walker.

The reality may be simpler. Wasserman Schultz is repulsive and repulsive people say and do repulsive things. She is Kate from *Taming of the Shrew*[231] without the pleasantness. That might explain her hostility. Whatever the reasons for her hysterical rantings — whether repressed sexual desires, projected violent fantasies, or cold political calculation — they were totally inappropriate statements from a woman who keeps saying totally inappropriate things. Debbie Wasserman Schultz is a most indecent woman. She heads an indecent party. Her comments are mainstream liberalism. There are no shades of grey in that.

The annual NOW Left-Wing Activism Conference

A worthless organization designed to elect political leftists convenes an annual conference dedicated to complaining about nonsense. The National Organization for Women infested a nice part of Tampa, Florida for one of those conferences.[232] Some delegates may have been trying out for the Tampa Bay Buccaneers, but most were there to cry on each other's oversized shoulder pads and insist they were relevant.

One look at the speaker lineup should relegate NOW's relevance claim to the ash heap of history along with New Coke and taco-flavored lip gloss (one of my brilliant but failed ideas). Here are some of their conference profiles, edited only for length.

Marleine Bastien is the founder and executive director of Fanm Ayisyen Nan Miyami, Inc. (FANM, Haitian Women of Miami) — Discusses the devastating effect that prolonged detention at Guantánamo had on Haitian children.

Let the terrorists loose in Tampa during the NOW Convention and see how the attendees like it.

Sam Bennett - In November 2008, Bennett ran for the U.S. House of Representatives in Pennsylvania's 15th district. She is the Director for America Coming Together (ACT), a non-partisan voter registration group.

She lost her race. ACT is a left-wing George Soros project.

Melanie Campbell is the president and CEO of the National Coalition on Black Civic Participation. She is a member of the inaugural class of the Progressive Women's Voices at the Women's Media Center.

There is no word on whether she considers Clarence Thomas or Condoleeza Rice to be black or female.

Kate Dillon is known in the fashion industry as a groundbreaker and passionate advocate for humanitarian and environmental causes. Her experiences as a mother and wife further solidify her respect for women all over the world.

Sarah Palin is a wife, mother and environment lover. There is no word on how Dillon feels about her.

Lois Frankel ran for the U.S. House of Representatives in one of the most important congressional races in 2012 - Florida's 22nd District. Her opponent, incumbent freshman Allen West, is a tea party favorite who has voted to destroy Medicare and let oil companies keep their deficit-busting tax loopholes.

Does Melanie Campbell believe that black civic participation means supporting Colonel Allen West? What do big oil and Medicare have to do with gender?

Latanya Mapp Frett is vice president for Planned Parenthood Federation of America's International Division.

By ensuring as many abortions as possible as quickly as possible, she is the raison d'etre for NOW to exist.

NAACP Legal and Education Fund … She is a founder of the Women's Equity Action League and Federally Employed Women, a charter member of Veteran Feminists of America, and was one of the longest-serving members of the Board of Trustees of the National Woman's Party.

This Queen of all trades is a master of few that matter.

Gabi Gregg - After graduating college in 2008, Detroit native Gabi Gregg created the blog, "Young Fat & Fabulous." She wrote, "Every Body is a Bikini Body."

Ask her how she feels about 300 pound NFL linebackers showing up at the NOW Convention wearing thongs. Not every body is a bikini body. Nobody wants to see my dad's chest scar from open-heart surgery.

Nancy Hogshead-Makar is one of the foremost exponents of gender equity in

education - including sports participation, sexual harassment, employment, pregnancy and legal enforcement under Title IX. In 2009, she brought a successful legal challenge against the Florida High School Athletic Association, whose cuts to competitive seasons discriminated against female athletes.

Colleges are canceling their football programs to avoid lawsuits from women's bowling teams and other groups with no popular support. The free market works.

Patricia Ireland - Today Ireland continues fighting for social justice. As a labor attorney in Miami, she represents unions and their members.

She gets paid to call Governor Rick Scott the devil while exploiting the proletariat. How liberal.

Celinda Lake is a prominent pollster and political strategist for Democrats and progressives.

She is useless but harmless.

Katie Makkai - In addition to poetry, Makkai teaches poetry to juvenile criminal offenders through "Art from Ashes" from 2000-2004.

Are you (redacted) kidding me? The long historical track record of converting rapists to nice boys through poetry is well known. Just kidding. I could not make up this woman's biography if I tried.

Sara Manzano-Díaz - From 1995 to 2002, Manzano-Díaz worked at the Department of Housing and Urban Development as deputy general counsel for Civil Rights and Litigation.

HUD is a disaster only a civil rights lawyer and Barney Frank could love. Perhaps she could sue George W. Bush for the housing collapse despite black home ownership peaking on his watch in 2007.

Dr. Maya Rockeymoore is president and CEO of Global Policy Solutions, a social change strategy firm based in Washington, D.C. Rockeymoore previously served as chief of staff to Representative Charles Rangel (D-N.Y.), among other positions.

Maybe she taught minorities that taxes were only for oppressive white men to pay. Then again, Timothy Geithner never paid his. I wonder if she knows that tax cheats hurt her constituents.

Pat Schroeder in 1988 ran and discovered the country wasn't yet ready for a woman president.

Whenever a liberal fails, they claim victimhood and blame the glass ceiling. Perhaps she was a lousy candidate, which says a lot for 1988 Democrats. There is no word on how she feels about Michele Bachmann or Sarah Palin.

Pam Spaulding is the editor and publisher of Pam's House Blend, honored as "Best LGBT Blog" in the 2005 and 2006 Weblog Awards.

Now that gay marriage is gaining acceptance in many circles, can she shut up (complaining) and shut down (the blog)? If she wants to see real bigotry, try being a Jewish Republican.

Eleanor Smeal - Founder and president of the Feminist Majority Foundation ... Smeal has pushed develop a feminist budget. Smeal and FMF were the first to draw world attention to the Taliban's brutal treatment of women in Afghanistan.

A feminist budget? Again, really? Assuming she really does care about women in Afghanistan, did she ever praise George W. Bush for liberating them? Will she criticize Barack Obama for all but ensuring that the Taliban returns to use their women as Piñatas?

Olga Vives - An outspoken leader in the feminist movement for decades, Olga Vives served as NOW's executive vice president from 2005-2009. Vives worked on the campaign that elected Carol Moseley-Braun as the first African-American woman in the Senate. She also participated in efforts to block the confirmation of Supreme Court Justice Clarence Thomas. Vives is a coalition builder.

When are feminist leaders not outspoken? She is a coalition builder who hates Clarence Thomas and thinks Walmart is the enemy. Moseley Braun set back her race and gender by being at the heart of a corruption scandal so bad that a conservative white male Republican won the next election in liberal Illinois.

These eighteen women contribute little if anything to the economy and provide no useful goods or services. To be fair, there were three additional women speakers who held real jobs in medicine and law enforcement. This almost fifteen percent usefulness ratio makes even Gloria Allred look relevant and successful next to these women.

A real conference for women would include women with actual accomplishments that matter. Sarah Palin ran an entire city and then became Governor. Nikki Haley was elected Governor twice. Michele Bachmann took in 23 foster children while running a business as a tax attorney and raising five biological children. This was before entering Congress. Dr. Condoleeza Rice is a former Secretary of State, National Security Advisor, Provost at Stanford, and accomplished classical pianist (in addition to loving the NFL, which the NOW may wish to pretend to learn about).

Phyllis Schlafly has enacted real change as the head of the Eagle Forum. Tanya Metaksa was a top executive with the National Rifle Association (which more than any other organization has stopped rapists in their tracks). Margot Dorfman is the CEO of the U.S. Women's Chamber of Commerce. Before that she held other real jobs.

Pat Summitt is one of the most successful coaches in any sport in history. The Tennessee Republican won on the basketball court without crying to the real courts. Jeanine Pirro is a tough New York prosecutor who stands up for the rights of women against male predators.

These women would give the NOW some real credibility. The NOW won't which is why they don't. This is why their conference is just more sniveling, crying, left-wing activism and crusading about the unfairness of life.

It is totally sensible to have enormous respect for real women while having utter contempt for the NOW. Their annual convention is an asterisk. Their members are not even that.

Nancy Pelosi, the new Edith Bunker

Pelosiraptor synapses do not work in typical fashion. In plainspoken English, Nancy Pelosi is a complete and total dingbat, a dolt's illiterate cousin. She is Jean Stapleton's Edith Bunker without the warmth. The *All in the Family* actress drove Carroll O'Connor's Archie Bunker crazy with her odd commentary that made sense only to her.

This reached its zenith when Archie pointed out that Jews changed their last names to blend into Christian society. He cited Morris Smith, Izzy Watson and others. When son-in-law Mike Stivic tried to disprove the theory by mentioning President Abraham Lincoln, Edith replied, "I didn't know Lincoln was Jewish."

There was only one thing Archie could say, and he said it often. "Stifle yourself, Edith."[233]

What else can one say when confronted with idiocy? At some point there have to be universal standards, no matter how low the television sound-bite era has sunk.

Nancy Pelosi was the woman who said of Obamacare that, "We have to pass the bill to find out what's in it." This is the woman who flew to Syria and put on a burka to sip tea with murderer Bashar Assad. As Speaker of the House, she lost the Democrat majority in only four years. Republicans nationalized the 2010 elections largely around making her the face of the Democrat Party.

She even accused Republicans of racism for investigating a corrupt Attorney General covering up an investigation of a dead border agent. South Carolina Congressman Trey Gowdy called Ms. Pelosi's remarks "mind-numbingly stupid."[234] While Gowdy is right, maybe Pelosi simply is unable to help herself. Maybe the water in San Francisco truly does have a higher lead content than the law allows. Maybe she really is just the Queen of Dingbatistan.

To the Pelosiraptor, there is just one thing to say. Nancy, stifle yourself.

Will feminists ever complain about something important?

Is there one feminist anywhere in America complaining about anything important?

Do feminists realize that their entire movement is the child of a cliché mated with a caricature? If they know this, do they care?

Every June 21, I kick off summer by publishing my list of the Top 30 Hottest Women in Politics. The only opinions I value are those of the women on the list. Many of the women privately contact me and thank me for the compliment. Some even thank me publicly. Others demand to know why they were not on the list. Usually those complainers are right, and I apologize for the oversight and promise to add them next year. Some women contact me before the list is released and let me know they expect to be included. This list is all in good fun and nobody gets hurt. Who could possibly be offended by such harmless fun?

Why liberal feminists, of course.

Rush Limbaugh once pointed out that feminism was created to give ugly women a chance in society.[235] Feminists despise hot women because hot women don't need feminism.

The inevitable charges of sexism came, and one of them will be given more attention than it deserves. The woman did not write her temper tantrum until July 10th, 2012, about three weeks after that year's column was published and four years after the original version. She claimed that she tweeted me with no response. Twitter is the apocalypse. My life does not revolve around tweeting twits.

An act of vanity brought on by boredom was the only reason her criticism was discovered. Late night insomnia led to an act of self-Googling. Everyone does it. Most just won't admit it. After I scrolled through about thirty pages (very bored), her criticism reared its ugly feminist head. That told me that in the big scheme of things, she was not widely read. Being attacked by *CNN* caught my attention. Being attacked by unknowns is boring.

For those building successful online presences, never argue downward. Do not elevate those who attack you from below. Those who can only build up by tearing others down deserve their anonymity. At some point she will scream to the blogosphere that she matters, to which my reply will be, "You're welcome."

(Her website is an amusing feminist community organizing site that actually teaches women how to write complaint letters. That will look fantastic on a resume. Most prospective employers are dying to hire professional complainers.)

The woman writes under a screen name and does not post a picture. Rush Limbaugh is starting to look like an even bigger genius. She referred to my column as the "Misogynist musing of the month." A day after her ranting, there were no comments.

She wants me to judge women based on their personalities and not their looks. Her looks remain a mystery. Any comment about me finding her repulsive is solely based on her revolting personality. Despite her bra-burning call to arms, I did not receive a single piece of hate mail. Finally, 48 hours later, exactly four emails arrived. They all said virtually the same thing, and had the same email suffix.

A few college girls at Brandeis University training to be future Sandra Flukes were the offended ones. Their astroturfing was pathetic. Ron Paul supporters can get hundreds of pieces of hate mail out in seconds. Feminists need to understand that if you are going to organize a hate mail campaign, at least be good at it. Even French people have sent me better hate mail in quality and quantity.

"(redacted) commits an egregious crime with his misogynistic and pompous pontification."

A crime? Beneath the failed onomatopoeia and the hysterical hyperbole is a simple solution for this woman. She may not need a man, but she certainly needs to take a law class. This woman is just a symptom of a much bigger disease that has reduced feminism from a struggle for equality to hyper-sensitive crybabies with their priorities anatomically upside down. As usual, it takes a conservative male oppressor to explain to feminists what they should care about.

1. Radical Islamofascists are trying to kill us all. Women subjected to radical Islam are beaten, stoned, raped, and shot for trying to drive a car or walk outside unaccompanied by a male. Those who take a tough stand against this are the good guys. Those who do nothing about it are not. George W. Bush is a feminist hero for freeing millions of women in Iraq and Afghanistan. Barack Obama is a zero for leaving women in Syria to get murdered for sport.

2. Global trafficking of young girls is evil. George W. Bush spoke about this throughout his presidency and took active steps to combat it. Barack Obama

does not bother to wax poetic about the subject, since there are no electoral votes at stake. Once again, George W. Bush is the feminist hero on this one.

3. Sexually abusing women and leaving them to die excludes politicians from being feminists, even if those politicians are pro-choice on abortion. Bill Clinton and Ted Kennedy are not feminists. They are (were) serial abusers with zero respect for women once the fetuses were carried to term.

4. Being pro-life on abortion does not disqualify a woman from being a feminist hero. Neither does being a homemaker. Sarah Palin, Michele Bachmann, and Ann Romney are what feminism is all about.

5. Any woman who spends one minute of her life harping on my lighthearted column admiring female beauty should be forced to live in Saudi Arabia for one month to be given a reality check on what misogyny really is.

Given the popularity of the column, some of my female colleagues talked about putting together a column of the hottest males in politics. There is a word to describe their idea. Harmless.

Modern feminism is not harmless. Feminism in the twenty-first century is like Islam. Radicals hijacked the movements and crowded out the moderates. This turned the feminist movement into the man-hating, unappealing stereotype that vacillates between being annoying and boring.

Since lists of hot women are sexist, there was only one thing to do. Dedicated to Helen Thomas and Brandeis feminists, I created the Top Ten Ugliest Women in Politics. It ran only once because nobody wants to look at or listen to them.

To hot political women everywhere, thank you for being you. Every dream about you allows my thoughts to steer away from the nightmares of those women wishing they could join you on any admired list of any kind.

The Top Ten Ugliest Women In Politics

Not all of these women are physically repulsive. They are ugly on the inside. Ugly truly does cut straight to the bone. Here are the Top Ten Ugliest Women in Politics.

10. Hillary Clinton. She rode the coattails of her charismatic husband to the highest levels of power. She made excuses for his decades of abusive behavior toward women, from sexually harassing an intern to various sexual assault and rape allegations.

She pretended to be a feminist heroine despite taking orders from a man who holds her in low regard. Given what a lightweight he is, that is quite the indignity, but power matters to her more than self-respect. This is why she flew hours on an airplane to ask Syrian President Bashar Assad whether he wants her to serve him Mint Medley or Earl Gray Tea. After she left he shot a few more of his citizens to remind her how little she matters.

She blames Israel frequently because her boss told her to. She left four heroes to die in Benghazi and covered up the truth. She wants to be President because she wants to be President. In past years she would have topped this list, but the ultimate indignity is her sliding to the oversized bottom.

9. Arianna Huffington/Joan Walsh. Ms. Huffington made her money the old-fashioned way. She married it. Huffington was conservative when conservatism was popular, then a populist when that was fashionable. She moved leftward when liberalism briefly ascended. She is really a capitalist who bashes capitalism, a Lear Jet Liberal.

She made millions selling to AOL and selling out her unpaid writers. She does not censor hate speech, prizing blog traffic and advertising revenue above decency. Her *Huffington Post*, with the *Daily Kos* and *Moveon.org*, forms the Axis of Anti-Semitism.

Joan Walsh represents the angry, screaming left. Ideological bigotry is her hobby. She is the editor of *Salon*, which may be a magazine about nail care. She has no power, influence, or abilities. Typing, "I hate Republicans" twice a week entertains her noxious fans, but it does not affect policy. She would say that pointing out her irrelevance is sexist and racist. She is not fit to clean most men's cuticles, much less opine on why everyone else but her poisons the political discourse.

8. Rielle Hunter/John Edwards. What is worse than a woman who sleeps with a married man, knowing his wife has terminal cancer? Edwards did it while

running for president and then used campaign money to cover it up. He made his money lying to juries and damaging the medical industry. His courtroom antics led to the drastic increase in unnecessary defensive medicine.

Rielle Hunter made her money blackmailing Edwards. Edwards makes this list as a hybrid metrosexual/effeminate pretty-boy. He's more feminine than many women. His unholy union with Rielle Hunter was a lesbian relationship. The lesbian Edwards, who with his ex-paramour are the only daughters of Sappho on this list, displaced Rachel Maddow from the list.

7. Christiane Amanpour. Ms. Amanpour criticizes all things Jewish or politically conservative. She married a leftist Jew, giving her cover. Every act of radical Islamic fundamentalism is due to the intransigence of Jewish settlers. She probably awakens from deep sleep murmuring about Jewish settler intransigence. Those words come to her the way other people say, "Hello" and "Nice day today." No act of Palestinian terrorism is too wicked for her to whitewash. Luckily she reports on a network that people stopped watching ages ago.

6. A pair of Barbaras, Boxer and Mikulski. Along with Streisand, these women make up the three worst Babsies in the country. At least the two leftist Senators from opposite coasts spell their first name correctly. Boxer is a former stockbroker who hates business. Mikulski will most likely become the next defensive standout for the Baltimore Ravens since the team has not won a Super Bowl since Ray Lewis retired.

These women spent their careers pretending to care about women. Their feminism is restricted to sticking up for politically liberal pro-choice women. These loudmouths shut their traps when a liberal man abuses a conservative woman.

They ignore radical Islamofascist violence against women. When beauty pageant contestants are attacked, they don't care. Boxer and Mikulski announced their retirements effective 2017 after a combined eight decades on the public dole. Most Republicans thought the gigantic seats had been vacant for most of that time anyway. Retiring after a lifetime of paid vacation is a pretty sweet gig if one can get it.

5. Sheila Jackson Lee. When Barack Obama holds his State of the Union, this Texas Congresswoman hurdles past everybody like a linebacker to get the aisle seat so she can kiss him. In private her hobbies include screaming at members of her staff until they cry. If verbal abuse does not get the message across, office supplies make for great projectiles.

When not railing against the young people working for her, she rails against Republicans. She calls them mean-spirited and claims they do not care about ordinary people. She makes racially charged comments, though less often than others higher up on the list.

4. Nancy Pelosi. During the 2006 election season, Pelosi made so many gaffes that she was given an order of silence from her own side. The Democrats won Congress in 2006 and she became Speaker of the House. She immediately became a lightning rod. Unfortunately, she removed the burka when she came home from her drink date with Bashar Assad.

When Obama was ready to give up on Obamacare, her heavy-handed tactics to pass it helped poison the well of Congress for years to come. The public still hates the law, and her speakership lasted only four years. When most people preside over devastating losses, they resign. Ms. Pelosi remained as House Minority Leader.

She rambled on about having Newt Gingrich arrested and other nonsense. She falsely believes that her San Francisco district represents America. Republicans gleefully note that most people understand she represents Democrats perfectly. That is not a compliment. Pelosi is an ideological bigot, but not a racial or ethnic one. Her comments about Republicans "exploiting" Jews dangerously approach the line.

3. Samantha Power. Anybody who thinks Obama is pro-Israel needs to know about Samantha Power. The Obama campaign in 2008 denied that she was an integral part of the team. She was forced into the background, but not because of anti-Semitism.

She made the mistake of truthfully referring to Hillary Clinton as a "monster."

Once the election was over, Obama brought Power back into the fold, knowing that liberal Jews would never stand up for themselves against a liberal black president. He needed to kick Israel in the teeth without leaving his own footprints behind. Ms. Power with her lifetime of pro-Palestinian writings was a perfect proxy.

In addition to fomenting Jew-hatred, Power is married to Cass Sunstein, Obama's regulatory czar. Glenn Beck repeatedly pointed out people in the Obama administration who operated in the shadows, and Sunstein and Power were at the top of that danger list.

Those who fear the green agenda should fear Mr. Sunstein. Those who fear the eradication of Israel should fear his wife, who never misses a chance to blame Israel for Palestinian suffering. Hamas and Hezbollah blowing up innocent Jews bores her as a topic.

2.) Maxine Waters. The constituents in her Los Angeles district were black and poor when she arrived in Congress. Now they are even poorer as Waters has become wealthy. She referred to House Speaker John Boehner, Majority Leader Eric Cantor, and many other Republicans using racially charged language. Her career pattern is to fail at everything, blame whitey, get worked up into a phony lather, wash, rinse, repeat. She praised Occupy Wall Street because leftist violence is justified in her vicious world.

1.) Debbie Wasserman Schultz. This woman is truly the very worst of the very worst. She was Obama's choice to head up the Democrat National Committee. The qualifications for the job are to get in the gutter, ignore policy, and make everything personal. Ms. Wasserman Schultz is a perfect fit.

Wasserman Schultz is a leftist Jew, which gives President Obama cover to knock Israel around at will. She would happily throw everyone from Eric Cantor to Israeli Prime Minister Benjamin Netanyahu to the wolves because they are not her people. Her people are leftists, and everything with her is personal. Like many angry, vicious people, she is not very bright. She acts like she knows everything. Like her husband Sergeant Schultz from *Hogan's Heroes*, she knows nothing. Unconfirmed rumors have her giving birth to their angry, screaming leftist child, *MSNBC*'s Ed Schultz.

Her hobbies include demonizing minority conservatives from Cantor to Colonel Allen West, who fought for his country and became a Florida Congressman. She ran her mouth off and occupied a neighboring South Florida district, where character takes a back seat to liberal ideology. She treats black conservatives like Colonel West as Uncle Toms, not noticing the irony of her being a leftist Jewish Obama shill.

Her accomplishments? None. The times she comes to the microphone and says something positive? None. She represents every stereotype of the angry, liberal, feminist woman that no man in his right mind would want to associate with.

She has unrepentant rage at anyone who dares to disagree with her. She gets paid to tear people apart and call that unity. Her job is to pit people against each other and then lament the lack of GOP compromise. She is a throat-slitter who wonders why the discord in America is so poisoned. It is because of women like her. Debbie Wasserman Schultz is at the bottom of every rung of decency. She is the ugliest woman in American politics.

Chapter 11: Musical Lunacy

Music is the language of…well, something. For college students, singing, "This is what democracy looks like" is the language of idiocy. For the United States military, rock music was the language of triumph that brought down Manuel Noriega.

Politics is the home of some truly stupid ideas brought by even stupider people. Music can take the worst movie and give it a meaningful score. This is why so many liberals sing at protest marches. It allows them to feel that by saying things through song, that they are actually doing things.

In the 1960s, people sang, "We shall overcome"[236] during marches for racial equality. That song mattered because there was concrete action that mattered even more. That was the last time liberals ever sang or did anything meaningful in the political world. Now it is time for some conservative Republican songs. Enjoy the beat. Enjoy the substance.

Singing Doo-Wop With Black Panther Malik Shabazz

I found a picture of the new leader of the Black Panthers. He looks just like the mascot for the Carolina Panthers football team. Who knew that Charlotte was such a hotbed of controversy?

Liberals truly believe we can make everything better by singing folk songs and starting a "Love Train." For those who hate us, I am here to help spread the love.

2011 was the year for white Wisconsin labor union thugs to riot. In 2012 it was white college Occupy Wall Street agitators. In the name of equality, it was about time black people started rioting to avoid falling behind white liberals. 2014 was the year where Al Sharpton fomented race riots around the nation. Slogans based on fictional events such as "Hands up, don't shoot"[237] and "No justice, no peace" were an excuse for pre-planned riots to take place. This came straight from Barack Obama and Eric Holder. This is not what democracy looks like. It is what community organizing looks like. The riots were as spontaneous as Benghazi and the Palesimian Intifadas.

Since music is the language of love, singing sweet songs to violent agitators is no less crazy than pacifists singing, "If I had a hammer"[238] to Islamofascists trying to use that hammer to bludgeon the pacifists to death. Maybe Sharpton can be brought down with sweet soul.

Another leftist agitator is Malik Shabazz, head of the New Black Panther Party. His hobbies include wielding billy clubs at polling stations to intimidate white voters in the name of racial justice and tolerance.

This proves two things.

1. The word new, whether referring to *Coke* or Democrats, means worse.

2. Malik Shabazz needs somebody to lovingly sing him Doo-Wop music.

Here is my serenade to our new warm adorable racist fuzzball, courtesy of the 1950s group The Silhouettes.

"Sha ba ba ba, ba ba ba ba ba, ba bazzzzzz (Sung 3x), Sha ba ba ba, ba ba ba ba ba,

Yip dip dip dip dip dip dip dip, mm mm mm mm mm mm, Get a job.

Yip dip dip dip dip dip dip dip, mm mm mm mm mm mm, Malik Shabazz.

Sha ba ba ba ba ba."[239]

Maybe Mr. Shabazz needs to consult with Damon Wayans and Tim Meadows, who participated in a hilarious skit on *Saturday Night Live* called, *Perspectives, With Lionel Osborne.*

Wayans: The blood of the white man is going to roll as the revolution takes to the streets this weekend.

Meadows: What if it is raining this weekend?

Wayans: Then the blood of the white man is going to roll as the revolution takes to the streets next weekend.

Meadows: What if it is raining next weekend?

Wayans: Whose side are you on man?

Meadows (to the audience): There you have it America. This weekend the blood of the white man will roll as the revolution takes to the streets, unless it is raining, where the blood of the white man will roll next week. This concludes today's episode of *Perspectives.* Our diversity programming continues next at 4:00 a.m. with programming for the Spanish community. Up next is *Los Perspectivos* with me, your host, Lionel Osborne.[240]

Enough fun. What part of kill whitey cracker honky babies do guilty white liberals not understand?[241]

Maybe we misheard Shabazz. Maybe he wants to kill crack babies. At least that could be seen as an act of warped compassion if it was deemed that they would live miserable short lives anyway. Given that crack is particularly problematic in inner city black communities, he was advocating killing his fellow black people. If he truly hated whitey he would advocate killing powder cocaine babies, which is the rich Caucasian problem. Tougher sentences for killing crack babies rather than for powder cocaine babies would be racist. I will not rest until the penalty for killing all drug babies is equal.

My social justice work is done. Let's be liberals and give Shabazz what he wants. Let's bring back segregation.

Forget Plessy v. Ferguson or Brown v. Board of Education. Forget Thurgood Marshall. Let's go back to a very limited form of segregation.

First we arrest Shabazz, Sharpton and any of his cohorts that cross the line from peaceful protesting to violent mob behavior. Then we ask them if they want to take a loyalty oath to a separate black society. Anybody who accepts the oath gets put in lockdown segregated from the general prison population. A few days in lockdown may have some of them singing the praises of integration.

These criminals roam the streets because Attorney General Eric Holder is their ideological soul mate. Putting on a fancy suit does not make him less radical.

If Shabazz kills an 80-year-old tea party grandmother, he will be a hero for stopping the real violent threat facing this nation. I can say with statistical certainty that they are precisely zero percent responsible for what is ailing our nation from a crime and terrorism standpoint.

Shabazz has many Caucasian Americans like myself developing Minority Sympathy Fatigue. He and the rest of his leftist thugs need to celebrate my father's favorite holiday, "Shut the hell up and go to work" Day. It is the precursor to Christmas and Hanukkah. You work all year to earn money to buy presents.

Some will say that finding work is difficult. Has Shabazz even looked? Plenty of Doo-Wop bands could hire him. Perhaps The Marcels are hiring.[242]

"Bob buh buh bob, buh bob buh bob bob…buh buh bob, buh buh bob, duh dang duh dang dang,..Duh ding dong ding dong…Black (Panther) Bu-ffoooooooonnnn,

You saw me standing alone, without a dream in my heart, without a love of my own.

You saw me screaming at whites, while I wielded a baton, I only wanted love,

and my own telethon."

It is time for Shabazz to feel the rhythm and beat of the soothing sounds of Doo-Wop. Then law enforcement needs to actually enforce the law. It is time for a Doo-Wop lockup. Maybe a Klan member can shave "Ebony and Ivory"[243] into Shabazz's head in prison, and Shabazz can reciprocate to his new interracial lover. That is melody and harmony in perfect rhythm together.

Herman Cain, Barack Obama, Morris Day and The Time

Herman Cain rocketed out of nowhere to take the 2012 GOP presidential race by storm. Although he did not win, he impressed many people. The radio host and former CEO of Burger King and Godfather's Pizza shined in the debates. His 9-9-9 economic plan garnered significant attention.

Congresswoman Michele Bachmann joked that when it was turned upside down, "The devil was in the details."[244] For those who missed the joke, think 6-6-6. Comedian Dennis Miller liked Cain but had a hysterical take. He said the plan was German: N*ein, nein, nein,* means "No, no, no!" [245] While where are strengths and weaknesses to the plan, at least Cain had one. The threat from Cain to the Obama White House was so severe that Barack Obama had to finally release his own economic plan.

The Obama plan is the 7-7-7 plan. It reflects what he has done since the day he entered the Oval Office but without the formal name. Now the 7-7-7 plan is official.

7-7-7 is where Obama hires advisors with zero experience, rolls the dice, and hopes everything comes out ok.

Harry Reid is the Senator from Nevada, but it was President Obama who gambled America's entire future by betting it all on hope. Like a down-and-out gambler blowing on the dice before furiously throwing them to the end of the craps table carpet, Obama knows he is down to his last few rolls. Given his complete lack of substance, coming up with new ideas is impossible. The only solution is to repackage failed ideas with exciting new titles.

By embracing 7-7-7, Obama can use Common Core math to eventually calculate that this adds up to twenty-one. 21 = blackjack, proving that the plan must be a winner.

Obama originally wanted to add the Wesley Snipes slogan, "Always bet on black"[246] into the campaign, but was dissuaded from doing so given that Cain is black. Also, Snipes was convicted of tax evasion, which would remind the electorate of Timothy Geithner, Charles Rangel, Kathleen Sebelius, Hillary Clinton, Claire McCaskill, and many others in the Democrat Party.

Obama at some point will be pressed into explaining what the 7-7-7 plan is. It has to have working mechanics. Just kidding. This is Barack Obama. Of course it is a meaningless slogan. Obama could promise to raise the top tax rate on millionaires and billionaires to ninety-three percent. He could then use that revenue to lower taxes on the middle class to eleven percent. This would allow him to market the plan as 7-7-7-nine-three-eleven, guaranteeing him the votes of Morris Day and The Time.[247] This might be a bad thing. They sang "Jerk Out,"[248] which is what the GOP has been begging of Obama since he took office.

7-7-7 is also the symbol of love, so Obama could use his plan as a reminder of why everyone should love him. He could have revealed his plan on February 14th, 2012. He preferred to wait until after the 2014 election to offer specifics.

To make the plan fun, Harry Reid ordered that all Las Vegas and Reno slot machines replace the sevens with the Obama logo. Three Obamas equals tons of cash that his voters can use to find something to not do all day. Five Obamas adds a free cell phone.

Obama tried to order Reid to rig the dice at the craps tables until an exasperated Reid pointed out that there was no seven on a die. Obama instead ordered that his symbol replace the number one since he is the one. Reid told him that would not work because people would mistake the O for a zero, throwing off the calculations.

Obama remained unconcerned, noting that his economic advisors could bend the numbers enough until they were accurate. He mocked Cain by pointing out that if Cain were so talented, he would not have to turn companies around through earning revenue. He could just print more money and declare every failure a success. Obama laughed and declared that if Cain won the nomination, the attack on him would be that he is not a politician.

Obama strategists pleaded with him in a private meeting not to go this route. Obama then dropped his too cool facade and ran up and down the hallways yelling, "Watch me prance, I am romance, 7-7-7, I can make the numbers dance!" Once everybody started dancing, everything came full circle. Morris Day was hired as director of the National Economic Council. His first task was to go to Wall Street protesters and explain to them not to take *Graffiti Bridge*[248] literally.

(Day was hired accidentally. Obama asked Biden in a cabinet meeting if he had "the time." Biden rushed out of the meeting and spent weeks looking for Mr. Day. FBI agents seized Day from a recording studio and brought him to the White House in the dark of night [opposite of day, ironically]. Sasha and Malia explained to Biden that their dad wanted him to look at his watch and translate the numbers on the big hand and the little hand. Day was a smooth talker so he stayed on.)

When told of this, Herman Cain, replied that he preferred gospel music since he is a gospel singer. He once sang "Amazing Grace"[250] on the campaign trail, prompting Obama to ask, "Why is my campaign rival singing songs of praise to me?"

No, Mr. Obama. Wrong again. No, no, no. Nein, nein, nein. Make that 9-9-9.

Barack Obama: A pop president that has a great beat you can dance to

From his allegiance to his Blackberry to hip ads promoting danger-free promiscuity thanks to Obamacare, Barack Obama is our pop president. This brings many concerns.

Never has the world had to deal with a leader as detached from reality as President Obama. The reason the United States is fast…

going down the toilet is because decisions at the top are specifically made to hasten America's decline. From stubborn sluggish stagnation…

to global conflagrations, Obama has consistently made matters worse. A reverse Midas, everything he touches turns to ashes. The media…

give him a free pass, which only encourages him to become more emboldened. His certitude replaces empirical evidence. He insists that…

you the American people are seeing progress, but this is pure fantasy. He just makes up numbers. Falling unemployment? Skyrocketing…

up are the sheer numbers of people who have quit the labor force in frustration.

Never has one American president been given a free pass for so many failures. He declares Obamacare a success despite that it is soon…

going to collapse from too few enrollees. Seven million people looking at online paperwork does not mean they are anywhere near close…

to paying Obamacare's unaffordable premiums. When numbers favor Obama, he releases them. Awful numbers are met with shrugs of indifference and…

"Let me get back to you" and other platitudes. He is not stupid. His arrogance is in thinking that he can say whatever he wants because he believes…

you are stupid. Every government failure is followed by calls for more government. Rather than have faith in free markets, Obama doubles…

down on his ever increasing failed bets. He truly is the Solyndra President.

Never has so much failure been propped up as success. This is before getting to the various scandals roiling his administration. He is…

going to set the presidential record for malfeasance in terms of quality and quantity. From Benghazi, Fast and Furious, and IRS targeting…

to using the EPA to harass oil and coal companies, Obama's lust for regulation is out of control. This is a president who is determined to...

run everything from coal plants to the local hot dog stand out of business because he does not understand how business works. Never...

around to do the heavy lifting, he condescendingly tells businesses, "You didn't build that."[251] Small Businesses are closing up their doors...

and Obama responds by piling on more taxes and more regulations. He lectures Americans about how we must innovate but companies...

desert the workplace because his anti-business climate stifles innovation. He preaches sacrifice while taking luxury vacations. Meanwhile,...

you and ordinary Americans are asked to give more.

Never has so much failure been dressed up as success. When George W. Bush was in charge, $4 gasoline was outrageous. Now people...

going on that family vacation are supposed to just accept high gasoline prices as the new normal. America has oil. Obama just refuses...

to drill for it because his environmentalist leftist base cares more about trees than human beings. In Obamaworld, farmers trying to...

make a living are the bad guys when trying to feed the entire country interferes with a seventeenth century Russian sturgeon. Obama expects...

you the American people to be productive with one hand behind your back and his government's regulatory boot on your throat. You can...

cry to the heavens that being left alone is all you need, but daddy Obama and his ivory tower academics always know best.

Never have so many people opposed an American government's actions without that government listening. Obama still insists he is...

going in the right direction with his policies, but that is what any insular leader would say. Admitting even one little mistake is too much...

to ask of a man constantly told how perfect he is by sycophantic aides and liberal media toadies. Nobody in his cabinet has the gravitas to...

say to his face that he is wrong about anything. Even if they did, it is doubtful he has the ability or willingness to listen. As Crimeans said...

goodbye to their freedom, Obama insisted that Russia is a "regional power."[252] Vladimir Putin seized a sovereign nation with impunity.

Never has one man so bad at virtually everything that matters been so certain of his righteousness. The world burns while he is happily…

going on his thousandth vacation to play his millionth hole on his billionth golf course. Spending time meeting with advisers is too much…

to ask of him. Whether his economic team or his foreign policy team, he skips meetings like a stoned teenager cutting class. He loves to…

tell others to roll up their sleeves and get to work to accomplish things, but he is the one slacking off. Many critics insist he does not care.

A look in his eyes shows a man bored with his job. If that is the case, he can leave any time he wants. What he must not do is look at us and…

lie at every turn. Americans no longer believe in him. "If you like your healthcare plan, you can keep it" was the lie of 2013.[253] Fabrications…

and exaggerations led 2014 to be another year of unmet expectations. Forget his detractors. Obama's policies have caused the most…

hurt to his biggest supporters. Now he wants to raise the minimum wage to combat inequality. If you are a person seeking your first job…

you[254] will be hurt the most. Obama promised to unite us all, but hope and change united us in shared misery. 2016 is our only hope.

Chapter 12: Conspiracy Theory Lunacy

A close friend's experience with conspiracy lunatics came when a roommate of his believed that Jews were vampires. The guy poured garlic all over my friend's clothing.

Wackos are everywhere. In India a group of cultists were convinced that flat tires were the key to salvation.[255] They went around town slashing tires and bringing traffic to a standstill while letting the victims know that the lord loves them. Jews are frequent targets of conspiracy theorists. We supposedly control the world. I wish we did. I like power as much as the next guy. Chicks dig guys with power.

To handle and defeat global crackpots, another secret society was formed. Headquartered in an undisclosed location in a nice part of Los Angeles, the Zionist Crusader Alliance for World Domination is conspiring against the conspirators.

The Return of the Zionist Crusader Alliance for World Domination

Opinion columnist Dr. Charles Krauthammer is a trained psychiatrist and proud Jew. Known for his astute analytical skills and lacerating wit, he has on more than one occasion poked fun at conspiracy theorists.

"We meet every month on the full moon at the Masonic Temple. We have the ritual: Karl (Rove) brings the incense, I bring the live lamb and the long knife, and we began with a Pledge of Allegiance to the Trilateral Commission."[256]

The Trilateral Commission along with the Bilderberg Group[257] and the Illuminati[258] are secret powerful forces that supposedly control everyone in the world and what we do. Nobody knows their identity or if they even exist. They may be so secret that even they do not know their identity or if they exist.

The one thing linking these forces is that they are all Jews. Zionist merchants, bankers and moneylenders are responsible for everything from the Brinks heist to restless legs syndrome.

The world's crackpots do not sit idly by, so neither can we. Batman is busy rescuing Gotham from Bill DeBlasio. For love of country and because we get bored sometimes, the Zionist Crusader Alliance for World Domination has returned.

Bolder than the Bilderberg Group and more illuminated than the Illuminati, the ZCA may or may not be real in achieving its objectives that it may or may not have. While the ZCA did start out as a triumvirate, we only move onward, upward and forward, not laterally.

When Palesimians crashed a pro-Israel rally at the Federal Building and called me a "Donkey, Zionist aggressor infidel," mass confusion ensued. Well I was confused, anyway. I looked around for three other people until realizing I was supposedly all four of them. With help from the ZCA, I grabbed the megaphone and sprung into action. "You people do not need a homeland. You need a thesaurus. I have heard better insults at the school parking lot at 3:00 p.m. after school and during recess." Apparently my chanting, "Two, four, six, eight, you should never procreate" did not amuse them. It did get them to disperse, although the Los Angeles Police Department helped the ZCA that time.

Right now the ZCA is investigating the Jewish global financial conspiracy. Whoever these rich Jews controlling everything are, none of my friends have seven-figure bank accounts or sneakers made of gold. If my parents have been holding out on me all these years and really are wealthy, I will take back everything I ever said about public schoolteachers.

In addition to the BITs (Bilderberg Group, Illuminati and Trilateral Commission), Goldman Sachs is apparently part of the Zionist Conspiracy. Jon Corzine and Hank Paulson are supposed to be the evidence, but neither of them have ever been Jewish. Perhaps this is part of the conspiracy. J.P. Morgan-Chase is also somehow connected to this massive global Jewish Wall Street conspiracy. Mr. Morgan was not Jewish. Neither is the current CEO Jamie Dimon.

Bill Gates, Paul Allen, Warren Buffett and Donald Trump are not Jewish. Neither are the Saudi princes or the Mexican billionaire who purchased *The NYJBT*. Despite absolutely looking Jewish to people who have never seen a Jew, Michael Jordan, LeBron James and Tiger Woods are not Jewish. The Pope wears a Yarmulke but is definitely not Jewish.

At some point I may have to conclude that there are no rich Jews anywhere. The conspiracy nuts may then claim that the people who controlled everything used to be Jewish. My response is that whoever these non-Jews are who stole our money should give it back! I would blame Palestinians if they existed.

Another train of hollow thought is that while many public billionaires are not Jewish, the people secretly controlling them are Jewish. So who are these people? Where does one find them?

Apparently it all comes down to the Federal Reserve. Central Bankers Alan Greenspan, Ben Bernanke and now Janet Yellen are all Jewish. Greenspan and Bernanke were both bald. Perhaps it is an outrage that Yellen was hired instead of a non-descript cue ball with a Jewish-sounding name. This could be a conspiracy of the follicly challenged, which would again bring us back to Corzine, Paulson, Trump, Pope Francis and Jordan. Jordan may be the most powerful of all of them. He started out as a basketball player. Now he owns an NBA franchise. He even has an entire country in the Middle East named after him.

If Greenspan and Bernanke were so powerful, how could they have been replaced? Bernanke was fired. Jews supposedly control the media. Couldn't the most powerful man in the world at the Fed have his friends in the media spin the story and save his job? Nazis carrying pitchforks did not do in Bernanke. College kids worshipping some non-Jewish octogenarian gynecologist demanded that the Fed be audited and abolished. The Fed survived but Bernanke was ousted.

I have heard that Jews control the Internet, but if we did we would hopefully be smart enough to ban anti-Semitic websites. If a Jewish conspiracy existed, we would be the ninety-nine point eight percent and not the two-tenths of one percent. We would certainly own more land. At the very least we would have oil. We are the most powerful people in the world who control everything but we cannot even get a decent gusher of petroleum or natural gas. Maybe the conspiracy is so powerful that we have fooled people into thinking we control nothing. If that is the case, can somebody let my friends and me in on the joke and transfer a few billion dollars into our bank accounts? This whole financial struggle thing is irksome.

If there is no conspiracy, perhaps one day there will be no conspiracy theorists. Until then, the conspiracy nuts are so crazy that they make the anti-conspiracy nuts just as crazy with their craziness.

Now rumors abound. Zionist is an anagram for "Stizoni." Whack jobs are feverishly working to decode the secret global Italian conspiracy. Former French President Nicolas Sarkozy is married to Carla Bruni, who is Italian. Super Bowl champions win the Vince Lombardi Trophy, not the Jacob Greenberg Trophy. There is the plain Stizoni proof. Anagrams are more annoying than acronyms but less serious than angiograms. Oy vey, my heart can't take this topic anymore. It is all too crazy for me.

You may never encounter Zionist Crusader Alliance for World Domination leaders. We often hide in the shadows. We only come out of the shadows because it is dark and scary over there, and we prefer operating indoors away from the cold weather.

Barack Obama, Valerie Jarrett, and the other Manhattan Project

A newly discovered recording of a meeting had dangerous national security implications. General David Petraeus attended the meeting but Valerie Jarrett was the only one to speak. The illegally videotaped high-level cabinet meeting had profound implications. General Petraeus had just resigned and agreed to testify on the Benghazi matter. Now the truth is coming out.

Good evening. I called this emergency cabinet meeting because my presidency is at risk. David Axelrod and I have done everything possible to shield the American people from the truth about White House spokesperson Barack Obama.

Axelrod and I kept the truth from all of you. It's time you know what is going on so you can make contingency plans before the American people catch on. With the Libya situation exploding and Israel on the verge of all-out war with the Palestinians, the last thing we all need are inside problems. Barack's last press conference was a debacle. I'm amazed we've kept things hidden this long. The Obama experiment has developed a flaw and we can't fix it. Let me backtrack a few years.

In 1997, an IBM super-computer named Deep Blue defeated Garry Kasparov in chess.[259] *After that it became obvious that computers would replace human beings at every level of society. When the Clinton impeachment scandal broke a year later, top Democrats got together to create a long-term response.*

Bill Clinton's problem was his human frailty. The Democratic Party realized that we could govern perfectly if we had perfection in the White House. The solution was to make an actual computer with some human features as our nominee. We have been working on this project since then with IBM at their main laboratory in New York City. The top-secret operation was referred to as the "Other Manhattan Project." The original prototype was Al Gore. The American people never figured out that he was made with titanium lugnuts, not blood and plasma.

You see, Al Gore did not invent the Internet. Al Gore is the Internet. He is credited as one of the early investors in Google, but the truth is that he is Google. His inventor has been kept secret for national security reasons. Everything was going fine until the 2000 presidential debates. The facial recognition software malfunctioned, causing Gore to roll his eyeballs and offend voters. We tried again in 2004, but a glitch in the voice recognition software made John Kerry come across as a Brahmin patrician.

In 2008, Barack Obama was taken out of the laboratory. All of the testing showed him to be harmless and inoffensive enough to get elected. Just to be safe, we rigged a financial crisis. Unfortunately, he was taken out in the rain and got wet. One of his parts short-circuited. His voice recognition software has created what can best be described as a Milli Vanilli problem.

As you may remember, Milli Vanilli had their Grammy taken away when it was revealed they were lip-synching.[260] *The same malfunction is causing Barack Obama to repeat the same words ad nauseum. He keeps saying "Forward, fairness, balanced approach," and a few other words and phrases ad infinitum that David and I taught him. At some point very soon Americans are going to realize that replying, "Invest in education" and "green energy" to every single question does not make sense.*

We managed to keep him away from the media for eight months, and Jay Carney did a fantastic job as my other spokesperson. We tried letting Barack speak, and you all saw what a disaster it was.

The reason David and I have spent the last four years wrecking alliances with our allies is so that if this situation went bad there would be zero extradition treaties. David and I will be taking Air Force One to an undisclosed third world nation. We will be taking Barack Obama with us to see if we can fix the problem.

There will be indictments coming down, so Vice President Joe Biden will be promoted to President to handle this. This will cause a decent delay because nobody will understand what he is saying. If the American people want a flawed human as President again, now they will have one. Hillary Clinton and Susan Rice will be sent out to obfuscate the media. Do not worry about perjury, since you have my word we will be sending a plane for all of you if anything should go wrong. Right now only essential personnel will be leaving, which means me, David, and computer Barack. I want to thank all of you for your service, and I will make sure you have plenty of security in case the people get angry and storm the capitol. You will be fine, since we know how to take care of our ambassadors and cabinet members.

We understand this will put all of you in a compromising position, but such is life. Now do not discuss any of this with the media under any circumstances until my plane takes off and is over international waters. If the media actually learns how to ask questions, tell them this was all George W. Bush's fault. If that fails, make an irrelevant comment about Sarah Palin. The media will all laugh and get distracted.

You may not be computers, but I appreciate your automaton loyalty. Oh, and don't forget to feed and water Joe Biden. The limo driver just arrived, so you are all on your own. Goodbye.

President Valerie Jarrett and David Axelrod have not been seen since. Meanwhile, confused and stunned cabinet members are not sure whether to blame Bush, blame a video, or blame it on the rain.[261]

Chapter 13: Community Organizer Lunacy

In his press conference, President Obama said…oh, nobody cares. He is boring. On January 20, 2017, he will be out of our lives. We can undo the damage once he leaves. For now, get your favorite food and drink and enjoy life. You're not married to Michelle Obama. You can eat and drink what you want. Rather than be angry, let's have fun looking back at the First Imbecile-In-Chief and his various iterations.

The First Computer-in-Chief

He has been the First Crybaby-in-Chief, the First Gasbag-in-Chief, and the leader of Gasbagistan. He was BHO and even BHMO, the adorable cherub Barack Hannah Montana Obama. He is now BWO. His name is Barack Watson Obama. He is now the First Computer-in-Chief.

Picture what would happen if Mr. Spock mated with original IBM hardware. It was funny when Alfred E. Neuman asked, "What, me worry?"[262] The most recent 2009 version with the funny ears and condescending tone is no laughing matter.

Supporters made excuses, denying that he was cold and clinical. He was cool, calm and collected, a cool cat, too cool for school, but always prepared. No, he was not. Computers can spit out data but they cannot show empathy or feelings.

Enough politeness. President Barack Obama cares about almost nothing and nobody because caring is an emotion. He doesn't give a d@mn. He enjoys his life on the golf course and filling out his college basketball bracket. This is not about a man and his hobbies. If Obama desperately needs to try and convince people he is a guy's guy, the worst he can be accused of is protesting too much. Being effeminate is not a crime.

He went on television after the 2010 oil spill and said he needed to know "whose @ss to kick."[263] His icy manner made the average guy in the bar wonder if Obama has ever kicked anything other than the can down the road on serious policy issues. This guy is Aaron from *Primal Fear*. He couldn't kick his own @ss.[264] It's not like he can't reach it. His head is inside, an impressive contortion act.

Obama is not evil. Evil requires emotion. He is just unfeeling, uncaring, and uninterested in virtually everything. The suffering all around him is an inconvenience for him. Like the Tin Man in the *Wizard of Oz*,[265] perhaps he just needs a heart. Even a 1982 Jarvik 7 original artificial heart would be an improvement.[266]

Forget that a cold, heartless man is running this country. The real problem is that his deepest supporters are even colder and less caring. As the domestic economy fails to provide jobs and American foreign policy emboldens our enemies and castigates our friends, the elites in this country share Marie Michelle Obama Antoinette's sentiments about letting the peasants eat cake.

The elites are a lost cause, but maybe one day Mr. Obama will develop humility and empathy. First he needs to develop humanity. Then he needs to say and do something that matters rather than vacillate between empty words and no words. It is long past time for him to offer the right words in the right tone at the right time with the right temperament and mean it.

After 9/11 George W. Bush did not need a teleprompter when he called out to that crowd and picked up that bullhorn. He said what was in his heart. Americans rallied around him.

Obama is slipping deeper and deeper into isolation. Unfortunately, this may be exactly how he wants it. If this view were wrong, at some point he would make an effort to dispel it. Then again, computers can only regurgitate stuff inputted by others. They cannot make an effort.

The First Computer-in-Chief would be amusing to watch missing the answers on *Jeopardy*.[267] With the world in jeopardy, there is no joy in watching our First Computer-in-Chief in permanent blue screen of death failed shut-down mode.

The Real Obama Birth Certificate Scandal

Finally there is resolution to a non-scandal. Now America can get back to the only thing less important than Obama, that being the Royal Family. Ok, enough talk about the Royal Family.

Barack Obama is a Christian born in Hawaii. Despite what Common Core textbooks say, Hawaii is a state. Obama loved the birth certificate issue because it made his critics look like frothing lunatics.

Sometimes people conceal stuff to hide something. Bill Clinton hid his medical records and Hillary Clinton sealed off her college thesis. Actually, everything the Clintons did was concealed in Whitewater fashion. John Kerry did backflips to prevent people from seeing he had lower grades than George W. Bush. Al Gore did not want people knowing he flunked out of law school and divinity school. How do you flunk out of divinity school? Did he spell God's name G-A-E-A on the final exam?

Sometimes people conceal stuff because they have nothing to hide. Critics expend endless energy only to eventually look foolish. This was the pointless birth certificate issue. Even if Obama had been born in Kenya, he would not have been fired on the spot for lying about his ineligibility. A lengthy impeachment trial would have taken place. Sixty-seven votes are required for conviction. That never would have happened. Even if it did, Joe Biden would then have become President. Nobody wants that. Having him run for reelection as an incumbent would have only helped him. There was no political upside to pursuing the birth certificate.

The real issue is that Obama conceals virtually everything. His college transcripts did matter. A birth certificate tells people where Obama started his life. His transcripts give insight into his views. He could always say he was younger then, but it would have been a conversation worth having. Thesis papers matter.

Obama was pressured to release his social security number. If he does this every college fraternity will order pizza and beer and charge it to the White House. The FBI financial crimes division will have to spend hours monitoring every transaction at Bloomingdales for fraud. While Obama does confiscate our money and spend it on his own desires, that does not mean we should do likewise.

So what was the big deal? What was Mr. Obama trying to hide?

His mother. The issue was never Barack Hussein Obama. It was Stanley Ann Dunham.[268] That's right. His mother's name is Stanley. Stanley? Are you kidding me?

We knew it was gibberish when Obama said that if he had a son it would look like Trayvon Martin. If Obama had a son it would look like Lena Dunham. Stanley Ann could have had two children of indeterminate gender. This explains everything. Barack Obama's mother was obviously a hermaphrodite.

On the television show *South Park* we learned that Eric Cartman's mother was really also his father.[269] Matt and Trey Stone offered a thinly veiled clue to the truth about President Obama.

If my mom were named Stanley I would keep that quiet as well. On *The Honeymooners*, Art Carney's Ed Norton told Jackie Gleason's Ralph Kramden that if he wanted his son to grow up to be a fighter, "Why don't you name the kid Percy? With a name like that he will be fighting all the time."[270]

This explains why Barack Obama is the most effeminate man in American political history not named John Edwards. When Obama bowled his 37, it looked like the ball hurt his wrist.

Blacks insist that his Kenyan father was normal. Only the Caucasian part of Barack Obama may be hermaphroditic. This does not make Obama bisexual, although it is fabulous that Americans are ok with a transgendered president.

Then again, the father was not listed on the birth certificate. What if President Obama is not partially Kenyan? What if he is not even partially black? Look at the man's ears. His father was obviously either Ross Perot, Mr. Spock or Prince Charles.

Maybe we have our first Vulcan president. Perhaps Obama is a British subversive trying to give America back to the monarchy. What if Obama admires European-style social democracies because he is a closet European? Being British is not so awful. At least Obama is not like John Kerry denying his Frenchness. If Obama really is Prince Charles's son, that would explain his combination of arrogance and obtuseness. It would also mean something even more awful.

When he and Michelle renew their wedding vows, the world would have to suffer through another Royal Wedding. Please lord, no. Anything but that. Let's congratulate Obama on his mixed gender and one hundred percent American heritage and get back to what really matters. His policies are dreadful.

Obama's Africa celebration nearly ruined by Mandela corpse

President Obama's self-celebratory tour of Africa was nearly derailed by the deceased yet persistent corpse of Nelson Mandela. While many in the global media focused on Obama, others were determined to recognize an elderly departed leader who actually did things.

One can almost forgive Obama for treating the world like his personal playground where decorum and dignity are not required. Nobody near him discourages his behavior.

Nelson Mandela was awarded a Nobel Peace Prize for helping free millions of his countrymen from cruel oppression. Obama got his for change and hope before he unpacked his White House bags.

The media rushed past the casket of a hero to focus on zero, the One, the O.

Obama and his loyal media subjects are not shallow because shallow implies a bottom. Why would a leader shake hands with another leader who violates the rule of law? What was Raoul Castro thinking? Castro's Cuban poll numbers suffered for this. Castro should know better than to associate with people suppressing freedom.

Was Obama imitating San Diego ex-Mayor Bob Filner by snuggling with the Danish Prime Minister? When Obama took his selfie, Michelle looked angry.[271] Then again, she is a leftist. When doesn't she look angry?

Can a picture be a selfie if it has three people in it? Can all three world leaders in the picture be taking a simultaneous selfie? Can the three rock stars in the 1994 movie *Airheads* really call themselves the "Lone Rangers?" As Joe Mantegna told Adam Sandler, "There's three of you. You're not exactly lone." Sandler, in his best Obama impersonation, replies, "I have no idea what you're saying."[272]

This is the world of Obama, by Obama, about Obama, and for Obama. What little he tries to do, he does badly. His foreign policy evaporates faster than a Syrian red line turning into a Miley Cyrus and Robin Thicke blurred line. The media and Obama are twerking when he should be working.[273]

The issue is not whether Obama shakes hands with murderous despots. It is not whether he took a selfie at a funeral or likes to enjoy a Danish every now and then when his wife is not looking. It is not that Obama inserts himself gratuitously into every situation or that his narcissism makes even the 1960s kids blush and pause. All of this is what morally bankrupt leaders with no sense of propriety do.

The real issue is that the media continues to cover his every waking stirring and utterance. He belches below the waist and the media rushes with Ziploc bags to capture a posterior for posterity.

The American economy is a wreck and the world is on fire while media schoolgirls drool over the Katy Perry of politics for winking at them and flashing his grin.

As Obama returned home, the media had nearly twenty hours to dissect what Obama ate for lunch on Air Force One and who cleaned the airplane's lavatory when he finished. Given how full of it he is, like his speeches, that job is never finished.

Why was he in Africa again? Oh yeah, some dead guy.

Barack Obama's new full name

When Barack Obama descended from heaven and Messianically (invented word combining Messianic and maniacally) announced that, "We are the ones we've been waiting for,"[274] liberals literally swooned in his presence. He was a combination of Socrates, Solomon and Adonis, more feminine than Joy Behar but less angry than Paul Krugman. He was Will Smith except more cool.

The one thing that he was not now, then or ever was new.

His pigmentation was different from previous presidents, which to liberals meant he was special. Conservatives understood that while he did have a different ratio of melanin content, his outer coat hid an inner layer of emptiness. At his core was no core. There was no there there.[275] Liberals declared him postmodern, which conservatives understand translates into hollow, substanceless, nothingness.

Liberals looked at the box and saw Crayola. Conservatives heard his platitudes and recognized cr@pola.

In reality the multi-cultured fellow with the unusual middle name was just Barry Sotero. He was a slacker, a stoner, and a guy whose hobbies growing up included chilling out, hanging out, and getting his Otis Redding on by "Sitting on the dock of the bay, wasting time."[276]

This does not make him a bad guy, but it does make him ordinary. Picture the Choom Gang in college sitting in the stairwell enjoying some recreational pharmaceuticals and waxing about life. They think they sound deep, worldly, cool, and meaningful. They are actually quite boring.

It is time to call Barack Obama by his real name. He is now Barack Hussein Mondale Dukakis Gore Kerry Sotero Obama. Let's add another name to his list. He is also Zonker.

Smug liberals (redundant) worship hate speech disguised as a cartoon known as *Doonesbury*. Written by Gary Trudeau, who is every bit as pompous as his French-sounding surname, the purpose of Doonesbury is to demonize conservatives and Republicans.[277] The only likable character in the strip is an easygoing slacker named Zonker. The Zonk is just coasting through life, more concerned with his next relaxation session than in dealing with anything serious. He does not do anything. Zonk just is, and he gets away with just being because of his likability.

This is Barack Obama. He climbed the ladder by saying nothing, offending nobody, and keeping his few real beliefs hidden. Obama frequently describes himself as reasonable and his opponents as extreme. They are the past and he is the future.

What is Obama's past? He hung out, chilled out, fell off the grid for a while (The missing gaps were never filled in), and reappeared with a winning smile and good hair. Throw in a different melanin content and all of a sudden he was not the same tired Democrat retread.

He does not know how to do anything because he never had to do anything. With his supporters, results are irrelevant. He got elected saying the other guy was worse. He said had he not been elected, things would have been worse. He ran for reelection saying the other guy would be worse.

Nothing with a tangible metric is ever connected to him because verifiable statistics would give him a failing grade. This is as unsurprising and unremarkable as he is. He is a liberal. Liberals fail. He failed. Even some liberals understand this.

He is Barack Hussein Mondale Dukakis Gore Kerry Zonker Sotero Obama. For short, just call him Baracka Khan, twin brother of Chaka. When translated from the original Indonesian, it means, "The one with funny ears and nose out of joint."

The Obama speech drinking game

The Obama speech drinking game is out there for all to enjoy. While Obama remains drunk on power, the rest of America can just get drunk. Those abstaining from alcohol can use soda instead. A really great sugar rush can be just as fun.

The following phrases are to be immediately followed by Americans raising their beverage holders and imbibing healthy swigs.

"Let me be clear." Whenever Obama says this, his next few sentences are incoherent gibberish. If he were ever clear, he would not need to tell us he was being clear. Speaking of Everclear, that stuff should be downed whenever he throws in another qualifier. If he wants us to be crystal clear, perfectly clear or some other absolutist phrase, down some Crystal or Absolut Vodka.

"Make no mistake." This phrase means Obama messed something up royally. He is telling Americans not to see his mistakes as mistakes. We should ignore our lying eyes. He is right because he is him. Then we should accidentally drop the cup of alcohol and blame somebody else.

"The right thing to do." This is Obama's favorite expression that truly shows why he is an incredibly insufferable pompous gasbag. He says something is right but never offers supporting evidence. Something is right because he says so and he agrees with it. Anyone who disagrees with him is wrong. Every time he says this phrase, recline to the right and then drink. Those seeking balance by reclining to the left can wait for his Passover speech.

"We must act." Whenever he tells America that the time for talk is over, it means he has no idea what to say or that he briefly ran out of things to say. At this point he needs a drink himself. He keeps forgetting that he is the Commander-in-Chief. By telling us we must act, he shifts responsibility from his failure to do his job to our failure to demand that somebody do his job. Perhaps he means we must become actors and actresses. Those watching his speech in bars must jump on the stage and drink upon his ordering us to act.

"No time to wait." Not only must we act, but we must act now, this very instant, or there will be global collapse. Whenever he tells us we cannot wait, it means his issue is unbelievably unimportant. Usually this phrase is associated with incredibly boring people talking about climate change, free contraception, and the Washington Redskins name. While ISIS matters, it is Obama who waited for six years and then became concerned once the polls told him to worry.

"Everyone agrees." This statement is his way of telling us that the discussion is over. Everyone will either agree with him or he will demonize them as racist, sexist, bigoted homophobes who kick puppies and kittens. By everyone he means his supporters. Dissenters are not human beings with legitimate points of view. They can be ignored when crunching the numbers. When he says this phrase, everyone should drink until he makes sense. This will require plenty of alcohol.

"No time for politics." He is demanding that nobody criticize his job performance before an election or argument his side is expected to lose. Everybody must fall in line like North Korean children and obey Dear Leader. Anyone agreeing with Obama is acting in America's best interests while anyone disagreeing with him is playing politics.

Other phrases worthy of ingesting enough alcohol to cause blurred vision include "Invest in education," "I inherited a mess," "forward," "fairness," "right direction," and his all-time classic, "This is not about me."

Those wishing to stay sober should refuse to have a solitary drop of alcohol unless Obama says the phrases, "Benghazi," "IRS abuses," "Fast and Furious," "War on Terror," or "radical Islam." Those wanting to stay sober forever should wait for him to say the words, "I was wrong" about anything significant, ever.

After his speech he will take selfies and admire his golf swing in the mirror. While no action to deal with the threat of radical Islam is expected by this president, he would be willing to give another speech once he takes a nap after finishing this one. That should give college fraternities just enough time to sleep off the hangovers, clean the place up, and get ready for the next Obama speech drinking game.

Arizona Iced Tea and More Liberal Protester Stupidity

Liberals and Islamofascists often respond to accusations of violence by committing violence. Anybody who disagrees with them is an intolerant infidel. The madness has now descended upon Arizona. The only thing worse than mobs are stupid mobs.

In the 1990s, Senator Bob Dole waded into the dispute between Turkey and Armenia. His comments were seen as anti-Turkish. Turkey responded by ordering a boycott of the Dole Pineapple Company. Panicked Dole executives held a press conference to state that they were not Republicans or Democrats, and that they supported anyone who liked pineapples. This may seem funny, but companies spend money defending against this stuff. That leads to higher prices.

In 2010, amnesty supporters expressed outrage at Arizona Governor Jan Brewer for upholding the rule of law. Nationwide leftist astroturfers tried to organize a boycott of everything Arizona including the Arizona Iced Tea Company. The company quickly explained that they were a New York company based on Long Island. If they called themselves the Long Island Iced Tea Company they would be mistaken for an alcohol company (I was raised on Long Island, which is not worth bragging about). Then the leftist imbeciles wanted to boycott Arizona sports teams.

Does anybody see the irony in refusing to come to a state because the state passed a law trying to get people to stop coming to the state? This is as stupid as breaking the law due to anger at Arizona citizens wanting others to stop breaking the law. The protesters then decided to refuse to come to Arizona by showing up in Arizona and causing riots and throwing bottles. Illegal immigrants refuse to leave, protesters promise to refuse to visit, and then the protesters come anyway and they also refuse to leave. Arizona's economy should be booming because of this. Protesters can't just leave the state to get dinner and come back.

What happens if a second state passes a similar law to the Arizona law? Will liberals boycott both states? What if all fifty states pass such a law? Will the people leave America entirely? One can only hope. Protesters eventually run out of real estate.

In global commerce, puritans have no idea what truly belongs to Arizona. What is an American car? Is a Ford car made in Japan and shipped here American? What about Toyotas made in Michigan? Cars have hundreds of parts from all over the world.

Now take Arizona. When you sit in San Francisco and buy something on eBay, how do you know where the item truly comes from? What if you have something Fedexed to you? What if the driver goes through Arizona to get you the package?

Liberals at this point will say that, "You do the best you can." That is code for, "Our approach is half-@ssed, but symbolism over substance requires that we make ourselves feel good and pat ourselves on the back as we pretend that we matter."

The backlash came when conservatives helped Arizona with a buycott.[278] In the end it was a wash, which is something liberal protesters rarely do.

If pro-amnesty liberals really want to fight back, they should burn all copies of the movie *Raising Arizona*. Conservatives would be too mature to burn boxes of *Rice-a-Roni*, the San Francisco treat, headquartered in Chicago. As Cliff Clavin of *Cheers* once told us, "The Bermuda Triangle is actually a trapezoidal rhomboid."[279]

The law allows police to crack down on illegal immigrants. Bring in the military to restore order if necessary. Leftists and minorities were perfectly fine with military intervention in the 1960s to integrate the schools. That was also the right thing to do. The white mobs were dispersed. A mob is a mob in any color. The police need to have their tear gas and rubber bullets ready. More importantly, I hope their weapons are made in Arizona.

Left-wing bullies finally on the run

In 2011 Wisconsin became ground zero in the battle between fiscal sanity and financial breakdown. Leftist teachers who already get three months off every summer wanted more money. That money would finance protests where the cause will be the right to make more money, get more time off, do less work, and attend more protests.

America is on the way to becoming a nation of imbeciles. Hop on board the train and ride the circular track for hours to the land of the misguided myopic menaces wielding misspelled maniacal messages. Wisconsin Governor Scott Walker favored fiscal sanity. For this, he was compared to the Fuhrer.

Few striking Wisconsin teachers taught social studies or English. A simple history class would point out that Adolf Hitler tried to murder my father and grandparents by tossing them into ovens and incinerating them for sport. Thankfully they escaped. Wisconsin Governor Scott Walker does not have a mustache, did not live in Germany in 1945, and has never ordered any legislation designed to murder an entire group of people. If the rhetoric seemed rehashed and scripted, that is what happens when groups with ties to the Obama administration dial 1-800-RENT-A-MOB. Unlike real grassroots tea partyers, the Wisconsin protesters were less blood and plasma and more bile and venom.

When Governor Walker tried to enact painful budget cuts to save his state, Democrat lawmakers fled faster than their ideological soul mates dodged the draft in Vietnam. Rather than Canada, these dodgers fled to Illinois. They hoped that using mob tactics would intimidate Republicans into caving.

The Republican Party must either go Roman or go home. Call it political Armageddon, but it is time to remind these illiterate third cousins of 1980s air traffic controllers what happens when they throw temper tantrums at the expense of our children. Any teacher skipping work to protest should be fired. Let them sue and exhaust their own savings. Hire replacement teachers straight out of college at half the pay. At the very least, start docking teacher pay immediately.

In the future, dock the pay of fleeing legislators as well. Then declare them missing. If they do not return to work within forty-eight hours, call for special elections. When legislators die or are unable to fulfill their responsibilities, new elections need to be held. It is unfair to have the people go without representation.

Lastly, once it can be determined in places like Madison, Wisconsin that the protesters are white, let law enforcement hose them down. In the name of racial equality, let black police officers turn fire hoses on white protesters. Then conservatives need to get tough and really crack down hard. The way to stop a mob is to stop it.

Chapter 14: Racial Lunacy

How did Barack Obama become too black to fail? How did Eric Holder become too black to jail? How did violent lynch mobs become authorities on justice and peace? The only time some of the protesters ever saw justice was when they were in a courtroom being convicted of something. Defendants by definition get defensive.

The issue is ideological, not racial. Black conservative Republicans are every bit as valuable to society as their white counterparts. White liberals are every bit as destructive to social order as black liberals. For every Milton Friedman there is a Dr. Thomas Sowell. For every Al Sharpton there is a Bill DeBlasio.

Welcome to the world of racial lunacy, where failure is deemed success based on skin color.

Barack Obama: The affirmative action president

Barack Obama is the Affirmative Action President. Many Americans are looking forward to the day he gets his official AARP card as the Affirmative Action Retired President.

This is where the perpetually outraged left begins hyperventilating, followed by uncontrollable screams of racism. Water is wet, Hezbollah blows stuff up, and leftists throw utterly boring race-baiting temper tantrums.

Affirmative action is not always bad. When implemented properly it can work quite well. The National Football League understands this. The Rooney Rule requires that when a head coaching vacancy opens, at least one minority candidate must be interviewed. An interview does not guarantee a job.[280] The Rooney Rule has exposed NFL owners to quality assistant coaches. Upon getting hired, black head coaches face the same scrutiny as their white counterparts. Wins result in glory while losses get coaches fired. This is how affirmative action should work. Give a helping hand with the interview process but not with job performance.

This brings us to Barack Obama. He was not elected solely because of his race. Many blacks and guilty white liberals loved the idea of a multiracial leader, but most of his voters turned to him after Lehman Brothers burned. Upon taking office, something happened that is an insult to everybody who believes in affirmative action but also values merit. The standards were lowered for Obama with regards to his on-the-job performance. His defenders made excuses for him and never stopped. The worse he performed, the more he was propped up. Any criticism of Obama and Holder was deemed racist.

Those who expected results out of Obama should have noticed how substanceless he was on the campaign trail. His idea for budget cutting was, "Getting rid of programs that don't work." He offered nonsensical platitudes such as, "Tomorrow will be different from today." Of course it will. It is called a calendar.

He was given the job because people believed that hope and change would lead to solutions. With his presidency winding down, he still complains about the mess he inherited. This is where the lowering of the bar comes in. He takes credit for a lack of accomplishments. Non-achievements are called achievements simply because he says so, without his being challenged.

Presidents are usually graded on jobs created. He is judged by "jobs saved or created."[281] Jobs saved? There is absolutely no metric to measure this unprovable assertion that the left treats as gospel. He has not created jobs. Even he arrogantly admitted through laughter that, "Shovel-ready was not as shovel-ready as we expected."[282] That is failure. Claims that he saved us from the next Great Depression cannot be proven. Obama blames Bush for the 2008 financial crisis but then takes credit for the TARP that Bush and Paulson enacted to turn things around. When Obama was challenged on his many failed campaign promises, he had the unmitigated gall to say that he did or tried to do everything he promised.

Tried to do? When did trying become acceptable? Can anybody remember his predecessor being praised for attempting to do things and failing? This insidious "soft bigotry of low expectations"[283] infected Obama's entire presidency. Incumbents are supposed to run positive reelection campaigns. Ronald Reagan's 1984 "Morning in America" best campaign commercial was entitled, "Leadership that's working."[284] Everybody to the right of the *NYJBT* would laugh Obama out of the room if he made that claim. Obama's slash and burn campaign was, "Reelect me or things will be worse." This was uninspiring, unknowable and successful. He convinced just enough people his opponent was evil.

Obama is also held to a lower foreign policy standard. People who would normally demand that the leader of the free world do something now lament that maybe the job is too big for one man.[285] No, the job is too big for this particular man. He had a light resume, and has not risen to the occasion.

His failure is ideological, not racial. Herman Cain, Dr. Condoleeza Rice, Ward Connerly, Judge Clarence Thomas, and Michael Steele all achieved great heights based on merit. Conversely, George McGovern, Walter Mondale, Michael Dukakis, Al Gore, and John Kerry also failed to reach the top due to a lack of merit. None of those other men were propped up. Even liberals quietly grouse that Al Gore ran a lousy campaign and that John Kerry and his grating patrician accent are insufferable. Liberals need to pretend that Barack Obama is one hundred percent Caucasian. It is the only way they will be able to view him objectively as a man and not a demigod.

To refuse to allow any person, business, or entity to fail ensures greater failure in the long run. We see it with stocks and with companies. Obama was given the political equivalent of portfolio insurance. In the 1980s, portfolio insurance led to people taking ridiculous risks that led to the 1987 stock market crash.[286] In 2004, the repeated promotion of Jayson Blair despite widespread dissatisfaction with his work led to the destruction of *The New York Times*. The *NYT* was now forever the *NYJBT*. In 2005, liberals putting political correctness over sound business decisions led to the collapse of Fannie Mae and Freddie Mac that hurt us all by 2008. In 2009, the left's refusal to allow criticism of Barack Obama only encouraged him to see himself as invincible and pass policies that the left trumpeted as successes simply because he enacted them.

Nobody cares if Barack Obama is light-skinned or dark-skinned. His problem is that he is thin-skinned and unable to fulfill the responsibilities of the job. He delegates everything because he enjoys ribbon-cutting ceremonies but not lifting anything heavier than those plastic scissors. This is why the Obama presidency was crushed under the weight of unrealistic expectations. Liberals wanted to see Utopia at all costs rather than see the truth of one mediocre man never being more than that.

President Obama and Melanintelligence

President Obama rarely loses his cocky swagger, but the myth of his intelligence was punctured by his miserable performance in the first 2012 presidential debate.[287] Dazed liberals never grasped that the beliefs they projected onto him were fantasy. One myth about Obama is that his extraordinary intelligence is a given.

He was never as bright as his supporters insisted he had to be. Real intelligence and fake intelligence exist. Many otherwise bright people have elevated others to the level of intelligent undeservedly. Legions of examples of fake intelligence are everywhere.

Hot girls: Zero correlation exists between physical attractiveness and mental acuity. No man wants to admit that the girl he lusts after may be a bimbo. Her spectacular (redacted) and (redacted) means she must have a brain. The reverse is true for the other gender. No woman ever wants to be seen as confusing beefcake with substantive intellect. That would make women as bad as men, which according to women is the worst insult to be leveled at them.

European accents: Many liberals assume that anybody possessing a European accent is automatically worldly and sophisticated. Hollywood in particular worships Europeans just for the way they sound. This is in contrast to the ugly Americans who sound like riff-raff. It is possible that the entire continent of Europe contains more than a few utter imbeciles, and that is before even getting to the disproportionately large group of French people who comprise Doltistan. No connection exists between geography and brains.

Loud people: Some people think that loud people have energy and enthusiasm, and are therefore smarter. This is Chris Matthews Syndrome. Those who are quiet do not know anything, because if they did they would speak up and say so.

Quiet people: Another school conversely says that quiet people are brilliant because they are deeply contemplative. Supporters of this notion have never heard of the concept of spacing out.

Ideology: Although there is no connection between political ideology and intelligence, liberals do consider conservatives to be imbeciles simply for being conservative. Any conservative who fractures his syntax must be a complete moron. This affliction does not produce the same conclusion if one is left of center.

Real intelligence matters. Labels such as brilliant and exceptional should not be thrown around cavalierly. 95 percent of people are within two standard deviations of average. 99.7 percent are within three standard deviations. The truly exceptionally bright people in society are the remaining 0.15 percent at the top end of the distribution. Evaluating these people should be based on evidence, not blind worshipful idolatry.

Using honest metrics, Dr. Charles Krauthammer is intelligent. While nobody comes anywhere close to Dr. Krauthammer, Dr. Thomas Sowell is also exceptionally bright. Despite his moral failings, former President Bill Clinton is a bright man. No evidence exists to suggest Barack Obama deserves to be recognized as brilliant. Winning a Nobel Peace Prize changes nothing because Obama never contributed anything to world peace. Obama could be intelligent, but his college transcripts and thesis are sealed. Insight into the depth, breadth and width of his critical thinking is hidden from society.

In college he was a dope-smoking surfer. Those are usually not the best and brightest people. What does Obama possess that has his supporters in awe?

Obama has Melanintelligence.

Melanintelligence equates darker melanin content with intelligence. Long-discredited crackpot studies advanced the notion that darker pigmentation meant a higher intellect. Overwhelming evidence conclusively proved that no pigmentation combination makes any human being inferior or superior to another one.

Melanintelligence is only applied to politically liberal blacks. Supreme Court Justice Clarence Thomas is often derided for having below average intelligence. His conservative ideology offsets his pigmentation. Dr. Sowell is simply not mentioned.

The left praises melanintelligence because everything they believe in is wrapped up in one shallow, mediocre man. Obama is not a dummy in the very bottom fifteen-one-hundredths of one percent. He rests with the mere mortals somewhere within striking distance of the statistical median. He is average.

The left held him up as an intellectual titan, so he must remain one. It is not his house of cards that collapses by proving otherwise. It is theirs. If liberals backed a false intellect, then maybe they themselves are shallow pseudo-intellects who confused melanintelligence with impressive insight. If Obama is not as bright as they thought and cannot even communicate without a teleprompter, then maybe his supporters have bad judgment.

They are liberals. Of course they do. Everybody knows academics and Hollywood celebrities are overrated except for them. When Jonathan Gruber talked about the "stupidity of the American voter," he was speaking about Obama supporters. Conservatives saw through Obama. Republican rubes in Middle America never swooned over melanintelligence in an attempt to create segregation and segmentation by making us pigmentation nation.

Liberals should look up the word meritocracy. Obama's picture is not there.

Is President Obama lazy?

Times are serious and President Obama is not. The question of whether Obama is lazy evokes everything from discomfort to rage. Yet asking and answering questions provokes national conversations that Obama cherishes.

Calling blacks lazy is one way for racists to spread their message. Denying the connotation denies history. How can calling Obama lazy not be racist? The immediate leftist response is to cry racist wolf. Lazy is a dog whistle word along with Chicago and other verbiage only liberals and canines can hear.[288]

(Most liberals are canines. Only dogs can reach around to sniff their own backsides and admire their scent.)

President Dwight Eisenhower was called lazy. So was 2008 presidential candidate Fred Thompson. At my initial stockbrokerage firm, black stockbrokers often excelled because they grew up in tougher circumstances than their white counterparts. The white stockbrokers came from privilege, and coasted. Stockbrokers are not superior by birth or race. The weekly paychecks issued often showed that the black stockbrokers worked harder.

Supporters credit Obama for earnings by his being symbolic. Obama is not an entire race. He is one person who happens to be that race along with millions of others.

Americans should analyze Obama the individual rather than his racial composition in circumstances good and bad.

Obama is not a Kenyan Muslim subversive. He is a Hawaiian Christian. He is also not revolutionary based on any deeds. Barry Sotero was ordinary. In college, he represented nothing unique. He was typical, mainstream and generic. His hobbies included alcohol, drugs, and loafing. This is not an indictment. Many young people lack ambition.

He struggles without teleprompters, stuttering and stammering when veering from programmed scripts. Intelligence (or lack of) is not a work ethic. Intellectual laziness is not divorced from physical laziness.

He was the Harvard Law Review President (HLRP). Those advancing the affirmative action explanation are called racists, but the point of affirmative action is to give minorities access. Becoming president of anything, as Obama would later prove, is often a popularity contest. Obama can be an affable, inoffensive and blandly harmless campaigner. His supporters use circular logic.

He has intellectual merit because he was the HLRP and became the HLRP because he had intellectual merit.

Circular logic is not tautological proof. Nobody can find Obama's published documents, which would offer at least one indicator of his intelligence.

Barack Obama became an adjunct professor, lightly regarded by peers and students. He spent time community organizing before entering politics. He ran for political offices in Illinois against scandalized opponents. He was likable, dogmatically liberal, and non-controversial.

Does being President automatically convey hard work and brains? Would liberals concede those qualities to George W. Bush?

Not one example exists of anything significant happening specifically because of intense Obama engagement and effort. His political supporters often engage in fiction. "Saved us from a Great Depression" is sloganeering, not policy. Obama surrendered on Obamacare, and was bailed out by Nancy Pelosi. Obama is an introvert who eschews building relationships. He enjoys being President but prefers nights at home with his family. He dislikes doing the rigorous work of governing.

George Herbert Walker Bush constantly telephoned world leaders and built relationships. Bill Clinton spent all-nighters discussing policy with legislators. George W. Bush after 9/11 devoured all information necessary to deal with threats.

Obama loves speaking but appears to loathe governing. Speaking is glamorous. Governing is boring and tedious. He constantly tells everybody else to get to work while he is AWOL.

The fiscal cliff negotiations saw Mitch McConnell bypass him and work with Vice President Joe Biden. Obama vacationed and signed the bill electronically from Hawaii.[289] Significant positive events happened during Obama's presidency, but not because of anything unique he did. The narrative "Al-Qaeda is dead and GM is alive" has been discredited.[290]

Obama still floats through life effortlessly. He is the CEO who wants secretaries to work faster without understanding administrative functions. During crises like the BP oil explosion, he was helpless and therefore useless. Head coaches motivating players must know the playbook. Obama skips intelligence and economics meetings.

He hides any evidence refuting his shallowness. Worshipers elevate him based on their feelings of his merit, not his exhibited merit. He is not evil or godlike. He is just, like most people, unimpressive and unremarkable. His cult of personality is a post-modernism aura in a world craving real solutions.

Throughout his presidency, others did the heavy lifting while he took credit and deflected blame. This does not make him a bad guy. It just makes him unmotivated, or in simpler terms, lazy.

Maybe Barack Obama is just inferior

President Obama's presidency crumbled under the weight of scandal, mismanagement and public frustration. He keeps speaking as more Americans tune him out. While the left will never accept the truth, it is long past time to pose a theory. Maybe Barack Obama is just inferior.

Let liberal skulls explode and leftist talking heads scream racism. Obama is half-Caucasian. His white half is every bit as below mediocre as his black half. Obama's story of failure is his ideology, not race. He has terrible ideas, and he implements those terrible ideas terribly.

Inferior. What other word describes a man not good at anything? Those praising his campaigning abilities require clarification. What other word describes a man not good at anything that matters? He succeeded at something that personally benefitted him. What has he done to benefit the American people?

Even supporters are left to parrot excuses. Obama would have succeeded if not for unprecedented circumstances. Forget Washington leading the Revolutionary War to create America or Lincoln leading the Civil War to save the Union. Obama had to deal with a budgetary issue that could be solved in seconds with fiscal discipline.

Inheriting a tough situation is no excuse. Tough times got him the job. Obama was losing the 2008 election until Lehman Brothers burned. It is ludicrous for him to bemoan his lot in life when his very presidential existence rested on his ability to exploit human suffering and panic for personal gain.

His job was to govern. George W. Bush and Ronald Reagan governed without constant whining. They inherited messes and turned things around. People in many walks of life inherit bad situations and improve things. Herman Cain grew up black in the segregated South and became a brilliant turnaround artist. He turned losers into winners. That is what successful leaders do.

Average people plod along. Superior people lead. Inferior people fail and blame others for their own inabilities. From Jayson Blair to Barack Obama, liberals still refuse to separate skin color from character content. Americans are not interested in Obama's navel gazing. They want results that never arrived despite America's longest presidential grace period.

Liberals mercilessly speculate about Republican presidents, so let's psychoanalyze Obama. Maybe Obama took too many brain cell-frying hard drugs as a youth. Illegal drug side effects existed before Obama, will exist after him, and cross all racial and ethnic strata.

Perhaps Obama had awful teachers. He will not release his grades or college thesis. Leftist attack dogs dishonestly try to link this to his birth certificate. No claim of intelligence should be taken at face value. Nothing in Obama's public record suggests a deep thinker or analytical mind. He often substitutes his own ideology for empirical evidence.

He publicly admitted to growing up lazy. Intellectual laziness dovetails perfectly with his well-known aversion to the work of governing. This could be why everything he does fails.

Stimulus? Flaccid. Cash for Clunkers? Clunk. Green energy? Solyndra. Billions wasted forever. Obamacare? The disaster is exponential. The world's smartest man could not even get a website built in four years.

A man without one meaningful success on the job is a failure. Zero percent success is an F-. Those claiming failure is the opposite of success have met their match with Obama. If he had one success, supporters would have rightly touted it.

Those in the real world understand that a man whose hobbies in Hawaii included beach-bumming and joint-toking would not become a nuclear physicist. Politics was his avenue because merit matters in corporate America. One can smile their way to the political top and speak well with teleprompters.

Eventually the man who never did anything had to actually do things that mattered to ordinary people. He failed because he lacks the skills to succeed. He lacks abilities, aptitude, and an understanding of human nature and how things work. He understands nothing consequential. He is a community organizer who mishandled the American community and ran an administration that is completely disorganized.

He is the Chevy Volt of presidents who golfs frequently while his governing abilities require countless mulligans. He is over par on the golf course and subpar everywhere else, never quite up to par. He is just inferior.

Post presidential jobs for Barack Obama

With the world on fire and the global economy on the brink, President Obama has just enough time left to make matters even better. He is good at everything, as *MSNBC* and *The NYJBT* keep reminding us all.

Unfortunately, even Obama's godlike perfection cannot last forever. The Constitution is forcing the Democrat Party to replace an overqualified man coasting on his race with an overqualified woman coasting on her gender.

What is a current president bored with his job and the American people to do? When even going through the motions and mailing it in are too tough, what comes next for Obama? It is never too early to look at post-presidential jobs so that Obama may hit the ground crawling in 2017.

The easy way out would be for him to go back to being a community organizer, Democrat fundraiser, or lightly regarded college professor. Obama never takes the easy way out, except with anything involving responsibilities. While we can praise his mere being, it is time to see what he actually has the skills to do.

He could become a member of the media. *MSNBC* and *The NYJBT* are entities already set up to worship everything Obama says and does simply because he says and does it. He would fit in perfectly. Nobody self-praises like Obama, and these are the closest things to no-show jobs outside of Chicago.

He could become a first-time author and work on his memoirs. His name is listed as the author of two books, but Bill Ayers claimed to have written one of them. This time Obama could actually write a book. Given his skill level, it could be a picture book of his selfies.

He could continue on as a government employee. The Constitution prevents him from being President of the United States again, but every other position is permitted. He could become president of another country. Maybe if he leads a nation hostile to America, he could be so effective leading that other country that America might finally reap some unintended benefits.

If he insists on staying in America, he could become the next Chicago Mayor. Rahm Emanuel may not want to leave a job that has absolute power. Obama has predator drones and Emanuel does not, making replacement easy enough. Besides, Chicago has had white mayors for far too long. It is about time that Chicago corruption and graft be apportioned to leftists of other races. The problem with that job is that the Chicago Mayor has to actually do the work. Also, the climate is miserable.

217

If Obama prefers a warmer climate, he should become the ambassador to Hawaii. Right now this job does not exist. However, Obama is a master at issuing executive orders. Hawaii was given statehood, and that can be changed back. If Hawaii remains in the union, Obama can just appoint himself anyway. He has lived in Hawaii and is an expert in the lax culture and lifestyle. Obama would be far more qualified than his appointed ambassadors to other areas.

Obama could be a behind-the-scenes political operative as Michelle Obama's campaign manager. She never has to actually run for office, making this the perfect job to build a slush fund. His ego may not be able to handle staying in the background, but if Michelle orders him to do it he will meekly do so.

Obama loves talking about himself and having people gaze at him in admiration. He could work at the Obama Museum. As an Obama wax statue stunt double, he could sit for hours doing nothing. As the Obama Museum curator, he could spend all day telling people about all things Obama.

Obama could retire in 2017 from being a celebrity president and spend the rest of his life continuing to be famous just for being famous. He could be a celebrity golfer, television cameo guy, product endorser, or reality television star. He has more experience hawking insurance than the Geico Gekko. He could selectively edit out mistakes in his appearances without requiring the rest of the media to do it for him.

Obama's future is so bright, he has to wear shades. He is as cool as the other side of the pillow.[291] Despite the world he has wrecked, he will have endless opportunities that will allow him to rest comfortably while others suffer. Nothing will change from his current status, making for a smooth transition.

President Obama signs executive order declaring
himself relevant and successful

Over the strenuous objection of congressional Republicans, President Obama signed an executive order declaring himself relevant and his presidency successful. Former Senate Majority Leader Harry Reid changed the filibuster rules to cut off debate and end the discussion. Everything is now fine.

Like man-made climate change and unicorns playing xylophones, Obama's complete and total success is now settled law. The time for debate and discussion is over. He is more relevant than he has ever been, and his entire presidency has been successful. All Obama critics are in violation of the law, and will be indicted by Attorney Eric Holder faster than a tea party leader reading a Dinesh D'Souza book.

Common Core, a complete success in itself, will now have updated textbooks to reflect that in 2009 the rise of the oceans did recede faster than David Axelrod's hairline.

As a citizen of the world, the Obama success decree is to be immediately implemented worldwide. No global events are expected to change, but the perception of those events will be altered immediately.

Iran is no longer building a bomb. If they are, it is because *Fox News* is racist. Syria's Bashar Assad is no longer committing genocide. If he was, it would be because Jon Stewart thinks Sarah Palin is dumb. Russian President Vladimir Putin is no longer slapping around Obama the way Ted Kennedy and Bill Clinton slapped around cocktail waitresses. That is the fault of Rush Limbaugh and evil talk radio. The Middle East is no longer a problem. Obama's relevance extends to his entire cabinet. Secretary of State John Kerry is now the greatest Secretary of State in the history of Obama's second term. Deniers are responsible for the war on women.

The economy is rapidly expanding, but the evil Koch Brothers refuse to hire all 300 million Americans. This is why people do not feel the growth. The Affordable Care Act really is affordable and Obama cares deeply. Hillary Clinton's indifference over four dead bodies in Benghazi now translates into her husband's, "I feel your pain."

To avoid having to deal with thorny issues, Obama's edict now reverses the relevant and the irrelevant. Climate change and the war on women now matter. The global economy is small ball, along with worldwide terrorism.

The decree extends to anybody defending Obama. Barbara Boxer and Nancy Pelosi are intelligent. Debbie Wasserman Schultz is pleasant. Barbara Mikulski is a swimsuit model. John Kerry is interesting. Vice President Joe Biden has job functions where he does actual stuff. Lois Lerner teaches ethics at Harvard. The Benghazi four and the Fast and Furious border guard are alive and healthy due to Obama's spectacular results handling the tiny problems that come his way. Millennials supporting Obama have their heads above their necks and not below their backs. Jon Stewart is sincere without a hint of smugness. *MSNBC* and *The NYJBT* are civilized and respectful entities run by *Homo sapiens* who walk upright on two legs.

Although Republicans fought the order to the end, Obama declared the law passed by a 535-0 congressional margin and held constitutional by a 9-0 Supreme Court vote to preserve harmony and bring everybody together in binding agreement. Obama celebrated his newly declared success and relevance by playing eighteen holes of golf. He scored a seventeen, one stroke better than the previous record held by the late North Korean leader Kim Jong Il. To prevent evil Republicans from altering history books in violation of teachers' union standards, Obama declared all history before 2009 and after 2017 to be non-existent upon his leaving office.

Alcee Hastings for the U.S. Supreme Court

President Obama knows that his executive orders can be reversed. Establishing a permanent legacy requires altering the Supreme Court. Although there is no immediate opening, Ruth Bader Ginsburg has been around since the founding of the Republic and may wish to step down. Obama may decide to use his power to threaten one of the High Court's conservatives into resigning. He can pardon himself before he leaves office. Once there is an open conservative seat on the High Court, Obama should immediately nominate Alcee Hastings to fill the vacancy.

Obama has shown zero interest in merit, decorum, bipartisanship, or modesty. His least endearing traits are arrogance and a refusal to treat political opponents with dignity. Therefore, there is only one qualified nominee for the U.S. Supreme Court to cement the Obama legacy. Alcee Hastings must be nominated.

Hastings is a corrupt former judge who was impeached and removed from the bench.[292] He then became a member of the Congressional Liberal Caucus, where integrity is not a job requirement. There are several reasons why Hastings is the perfect choice.

1. He is black and liberal. He cannot be criticized for any reason. Anybody that brings up his impeachment and removal is a racist.

2. Although he is not a woman, his first name is Alcee. That is close enough. The National Organization for Women is not known for doing research. Hastings supports the abortion of the month club, so they would support him. Obama will state that Hastings supports women's issues, and is therefore a woman. Who can argue with someone named Alcee?

3. The right would be enraged that Obama would again spit in the eye of the rule of law. Hastings might know somebody who marched with Dr. Martin Luther King Jr., so he is beyond reproach.

4. Bill Clinton proved that impeachment doesn't matter. Stealing documents like Sandy Berger did also does not matter. Picture Clinton laughing and saying that Hastings was the victim of the right-wing smear machine, and that his misadventures were just Alcee being Alcee.[293]

5. Remember, Chuck Schumer and Joe Biden have long said that qualifications don't matter. What they actually said was that ideology can and should be factored in to the confirmation process.[294] Hastings is a liberal and therefore a legal genius.

Even by the typical mediocre standards of Obama and Congress, Hastings is below the bar. Intelligence, ethics, and merit are over-rated. Obama already dedicated his life to these principles, so he should prove how powerful he is. If he can get Hastings through, he truly can walk on water.

Obama is under intense pressure by the Congressional Black Liberal Caucus and the National Association for the Advancement of Liberal Colored People to place a black man on the Supreme Court. Conservatives argue that Clarence Thomas is black, but the CBLC and NAALCP disagree. Blackness is about liberal feelings and attitudes, not odd concepts such as pigmentation.

Since Hastings is a CBLC member, they will champion him. NOW hags and harpies will be too scared to object, blaming George W. Bush for the nomination.

Nominating judges to lifetime appointments based on knowledge of the law, judicial restraint, and honor is so 2008. It is time for some good old-fashioned liberal tokenism. A corrupt, black, impeached and removed judge with a liberal voting record and a feminine sounding name is the best possible choice in the age of Obama. He is the very best possible pure and true representation of the modern Democrat Party.

He is the anti-Antonin. Democrats want the non-thinking non-Scalia. Alcee Hastings and one more justice (Barney Frank perhaps) can help Mr. Obama pass any legislation he wants with zero judicial interference. Judicial corruption takes a back seat when a man is perfect for the job. Go, Alcee, go!

Eric Holder's Mystery Illness

Many Americans held Attorney General Eric Holder in contempt for being Eric Holder. Congress just made it official. Holder has gotten worse. From Iran to Arizona, Holder has engaged in very strange behavior.

First he rejected the concept of radical Islam since that does not fit a leftist narrative. Holder prefers the fictional lunacy of a wheelchair-bound eighty-year-old-grandmother bombing New York City due to her unhappiness with everything from reduced Medicare to reduced flavor in Sweet'N Low packets.

Then Holder spoke passionately against an Arizona law before conceding that he had not read or been briefed on it. He believes that the law will have unintended consequences. This would be revolutionary except that every law has unintended consequences. This is definitional.

Eric Holder obviously suffers from a debilitating illness. His undetermined affliction has been narrowed down to four suspects:

1. Glaucoma. 2. Diabetes. 3. Tertiary Stage Syphilis. 4. Self-love addiction below the waist.

(Regarding #4, my policy is that it is something people should not talk about. Only twice has it ever been a political issue, first with the enthusiastic support of Joycelyn Elders, and now with Holder.[295] This is not to be confused with the metaphorical version of self-love that infects many liberals including the Clintons and the Obamas.)

All of these illnesses have the same tragic effect in many victims: blindness. Eric Holder is blind. Buy the man a cane and a guide dog. He cannot see the forest for the trees or the jihadists for the bombs. It might not be his fault. Perhaps he had a laundry mishap and inhaled the bleach. That is certainly better than what happens when one gets what rapper Biz Markie calls, "The Vapors."[296]

There could be a musical element. It can't be breakdancing, which in the 1980s did plenty of damage to the skulls and vision of kids spinning on their heads. Mr. Holder was most likely coming of age long before *Breakin' 2 Electric Boogaloo* came out.[297]

Holder's vision will never improve. Obamacare does not cover elective procedures such as vision restoration or cranial-gluteal extraction surgery.

Should Americans care if Holder is found on a street corner with a tin cup and a dog with a sign that reads, "Will ignore common sense for food?" It matters because when the top law enforcement officer in America lacks credibility, he cannot effectively do his job.

Holder and Obama want to take the fight to an enemy without acknowledging who or what the enemy is. I can insist that a rum and Coke is made of vodka and apple juice. That is about as sensible as insisting that crimes committed by radical Islamofascists were really tea party reactions from Glenn Beck and Rush Limbaugh watchers worried about excessive government spending.

Radical Islam is the problem. Obama and Holder know this, but will not publicly admit it. They clearly see the problem. Then again, maybe they are truly blind. The only question is what causes willful blindness. Is it syphilis or self-love down there? Is this a canker, chancre or wanker problem?

Forget the root cause of Holder's malady. His illness does not require penicillin, therapy or surgery. Holder needs to simply snap out of it. For those not blind or dead from the neck up, it really is that easy.

Liberals become conservatives when they get mugged. Radical Islam opened our eyes on September 11, 2001. Only those with their heads located in the clouds clogging up their posterior cannot see this. Come to think of it, having your head up your hide also causes blindness. We can help Holder get better once a doctor not suffering under Obamacare can figure out where to administer the thermometer.

Gay marriage, climate change, and other white leftist movements

The ouster of Brendan Eich as Mozilla CEO allowed leftist "gannibals (gay rights cannibals)" to devour another carcass.[298] Eich was punished for his beliefs, since no actionable behavior warranted a dismissal. No discrimination or hostile workplace environment claims were filed against him.

In 2008 he donated to Proposition 8, the initiative banning gay marriage. The measure passed with fifty-three percent of the overall vote and seventy percent of the black vote.[299]

While Eich is already a footnote (#298 in this book), the issue surrounding his removal begs a larger question: Why is every leftist movement so overwhelmingly white?

Democrats love to portray Republicans as wealthy Caucasian plutocrats. The real truth is that white aristocrats lead almost every liberal cause.

The pro-gay marriage movement is far whiter than mere beige. Blacks are far more likely to be against gay marriage than their white counterparts. The left denies this because it risks fracturing their loosely held coalition of disparate groups with disparate grievances.

The climate change movement is more white than green. White hedge fund billionaire Tom Steyer yanks the leash and Senate Democrats heel. The Senate held an overnight talkathon after Steyer announced he would donate $100 million to politicians emphasizing climate change.[300]

Legalizing drugs is the obsession of white Hungarian billionaire George Soros. When not reminiscing joyfully about helping confiscate the property of his fellow Jews before they went to the gas chambers ("I would say that's when my character was made," he mused on *60 Minutes*),[301] Soros funds most leftist shadow groups in America. Liberals obsess over the Koch Brothers, but without Soros money many leftists would have to find gainful employment. The job market for unfunded think tanks and other navel-gazing pontification centers remains sparse.

The labor movement started by white Samuel Gompers eventually led to white union protesters in Madison, Wisconsin exploding in violence over Governor Scott Walker's collective bargaining law. Joined by bored, white college students, ultra-white leftist Madison went berserk. Protesters demanded more free benefits. Governor Walker was trying to keep Wisconsin from going bankrupt.

Sometimes, the left does not need an actual issue. With white leftists, protesting for the sake of doing so is sufficient. Decades ago, whites including Jack Kerouac and Timothy Leary convinced white America that beatniks, hippies and beat poets contributed positively to society.

The 21ˢᵗ century brought Occupy Wall Street, another overwhelmingly white leftist movement. OWS was not spearheaded by the downtrodden. Many protesters were upper-middle class white college students funded by their parents. More than a few white trust-fund babies helped break windows, commit sexual assaults, and rage against the man.[302] They are the man, which was lost on those surfing the Internet on their smartphones during breaks in anti-capitalist rioting.

Why are leftist rebels often without a cause or a clue whiter than the famous painting of Snow White caught in a snowstorm?

At the risk of inventing positive slander, blacks and Hispanics have better things to do with their time. Blacks and Hispanics have been marginalized in America. Marginalized people do not have the luxury of obsessing over white pet projects. Marginalized people focus on survival.

Fairly or not, the gay community is seen as affluent. There is wealth in gay-friendly enclaves San Francisco, Silicon Valley and Palm Springs. Blacks were once slaves. Mexicans sneak across the border to pick lettuce. People enduring real hardship are not concerned about rich white gay marriage ceremonies.

The last thing blacks and Hispanics want is the legalization of illegal drugs. Drugs have devastated inner cities. The crack epidemic that began in 1986 is still causing disproportionate pain in minority communities. While plenty of blacks favor reducing the disparity in sentencing laws for crack and powder cocaine, outright legalization of hard drugs is not a black priority.

Blacks attend college often just to escape rough conditions. They want to get an education. If they get thrown out of school for protesting, they are less likely than whites to have daddy's money get them a top-notch lawyer. Most blacks cannot afford to get arrested protesting over bunny rabbits, trees or wallabies.

White leftists obsess over climate change, which may or may not affect people in a thousand years. Blacks and Hispanics want to feed their families right now. They work hard so their children can reach the American middle class and their grandchildren can reach the upper class. New money has to be earned. Old money can sit back and hold tea parties to provide free contraception for lesbian vegan spotted owls. Old money is white. There is no black old money in America.

Liberals have spent decades pointing out that whites have more money than minorities. Overall, these liberal whites are not wrong. They are just detached.

Black inner city children worry about getting shot to death on the way to school or beaten up once inside the building. White liberals confiscate the sodas in the school vending machines because the children may get diabetes in a few decades. Until bullets are made of high fructose corn syrup, white liberals may wish to reprioritize their crusades.

Black Republican Frederick Douglass said that, "If there is no struggle, there is no progress."[303] Blacks and Hispanics still have to struggle, which causes them to frequently focus on what actually matters. Taxes, spending, crime, and terrorism matter. Those with too much money and far too much free time continue to prove that if the idle mind is the devil's playground, wealthy white liberals are America's amusement parks. Minorities do not buy bottled water for their pets.

The war on women, climate change, getting everybody hooked on drugs, and fretting about trees and animals are all great social causes for billionaire coffee parties. Wealthy whites focus on this stuff because they can. For these people, trendy social causes are the political equivalent of summer camp without the S'mores. Blacks and Hispanics, like the rest of Americans, do not have this luxury. The real world needs to be dealt with.

Chapter 15: Rancher Lunacy

Some call him George W. Bush. Others call him "Dubya" or "43." He is "The Dub." He clears brush on his ranch to relax. Whatever relaxation time he needs, he's earned it. I'd run through a brick wall for the man if he asked me to. While he swings an ax and cuts through tree bark, I take my keyboard and cut through the BS. Somebody has to tell the truth about this man since he is too modest to talk about himself. He was not a good president. He was a great one. Those who disagree can go pound sand.

My birthday wish: Meeting 43 by 43

On my 43rd birthday, there was only one thing for me to wish for. Call it "43 by 43."

If circumstances should allow for it, I want to meet President George W. Bush and shake his hand.

The message I delivered to Vice President Dick Cheney in 2013 is the same one I want to deliver to The Dub. I will go to my grave knowing they were right. On the big issues that mattered most, they were, are, and will be right. History will vindicate them because, to paraphrase Winston Churchill, I will help write that history.[304] I do not care if I am the last man standing next to these guys. I believe them, and am proud to still support them when others wavered. My one sentence to Bush would be the same one I said to Cheney.

"Sir, thank you for saving the world."

I have all the possessions a guy could need. My television set works and my computer works often enough. A burger and a soda is more than enough to satiate my hunger and slake my thirst. I want for virtually nothing in this world, except to meet Dubya.

Mr. President, I know you are a busy man who has been through a lot. Whenever I meet one of your staff, I ask how you are. They insist that you are at peace, with no regrets. Thank God for this.

To meet one of the greatest leaders of all time in one of the most consequential periods in American history is more than any man has a right to expect. Not every wish is granted, so some gratitude is in order. Thanks to my grandparents and parents for bringing me into this world, my friends for making it fun, "the boy" for reminding me what matters, and to George W. Bush and Dick Cheney for saving the world so everyone can enjoy it.

How social liberalism elected George W. Bush

In 2000, 537 votes in Florida sent George W. Bush into the White House and Al Gore in a downward spiral of madness from which he and his supporters never recovered.

I declared shortly after the 2008 election that January 20th, 2009, would be the death of the left. I was right.

The left needs a conservative to despise like the right needs oxygen to breathe. When the left failed at demonizing Rush Limbaugh and *Fox News*, they went after Sarah Palin. All that did was energize the right, and annoy the middle. None of the targets held any political office. The left was in trouble. They had to actually do something. They had to govern.

Naturally, they failed. Water is wet. The Sun rises in the East. Liberals can't govern. They fight amongst themselves because they are a collection of beggars with no coherent uniting philosophy other than hating Republicans. They turn on each other when more free money is given to tri-racial Latino pygmies than transsexual black obese women.

Yet the right has made its share of mistakes, especially the social conservatives. The social conservatives are flawed in that they insist on having principles and sticking to them. The left never lets principles get in the way of winning. Cheating, lying, and stealing are allowed because the ends justify the means.

I am not as principled as many social conservatives.

(I blame them because it is easier to criticize others for getting things right than me taking responsibility for my often totally inappropriate actions and even more heinous thoughts. That reminds me of a story about a college coed, some Vaseline, and a mountain goat, but I will save that for another time.)

For conservatives to dominate and build a lasting majority, they need to give liberals exactly what they want.

Start with abortion. Most people in America having abortions are liberals. Who is more likely to have an abortion, a social conservative obeying their biblical faith or a man-hating NOW member asserting her feminist rage?

(Let's say for the sake of argument that a NOW member actually had sex. It is a stretch, but some guys do get drunk and stoned and other guys are deaf, rendering the anger directed at them less problematic.)

If 538 liberal women in 1973 had decided not to exercise their right to choose an abortion in Florida, Al Gore would be president. Liberal ladies, keep choosing!

(Forgive me social conservatives. You are principled, and I will be burning in Hades for this.)

Now let's talk gay rights. I support the rights of all gay men and ugly gay women. Gay men reduce my competition for women, and ugly women know nobody cares. Hot lesbians are evil. Jesus hates them. They are not thinking about my needs.

While there are plenty of gay Republicans in America (I count several members of the Log Cabin Republicans as my friends, and am honored and proud to do so. Being gay somehow did not prevent them from wanting to cut taxes and kill terrorists.), the majority of homosexuals in America are politically liberal.

Leave them alone. They can't breed. They cannot bring new voters into the world to vote liberal.

Meanwhile, good religious families are having children. Religious Christians often have several children. Orthodox Jews rival bunny rabbits in terms of fertility, and their children are almost always sensible citizens. Apparently this belief in God stuff leads to a more moral life on many occasions.

(For those wanting to make remarks about priests and pedophilia, preaching about God and following his teachings are not the same thing. Actual believers do usually lead moral lives and are more charitable.)

Euthanasia is less of an issue because outside of Tony Randall and Anthony Quinn, most people over 70 do not breed. Maybe the left can reduce the euthanasia age to 20 from 80.

(That remark was too far even for me. It sounded better before I typed it.)

It is impossible to unite everybody on my side but it is possible to lose everybody. The left will never support me. The right has problems with my cold calculating desire to win elections at any and all cost to the greater social fabric. I am an island. That does not make me wrong.

Conservatives should keep living how they live. Liberals should do the same provided that for once in their miserable rotten leftist lives they stop trying to force their world view on the rest of us. If liberals want to reduce their own existence, I say let them. Democracy is wonderful.

Now if only I can persuade leftist billionaires to redistribute wealth so that conservatives can live in safer neighborhoods with expensive security systems and guards. That way when illegal aliens come across the border, the few who commit crimes will only be attacking liberals.

To those who say we cannot allow the liberals to destroy liberalism and lead to a more conservative future, I channel my inner vacuous liberal sloganeering and say…Yes we can!

Iraq 10 years later: George W. Bush is still right

Ten years ago, after seventeen broken United Nations resolutions, President George W. Bush enforced Resolution 1441.[305] America engaged in regime change designed to remove Saddam Hussein from Iraq. It took about three weeks to realize that goal, and in 2004 Hussein was caught in a spider hole. Soon after that Saddam was hung.

Like America in 1776, Iraq got off to a very rocky start. President Bush hired General David Petraeus to salvage things, and the 2007 surge of troops was a spectacular success. The Iraq War was won and Iraq was on its way to becoming a functioning if imperfect democracy. Bush's successor would squander all of the gains and then blame the original mission to hide that incompetence. The original mission was fine. Once again, never send a liberal to do a man's job.

Ten years later the Iraq War was still absolutely the right thing to do. Saddam was a madman and a monster. He had Weapons of Mass Destruction. He used them, and they are probably in Syria now. Liberals still hate the Iraq War and America's involvement in it more than they hated the genocidal lunatic we removed.

Their cries are still shrill, still false and still wrong.

"The war was illegal." No it wasn't. We went through the U.N. that liberals worship.

"The war was immoral." No it wasn't. We freed people held captive and liberated them.

"The war was for oil." No it wasn't. We could have taken the oil. We didn't.

"Bush lied." No he didn't. Liberals still cannot point out any actual lie. Perhaps they meant Fast and Furious or Benghazi.

"WMD." Nobody cares. That's not why we went to war. It's the excuse liberals invented to give themselves an out. Besides, Saddam had them. Republicans who apologized should be blamed for doing so when no apology was necessary. Saddam acted like he had them. If he lied, he got what he deserved anyway. Over time, some WMD were found, proving that the Neocons were right the whole time.

"We should have gone after Iran instead." Wrong. We should have gone after both of them. Vice President Cheney wanted to hit Iran in 2008 and the liberals howled about another war. In the several years since, the left had control and President Obama did nothing to slow Iran.

"It created more terrorists." No it didn't. It killed them. Days after Saddam was captured, Khadafi voluntarily turned over his weapons program. He got the message.

"Saddam had nothing to do with 9/11." Nobody said he did. Saddam did have everything to do with worldwide terrorism. He funded Palestinian suicide bombers to blow up Israeli citizens.

"We're not the United States of Israel." The anti-Semitic left is so classy, and not worthy of having their comments dignified.

"Afghanistan was the good war." The minute the left retreated from Iraq, the Code Pink Democrat Party planned the surrender from Afghanistan. The modern Democrat Party would have lost World War II if given the chance.

"I'm glad Saddam is gone, but…" No but. Liberals stood with Saddam over The Dub. I'll stand with The Dub every day of the week and twice on Sunday.

It is hypocritical for liberals to say they are glad Saddam is gone without praising George W. Bush for removing him. Saddam was not removed by osmosis. He was removed by force. Liberals wanted to lose the war because they hated Bush more than they loved their country.

The Bush-bashers lost and the Saddam-bashers won. The Neoconservatives were validated everywhere but in the liberal media. Where it mattered, on the battlefield, the Neocons got it right. Liberals unable to accept this should break out their peace pipes and Ouija boards, hold séances, bring Saddam back, and live under him in Iraq.

Bush Derangement Syndrome prevents liberals from living principled lives. Human rights go out the window if it means giving Bush an ounce of credit. Liberals wanted to lose the war so they could win the White House in 2004. Bush refused to allow any of that to happen.

In another decade, liberals will still be bashing what Dianne Feinstein called, "Bush's war." She was right about that. It was his war. Thanks to his leadership and the greatest military on Earth, it was won.

Forcibly removing Saddam Hussein was, is still now, always, and forever will have been the right thing to do.

George W. Bush: Great President, even finer man

The George W. Bush Presidential Library is now living history. The Southern Methodist University campus houses some of the most important documents spanning one of the most critical periods in American history.

Governor George W. Bush entered the Oval Office after a disputed election. His first few months saw him pass supply-side tax cuts that turned around a slowing economy he inherited from his predecessor. Despite a Clinton NASDAQ collapse, Bush did not spend one minute complaining about his circumstances or blaming anybody else. He rolled up his sleeves and went to work. His promise upon taking office was to "restore honor and dignity to the White House."[306] After eight years of endless scandals during the prior administration, he did exactly that.

On September 11, 2001, radical Islamofascists from al-Qaeda hijacked American airplanes and flew them into the two World Trade Center towers and the Pentagon. A fourth plane destined for the White House was diverted when brave passengers took the plane back. United 93 would crash in a field near Shanksville, Pennsylvania. New York was ground zero of a war America never asked for. Yet after almost four decades of presidents unwilling or unable to take the fight overseas, President George W. Bush launched a Global War on Terror.

He left office with toxic poll numbers, but has seen a revival as Americans come to appreciate and respect the hard choices he made during the toughest of times.

The left always hated him, felt he stole the 2000 election, and never gave him the decency and respect that an American leader deserves. An honest look at his presidency reveals not a good leader, but a great one.

After 9/11, Bush took the fight to Afghanistan. The Taliban was routed in less than one month. Ruthless killer Abu Musab al-Zarqawi was killed and 9/11 mastermind Khalid Sheik Mohammed was captured and placed in Guantanamo Bay. The Bush-Cheney interrogation methods extracted valuable information from KSM that led to the eventual killing of Osama bin Laden. When the war was floundering, Bush advocated a surge when Democrats were accepting defeat as inevitable (and in some cases openly rooting for it).

Liberals claimed the Iraq War was a failure based on a lie. Wobbly Republicans called the situation an honest mistake. Both of these groups are wrong. Iraq was the right war at the right time, led by the right President.

Those who disagree can judge Bush's Iraq War and compare it to his successor's approach in Syria.

Those who criticized Bush's handling of Katrina were given a heaping dose of humble pie with revelations by one of his former toughest opponents that his conduct saved many lives. Al Gore's former campaign manager Donna Brazile told the truth years too late, but late is better than never.[307]

Bush's heroism during Katrina stands in stark contrast to his successor's inability to fix Staten Island years after the devastation of Hurricane Sandy.[308] Blacks in Africa know that Bush did far more to combat AIDS than his predecessor or successor.[309]

Bush's integrity meant eight years of governing without a single significant scandal. His opponents had to invent scandals from Enron to Valerie Plame, yet neither of those situations showed any wrongdoing by President Bush. Nobody died, that's for sure. Compare this to Fast and Furious and Benghazi.

If there was one valid criticism of the Bush 43 administration, it would be lousy public relations. Dubya was far too gracious, polite, and dignified toward many critics not fit to lick his boots.

Bush's Press Secretary Dana Perino provided the measure of the man at a private dinner in the last month of his presidency. Given that the political scene felt like a boxing match where only one side was throwing punches, I asked when President Bush was going to finally start hitting back. She replied, "never."[310] Not only was he going to be gracious to the end, his entire staff would be as well. Anybody violating his edict of politeness in the face of hostility would be immediately fired. That order came straight from the top. His staff loyally obeyed.

He kept his word not to criticize his predecessor or his successor. He kept his word about everything he said. When he spoke, his critics and supporters alike knew that he meant what he said. His library deserves to be a tribute to a man who let his deeds triumph over the many short-term revisionist historians wanting to grind him into dust before he ever took office.

His rising poll numbers will only go higher as time goes by and others tell the real stories of the Bush White House that he is too modest to share himself. It needs to be said right now that George W. Bush was a great President and an even finer man.

Chapter 16: Laughable Lunacy

There is normal crazy and extra special crazy. Most things the left does are the standard garden-variety lunacy. This involves being wrong on almost every policy and responding to being wrong with atrocious child-like behavior. Some episodes are so bizarre that even the category of miscellaneous cannot contain them all. For those who fall beyond the bounds of miscellaneous, there is just laughable lunacy. To quote a former football player who knew about controversy and crossing the line, "Get your popcorn ready."[311]

New York Democrats... The real disgrace

New York Democrats have become a disgrace. However, most people fail to understand the real disgrace. After dispatching them them one by one it will be necessary to get to the scandal nobody in New York wants to discuss.

Eliot Spitzer was a scuzzbucket. None of the other New York Democrats compare to him. He is a horrid human being. Forget his prostitution scandal. His harassment of Wall Street firms punished many innocent people without enough money and power to fight him.[312]

Charles Rangel deserves all the credit in the world for having served America honorably in the Korean War. Unfortunately he has repeatedly played the race card and compared conservative tax cutters to the KKK.[313] He gets away with it because he smiles. He is "Good ol' Charlie," the lovable rascal. He was censured by the House but smiled his way out of a prison sentence for tax crimes.[314]

New Yorkers had high hopes for David Patterson. He broke down barriers by showing that a blind man could lead New York. Patterson was black, but his race took a back seat to his breaking the handicap barrier. When Governor Patterson immediately disclosed his past infidelities and drug use, people saw an ethical man and the anti-Spitzer. Unfortunately, because he was a liberal, he and his supporters truly were the blind leading the blind.

Initially he seemed to be like David Dinkins, a good guy not tough enough for the job. He was weak. Yet his intervening on behalf of a subordinate who beat up a woman was stupid, reckless, and possibly illegal.[315] Richard Nixon taught us that blind loyalty is not the answer. Sometimes friends have to be cut loose, especially when they break the law.

Congressman Eric Massa was slime. He also served his country honorably, but his short congressional career has been dishonorable. His inappropriate and bizarre public bad behavior with his staff members led to his resigning in disgrace.[316]

Congressman Anthony Weiner was in a class by himself.

Assembly Speaker Sheldon Silver was indicted on corruption charges in January of 2015. The charges came along twenty years too late for a guy who made Boss Tweed seem like Mother Theresa. The next time we see that commercial about investing in silver, let the marketers know that New Yorkers have given him enough. He wasted it on graft. For liberals, that is called investing.

Republicans are not blameless. Congressman Michael Grimm resigned after being indicted for financial misdeeds.[317] New York is mostly a one-party state controlled by liberals, reducing Grimm to a statistical aberration. Corruption among New York Democrats is a way of life. To show they learned nothing, Democrats allowed a judge who resigned his office under pressure, Frank Seddio, to head the Brooklyn Democrat machine.[318] One of his first acts was to back a Democrat lawmaker facing criminal charges for embezzling nearly half a million dollars from the sale of foreclosed homes.[319] Accused John Sampson is black, but the race card may not work in a Democrat primary in a heavily Democrat area.

These corrupt New York Democrats should make all New Yorkers angry. Their repeated screw-ups are offensive for a reason that nobody is talking about. The whispers are already beginning. People are saying that New York politicians are becoming like "those people." That's right, I'll say it. New York is on the verge of being seen as…New Jersey.

This cannot ever happen. New Jersey gave us Jim McGreevey, Jon Corzine, and a million other corruptocrats ranging from crooked politicians to clergymen on the take. New Jersey Democrats make Pinochet's Chile seem ethical.

I don't care if Rangel, Patterson, and Massa go to jail. Just get them out of New York. Deport them to Trenton.

When football coach Sam Wyche saw the home crowd at a Cincinnati Bengals game throwing trash on the field, he angrily picked up the microphone. He yelled at the crowd to be civilized, thundering, "You don't live in Cleveland, you live in Cincinnati."[320]

My message to these New York politicians is to knock it off. You represent New York, not New Jersey.

I live in Los Angeles, but I am a New Yorker until the day I die. I was born and raised there. New Yorkers are my people. When somebody does something stupid in California, making it the national laughingstock, I emphasize that I am a New Yorker living in California. I am proud of my Brooklyn heritage. I am proud to be from New York. I never want being a New Yorker to be a source of shame.

Deport Spitzer, Massa, Patterson, and Rangel to Atlantic City.

Forget Obama's birth certificate. New Yorkers need to obsess over the birth certificates of New York politicos. Find evidence that they are really Jerseyites. Perhaps they would then under the state constitution be ineligible to serve.

The day the New York Jets and Giants call themselves New Jersey, NYPD and FDNY will engage in cross-border violence. This must be prevented now.

New York Democrats can either act like New Yorkers or move to New Jersey.

Tony Soprano is from Jersey. The Statue of Liberty is a New Yorker. That settles it. New Yorkers will tolerate many things, but being compared to New Jersey is not one of them.

New York civilization is on the line. Clean up your act guys. We are not them. The whisper campaign must stop. The next New York politico to screw up should be waterboarded behind the Log Flume at Six Flags Great Adventure, located in…you know…the place where hidden crimes are a way of life.

Do Nothing–Appoint a Commission

Before getting to the deep science of doing nothing today, it is now time to do my impression of Barack Obama testing out a hammock in the local mall. There, that was easy. Now back to doing nothing.

Rather than quietly just admit I am doing nothing, I am going to give the illusion that I am doing something productive. I am going to appoint a commission to study the problem. Appointing a commission is actually worse than doing nothing because it costs taxpayer dollars. Politicians appoint commissions when they want to delay doing anything so they can ignore their responsibilities while looking busy.

The only thing more useless than a commission is a blue ribbon commission, also known as a blue ribbon panel. The most useless panel is a panel of experts.

If politicians really cared about certain problems, they would just get to work on solving them.

I worked on Wall Street for 15 years. When I wanted to get nothing done, I participated in a meeting. Nothing gets done in meetings. First the equipment does not work, so teleconferences are spent trying to work a telephone. The sandwiches can't be eaten because nobody brought napkins. Arguments take place over whether business cards should say, "Management Lackey," "Management Flunky," or "Management Shill." I prefer shill because it is easiest to spell.

President Obama appointed a commission to study how to reduce the debt. We do not need a commission to stop spending so much money on nonsense! I can save half a million dollars by canceling the commission. The president's debt commission had no enforcement powers. Their predetermined recommendations were in complete agreement with the president on his orders. Otherwise they will be ignored.

A commission of lethargy experts can spend hours determining why I am asleep at noon on a Sunday. I can sum it up for you. There is no football on so I am being lazy.

If the president would just admit that he does not want to be bothered with the issue, that could save us all time and money. I could talk about his speech at the White House Correspondents Dinner, but the only person going through the motions more than him would be me describing his inaction.

I could insult your intelligence by pretending to care. Then I would be qualified to be president. Thanks to Obama that job is now a pay cut and a loss of prestige.

I have bigger things to do. I have been awake for an hour or so and it is time for a midday nap. As for why I need a nap, I have the best and brightest studying the issue. They will report back to you never because the truth of my laziness cannot get out, so I will suppress the report. A successful day and a successful nap…I am that good. Now to fly on Ear Force One and ask Michelle what is for dinner while pretending to listen. Then I will meet with some business leaders on my commission and pretend I know, care or listened to one word they said.

The Otter Picnic

While attending the Idaho State GOP Convention, I was invited to partake in a very strange custom. As somebody who has only lived in metropolises like New York and Los Angeles, I am unfamiliar with Mountain West rituals. I was unprepared for what seemed like something different for a lover of animals like myself. I was invited to the 2010 Idaho Otter picnic.

I have dined on elk, buffalo, and venison, but I had never eaten otter before. It actually seemed a tad barbaric. Maybe living in progressive (translation: screwed up beyond recognition) areas made me snobbish to those with different dining tastes.

I did not see the otters running around before the picnic, which made me wonder where they would be obtained. I hoped I was not being invited to participate in an otter hunt. Kill it and grill it is a great slogan but I prefer my animals served to me already dead. I don't care how the cow gets slaughtered. Just serve me a steak. I wondered what otter steak tasted like. I bet people would say chicken, since everything including chicken tastes like chicken. What would the dietary laws be. I am Jewish. Is otter meat even kosher?

I staunchly support the Second Amendment right to keep and bear arms, but I am not an otter hunter. Like Dennis Leary, I prefer we kill only the ugly animals.[321] I don't mind clubbing baby seals or nuking the whales, but I draw the line at blasting baby otters to smithereens. These Idahoans seemed barbaric, not like enlightened coastal people such as me.

I do like meat and potatoes, and Idaho is the potato capital. I did once receive some delicious Idaho steaks in the mail. They know their meats so I owed them the benefit of the doubt. Maybe otter meat was a secret delicacy that those far away from Idaho had yet to experience. The whole thing made me queasy. I could barely pick up my knife and fork. Then somebody brought me the sandwich. It tasted like ordinary cold cuts. Come to think of it, it was cold cuts. Who knew that otter tasted like salami? It turns out that was just salami. Otter was the main course.

I looked around for a warm furry creature, but instead a tall man with perfect hair that would make Mitt Romney envious walked in. People called him over and shook his hand.

"Good to see you, Governor Otter."

Governor Otter? Did an Otter lead the state of Idaho? Apparently he did. He seemed quite human and rather pleasant. The Otter Picnic focused on the governor's speech about low taxes and creating a better business climate, without any shooting or eating of adorable little animals.

I jumped the judgmental gun like too many coastal elites tend to do. The sandwiches were as normal as anything I have tasted in California, although thankfully this picnic had no tofu. I would sooner eat otter. After the meal I was prepared for them to call in the dogs, but the only thing resembling a canine came in the form of a Labrador.

The Labrador is their congressman.

They also have Bengal Tigers running around, which either means that Idaho state has a cool mascot or the state has lousy hunters and dangerous game running wild.

I had to cut my lunch short because the Idaho state police were looking for me. Just because an Otter and a Labrador lead the state does not mean it is ok to pet them without permission. Their security details were not pleased.

Governor Otter's first name is Butch. With his perfect hair and jaw he should run for President. At the very least the next Republican president should make him Director of Homeland Security or Attorney General. After the twin Janets Reno and Napolitano, Otter is well qualified. He is already a Butch.

Otters, Labradors, and tigers, oh my! Hey, it beats the political vermin in California. Long live Idaho, home of the Otter and the Labrador!

Schoolchildren exploit President Obama to get on television!

In an outrageous move that should have perpetually outraged individuals outraged, several young children exploited President Obama by writing him letters just to get on television. These hooligans know that he sees them as props and photo ops, yet they took advantage of him anyway. These kids should be ashamed. Bringing a room filled with carefully screened, multicultural politically correct kids to a narcissist leader is like giving a crack pipe to a recovering drug addict.

President Obama and the Choom Gang did consume copious amounts of recreational pharmaceuticals in college, and the kids had to know about his predilection to addiction. The most dangerous narcotic is ego, and Obama has zero interest in attending rehab. For these children to take advantage of his vulnerability is sickening. They should be condemned for exploiting Obama's reverential self-worship.

Some people are trying to make excuses for the children, claiming the parents wrote the letters. If that is true, then these kids should be further condemned for forcing their parents into doing what they should have to do for themselves. These are some seriously sociopathic, manipulative children!

The way to get to the bottom of this scandal is to find out if the grammar and spelling in the letters was accurate, and whether the letters were written in block letters or cursive. If so, then the children did not write them because there is no way they could have learned such skills at public schools. If these kids were home-schooled or attended a charter or private religious school, Obama never would have allowed them on the stage. Their parents are old enough to have been instructed in cursive writing (Attention young people: Cursive does not involve using expletives).

However, if some of the letters said, "Guns are badd and Obama is kewl," then either the kids or child predators wrote them.

These kids are no angels. Some of them probably play violent video games. In five years at least one of them will wear a baseball cap and maybe even their pants on backward. They know Obama wants to move forward, so their attempt to use their cuteness on camera to sabotage the Obama agenda is the biggest tragedy in American history.

These kids knew what they were doing, and now have the potential to be the biggest liability to Obama not counting his entire cabinet. Obama is a naive man who has done everything to rise above the cynicism of American politics.

These kids may not have blood on their hands, but who knows if one of them ever burned ants with a magnifying glass?

These cold, calculating youngsters took advantage of a man trying his hardest to instill martial law on the American people. Now that they have been on television, they will most likely try and parlay that into a reality television series such as, "All the President's children." Rapper Shawty Lo could guest star. Americans should shudder at the potential fallout if the X-rated-sounding program *Romper Room* returns.[322] Obama supporters will insist that everybody loves Mickey Mouse, but again, Obama's cabinet has nothing to do with this.

Anti-child exploitation legislation must be passed to ensure that no children ever exploit Obama again. After all, he keeps insisting that, "This is not about me." Of course it is all about him, and the Secret Service is taking a break from their other responsibilities to investigate. This cannot become another Benghazi or Fast and Furious scandal. Americans must know the truth about how future Salahis[323] got past the White House security detail and into the national spotlight reserved only for Obama.

WKRP in Cincinnati: Random Radio Weekend

First came dinosaurs, then Adam and Eve, and finally radio. Civilization was complete. In the 1980s, sitcom *WKRP in Cincinnati* began each episode with an unidentified hand flipping through the radio stations. One news station calmly stated that, "The senator, while insisting he was not intoxicated, could not explain his nudity."[324]

To avoid the problem of radio static, it is best to get rentals with *Sirius XM Satellite Radio*. *Fox News* and *NFL Network* can get me through the longest of drives and traffic jams. Otherwise, on the AM dial, Rush Limbaugh or Sean Hannity can suddenly turn into any program of any kind in any language, eventually fading into the inevitable radio static.

On a six or seven-hour drive from Des Moines, Iowa, to Chicago, the stations melded into each other. It was late at night, so this transcription may not be entirely accurate. This is a fancy way of saying it is mostly wrong. The following is what I clearly heard while changing stations, unless I did not hear it at all.

(**Politics**) "President Obama keeps giving speeches and the problems keep getting worse. People are not seeing results. All they hear from politicians are unfulfilled promises. President Obama needs to be…

(**Cooking**) …stuffed with giblet gravy. For a thicker brown sauce, go with that rather than country gravy. Make sure to stir it frequently. Nothing lays it on a turkey real thick like…

(**Politics**) …President Obama…He said we needed to take a scalpel to the budget and not a machete. He keeps scratching at the surface but does not get to the underlying cost drivers that are killing this economy. He scratches around the edges. I think President Obama…

(**Pet care**) …has fleas. Pets are not immune from fleas and ticks in the winter. Simple dog collars are often not enough of a solution and medical remedies from veterinarians can be very expensive. Sometimes the only way to afford adequate medical care for canines and kittens is to…

(**Financial**) …Sell China. The country as a whole is overvalued right now. The Yuan is pegged to the dollar and the Chinese government needs to stop manipulating their currency. If the Yuan were to reach its true value, it would be worth…

(**Sports**)…a third-round draft pick. As for the Packers, Aaron Rodgers guided Green Bay to a Super Bowl win, beating Brett Favre along the way. Favre had twenty mostly great seasons but it was time to retire. He almost came back again but at that point he was older than…

(Politics) …Nancy Pelosi…she still does not get the message. The 2010 and 2014 elections were crystal clear. The American people voted for…

(Cooking) …basted breast meat with thick country gravy. The stuffing is added to create an extra layer to the meal. Make sure to clean the turkey beforehand thoroughly so that you don't taste the aftereffects of a…

(Pet care) …fine coat of hair. By using a softer roller rather than a hard brush, your dog will look happier, and not be howling in pain. You want your dog sitting next to you, not fleeing like…

(International News) …Moammar Khadafi…He vowed to fight to the death, and the rebels gave the Tripoli terrorist his wish. Just before Khadafi was killed, his only hope was that people would think he was…

(Music) …Carlos Santana. His big hit "Smooth"[325] goes down like…

(International News) …death to the Zionist entity. Hezbollah and Hamas will ensure that Little Satan Israel shall be eliminated and replaced with…

(Cooking) …a healthy heaping of scallions and a touch of cilantro for garnish. Paprika adds some coloring and voila…a delicious…

(Politics) …Satan sandwich. The budget deal was a disaster. The cuts may never materialize and unrealistic growth assumptions are used. The CBO took one look at it and scored…

(International News) …more cocaine than has been seen in some time. The DEA is calling this the biggest attempted heist since…

(Politics) …Al Gore tried to use selective recounts to try and take the 2000 election. Gore was recently caught on tape screaming and cursing while apparently intoxicated. Gore has had a troubled few years. He divorced his wife after four decades of marriage and faced accusations by a masseuse that he was a crazed sex poodle.[326] On each of these occasions, the former Vice President and Tennessee…

(WKRP in Cincinnati) …Senator, while insisting he was not intoxicated, could not explain his nudity."

Chicago's Robin Kelly: Never indicted, elected anyway

In a stunning turn of events, Chicago voters elected someone to Jesse Jackson Jr.'s congressional seat who is not under indictment. Congresswoman Robin Kelly has never been indicted nor ever been accused of any wrongdoing of any kind. Chicago voters may wonder how she can be an effective leader in Washington and in Chicago if she is a law-abiding citizen. Kelly won the seat in a special election after Jesse Jackson Jr. pled guilty to financial crimes.[327] Jackson took over the seat from Mel Reynolds, who went to prison for statutory rape.[328]

Party bosses and power brokers may privately be expressing concern about Kelly's lack of a criminal record. Her clean record and apparent disinterest in breaking the law have led some to speculate that she may not be a Chicago Democrat at all.

Those fretting she may be a closet Indiana Republican should stop worrying. Her first speech attacked the "tea party Congress" and accused the National Rifle Association of holding the American people hostage.[329]

While she is not out shooting citizens, she will at least support legislation that will get many of her constituents killed. However, being a wrongheaded liberal Democrat from a failed liberal city is perfectly legal and expected.

Adding to the confusion is that in the 1980s, she was a community activist. President Barack Obama and Reverend Jesse Jackson Sr. are lifelong community activists. Community activism involves taking money from those who legally earned it and giving it to those who will waste it and never produce anything. Most of the money is supposed to be skimmed off the top by the activist for the activist.

In forty-nine states this is done through extortion. In Illinois it is just the Chicago way. Even when she was a community activist, Kelly never, to the best of our knowledge, contributed in any way to a criminal enterprise.

The staggering improbability of that may force Illinois Republicans to demand an investigation into Kelly's non-record. The Chicago Tribune might want to launch its own probe into her past. No one will want to appoint a special prosecutor, because that could lead to scrutiny of other Chicagoans, past and present.

Honesty in Congress is as common as sobriety at a frat house. Republican Speaker John Boehner united with Democrat Minority Leader Nancy Pelosi to avoid any investigation of Kelly in order to protect the other 434 House members.

Kelly has spent her entire life in the public sector living off of the taxpayers without crossing the line. She has not embezzled from a single foundation or steered any no-bid contracts to anybody while on various boards. Even as an education trustee, she managed not to violate the public trust. She has not contributed much to the American economy but she has not detracted from it either.

Kelly was sworn into Congress on April 11, 2013. Her first forty-eight hours were entirely scandal-free. She is now the most ethical member of Congress from her district in decades.

Those wanting her to run for Governor of Illinois have warned her that unless she can spread around graft like the Daley Machine or curse like Rahm Emanuel, she will never make it as an imprisoned chief executive. Rod Blagojevich of the Planet Bloggo section of Chicago had no comment[330].

Chapter 17: 2016 and Future Lunacy

For six years, Republicans went after President Obama. The criticism was policy-based, never personal. He took it personally because he takes everything personally. On January 20, 2015, Obama gave his sixth State of the Useless address. He said stuff. We ignored him. He is irrelevant. Focus on the many qualified Republican presidential candidates and what they stand for. Offer a conservative vision. Meanwhile, the Republican candidates have to stay out of trouble. For the good of the nation, I will be monitoring them.

The 2016 GOP presidential candidates are
not partying in Las Vegas nightclubs

In January of 1981, the Oakland Raiders were preparing for the Super Bowl in New Orleans. The hard-partying Raiders were told not to be out all night on Bourbon Street. Curfew was 11:00 p.m. every night. John "The Tooz" Matuszak was out partying until 3:00 a.m., and head coach Tom Flores was not happy. When Tooz was asked why he broke curfew, his answer was one for the ages. He insisted that he was on Bourbon Street all night making absolutely sure that everybody else was obeying curfew. Once he was finally assured that not a single player was on Bourbon Street, he felt comfortable coming back to the hotel knowing they were all being responsible. Coach Flores just shook his head. The Tooz was not suspended, the Raiders won the Super Bowl, and the matter was dropped.[331]

Today we live in a world of Facebook, Twitter, and camera phones that clear photos. Everything can be publicized. Reputations have been wrecked. In sports this can cause embarrassment. In politics it can put the nation at risk. Leaders cannot subject themselves to being blackmailed. With several sex scandals having rocked the nation, it is vitally important that presidential candidates stay out of trouble.

In 2012 in Florida, I made sure that Mitt Romney, Rick Santorum, Newt Gingrich, and Ron Paul were not partying in South Beach. GOP candidates cannot be caught in hot tubs with college coeds. Thankfully the candidates were not in Miami Beach.

The candidates went from one *Temptation Island* to another due to the Nevada Primary. For the good of the Republican Party, my stay in Las Vegas had me checking the nightclubs. I am absolutely sure that the candidates went on to Colorado and Minnesota like they said they did.

It is critical that none of them be caught in the nightclubs. The outfits the girls are forced to wear are a tad risqué, perhaps even objectifying. It was so inappropriate that I had to turn away from them after a brief look of approximately five hours. It is with great relief that none of the other candidates were inside the hotel nightclub doing the same. I was looking out for them, but they would not be given much latitude had they gone there trolling for votes.

Ron Paul was the one most likely to get into trouble. Many of his supporters are the types of young women who dance at these clubs. After carefully checking Tao, Dr. Paul has now been exonerated. He was not there.

Mitt Romney has five sons, and it took much longer to comb through nightclub RPM at the Tropicana Hotel. Despite one woman calling out Romney's son Tagg, it was a false alarm. She was just slapping her friend on her (redacted) and saying that the other girl was "it." This game of tag was slightly less innocuous than the game I played on the school playground. None of the Romney men were at RPM.

Rick Santorum is constantly preaching family values. To find out he was at Spearmint Rhino would have been a death knell for his presidency and a disappointment to social conservatives everywhere. After scouring the place from (tight) top to (apple) bottom, it can be said with certainty he was not there. Unconfirmed rumors have him once chewing Spearmint gum.

Newt Gingrich once ate a bag of Cheetos, but he was not hanging out at Cheetahs. Gingrich did not buy dances from any of the women. None of the women confessed to knowing any fellow named after either a newt or a salamander.

Former New Mexico Governor Gary Johnson was getting stoned somewhere, but in all fairness toking up was his public platform. He dropped out of the GOP primaries and ran as a Libertarian, so he gets a pass for fulfilling the mission of that party. Libertarians are Republicans who want to get stoned.

My surveillance was hard work. Thankfully all of the Republican candidates stayed out of trouble. While I am happy to help in any way I can, it would simply be better if somebody else would relieve my burden. The Hawaii Caucus was in March, and I arrived in Honolulu in late February. It is just too burdensome to check every single Waikiki club, much less canvass all five islands to make sure the GOP presidential race is free of sex scandals.

The candidates are morally practicing what they preach. So far, so good. It is imperative that my level of analysis is augmented just to make sure the statistical sample size is valid. There will be many more candidates running in 2016 than in 2012. This means I will have to do twice as much monitoring of South Beach, Bourbon Street and Sin City. It is a dirty job, but someone's got to do it.

In case I ever embark on a political career of my own, I was really in bed in my hotel room by 10:00 p.m., five hours before this column somehow got published without my knowledge. To the person monitoring me to make sure I am properly monitoring the candidates, sorry you were bored. Next time do a better job of writing my column. Had you not been in those inappropriate places looking for me, you would not have been so tired.

Election 2016 South Beach, Miami GOP Caucus

With the Republican Party winning the 2014 elections and building momentum into 2016, trouble lurks on the horizon. In 2014 my surveillance of Bourbon Street in New Orleans, Louisiana was productive. It can be said with certainty that Rick Santorum was not at the Bourbon Cowboy watching young women in miniskirts ride the mechanical bull.

With spring break in full bloom, thousands of people descended on Florida party havens from Daytona Beach to Fort Lauderdale. Miami Beach is the most tempting, so that is where that week's surveillance took place. A quick check of South Beach showed that Ted Cruz was not at Ocean's 10 Nightclub. Rick Perry was not dancing inappropriately with coeds at the Clevelander. Despite being the candidate of the stoners, Rand Paul was not lighting up marijuana joints on Collins Avenue. Although he lives in Florida, Marco Rubio was not in Fat Tuesday on Wednesday at 2:00 a.m. Chris Christie was not hanging out at the Versace house. Bobby Jindal was not drinking on top of the roof of one of the Tenth Street hotels.

The Republican Governors Association did have a meeting in Palm Beach County. None of the thirty Republican Governors made their way down to the clubs in Miami-Dade County. Rick Scott did stay in Florida, but the Scott team insisted he was the Governor of Florida. He drove North to Tallahassee to avoid the temptations of South Florida.

The candidates may have known about the surveillance, so it will be necessary to monitor them again in the weeks and months to come. The last thing the GOP can handle is Mike Huckabee walking down Ocean Avenue with two women on each arm. The paparazzi are everywhere looking for Republicans to make mistakes. Once this phase of the campaign ends, it will be necessary to cover every strip club in Las Vegas again just to be safe.

Election 2016 New Orleans Bourbon Street Caucus

Monitoring Miami Beach and Las Vegas is complicated enough. In those cities the action is mostly indoors in dimly lit back rooms. Bourbon Street is tougher to monitor. The action takes place outdoors in plain view, but people throw beads to distract from political caucusing. Women now throw beads at men, a completely sexist and deplorable act. This is another example of how traditionalism has been destroyed. Meanwhile, my monitoring of Bourbon Street in December of 2014 was productive.

Nobody in South Beach or Bourbon St. was rioting or yelling. Gorgeous weather and non-stop partying make a great antidote to violence. Cities with miserable weather lead to grouchy people. There were people in Miami and N'Awlins concerned about Ferguson. They just care about dancing and partying more. When people are happy, violence goes down. It's hard to protest when everyone is having such a good time.

The only downside to Bourbon Street and other party places is the scourge of humanity known as the "selfie." Almost every selfie-taking woman makes the same pose. I never had the romantic desire to mate with a duck.

I monitored the Democrats and the Republicans on Bourbon Street. In addition to the 2016 presidential candidates, there was also a Senate runoff between Democrat Mary Landrieu and Republican Bill Cassidy.

Club Déjà Vu has the slogan, "1000's of Beautiful Girls and 3 Ugly Ones." Apparently this is where the Pelosiraptor, Debbie Wasserman Schultz and Elizabeth Warren were hiding out after the November 2014 elections.

At 3:00 am an EMT rushed to the hospital but it was too late. The patient was identified as Mary Landrieu's campaign. Obama offered to drive but other passengers wanted to avoid crashing. He was allowed to honk the horn once. He played taps.

Lesbians held up signs saying they needed funds to pay for strap-on devices. The Obama coalition got lovelier as the night went on.

Landrieu was winning Bourbon Street but Cassidy was winning everywhere else. Three people were spotted in the French Quarter wearing t-shirts with the slogan, "I'm for Mary." Two of them were Landrieu supporters. The other one was a satire shirt endorsing Mary Jane, the code name for marijuana. While Landrieu led two votes to zero among those disclosing, the remaining ninety-nine point ninety-nine percent of Bourbon Street revelers were less concerned at night about red states and blue states than about purple, green and yellow beads. Cassidy won the runoff election.

The Republican presidential contenders were staying out of trouble. Neither Scott Walker nor Marco Rubio partied at Lipsticks Men's Club. Rand Paul, John Kasich and Paul Ryan were not at Bourbon Vieux. Kasich was not doing Jell-O shots off a coed's belly at the Beach on Bourbon. Jeb Bush was not at Mangos playing with a young girl's bongos. Initial reports of Mitt Romney tossing beads at women from the Hustler balcony turned out to be false. It was another white guy with perfect hair.

Two guys got into a fight in the street near me. A stripper pulled me near her only to keep me from getting decked. After being rescued by a girl, I turned in my alpha male card. The guys fighting outside the club could have been Huckabee and Santorum except both fighters were black. Further investigation was needed.

Women are more likely to get lusty if a guy tosses beads rather than yell, "End the Fed." Sorry, Senator Rand Paul, or your slightly drunk lookalike.

In late 2015 and early 2016, the candidates are expected to spend time in freezing cold weather in Iowa and New Hampshire before heading to the Bible Belt in South Carolina. I will still be monitoring Miami Beach, Waikiki and Bourbon Street for consistency. This will ensure that Iowa and New Hampshire are not a ruse. Nobody in their right mind trudges through snow begging for votes in the age of teleconferencing. I will rejoin the candidates in Las Vegas when the Nevada Caucus rolls around again. The strippers have been instructed not to harass the candidates. I will intercept them for the safety of America and the Republican Party.

Election 2016: Already Decided

Election 2016 is already decided. Primaries are a waste of time. For Republicans, the outcome is always as predetermined as an Obama opinion. There is no room for flexibility. The GOP nominee is selected four years before the election is held. The Republican Party is not a democracy. It is a hierarchy. We always one hundred percent of the time choose the person who is next in line. Six Powerful Bald White Guys (PBWGs) get in a room and say, "Ok, you're up next. It's your turn." That is how the GOP gets awe-inspiring nominees like Bob Dole. The PBWGs know nothing but control everything. For conspiracy theorists taking a survey, the PBWGs are not Jewish.

Democrats are wrong about virtually every policy, but at least they have real primaries. Hillary Clinton was not anointed in 2008. Barack Obama came out of nowhere. For those wondering, Hillary is far worse than Obama ever could have been. Hollywood made a movie about the American people suffering if Hillary succeeds Obama for what would be Obama's third term. The movie was called *Twelve Years a Slave*.[332] To avoid being kept in bondage until we give up in despair, defeating Hillary again in 2016 is vital.

She will be the nominee. Obama will leave office on time to avoid Hillary getting past the presidential food taster and lacing his dinner. Other Democrats will not dare challenge her because her apparatchiks will destroy them. Unless another black candidate shows up, Hillary can destroy anybody she wants without consequences. Democrats are especially tolerant of women savaging other women. Elizabeth Warren knows this and will opt out. Republicans desperately want her to run as the heir to the Howard Dean lunatic fringe. Her campaign slogan could have been taken from rock group Jackyl. She is "bigger than life and twice as ugly."[333]

Other white males will run, but as John Edwards and the also-rans found out in 2008, Democrats will not choose another white male for a while. The party of identity politics is not going to choose someone from the oppressive heterosexist heteronormative power structure. Hillary is entitled. The nomination is hers.

Republicans pretend to create excitement, but the primaries are a show. Iowa goes to a Christian activist. Spend every day opposing abortion as loudly as possible. New Hampshire goes out of its way to contradict Iowa. They are anti-tax advocates with a libertarian streak. Then South Carolina attempts to reduce both Iowa and New Hampshire to irrelevancy. South Carolina has a strong military contingent, so foreign policy matters.

In 2012 social conservative Rick Santorum won Iowa. Fiscal conservative Mitt Romney took New Hampshire. Foreign policy conservative Newt Gingrich took South Carolina. Ron Paul and his libertarian contingent flopped in Iowa, did well in New Hampshire, and faded in South Carolina. He hung around collecting his ten to fifteen percent of the vote as his supporters insisted the system was rigged against them. They screamed at the other eighty-five to ninety percent of GOP voters and then wondered why they did not make inroads. At least not all Paulbots blamed the Jews.

Rick Perry was the Southern conservative. Michele Bachmann was the tea party conservative. Herman Cain provided racial diversity and a strong business background. Gary Johnson was there for people who just wanted to get stoned. Every niche of the GOP was represented. In the end, the establishment candidate won because the Republican Party always goes with the establishment candidate.

Unless one has a reason to run, they fail quickly. Tim Pawlenty was the competent white governor with good hair. Jon Huntsman was the white Mormon governor who came across as a slick insurance salesman. Romney was already in the race. He was tougher than Pawlenty and far more likable than Huntsman. Nobody figured out why Huntsman was running. He tried to run as a member of *The New York Times* wing of the GOP, which is why nobody liked him.

2016 is no different from 2012. The PBWGs already decided who the nominee was ages ago.

There is only room for one establishment candidate. The big money donors do not divide their votes. They unify quickly and force other establishment candidates out of the race.

Initially it seemed that Paul Ryan was guaranteed the nomination. He was tall, had good hair, and was inoffensive. He was next in line after Mitt Romney selected him in 2012. Ryan was anointed. Then Jeb Bush upset the entire apple cart. Americans can say they dislike political dynasties, but they supported several Virginians for the first few presidencies. The Kennedys refuse to go away and get jobs. Dynasties exist in America.

Jeb getting in immediately eliminates Romney, Ryan and Chris Christie. Romney made noises about getting in, but the Bush family connections and Karl Rove's apparatus will be behind Jeb. Ryan grew a beard and dropped out a few days after Jeb unofficially got in. Conservatives disagree with Jeb about some policies, but primaries are not about ideas. Jeb gets the nomination handed to him. This is just the way it is.

The insurgents have plenty of candidates. Ted Cruz, Marco Rubio and a bunch of other Senators will run. So will Scott Walker, John Kasich, Mike Pence, Rick Perry, Bobby Jindal and every other Republican Governor. Donald Trump will pretend to run even though the entire world knows he is not running. You don't give up the absolute power of being a CEO to trudge through a blizzard and get grilled by ordinary people. Sarah Palin and Colonel Allen West will opt out so they can make millions on the speaking circuit.

In 2016, Rand Paul will get his father's ten to fifteen percent. The conservatives will fight it out. Iowa does not have room for both Santorum and Huckabee. The conservatives will all split their vote. Jeb will struggle in Iowa, rebound in New Hampshire, and cruise to the nomination. When something happens one hundred percent of the time, expect it to happen again until the cycle is broken.

The insurgent candidates who run should make sure not to beat the daylights out of the front-runner. Make some noise, get beat, drop out graciously, and then campaign for the nominee vigorously. Then the PBWGs will demand that an insurgent be the vice presidential nominee to ideologically balance the ticket. A very conservative number two takes all the slings and arrows and allows the top of the ticket to stay above the fray.

Voters should go with the candidate they believe in regardless of what the media promotes. Voters say they understand this every four years but never listen. With all respect to the twelve dipsticks in Dixville Notch, New Hampshire who think they run the world, they do not deserve to speak for sixty million Republicans. These are people who wake up at 4:00 a.m. and put on a tuxedo to go out in subzero February weather to get advice from a groundhog. Californians are far from the best and brightest but at least they are smart enough to live where the weather is nice.

Now to enjoy the primary season and pretend the outcome has not already been decided. As for the general election, flip a coin. It is tough to win three straight elections, which shows how amazing Ronald Reagan was in getting George Herbert Walker Bush over the hump. Bill Clinton could not get Al Gore over the finish line despite relatively good times. Now times are awful, and Obama could drag Hillary down. She is unlikable, but the media will force itself to like her out of fear. She is beatable but she can win. Jeb can take her down, but it will not be easy.

Once the 2016 election is over, the schizophrenic electorate can undermine their new leader by giving the other party control of Congress in 2018.

Chapter 18: My American Lunacy

America is the greatest nation on Earth and was founded by white men adhering to Judeo-Christian values. Minorities of all stripes should kiss George Washington's waxed feet in every museum that houses him. Americans have the freedom to complain about garbage because the Founding Fathers risked their lives for that very freedom.

My American Lunacy leaves just enough time to ridicule the worst aspects of society who desperately deserve that ridicule. It was God, not nature, who "done shed his grace on thee."[334] Ray Charles said so, ending the discussion.

Muhammad is…me?

The revelation was shocking even to me. I have brought to my attention and am now bringing to the world the unmistakable truth that will affect everything and everyone from now until Armageddon. I am the prophet Mohammed.

I am also Muhammad. Hanukkah can be spelled Chanukah. As the prophet, I decide the spelling. My first fatwa is that U's shall be replaced with O's everywhere until further notice. Usama is Osama.

Some will say I am insulting one billion people. Nonsense. I am declaring myself their spiritual leader. Why would I do this if I disliked them? Islam has many beautiful traditions and a billion followers. I would love a billion followers, provided they do not keep contacting me on Twitter (On Facebook they can go to my fan page).

Drawing a picture of Mohammed is forbidden. Therefore, nobody has ever seen a real picture of Mohammed. Since nobody knows who Mohammed actually is, nobody has proof to refute my claims of being Mohammed. To do so would be blasphemous.

As the new spiritual leader of Islam, I am declaring that Jews and Christians are good people to be treated with respect at all times. Jews are the people of the book.

I have not converted to Islam. I am still Jewish. How can I be Jewish and lead Islam? I am the prophet. I can because I said so.

(Who knew Mohammed was as arrogant as a twenty-first century American liberal?)

To radical Islamofascists choosing Jihad as a hobby over macramé or golf, you will burn in hell. I will make the seventy-two ladies you receive as hideous as the offspring of Helen Thomas and Danny Thomas, and they won't be virgins.

(Scratch that remark. Danny Thomas was a nice guy, and unrelated to Helen Thomas even though both were Lebanese. Even supreme leaders can be uninformed when they have not read the paper with their morning beverage.)

The ban on showing my face will be lifted. I want everyone to honor me with visuals. I could use the publicity.

I am now declaring myself the only Mohammed. Anybody else claiming to be me will be rejected out of hand along with the millions of people falsely insisting they are Spartacus.

To blend in with American society, I will not be using my name of Mohammed. I have decided to choose an American name. To the public, I shall be known as Eric.

(I will frequently spell it with a lowercase e. Supreme leaders are not bound by grammatical constraints.)

I now embrace capitalism, so buy my books. I use the pen name *Tygrrrr Express*.

Normal Muslims shall continue living their lives exactly as before my revelation. No changes need to be made with their faith. It works perfectly fine on its own. I am not going to be one of those consultants who comes in and blows everything up (bad choice of words). I will just tinker around the margins.

The margins are the radical Islamofascists who have hijacked the Muslim faith. They shall be banned from Mecca and Medina and relocated to Cleveland. The people of Cleveland are dealing with false prophet issues of their own and could use some replacements.

Being a supreme leader is not easy for me. To avoid being a hypocritical leader I am going to have to start obeying the Ten Commandments at some point soon. I will start with the "Thou shalt not murder" commandment. That one is so easy that anybody other than a genocidal religious lunatic can understand it.

I will not covet my neighbor's wife's @ss (No matter how juicy, luscious and delicious it looks), but if you defy me I will kick yours.

Once I have punished all the Islamic fundamentalist infidels, I will then step down. After all, a Jewish leader of Islam is so retro. The Christians already have their leader, and leading the Jews is a thankless job nobody claims. It is not for me.

I implore the people of the world to help me eradicate the evil Islamofascists who have kidnapped the real true Islam so that I may relinquish my role as supreme leader. This must be done before September when the NFL football season starts. I hate it when my subjects and their complaints and needs interrupt my ballgame.

There is much work to be done. I expect you all to work hard. Until the day of reckoning, may peace be upon me, and you're welcome.

I am Rosa Parks

Good morning, ladies and gentlemen of the media. I will begin this *Tygrrrr Express* press conference with a brief opening statement concerning my act of heroism as the new Rosa Parks. After congratulating myself, I will deign to take questions from you mostly worthless parasites. You will then refer to me as post-racial, which means anything and everything I do will be above criticism.

MSNBC reporters are not in the room to cover my remarks due to a medical crisis. Their heads got lodged up Barack Obama's (redacted), and surgeons are performing the first non-Siamese operation.

Your questions must be in the form of a question. You will not be making statements. This is not your press conference and nobody cares what you have to say. This is about me.

Arab Jihadist Helen Thomas finally blew herself up, so she will not be in the front row to ask anti-Israel questions.

With that, I am proud to discuss the events of yesterday. In an act of racial solidarity, I became the second coming of Rosa Parks. I gave up my seat to a black woman. She was denied the right to sit. This cannot happen in America. This is the twenty-first century, and I will not tolerate a land where a black woman is denied a seat. I voluntarily gave up my seat so she could sit down. Not since King has somebody like me come along. Of course I refer to Don King, who understands that only in America could I do what I did.

I endured uncomfortable positions, but the black woman was comfortable, and that is all that matters. I will now take your questions.

Larry King, *CNN*: My eyes are not what they used to be. Actually, nothing is what it used to be. Are you absolutely sure she was black?

TE: Larry, it is wrong to judge a woman's race by the color of her skin. However, since you are obsessed with race, I will say that the evidence indicated she had a significant amount of melanin content. In short, she was what the Rolling Stones called *Brown Sugar*.[335] Next question.

Amanda Carpenter, *Townhall*: Why did you give up the seat?

TE: That was an intelligent question. Insightful as always, Amanda. The airline asked for volunteers. The flight was oversold. Given how black people have been treated since the beginning of time, I felt it would be an act of racial healing.

I laid down my seat for her the way Sir Walter Raleigh laid down his coat.[336] I figured if I did this, we could finally stop talking about race.

Richard Cohen, self-loathing Hebrew, *Washington Post*: Were you compensated for giving up your seat? If so, isn't this all about money?

TE: Once again the liberal media takes a feel-good story and injects poison into it. The significant compensation I received does not change the fact I gave up my seat for a black woman. I expect a monument to be built in my honor in Washington, DC.

Thomas Friedman, *New York Jayson Blair Times*: Given the compensation you received, wasn't the race and gender of the other passenger irrelevant?

TE: Are you saying she is irrelevant because she is a black woman? I find your insinuation racist and sexist. She should be proud of who she is, the same way you should be proud of who you are. Actually, never mind, you work for the *NYJBT* so you should feel shame. If you were not so insensitive you would have remembered that the late Johnny Cochran once said that race is a part of everything we do.[337] In a nation of Barack Obama, Eric Holder, Henry Gates, and Shirley Sherrod, everything is racial. To question this is racism.

Maureen Dowd, *New York Jayson Blair Times*: Rosa Parks refused to give up her seat. Doesn't that ruin your analogy in the same way that my attitude ruins my chances of having a man warm my seat?

TE: Are you implying I should have refused to give my seat to a black woman because she is a black woman? That is racist. I expect sexist, man-hating drivel from you, but your racism is too much for me to bear. You need to get past your venom and stop trying to hinder civil rights.

Rich Eisen, *NFL Network*: What do you think Drew Rosenhaus should do regarding Terrell Owens and the upcoming season?

TE: Next question.[338]

Bob Herbert, *New York Jayson Blair Times*: Do you think your situation is proof that reparations for slavery are in order?

TE: Excellent question. This compensation was a form of reparations for my being enslaved many times at various airports with inadequate remedies. My luggage has been lost. I have been stranded on the tarmac and even been forced to sleep on airport floors without redress. While this compensation today does not make up for all the past injustices I have faced, it is a good start from a reparations standpoint.

Major Garrett, *CBS News*: President Obama flies around on a private jet while you fly coach. Is this reverse racism?

TE: The question Arianna Huffington planted on you to make you look bad worked perfectly. You are usually better than that. It is not just an issue of reverse racism. It is also class warfare. Obama promised to share the wealth, yet he has not one time given up his seat on Air Force I for me. I have not even ridden on Air Force II, and that plane is not used for anything. They could fly coach, but they do not care about the people. It is all talk coming from them.

Ellen Degeneres, *Gay and Lesbian Monthly*: Was the black woman gay, and if so does this mean we should have gay marriage?

TE: I do not know her sexuality, rendering me unable to comment in terms of broader social policy. I do not know if any clergy were on the flight since I did not board the flight. I am not sure if a gay or straight marriage could have taken place in the air. I do not know what the rule is regarding nuptials and sky miles. Regarding potential honeymoons, joining the Mile High Club is frowned upon except on redeyes when other passengers are asleep.

Wendell Goler, *Fox News*: Will you be having a holiday named after you due to your heroic act?

TE: Wendell, I cross every racial and ethnic strata. Now that I have healed the entire country, I am declaring an end to every grievance of every kind by every human being. There are now no more problems, and bigoted liberal bomb-throwers will be forced to learn skills that would make them remotely employable. As for this holiday thing, who am I to argue with the media?

Greta Van Susteren, *Fox News*: Do Paris Hilton and Lindsay Lohan think…

TE: No, they don't, not in the least. Rumor has it that a couple of them offered to give up their jail cells including the seats to black inmates in a very generous racial gesture. When asked if they would do the same at their own mansions, they seemed less tolerant. They really do seem like mean girls.[339]

Hillary Rodham Clinton, *Arkansas Democrat-Gazette*: Since you will still be flying to Little Rock, Arkansas, will you be speaking to any state troopers slandering my loving husband?

TE: I always suspected you and the rest of the State Department did nothing all day, but posing as a reporter is a new low even for you. I will not be delving into your husband's trousers literally or metaphorically because the last thing I need is for you to ever get near mine. It would be mutually assured destruction in the bimbo eruption department. If you wanted a better marriage you should have stopped pushing gun control legislation. My girlfriend, her parents, and my parents all support the NRA. Believe me when I say that is the best way to eliminate infidelity.

Keith Olbermann, *MSNBC*: The operation was partially successful, so forgive my showing up all filthy and disgusting. I still have President Obama's umbilical cord wrapped around my waist, but I am here. Don't you think it is wrong to turn every little incident into a racial issue?

TE: That would be Barack Obama. Keith, once again you "acted stupidly."[340] I see the umbilical cord, you sweet liberal boy. I would get the scissors but you might die, and nobody wants that. Unlike liberals rooting for conservatives like Rush to die, I want you to live so I can point out your idiocy.

I would take more questions but most of you are not fit to shine my shoes. My sneakers are black, which proves something you can't understand. I just hope I have shown young people the importance of volunteering. When you give, you get back so much more.

It is time to invest one percent of my compensation in an overpriced airport soda. Normal people would consider that an expenditure, but in liberal fantasyland expenditures are investments. I will further the cause of healing by buying Coke Zero, which is black. Those who claim that the beverage is actually red are trying to drive a wedge between blacks and American Indians. I am tired of liberals and their racial division strategy. You're welcome America.

My animal rights heroism

I spoke to a woman recently without staring at her cleavage. She was hideous, but that is immaterial. I did not look at her at all, champion of feminism that I am.

I became a hero of the gay rights movement by offering a brilliant compromise of allowing gay rights for homosexual men but condemning the behavior for lesbians. I even compromised further, allowing ugly lesbians to do as they pleased. Critics accused me of just trying to get more hot women for myself. Those critics have no idea the burdens I bare being a bra-burning feminist.

(I hope whoever owned that bra does not want it back.)

It is in this vein (vain perhaps) that I reveal my animal rights heroism. I am a hero to the animal rights movement. I admit to being to the right of Ted Nugent when it comes to the philosophy of beef, which is kill it and grill it.

(On Thanksgiving Thursday, stabbing a turkey with a fork is a guilty pleasure. The turkey is already dead and quite flavorful thanks to the makers of Swanson dinners.)

I also agree with Nugent on his philosophy of *Wang Dang Sweet (redacted)*, but that is for another day.[341] Anyway, back to me being a hero and animal lover.

The year was 2006. The country bar in Honolulu was Nashville Waikiki.

For those confused, I was on Kuhio Avenue in Oahu, Hawaii, not Tennessee. I saw her. She was your standard hot raven-haired goddess.

Nothing warms the hearts of most women like trees and animals. For some reason flora, fauna, and furry fuzzies make them want to visit the island of fornicatia.

As for me, abuse of animals gets my hackles up. It is one thing to eat beef, but barbecuing dogs and cats is totally unacceptable!

(This is how liberals operate. They make a statement nobody could possibly disagree with. They then accuse you of being insensitive for not saying it first, meaning you support the evil action. I am against using goat horns to violate women. This means everybody I dislike supports doing this and are misogynists for not taking up the cause without me prodding them.)

Some barbarians actually eat horsemeat, which is illegal. According to my Denis Leary handbook on animals, we are only supposed to care about the cute ones. Otters and seals get to live. Cows are steaks and baseball gloves.[342]

Horsies are adorable, and it is high time somebody stepped in and saved them all. In the spirit of protecting these noble creatures, I let this brunette goddess know how I felt about combating the evil and brutality involved with hurting these animals.

I walked toward her, and with inspiration from animal lovers Big and Rich, showed my compassion.

"Sweetness, 'Save a horse, ride a cowboy.'"[343]

She understood my message of lustful humanitarianism.

To that cowgirl who was part Nashville, part Waikiki, and one hundred percent brunette goddess, thank you for helping me spread my...cause. Even a sixty-five-inch guy can be tall in the (side) saddle.

I will not rest until every animal is saved or I am exhausted, whichever comes first. No need to thank me. I just do what I (lust) love.

To all those horses (and horses' hides known as animal rights activist zealots) alive today because she decided to save a horse and ride a cowboy, there is only one thing to say. You're welcome. I would do it again...and again...and again.

Election 2016: The conservative Republican path to victory

On January 20, 2015, President Obama gave his annual State of the Useless address. He intoned, "Blah, blah (look in confusion at the teleprompter), blah." It had a shelf life of eleven years before it was given. It was the greatest speech in the history of history except for every other speech by anyone, anywhere. This concludes coverage of the inconsequential man with inconsequential words.

The day after his speech should be the last day that Republicans and conservatives ever mention his name. Let Barack Obama go. Look forward to the future. He is the past. Take away the media oxygen that he needs to breathe. Ignore him.

As the media turns to Election 2016 and the many caucuses and primaries, President Selfie Pajamaboy Obama will be seething in front of the mirror. He will be angry that the media is focusing on others. He will be arguing with himself in front of his mirror.

"Joe Biden does not inspire his own family. Hillary Clinton is toxic. The former Governor of Maryland is such a boring non-descript white guy that even he does not know who he is. He could be standing in my living room right now. Security should remove him. Are these the losers who want to take my job?"

Obama will fail to notice the irony. Hillary muttered those exact same words in 2008 about him.

He will be desperate to pick fights. Republicans can govern, but they must let Obama come unglued. They must ignore him like you would any other child throwing repeated temper-tantrums. He will be grounded soon enough as his plane and all his other toys are taken away.

The time for bashing Obama ended with the 2014 elections. The 2014 message was very simple. "Democrats suck. They're in charge. We're not them."

The 2016 message must be a positive one. America already knows that Obama sucks. They want answers on how to fix his failures. People will come up to you saying, "I don't know what I was thinking. I voted for Obama." Do not make them feel worse or tell them you were right all along. Smugness is for liberals. Be conservatives. Be respectful. Turn on the one quality that liberals lack: empathy.

"It's ok. A lot of people voted for President Obama (Be respectful at this point, use his title). I understand you're hurting. A lot of people are hurting. That is the past. Let's talk about the future. Let me tell you about (insert your GOP candidate of choice)."

Talk about your own candidate for an hour. Do not mention the president's name once. He is yesterday's news.

What matters is not ideological purity. Winning elections and governing is key. Even President Ronald Reagan raised taxes in 1982. Stop looking for perfection. Only God is perfect. The media will try to convince conservatives that the GOP candidates are a bunch of losers. The GOP bench is phenomenal and keeps getting better.

Do not worry about Obama trying to govern by vengeance in his final two years. If he governs against the people, get your microphones and force Hillary to go on the record with her opinions. Smoke her out. Make her tell us that she remains the terrible person she has always been. The more voters see and hear of her, the less they like her. She must pay the price for every Obama sin. When Obama goes crazy in his final two years, Hillary's people will undermine him to protect her. Let her do the dirty work for us. Let her sabotage the end of the Obama presidency.

Lastly, remember that building a majority coalition requires advocacy. With advocacy, do not tell people what they should care about. Ask them what they do care about and show them how the conservative Republican message fits in with what matters to them. If all somebody cares about is abortion and you talk about illegal immigration, their eyes will glaze over.

Obama spent his entire presidency ignoring people and pursuing his faculty lounge utopian pipe dreams. Do not repeat his reign of error. Find out what is in the hearts and minds of those you want to persuade. An assistant coach can draw plays on a blackboard. Be a head coach. The head coach is somebody you would go through a brick wall for because you want them to lead you. Be leaders, not wonky technocrats. Liberals are boring. Do not be boring. Obama managed to hide his boring side just long enough. Now he is seen as the Sominex he always was.

Conservatives are alphas. Liberals are betas. Conservatives, go kick their @ss. They need it. They deserve it. They are too weak and pathetic to fight back unless you cower first and let them punch you. When conservative Republicans fight back against liberal bullies, we win easily.

State of the Useless: My Summit With Barack Obama

It is time for a presidential summit featuring a half-black and half-white leftist fellow with big ears and a pasty white vertically challenged Republican Jewish alpha male, both with winning smiles.

President Obama, I listened to your State of the Union speech. It is time for you and I to engage in an athletic competition. Don't worry. It won't be bowling. I want your best, not your worst. It will be like the Nathan's Hot Dog Eating Contest at Coney Island, only we will eat at a much more leisurely pace.

I would like to have a navel gazing competition with you.

January 21, the day after his speech, should be a nationwide event: STATE OF THE USELESS: NAVEL GAZING SUMMIT!

Before people get excited, this is not where we sit on the beach and ogle women in bikinis. Also, we will not be staring at each other's bellies. That would be creepy. No. We will both sit outside in lawn chairs and deeply contemplate our own respective navels.

I warn you, sir. I am prepared. I went to a liberal arts college. I know how to navel gaze with the best of them. For the record, my navel is round and symmetrical with zero imperfections. Whoever cut that cord did a great job. There is also not an ounce of lint in my belly button, although your policies have left plenty of it in my pockets.

Like the Miss America pageants, there will be more to this contest than just looking spectacular with our shirts off in self-admiration. There will be a talent contest where we spout meaningless phrases that on the surface seem deep and meaningful but really mean actually nothing. You say several of them repeatedly. Your supporters consider them brilliant solely because you say them. This allows you to be for and against the exact same thing and always be right. This is impressive.

Obama finds privatizing Social Security to be a risky stock market scheme while celebrating the rise of the market. We should like teachers, as if people run around saying they hate them. Parents should help kids with their homework, as if there is a powerful lobby against that. Americans should favor innovation despite that viewpoint never being challenged.

Obama celebrates innovators while absolutely burying the very essence of what innovation is about. He lauds entrepreneurship yet insists the public sector creates anything of value. Governments destroy value. Limited government is necessary to prevent anarchy, but preventing destruction is not the same as creating something.

Obama wants to take from oil companies to create a green utopia without any contingency plan when unproven green technologies fail. The fact that oil actually works is lost on him. He is so far above the rest of us mortals because he thinks decades into the future. Somehow all of his pontificating never explains to people what to do to get people back to work now.

Increased education may help somebody several years from now, but plenty of educated people need jobs now. High-speed rail will get people places fast, but if they have no place to go and nothing to do, they will not travel. All the government money poured into electric cars will fail because people are not interested in a green revolution right now. The only green they care about is money. They don't have it because liberals keep taking it from them.

Mr. President, I know you are a magician who walks on water. I accept that you can recycle your toilet paper because your (redacted) don't st@nk. This is why I believe you can spend into the stratosphere and save at the same time.

Just because you failed to name a single program you would cut does not mean you are full of (redacted). You truly believe what you say. In your world, freezing spending really does mean cutting.

I used to think that you were a cold, clinical Vulcan. Spock lacked empathy, but at least he was logical. I am not sure what you are. Your proposals are illogical, but you also fail to exhibit any human emotion. Perhaps you really do care more about trees than people. You would not be the first liberal blessed with this vision.

This is why it is so important for us to spend time together. You can wax poetic for hours on why everything you are doing is working while the world burns. We can ignore everything around us like worldwide radical Islamic terrorism.

We can watch people beg for jobs as you respond with destroying their health care, harassing small businesses, and beating people into submission in the name of bipartisanship. Not to worry you sir, but some of the people blown to bits were driving hybrids. Trees also suffered.

Rather than attack your many deficiencies, I think I should be fair and highlight your strengths. Your shirts and ties are crisp and you have good hair. Let's celebrate what you love to celebrate most, you being you. It is not about your doing anything. Your very being is an invaluable enough gift.

If I win this navel gazing competition with you, don't worry. I know you have nothing to get back to, and Joe Biden will be just fine managing absolutely nothing. We can make it a best two out of three.

At the end of the evening we will have the final contest where we lay back in the lawn chairs, pour water in our navels, slap our stomachs, and see who can make the water jump higher. Think of it as golf, but with action. Then we will gaze into the future with very serious poses so that observers think we are really doing important things that matter.

We can even bring schoolchildren in to wave pompoms and shout praise to you like your supporters do at memorials and other campaign events.

I challenge you, Mr. President. May the best navel gazer win. I suspect it will be you, but your very essence and speeches inspire me so much. I now have hope that I can change the results, win the future, and defeat you in this contest every bit as important as anything else you do daily.

Bring your navel gazing best sir. You are a man of slogans, and our navel gazing contest has an official slogan: Whether innie or outtie, it's onnie!

INSANE CONCLUSIONS

My views are based on a simple premise: My critics are mostly raving lunatics who confuse emotions with facts, pompousness with accuracy, and close-minded certitude with empirical evidence. I am not always right. My critics are virtually always wrong. They are uninformed on a good day, and crazy people do not have that many good days. Feedback is valuable from people with good intentions who matter. My liberal critics are malevolent and therefore irrelevant.

In football and in politics, players do not have time to discuss diplomacy. Somebody is coming at them trying to knock their block off. They either defend themselves or get belted to the ground. The opponent does not want to dialogue. People yammering during the game and then demanding silence during the commercials often ruin Super Bowl parties. The rules in my home for football are the same as for politics. If you have no idea what you are talking about, stifle yourself. Then leave.

Love and sports are fun and fantasy. The real world is about trying to keep a toxic cocktail of Islamofascism and leftism from getting us blown to the afterlife. It is not possible to reason with and develop an understanding with the lunatic fringe. The best one can hope for is that somebody will verbally shake the stupidity out of these miscreants while yelling, "Knock it off!"

We need to support our troops. The next time a member of Congress says that they support the troops and want them to come home, let that soon to be ex-politico know that the troops feel the same way and want Congress to go home and stay there.

God created imbeciles, and they begot more imbeciles. All Adam had to do was avoid a tree. He was a guy. He had no interest in trees. He made the mistake of listening to Eve, the world's first feminist environmentalist. Then the snake showed up and we had animal rights activists. Adam was a conservative. He minded his own business. Eve was a liberal activist. She and her liberal descendants of both genders are proof that one can eat from the tree of knowledge, have an inflated sense of intellectual importance, and yet know virtually nothing that benefits anybody in society.

I do what I do so the next generation gets it. I asked "the boy" to show his parents how they play *Star Wars* lightsabers in France. He dropped the lightsaber, fell to his knees, and said, "I surrender." I love that kid. He melts my heart.

As for me, my battle cry remains the same. *Hineni*. Here I am. Jewish, proud, politically conservative, and morally liberal. So what next?

I'll be flying down the highway headed west …In a streak of black lightning, called *The Tygrrrr Express*. On to the next adventure. God bless.

eric

Acknowledgements

My grandparents are gone, but with me always. My parents were never wealthy, but I was raised right.

Without love, there is no life. Romantic administrations past, present and future all brought something positive into my life, although some far more than others. To any woman whoever loved me that I did not appreciate enough, I tried my best and did care. Thank you for love, no matter how fleeting it may have been.

My friendships are lifelong and alphabetized: Leeor Alpern, Gary Aminoff, Seth Arkin, Brian Arnold, Rachael Aron, Richard Baehr, Michael and Ann Benayoun, Lara Berman, Leo Bletnitsky, Shane Borgess, Sherry Caiozzo, Johnny Ceng, Ligang Chen, Lisa and Bob Cohen, Nim Cohen, Colonel Bill Cowan, Chaim and Tova Cunin, Val Cymbal, Toni Anne and Tom Dashiell, Ari and Fini David, Aaron Deutsch, Chuck and Diane DeVore, Seth Edelman, Brian Elfand, Sharon Elias, Jason Elman, Uri Filiba, Ken Flickstein, Deron Freatis, Brian Gerson, Eric and Jennifer Goldberg, Steve Goldberg, Eugene Grayver, Molly and Leonard Grayver, Meri Testa, Elyse and Aaron Greenberg, Larry Greenfield, Alan Greenstone, Celeste Greig, Danny Halperin, John Heller, Tamara Holder, Kevin Jackson, Julia and Marc Jaffe, Jason Kenniston, Tarik Khan, Jamie Krasnoo, Jerry Krautman, Jacquie Kubin, Jeff Kuhns, Amy and Gene Laff, Elana Landau, Trevor Loudon, Lisa Macizo, Mendy and Dinie Mangel, Jason Margolies, Leslie Marshall, Margie and Tom Mergen, Carl Merino, Mike Monatlik, Izzy Newman, Greg Neyman, Erica Nurnberg, Doris Ohayon, Terry Okura, Brian Ozkan, Mike Patton, Harold and Sharon Rosenthal, Jeanie (RIP Bernie) Rosenthal, Ron Rothstain, Michael Rubinfeld, Peggy Sadler, Beverly Sandler, Daniel Savitt, Evan Sayet, Alan Schechter, Steven Slade, Ryan Szackas, Ruth and David Tobin, Dov and Runya Wagner, Grant Wallensky, Adam Wasserman, Doug Welch, Laura Wolfe, Woody Woodrum,

Nate and Janna Wyckoff, Oliver Young, Marc Zoolman. RIP Borah Van Dormolen.

My extended family includes the Arzillos, the Diels, the Katzs, the Mouradians, the Rossis, and the Weitzs. RIP Janice Rossi and David Malakoff.

Lara Berman convinced me to start a blog. Jamie Krasnoo provided the technological advice. Eliot Yamini of Hotweazel developed it. Hugh Hewitt, Armstrong Williams, Ward Connerly, Evan Sayet, and Larry Greenfield all helped my blog expand. Celeste Greig, Colonel Ralph Peters, Peggy Sadler, Toni Anne Dashiell and (RIP) Borah Van Dormolen all helped my speaking career. Chabad, USC Hillel, the Republican Jewish Coalition, and the Zionist Crusader Alliance have all nourished and inspired me.

Thank you Ronald Reagan, George W. Bush, and Dick Cheney for your leadership.

Almighty God, thank you for tolerating me.

eric, aka *The Tygrrrr Express* http://www.tygrrrrexpress.com @TYGRRRREXPRESS

ENDNOTES

CBS News is fine with "Fake but accurate" memos. *NBC News* is happy with doctored video footage. *The New York Jayson Blair Times* and *MSNBC* may have gotten a story right once, but that could have been an accident. Conservatives are like *Hebrew National* hot dogs. We are held to a higher standard. Everything is sourced.

(1)   Sowell, Thomas. Ferguson protest "hands up, don't shoot" "lie" like Joseph Goebbels. *Tablet, Washington Times*, December 3, 2014

(2)   Wittrock, Angela. Lansing business owner alleges racial abuse, loses equipment in Right to Work protest at state Capitol. *Mlive.com*, December 12, 2012

(3)   Liberal hate speech. *Conservapedia.com*

(4)   Alinsky, Saul. *Rules For Radicals*, 1971

(5)   Baldwin, Alec. *Late Night With Conan O'Brien*, 1998

(6)   Crowder, Steven. No Laughing Matter—From Wonkette to Louis CK, Attacks on Sarah Palin and her Son Trig Are Despicable. *FoxNews.com*, April 21, 2011

(7)   Merica, Dan. Comedian tells 'special needs' joke at Palin event. *Politicalticker.blogs.cnn.com*, September 3, 2011

(8)   Queen. We Will Rock You. *News of the World*, 1977

(9)   Hoft, Jim. Tea Party Protesters Attacked—1 Black Conservative Seriously Hurt in St. Louis! 6 Arrested Including SEIU Members. *GatewayPundit.com*, August 7, 2009

(10)   Man accused of trying to run down Rep. Katherine Harris. *CNN.com*, October 27, 2004

(11)   Troubled Asset Relief Program. *Wikipedia.org*

(12)   Obama, Barack. Speech to his Jobs and Competitive Council in Durham, North Carolina, June 13, 2011

(13)   Government Accountability Office official report. February 26, 2013

(14)   Navellier, Louis. Ford (F) Turns a Profit after Turning Down Bailout. *Nasdaq.com*, 2010

(15)   Dean, Howard. *Washington Post*, 2005

(16)   Dean Defends Criticism of GOP. *Associated Press*, June 8, 2005

(17)   Self-executing rule. *Wikipedia.org*

(18)   Mitchell, Alison. Clinton, Gingrich and Dole pledge a deal on budget. *New York Times*, December 20, 1995

(19)   Clark, Nicola. Soros Loses Challenge to Insider Trading Conviction. *New York Times*, October 6, 2011

(20)   Soros, George. Steve Kroft Interview on *60 Minutes*, December 20, 1998

(21)   Kurson, Ken. The Tyranny and Lethargy of the Times Editorial Page, *New York Observer*, February 4, 2014

(22)   Taranto, James. Happy Enroniversary. *Wall Street Journal*, January 27, 2012

(23)   Berrin, Danielle. Jon Stewart's version of Judaism, *Jewish Journal*, October 15, 2010

(24)   Katy Perry on 'Sesame Street'--See her cleavage for yourself, *Los Angeles Times*, September 23, 2010

(25)   Metrosexual. *Wikipedia.org*

(26)   Ibid.

(27)   Beaches. *Wikipedia.org*, December 21, 1988

(28)   Steel Magnolias. *Wikipedia.org*, January 1, 1989

(29) Fried Green Tomatoes, *Wikipedia.org*, December 27, 1991

(30) *South Park: Bigger, Longer and Uncut.* June 30, 1999

(31) Williams, Robin. Robin Williams Jokes, *Jokes4us.com*

(32) Obama, Barack. Speech on May 19, 2011

(33) Netanyahu, Benjamin. Speech to AIPAC on May 23, 2011

(34) Golding, William. *Lord of the Flies*, September 17, 1954

(35) Mathers, Marshall. Without Me, *The Eminem Show*, May 14, 2002

(36) Ibid.

(37) Karl, Jonathan. Obama and His Pot Smoking Choom Gang, ABCNews.com, May 25, 2012.

(38) Shakespeare, William. *Hamlet*, 1600

(39) Sayet, Evan. *EvanSayet.com*

(40) Cornwell, Tim. George Michael arrested over "lewd act." Independent.co.uk, April 9, 1998

(41) Murdock, Deroy. Remember Fast and Furious's Mexican Victims. *National Review Online*, July 6, 2012

(42) McKibben, Bill. Time for climate scientists to go on strike. *MSNBC.com*, March 31, 2014

(43) Ibid.

(44) Kelly Bounces Back. *Married With Children*, October 28, 1990

(45) Nation's Experts Give Up. *The Onion*, June 16, 1999

(46) C-Span. *Road to the White House*, Debuted 1987

(47) Gruber, Jonathan. Remarks to University of Pennsylvania's Leonard Davis Institute of Health Economics, October 17, 2013

(48) Sandler, Adam. *Saturday Night Live*, February 5, 1994

(49) Hall, Rich. *Sniglets*, 1984

(50)   Biden, Joe. Barack Obama speech, March 23, 2010

(51)   Obama, Barack. Obama Montage. *Youtube.com*, March 14, 2014

(52)   Pelosi, Nancy. Speech to Legislative Conference for National Association of Counties, March 9, 2010

(53)   Obama, Barack. Speech to M. Luis Construction Company, October 1, 2013

(54)   Jackson, Andrew. *Wikipedia.org*

(55)   Bush, George W. White House Press Conference, July 2, 2003

(56)   Krauthammer, Charles. The Obama Doctrine: Leading from behind. *Washington Post*, April 28, 2011

(57)   War on Terror. *Wikipedia.org*

(58)   Blake, Mariah. The White House Broke its Promise to the Victims of the First Fort Hood Shooting. Will History Repeat Itself? *Mother Jones*, April 10, 2014

(59)   *The Men Who Stare at Goats*, 2009

(60)   200. *South Park*, April 14, 2010

(61)   Jewbilee. *South Park*, July 28, 1999

(62)   Fantastic Easter Special. *South Park*, April 4, 2007

(63)   Thrilla in Manila. *Wikipedia.org*, October 1, 1975

(64)   Leyden, John. Cyber-jihadists deface home of teddy bears' picnic. *TheRegister.co.uk*, September 2, 2010

(65)   Bratton, John Walter/Kennedy, Jim. Teddy Bears' Picnic, Melody 1907, Lyrics 1932

(66)   *The man with one red shoe*, Debuted July 19, 1985

(67)   2005 Koran Desecration Controversy. *Wikipedia.org*

(68)   Curren, Kevin. *Wikipedia.org*

(69)   Clinton, Hillary. Testimony before Senate Foreign Relations Committee, January 23, 2013

(70) *bringbackourgirls.us*, April 14, 2014

(71) Letterman, David. Interview with Dan Rather. *Late Show With David Letterman*, September 17, 2001

(72) Giuliani, Rudy. Saturday Night Live, September 29, 2001

(73) Gottfried, Gilbert. October, 2001

(74) Clark, Anthony. *Half Hour Comedy Hour*, 1991

(75) Benjamin, Bennie/Caldwell, Gloria/Marcus, Sol. Don't let me be misunderstood, 1964

(76) LMFAO featuring Lil Jon. Shots. *Party Rock*, October 13, 2009

(77) *Austin Powers: International Man of Mystery*, May 2, 1997

(78) Choate, Rufus. *Wikipedia.org*

(79) Kerry, John. Testimony before Senate Foreign Relations Committee, April 12, 1971

(80) Dennis, Brady/Wallsten, Peter. Obama joins Wisconsin's budget battle, opposing Republican anti-union bill. *Washington Post*, February 18, 2011

(81) Miller, Zell. Keynote Speech to Republican National Convention, September 1, 2004

(82) Thomas, Helen. Interview with Rabbi David Nesenoff. *RabbiLive.com*, May 27, 2010

(83) Hillary's Kiss-Off to Israel, *New York Observer*, November 22, 1999

(84) Cohen, Tom/Labott, Elise. Kerry's apartheid remark hits pro-Israel nerve. *CNN*, April 30, 2014

(85) Duke, David. *Wikipedia.org*

(86) Seahawks blow out Cardinals in record fashion. *NFL.com*, December 9, 2012

(87) Arafat, Yasser. *Biography.com*

(88) Ibid

(89)   Black September in Jordan. *Wikipedia.org*, Disputed claim of Yasser Arafat, September, 1970

(90)   Fiallo, Fabio Rafael. Ariel Sharon's Masterstroke: The Gaza Withdrawal. *RealClearWorld.com*, January, 12, 2014

(91)   2000 Camp David Summit. *Wikipedia.org*

(92)   Muslims in Miami Scream: 'We Are Hamas'. *Breitbart.com*, July 23, 2014

(93)   Concert For Kerry/Edwards Raises $7.5M. Billboard.com, July 9, 2014

(94)   Flashback: Sean Penn Beat Madonna for 9 hours in 1987; Charged with Felony Assault. *LipstickAlley.com*, May 2, 2011

(95)   Alec Baldwin's Threatening Message to Daughter, *TMZ*, April 22, 2007

(96)   Penn, Sean. *Milk*, November 26, 2008

(97)   The Vagina Monologues. *Wikipedia.org*, 1996

(98)   *Frost/Nixon*, Debuted October 15th, 2008

(99)   *Batman: The Dark Knight*, Debuted July 14, 2008

(100)   ecksmanfan. Did Heath Ledger *Really* Deserve the Oscar for Playing the Joker? *Comicbookmovie.com*, January 20, 2011

(101)   *Crouching Tiger, Hidden Dragon*, Debuted December 8, 2000

(102)   *Slumdog Millionaire*, Debuted November 12, 2008

(103)   *The Expendables*, Debuted September 14, 2010

(104)   *Judge Dredd*, Debuted June 30, 1995

(105)   Ibid

(106)   *Over the Top*, Debuted February 12, 1987

(107)   *Kumbaya*, Debuted 1926

(108)   *The Expendables 2*, Debuted August 17, 2012

(109)   *Wiseguy*, Debuted September 16, 1987

(110) *The taking of Beverly Hills*, Debuted October 11, 1991

(111) *Jersey Shore*, Debuted December 3, 2009

(112) *Real Housewives of New Jersey*, Debuted May 12, 2009

(113) Parloff, Roger. How MF Global's 'missing' $1.5 billion was lost--and found. *Fortune*, November 15, 2013

(114) Sutherland, Kiefer. *24*, Debuted November 6, 2001

(115) Nicholson, Jack. *A Few Good Men*, Debuted December 11, 1992

(116) Theismann, Joe. Super Bowl XVIII Post-Game comments

(117) *The Expendables 3*, Debuted August 15, 2014

(118) *Batman: The Dark Knight Rises*, Debuted July 20, 2012

(119) Jones, Tashara.The rocky life and true romance of Michael Sam, *New York Post*, January 12, 2015

(120) Page, Ellen. *Wikipedia.org*

(121) *Canadian Bacon*, Debuted September 22, 1995

(122) Blame Canada. *South Park: Bigger, Longer and Uncut*, Debuted June 15, 1999

(123) Seger, Bob. Turn the Page, *Back in '72*, 1973

(124) Opcit, 83

(125) Allah Pundit. Helen Thomas: What else should a reporter be but a liberal? *HotAir.com*, January 20, 2009

(126) Snow, Tony. White House press conference, July 18, 2006

(127) Goldberg, Bernard. Helen Thomas Speaks: Unfortunately. *BernardGoldberg.com*, June 7, 2010

(128) Perino, Dana. Speech to Republican Jewish Coalition, December 16, 2008

(129) Balleza, Maureen/Zernike, Kate. Memos on Bush Are Fake but Accurate, Typist says. *New York Jayson Blair Times*, September 14, 2004

(130) Pickett, Bobby. Monster Mash. *The Original Monster Mash*, August 25, 1962

(131) Restoring Honor Rally. August 30, 2010

(132) Rally to Restore Sanity and/or Fear. October 30, 2010

(133) Ibid

(134) Restoring Courage Rally. August 24, 2011

(135) Kerry, John. Appearance on *Viewpoints*, November 6, 1971

(136) Plastic Ono Band. Give Peace a Chance, July 4, 1969

(137) Stewart, Jon. *Daily Show*, June 10, 2011

(138) Clinton, Hillary. MLK Day Speech to Canaan Baptist Church of Christ in Harlem, January 16, 2006

(139) *In Living Color,* Debuted April 15, 1990

(140) Carrey, Jim. *Ace Ventura, Pet Detective*, Debuted February 4, 1994

(141) Carrey, Jim. *YouTube* video, March 25, 2013

(142) Opcit, 141

(143) Carrey, Jim. *The Mask*, Debuted July 29, 1994

(144) Obama, Barack. Dreams from my father, Debuted July 18, 1995

(145) Damon, Matt. *Promised Land*, Debuted December 28, 2012

(146) Carrey, Jim. *The Cable Guy*, Debuted June 14, 1996

(147) Schneider, Rob. Deuce Bigolo, Male Gigolo, Debuted December 10, 1999

(148) *The View*, Debuted August 11, 1997

(149) Remy. Jim Carrey's Cold Dead Hand--A Rebuttal. *ReasonTV*, March 28, 2013

(150) Lott, John. Democrats supposedly never Demonized Republicans during budget battle, *JohnRLott.blogspot.com*, April 19, 2011

(151)   *Weekend at Bernie's*, Debuted July 5, 1989

(152)   Parks, Bert. *Wikipedia.org*

(153)   Leary, Timothy. *Wikipedia.org*

(154)   Douglas, Michael. Wall Street, Debuted December 11, 1987

(155)   Black Eyed Peas. Let's get it started. *Elephunk*, 2003

(156)   *The Beverly Hillbillies*, Debuted September 26, 1962

(157)   *Barnaby Jones*, Debuted January 28, 1973

(158)   Stewart, James B. *Blood Sport*, 1995

(159)   Sen. John Kerry docks new boat in Rhode Island, saving taxes. *Associated Press*, July 23, 2010

(160)   The Travails of Tom Daschle. *New York Jayson Blair Times*, February 2, 2009

(161)   Montopoli, Brian. Another Obama Nominee has Tax Issues. *CBS News*, March 31, 2009

(162)   Weiner, Rachel. Claire McCaskill admits to $287,000 in unpaid taxes on private plane. *Washington Post*, March 21, 2011

(163)   Bresnahan, John/Allen, Jonathan. House censures a defiant Charles Rangel by overwhelming vote. *Politico*, December 2, 2010

(164)   Geithner Apologizes For Not Paying Taxes, *CBS News*, January 21, 2009

(165)   Biden, Joe. Interview on *Good Morning America*, September 18, 2008

(166)   Matthews, Chris. 2008 Potomac Primary Coverage, *MSNBC*, February 12, 2008

(167)   *The Biggest Loser*, Debuted October 19, 2004

(168)   Goldfarb, Zachary. S&P downgrades U.S. credit rating for first time. *Washington Post*, August 6, 2011

(169)   Henderson, Nia-Malika. Maxine Waters to tea party: Go to Hell. *Washington Post*, August 22, 2011

(170)   *Driving Miss Daisy*, December 13, 1989

(171) Gates, Dominic. Boeing will build largest 787 model only in S. Carolina. *Seattle Times*, July 30, 2014

(172) 1999 Seattle WTO protests, *Wikipedia.org*

(173) Enola Gay, *Wikipedia.org*

(174) Bash, Dana. Weiner resigns after sexting scandal. *CNN*, June 16, 2011

(175) Cohen, Debra Nussbaum. Weiner's Jewish Problem, *The Jewish Daily Forward*, June 7, 2011

(176) Hatcher, Teri. The Implant. *Seinfeld*, February 25, 1993

(177) Desperate Housewives, Debuted October 3, 2004

(178) American Idol, Debuted June 11, 2002

(179) Celebrity Apprentice, Debuted January 3, 2008

(180) Platt, Larry. Pants on the Ground. *American Idol* audition, January 13, 2010

(181) Lopez, Jennifer. I'm Real, *J.Lo*, September 4, 2001

(182) Aerosmith. Walk on Water, *Big Ones*, 1994

(183) Adkins, Trace. Honky Tonk Badonkadonk. *Songs About Me*, October 3, 2005

(184) Rich, John/Fallon, Jimmy. Sung on *Celebrity Apprentice*, May 8, 2011

(185) Lady Gaga. Telephone, *The Fame Monster*, January 26, 2010

(186) Lady Gaga. Just Dance, *The Fame*, Debuted April 8, 2008

(187) Weiner apologizes to wife, family, Andrew Breitbart. *CBS News*, June 6, 2011

(188) Miller, Dennis. Appearance on *The O'Reilly Factor*, November 18, 2009

(189) SlutWalk. *Wikipedia.org*

(190) Old School, Debuted February 13, 2003

(191) Digital Underground. Same Song, *This is an EP Release*, July 1, 1991

(192) Divinyls, I touch myself, *diVINYLS*, December, 1990

(193) Jams. *Wikipedia.org*

(194) Barron, David H. *Days of Wine, Women and Wrong: The Further Scandals of Ted Kennedy—It Didn't End With Chappaquiddick!*, 1990

(195) Kardashian, Kim. Break The Internet. *PaperMag.com*, November 12, 2014

(196) Lewi, Marshall I. From Russia With Love. *The Harvard Crimson*, February 19, 1998

(197) Dallas, Debuted April 2, 1978

(198) Hagman, Larry. Interview on *BBC*, April 15, 2012

(199) Dynasty, January 12, 1981

(200) Falcon Crest, December 4, 1981

(201) Knots Landing, December 27, 1979

(202) Boteach, Shmuley. *Kosher Sex: A Recipe For Passion and Intimacy*, 1999

(203) Shane, Scott. Pornography is Found in Bin Laden Compound Files, U.S. Officials Say. *New York Jayson Blair Times*, May 13, 2011

(204) New York v. Strauss-Kahn. *Wikipedia.org*

(205) VandeHei, Jim. Kerry Drops Ball With Packer Fans, *Washington Post*, September 15, 2004

(206) Gore, Al. Speech at D.C. Fundraiser. *Chicago Tribune*, June 17, 1998

(207) Cillizza, Chris/Blake, Aaron. What President Obama's skeet shooting photo tells us. *Washington Post*, February 4, 2013

(208) Jacoby, Jeff. Obama's swelling ego. *Boston Globe*, November 14, 2009

(209) Goldsmith, Jonathan. *Wikipedia.org*

(210) Obama, Barack. Bowling at Altoona Bowling Center in Pennsylvania. *YouTube*, March 30, 2008

(211) Obama, Barack. Remarks at Baseball Hall of Fame in Cooperstown, New York, May 22, 2014

(212) Obama, Barack. Shooting hoops at annual White House Easter Egg Roll, *ABC News*, April 1, 2013

(213) Obama, Barack. Football toss with Chris Christie at Jersey Shore. *CBS News*, May 28, 2013

(214) Ifill, Gwen. Clinton Hunts, Making Point on Guns. *New York Jayson Blair Times*, December 28, 1993

(215) Palance, Jack. Doing one-armed pushups at the Academy Awards. March 30, 1992

(216) Murray, Bill. *Caddyshack*, Debuted July 25, 1980

(217) *Happy Gilmore*, Debuted February 16, 1996

(218) *Tin Cup*, Debuted August 16, 1996

(219) Pavlich, Katie. Anti-Islamic Filmmaker Sentenced to Year in Prison, *Townhall.com*, November 8, 2012

(220) Williams, Robin. *Live on Broadway TV Special*, July 14, 2002

(221) Roebling, Paul. Why Are Liberals Called Useful Idiots? *Mr. Writing*, 2012

(222) Youngman, Henny. Henry "Henny" Youngman, 1906-1998, *Qotd.org*

(223) Feinstein, Dianne. Senate Judiciary Committee Hearing, March 8, 2013

(224) Feinstein, Dianne. Appearance on CNN's *State of the Union*, January 27, 2013

(225) Cohen, Patricia. After 34 Years and Many Diets, "Cathy" Comic Strip to End, *New York Jayson Blair Times*, August 12, 2010

(226) Rock, Chris. *Chris Rock: Bigger and Blacker*, 1999

(227) Whitehead, Barbara Dafoe. Dan Quayle Was Right. *The Atlantic*, April 1, 1993

(228) Sally Forth, *Wikipedia.org*

(229) Wasserman Schultz, Debbie. Remarks at Milwaukee Athletic Club, September 3, 2014

(230) James, E.L. *Fifty Shades of Grey*, Debuted June 20, 2011

(231) Shakespeare, William. *Taming of the Shrew*, 1592

(232) NOW.org

(233) Boe, Eugene. *The Wit and Wisdom of Archie Bunker*, 1971

(234) Gowdy, Trey. Trey Gowdy Calls Nancy Pelosi "Mind-Numbingly Stupid." *On the Record With Greta Van Susteren*, February 16, 2014

(235) Limbaugh, Rush. *See I told you so*, November 1, 1993

(236) We shall overcome. *Wikipedia.org*

(237) Hands up, don't shoot. *Wikipedia.org*

(238) If I Had a Hammer. The Weavers, *If I Had a Hammer*, 1950

(239) Get a Job. The Silhouettes. *Get a Job*, October, 1957

(240) Saturday Night Live, April 8, 1995

(241) Shabazz, Malik Zulu aka Lewis, Paris S. *Wikipedia.org*

(242) Rodgers, Richard/Hart, Lorenz. Blue Moon, 1935

(243) McCartney Paul/Wonder, Stevie. Ebony and Ivory, *Tug of War*, March 29, 1982

(244) Bachmann, Michele. GOP Presidential Debate in New Hampshire, October 10, 2011

(245) Miller, Dennis. Appearance on *The O'Reilly Factor*, October 12, 2011

(246) Snipes, Wesley. *Passenger 57*, Debuted November 6, 1992

(247) The Time. 777-9311. *What time is it?* May, 1982

(248) The Time. Jerk Out. *Pandemonium*, 1990

(249) Prince. *Graffiti Bridge*, 1990

(250) Newton, John. *Amazing Grace*, 1779

(251) Obama, Barack. Campaign Rally in Roanoke, Virginia, July 13, 2012

(252) Obama, Barack. Press Conference in Holland, March 25, 2014

(253) Holan, Angie Drobic. Lie of the Year: "If you like your health care plan, you can keep it." *Politifact*, December 12, 2013

(254) Astley, Rick. Never Gonna Give You Up. *Whenever You Need Somebody*, July 27, 1987

(255) Flat Tire Cultists End up Deflated. *Associated Press*, December 29, 1992

(256) Krauthammer, Charles. *O'Reilly Factor*, 2012

(257) New World Order Conspiracy Theory. *Wikipedia.org*

(258) Ibid

(259) Deep Blue. *Wikipedia.org*

(260) Milli Vanilli, *Wikipedia.org*

(261) Milli Vanilli. Blame it on the Rain. *Girl you know it's true*, July 13, 1989

(262) Alfred E. Neuman, *Wikipedia.org*

(263) Obama, Barack. Interview on *Today*, June 7, 2010

(264) Norton, Edward. *Primal Fear*, Debuted April 3, 1996

(265) Haley, Jack. *The Wizard of Oz*, January 1, 1939

(266) Jarvik M.D., Robert. Jarvik 7, *JarvikHeart.com*, 1982

(267) Jeopardy, Debuted March 30, 1964

(268) Stanley Ann Dunham, *Wikipedia.org*

(269) Cartman's mom is still a dirty slut. *South Park*, April 22, 1998

(270) Carney, Art. The Expectant Father. *The Honeymooners*, 1952

(271) Soltis, Andy. Michelle not amused by Obama's memorial selfie. *New York Post*, December 10, 2013

(272) Mantegna, Joe/Sandler, Adam. *Airheads*, Debuted August 5, 1994

(273) Thicke, Robin/Cyrus, Miley. Video Music Awards, *MTV*, August 25, 2013

(274) Obama, Barack. Speaking at Campaign Rally in Chicago, Illinois, February 5, 2008

(275) Stein, Gertrude. *Wikipedia.org*

(276) Redding, Otis. Sitting on the dock of the bay, *Dock of the Bay*, January 8, 1968

(277) Trudeau, Garry. *Wikipedia.org*

(278) "Stand with Arizona Buycott" draws thousands to the Valley. *Phoenix News*, May 29, 2010

(279) Bjorklund, Dennis. *Toasting Cheers*, 1997

(280) Rooney Rule. Wikipedia.org

(281) Wong, Kristina. Farewell "Saved or Created": Obama Administration Changes the Counting of Stimulus Jobs. *ABC News*, January 11, 2010

(282) Obama, Barack. Remarks in Durham, North Carolina to his Council on Jobs and Competitiveness, October 13, 2010

(283) Gerson, Michael. *Wikipedia.org*

(284) Morning in America. *Wikipedia.org*

(285) Newsome, Hughey. Too Big for One Man, or Just Obama? *NationalCenter.org*

(286) Norris, Floyd. A Computer Lesson Still Unlearned. *New York Jayson Blair Times*, October 18, 2012

(287) Blake, Aaron. Six reasons Romney won the first debate. *Washington Post*, October 4, 2012

(288) Matthews, Chris. Hardball. *MSNBC*, August 30, 2012

(289) Obama signs fiscal crisis deal from Hawaii with autopen. *Fox News*, January 3, 2013

(290) Biden, Joe. Speech to Democrat National Convention in Charlotte, North Carolina, September 6, 2012

(291) Scott, Stuart. *ESPN*

(292) The Impeachment Trial of Alcee Hastings U.S. District Judge, Florida. *Senate.gov*, 1989

(293) Drudge, Matt. Clinton: Laughing about it. *Drudge Report*, July 20, 2004

(294) Marra, William C. Schumer Says Ideology is Fair Game in Judicial Confirmations. *The Harvard Crimson*, November 10, 2003

(295) Jehl, Douglas. Surgeon General Forced to Resign by White House. *New York Jayson Blair Times*, December 10, 1994

(296) Biz Markie. The Vapors. *Goin' Off*, 1988

(297) Breakin' 2: Electric Boogaloo, Debuted December 21, 1984

(298) McBride, Sarah. Mozilla CEO resigns, opposition to gay marriage drew fire. *Reuters*, April 3, 2014

(299) Vick, Karl/Surdin, Ashley. Most of California's Black Voters Backed Gay Marriage Ban. *Washington Post*, November 6, 2008

(300) O'Keefe, Ed. What the Senate's all-nighter on climate change is really about. *Washington Post*, March 10, 2014

(301) Greenfield, Daniel. The Jewish People vs George Soros. *Sultan Knish*, November 13, 2010

(302) Newcomb, Alyssa. Sexual Assaults Reported in "Occupy" Camps. *ABC News*, November 3, 2011

(303) Douglass, Frederick. If There Is No Struggle, There Is No Progress. *BlackPast.org* 1857

(304) Churchill, Winston. History will be kind to me for I intend to write it. *Brainyquote.com*

(305) United Nations Security Council Resolution 1441. *Wikipedia.org*

(306) Bush, George W. Interview with Candy Crowley. *CNN*, March 9, 2000

(307) Brazile, Donna. Brazile: Bush came through on Katrina. *CNN*, April 25, 2013

(308) Gurian, Scott. Two Years After Hurricane Sandy, New Jersey's Recovery Trudges Along. *NJSpotlight.com*, October 29, 2014

(309)   Raghavan, Sudarsan/Nakamura, David. Bush AIDS policies shadow Obama in Africa. *Washington Post*, June 30, 2013

(310)   Opcit, 129

(311)   Owens, Terrell. Terrell Owens most memorable moments. *FoxSports.com*, October 26, 2011

(312)   Cunningham, Lawrence. The Wild Eliot Spitzer. *Concurring Opinions*, July 30, 2013

(313)   Rangel, Charles. Appearance on *Hardball*, July 2, 2014

(314)   Kocieniewski, David. Rangel Censured Over Violations of Ethics Rules. *New York Jayson Blair Times*, December 2, 2010

(315)   Rashbaum. William K./Hakim, Danny/Kocieniewski, David/Kovaleski, Serge F. Question of Influence in Abuse Case of Paterson Aide. *New York Jayson Blair Times*, February 24, 2010

(316)   Leonnig, Carol D. Staffers' accounts paint more detailed, troubling picture of Massa's office. *Washington Post*, April 13, 2010

(317)   Bash, Dana/Jaffe, Alexandra. Michael Grimm announces resignation. *CNN*, December 30, 2014

(318)   Brooklyn Democratic Boss Seddio. *True News (The Bund),* September 27, 2012

(319)   Blau, Reuven. Brooklyn Democratic Party boss supports scandal scarred lawmaker, forcing other candidates with county support to run for cover. *Daily News*, July 30, 2014

(320)   Wyche, Sam. Speech in Cincinnati at Bengals Game. December 19, 1989

(321)   Leary, Dennis. *No Cure for Cancer*, Debuted January 12, 1993

(322)   Shawty Lo. *Wikipedia.org*

(323)   Salahi, Michaele. *Wikipedia.org*

(324)   *WKRP in Cincinnati*, Debuted September 18, 1978

(325)   Santana, Carlos. Smooth. *Supernatural*, Debuted June 29, 1999

(326) Hernandez, Sergio. Meet the Masseuse Who Says Al Gore is a Crazed Sex Poodle. *Gawker.com*, June 30, 2010

(327) Jesse Louis Jackson, Jr. *Wikipedia.org*

(328) Geiger, Kim/Skiba, Katherine. Ex-Illinois Congressman Mel Reynolds arrested in Zimbabwe. *Chicago Tribune*, February 18, 2014

(329) Robin Kelly: Conceal and Carry Failed in Aurora Shooting's Gun-Free Theatre. *TeaParty.org*, April 5, 2013

(330) Blagojevich, Rod. *Wikipedia.org*

(331) Plunkett, Jim/Newhouse, Dave. *The Jim Plunkett Story: The Saga of a Man Who Came Back*. September, 1981.

(332) *12 Years a Slave*, Debuted October 18, 2013

(333) Jackyl. Twice as Ugly. *Cut the Crap*, Debuted October 14, 1997

(334) Bates, Katharine Lee. *America the Beautiful*, 1895

(335) Rolling Stones. Brown Sugar. *Sticky Fingers*, April 16, 1971

(336) Raleigh, Walter. *Wikipedia.org*

(337) Cochran, Johnny. *Biography.com*

(338) Rosenhaus, Drew. Press Conference with Terrell Owens on November 8, 2005

(339) *Mean Girls*. Debuted April 30, 2004

(340) Obama: Police who arrested professor "acted stupidly." *CNN*, July 23, 2009

(341) Nugent, Ted. Wang Dang Sweet Poontang. *Cat Scratch Fever*, Debuted May, 1977

(342) Opcit, 321

(343) Big and Rich. Save a Horse, Ride a Cowboy. *Horse of a Different Color*, Debuted April 19, 2004

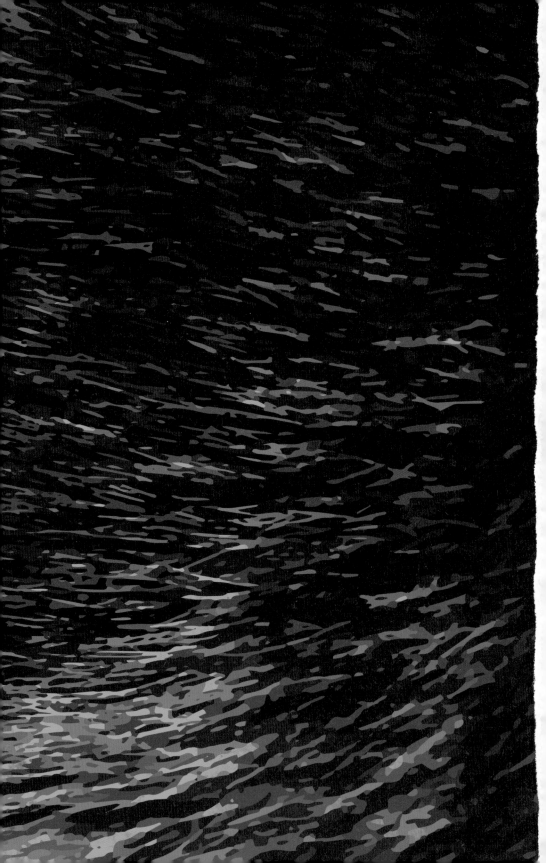

THE DAY THE RATS
VETOED CONGRESS

Publisher: GARY GROTH
Senior Editor: J. MICHAEL CATRON
Designer: JUSTIN ALLAN-SPENCER
Production: PAUL BARESH
Associate Publisher: ERIC REYNOLDS

Fantagraphics Books, Inc.
7563 Lake City Way NE
Seattle WA 98115
(800) 657-1100

Fantagraphics.com • Twitter: @fantagraphics • facebook.com/fantagraphics.

The text of *The Day the Rats Vetoed Congress* is slightly abridged from
Ralph Nader's *How the Rats Re-formed the Congress* (CSRL, 2018).
The illustrations by Mr. Fish are unique to this edition.

First Fantagraphics Books edition: August 2020
ISBN 978-1-68396-321-9
Library of Congress Control Number: 2019953941
Printed in the Republic of Korea

THE DAY THE RATS VETOED CONGRESS

A Fable of Citizen Action by RALPH NADER

Illustrations by MR. FISH

FANTAGRAPHICS BOOKS

SEATTLE

⊙ ⊙ ⊙

To Russell who provided the empiricism.

To the spirit of Voltaire and Mark Twain.

*To Molly Ivins, Dick Gregory, Jim Hightower,
and Victor Navasky who taught us how to laugh
ourselves serious.*

⊙ ⊙ ⊙

1 · Invader

IT WAS ONE of those uncomfortable morning strategy sessions with his senior staff. For House Speaker Reginald Blamer, the discomfort was in having to figure ways to continue blocking a long overdue raise in the federal minimum wage for many millions of low-income workers when he knew in his gut that it was not the right thing to do.

"We're in the crosshairs," he would say, starting such Congressional meetings in his spacious office.

Not that his anxiety would cause him to renege on the implicit promise he'd made to the Big Boys to stop the move in Congress to raise the minimum. But there was still background anxiety. After all, politicians are only human, and, like many, Speaker Blamer came from a large family that had lived through tightened circumstances. His father was a tavern keeper and his mother a seamstress. Deep anxiety, however, did have one inherent comfort at such morning gatherings; it tended to work in mysterious ways to overcome his morning constipation — the constant bane of The Speaker's existence. Holding down 30 million American workers — including among them many conservative voters, who are making less today than workers made in 1968, adjusted for inflation — bothered the very private, self-censored psychosomatic recesses of The Speaker's conscience.

And, so, not surprisingly, Speaker Blamer felt the onset of a solid bowel movement. He excused himself and repaired to his large private bathroom. As he sat down on the broad porcelain toilet, he felt that the expected discharge would be ample and prompt — no straining today. After quick breaks of the wind, The Speaker heard a sound inside the toilet. But it wasn't from his bowels. Lifting himself up a bit, he looked down and saw the head of a mostly submerged black rat closely eyeing his bottom.

"YEEEOW! YEEEEOW! YEEEOW!" bellowed The Speaker as he straightened up, slammed the cover down, and flushed.

Alarmed, the staff rushed to the bathroom door to respectfully call, "Speaker Blamer, are you all right? Do you need help?"

They dared not open the door. The Speaker did not tolerate any exposure of his privacy, especially being seen in his corpulent native suit.

Another, more normal person might have replied, "Yeah, I'm OK … it's just that there was a rat in the toilet bowl."

But Speaker Blamer was not a normal person. He had had to be super-cunning to get to his present station in life. Being cunning means you can instantly sense danger, being as alert as, say, a rat. And Speaker Blamer was already imagining the derisive headlines and the late-night-show jokes if he disclosed what really prompted his impulsive cries of sheer terror as he leapt from the "throne." So he replied, "Nothing much, boys, just one of those sudden spasms I get once in a while. Sure comes on fast — and goes away fast, too. I'll be right out."

Rejoining the staff at the head of the conference table, albeit full of gas and undischarged waste, The Speaker went through the checklist for crushing the hopes of the downtrodden multitudes. His Chief of Staff reviewed the usual elements of the campaign against workers. First off, The Speaker will say, "I always thought that if you raise the price of anything, you get less of it. The proposal to raise the minimum wage is a Job Killer!"

"Good sound bite," said his research assistant.

The Speaker nodded gravely, though when he heard the work "bite" he silently winced.

The operations assistant counted off the usual, reliable economics professors who would supply "objective" warning about losses of jobs and recession. The fast-food and big-box retailer associations had begun the large ad buy on television and radio with the announcers' stentorian voices of dire gravity. The K-Street lobbyists were already in action on Capitol Hill, marshaling the corporate PACS to make sure that this issue was on the front burner, hinting to legislators that their employers might see this as a litmus test as a condition for their donations. Op-eds, letters to the editors, and editorial condemnation of economically disruptive higher wages and layoffs were already in the pipeline.

About to burst, The Speaker could not wait to end the meeting. "OK, fellows, you seem to have the situation well in hand — it's not the first time we had to fight off this wage grab. Get to work."

They all scattered, including an irreverent intern who wondered to herself whether paying members of Congress more would mean the government would end up with less of *them*.

The moment the door to his spacious office closed, The Speaker lunged to his private toilet, whereupon he unloaded a vast quantity of feces: soft and semi-hard. Three bursts worth. Before he could enjoy a moment of quiet satisfaction, a shrill shriek lifted him up as his eyes bulged. It was the black rat swimming in the bowl propelling the terrified cry — "YEEEOW! YEEEOW! YEEEOW!"

Again he slammed down the toilet seat. He flushed and kept his hand on the flush handle, gritting his teeth as if to say: "On the way to oblivion, you dirty rat!"

His longtime secretary heard his yell and rushed to his bathroom. "Mr. Speaker, Mr. Speaker, what happened? Are you OK?"

Recovering his composure, he replied, "I'm OK, Sarah, just more of those sudden spasms. I've got to get some physical therapy. By the way, did you schedule that fundraiser next week for an hour later?"

"Yes, I did, Mr. Speaker," Sarah replied, sounding very relieved.

✳ ✳ ✳

Arriving home early that evening, he sat down to a healthy-diet supper prepared by his adoring wife, Regina. Their three children were grown up, living in distant states, and so they were "empty nesters."

"You seem unusually agitated, honey," said Regina. "Did you have a hard day?"

"It seems every day is a hard day in these times," he replied, shrugging off her concern. "What a great meal, as always, Regina! Now I need some relaxing reading. Do you know where we put that colorful book of animals that we got as a wedding anniversary gift years ago?"

"Why, yes, Reginald. It came in three volumes: mammals, reptiles, and insects. Tell me which one you want, and I will get it for you."

"Mammals," he replied.

Sitting in his study, The Speaker started reading about the rat.

> The word "rat" is derived from the Latin *rodere* which means "to gnaw." Rats produce litters several times a year, with high infant mortality. If seen as weak, newborns are eaten by their parents and their stronger siblings. Over the centuries, rats have developed uncanny abilities to survive dangers everywhere, especially those produced by their proximity to humans whose detritus and garbage ironically provide the means by which they prosper and create new nests. Rats live everywhere underground — under sewers, in buildings, highways, yards, cellars. They also wander to get food, which may involve killing any mammals smaller than they, including mice. They also eat insects. Their appetite is immense, facilitated by their sharp teeth. This leads some intrepid rats to wander into little known crevices and, yes, pipes. Restaurant kitchens and their refuse attract them since these animals have a strong sense of smell.

Then The Speaker, saw the words, "They even like feces." The Speaker had enough. But before he closed the book, he saw a footnote citing conversations that bloggers had with frightened people asking about rats swimming up the toilet bowl. The Speaker went to the sites. He learned that when sewer lines are in disrepair or when storms overpower the sewer system, rats see an opportunity. Most everybody knows that rats can run, climb, and leap up to three feet. Fewer know that rats can gnaw through concrete. Even fewer know what an impossibly tiny space rats can squeeze through when they smell food or prey. And who knows that rats can tread water for three days and can swim over a half mile to reach dry ground?

Flushing is only a temporary fix, for a rat can hold its breath until the water passes. Rats can even gain entry through the soil pipes (the pipes that carry "soiled" water from the toilets), then through the vent in the roof and down the pipe into the toilet. "Rats can always find a way if there is one," one plumber was quoted as saying.

The Speaker scrolled down to a section titled "Rats and Bubonic Plague, Typhus, and Rabies…" This time he really had enough and switched off his computer, retiring to his chambers, somewhat nauseous.

2 · Repeat Performance

THE NEXT MORNING AT THE OFFICE, he felt the urge and went into his bathroom, flushed the toilet three times, and sat down to do his business. It took about four minutes for the bowel movements to seriously commence, thanks to the unsung sphincter, when he felt something brush across his testicles. Springing up and looking down, he saw the black rat waving its whiskered head back and forth.

"EEEEYOW! EEEYOW!" The Speaker shrieked at the top of his lungs. Once again, his secretary rushed to the door to see if he was in need of help.

"It's that awful spasm again, Sarah. I'd better see the house doctor. Can you get me an appointment early tomorrow morning?" (He felt awful about lying, but there was no choice.)

The rat was still splashing around languidly, as if it were taking a bath, when he slammed down the toilet cover. He kept flushing the toilet until his back hurt. Quickly, he got a bottle of alcohol from the cabinet, poured it into his hand, and cuddled his balls to disinfect what he could. For good measure, he poured hydrogen peroxide into a cupped hand and rested his balls in that antiseptic liquid.

It turned out that as Sarah returned to her desk, she found The Reporter waiting for one of The Speaker's assistants who had agreed to be interviewed about some appropriations earmarked for The Speaker's district. He, too, heard the "EEEYOW! EEEYOW!"

"Who's that?" he asked, knowing it came from The Speaker's suite.

"Sometimes, the water comes out scalding hot, and it catches the person under the shower unaware," Sarah answered. (She felt awful about lying, but there was no choice.)

Meanwhile, The Speaker, about to burst, had to find an outlet to receive his deposits. Terror-stricken, he sat down on the edge of the bathtub and let it all out, come what may. Fortunately, the stools were very loose, and he quickly washed them down the drain with a tumbler filled with water. He then showered, dried himself, and dressed.

He was late for a meeting over the bill to weaken the Endangered Species Act. The get-together was with The Chairman of the Committee, a guy who hated wolves, a prejudice he had picked up from his upbringing on a cattle ranch in Montana.

The Chairman, whom The Speaker found surrounded by four grim-looking staffers, was determined to gut the law. The Speaker asked him whether he would add an amendment to make rats and cockroaches *more endangered* as species. Everyone thought The Speaker was being funny and didn't reply. The Speaker did not persist, going along with the chuckles to mask his inner turmoil.

3 · More Bathroom Business

OVER AT THE MINORITY LEADER'S SUITE, the dignified Marcy Melosay was finishing some camouflaged fundraising calls (ones absent a direct ask) when she felt nature's call. She, too, had trouble moving bowels early in the morning. She had always admired colleagues who could immediately defecate upon rising from bed. Never in her 28 years in the House could she acquire that blessing, that relief from feeling bloated and gassy. As a female public official, she had to be especially careful about farting, even when the gasses were building up to the breaking point. At extreme moments, she would excuse herself by appearing to have a coughing jag, go to her spacious bathroom, and sonorously break the wind.

"Ahh, thank goodness, I made it in time!" she would say to herself.

Today, it was almost noon when she excused herself, but not before telling her assistant to call her sister-in-law and cancel tomorrow's breakfast. The Minority Leader made a beeline to her own toilet, plunked herself down, and commenced serious discharge. She heard a noise. Lifting herself up and looking down, she saw a black rat smothered with fresh feces.

The reaction from her was an earsplitting, prolonged scream, "Ahhhh-hhh, ahhhhh, ahhhhhkheee!"

Startled, the rat scurried back down the pipe as The Minority Leader ran from the throne, soiling the floor and nearly tripping on her panties. She rested her trembling hands on the sink. Her longtime assistant, Velvet, rushed to the bathroom door exclaiming, "Miss Melosay, Miss Melosay, do you need anything?"

"Yes, please," The Minority Leader responded just above a whisper. Velvet rushed in and her beloved boss told her what happened between gasps of breath.

A matronly 66-year-old, Velvet cradled Ms. Melosay in her arms and assured her that all is well when it ends well. The rat was probably scared, too, Velvet added reassuringly. The Minority Leader managed a wan smile, but she continued to shake uncontrollably.

"You may wish to take a shower to calm down and soothe your nerves, Ms. Melosay," Velvet suggested. The diminutive Minority Leader nodded. Velvet turned on the spray and adjusted the temperature so The Minority Leader could take a very long shower.

Again, The Reporter just happened to be in the sitting room and heard the screams.

4 · Synchronicity

THE NEXT NOON, The Speaker and The Minority Leader found themselves together at a Joint Session of Congress to honor the return of American Israeli soldiers from crushing Gaza again with weapons made in America. The keynote speaker was the Prime Minister of Israel, whose past addresses to this august body had rated standing applause, coming (on the average) after every 35 words.

Going through the minds of both The Speaker and The Minority Leader was the fear that standing ovations of such frequency would trigger an uncontrollable surge of defecation. Excusing themselves in the midst of this command performance would be disastrous, for without admitting the cause, which would have provoked muffled guffaws, The Speaker and The Minority Leader might be unfairly accused of thinly veiled anti-Semitism. Talk about being between a rock and a hard place.

The standing ovations continued with staccato predictability and reached a crescendo when The Prime Minister declaimed loudly that he was amazed that people didn't realize Iran was the biggest threat to the world since Hitler. It was also amazing, if of less global significance, that when under enormous pressure to contain one's bodily emissions, there is an impressive display of the discipline known as mind over matter. Immediately after the

32nd and last standing ovation, The Speaker quickly and profusely thanked The Prime Minister and the soldiers and adjourned the session. Both he and The Minority Leader raced to their respective restrooms for immediate relief. The Reporter noticed their respective beelines and began to wonder.

For a couple of days, whenever nature called, The Speaker and The Minority Leader made some excuse to use their staffs' toilets, because they couldn't stand the return of the cold fear they'd each experienced in their boudoirs. Lo and behold, one day the staff toilets were occupied, so The Speaker and The Minority Leader both nervously sat down in their own respective spaces, and, once again, in the midst of doing their business, they heard, they rose, they looked, and they screeeeeched at the top of their lungs. There was a black, grinning rat in each bowl.

They did what they had to do. The Speaker drained his bathtub. The Minority Leader had to finish her business in her shower stall since, being in the minority, she was not allotted a bathtub. The Minority Leader's confidant, Velvet, learned what had happened to her leader while The Speaker's staff heard about his "spasm" again.

Having not gotten his interview earlier, the same Reporter had returned and once again heard the screams coming from The Minority Leader's interior office suite. His wonder turned into operational curiosity.

The Minority Leader warned Velvet to tell no one about what happened. "NO ONE!"

"Why, of course," Velvet replied in a tone that suggested such an admonition was not needed. Leader Melosay told Velvet to get The Speaker on the phone immediately.

5 · A Call to Action

THE SPEAKER PICKED UP HIS PHONE to take the call from The Minority Leader. "Speaker," she told him calmly, "we have a rodent problem. They've been seen scurrying around the carpets in recent days, both rats and mice, which means there are nests. They are probably coming up from the Catacombs beneath the Capitol." (The Minority Leader hated to lie, but there was no choice.)

She asked The Speaker to request an inspection by the rodent and insect extermination unit, which was under the House Administration Committee's jurisdiction.

Of course, The Speaker assured her he would do so immediately and revealed that he, too, had been told by staff that the little creatures were running all over their carpets, as well. (He hated to lie, but there was no choice).

The Minority Leader asserted that the rodent invasion must be systemic, and she joked about the rare bipartisan display of remedial action to come. Lowering his voice, The Speaker suggested that the requested action should be seen as a very routine inspection to avoid the press making more of it than was deserved. The Minority Leader, possessed of similarly sensitive political antennae, agreed and, before closing, requested that her office be given advance notice of the inspectors' arrival and be told what kinds of rodenticide would be employed.

"Will do," said The Speaker. "Talk to you soon."

However, for The Speaker, the matter was not so simple. Suppose the inspectors found nothing — not a hole, not a hair, not a dropping — but, not wanting to disappoint their superiors, they recommended that rat poison be placed around the suites. The Speaker knew that would not solve his problem, which was The Toilet! He could not, would not, give away his secret to the inspectors that rats were bobbing around in his personal commode, for then there would be the inevitable leak. Between the rat in the toilet and the yelling, people would start putting two and two together. With over 450 full-time, snooping reporters covering Capitol Hill — "ditto heads," he derisively called them — plenty would rush to pursue this story.

"They always have an anal complex," The Speaker thought to himself, chuckling over his own wit.

He decided to let his Exterminators do what they urged, if only because their application provided a cover for any later media inquiry. Within a few hours, poison bait and rat traps were situated in circumspect locations around his suite. The Speaker called and told The Minority Leader to schedule a similar remedy for her offices.

Both The Speaker and The Minority Leader knew that this was not going to solve their own very personal problems. The individual rats were entering the toilet bowl from a pipe that was far removed from the rat traps. Neither politician could think of a way to tell the other what each was going through since they did not know they shared a common, horrifying experience. Such was their conundrum.

6 · In the Underground

MEANWHILE, DOWN DEEP in the Capitol's underworld, activity of another sort was taking place. It was going on in a vast subterranean area where gigantic steam pipes sweat side by side with other engineering systems that keep the vast buildings above operating technically, if not legislatively. This is terrain so occupationally hazardous that no member of Congress, regardless of position or seniority, is allowed to enter the elevators and descend to the bottom. Heavy metal particulates, including asbestos, and noxious emissions have long plagued the small number of security-cleared, skilled workers who complain, to no avail, about their chronic health problems.

For rodents and insects, however, the immense space was a favorite scampering (and camping) ground, but one with few ascending apertures. Except, that is, for the odorous sewage pipes. Rats and mice were curious about these laden pipes, but the water that washed down them irritated their fur. Far more tempting were the crumbs and foodstuffs left overnight or discarded by the workers.

Very recently, however, a startling development had opened new opportunities for the rodents in their nonstop quest for nutrients. (Rats, as noted previously, were known to gnaw through concrete to get to something tasty.)

Both The Speaker and The Minority Leader, importuned by salespeople, had agreed to install electric garbage disposals in their kitchenette sinks. This was for the politicians' convenience when they did not have time to go to lunch or dinner and didn't particularly relish takeout. Their staff could cook something up reflecting their bosses' tastes at the moment. Also, exercising a little *noblesse oblige*, our solons let the cleaning people use the cooking facilities in the evening if those workers had to heat their takeouts.

The cleaners were sternly instructed to leave no crumbs behind. But they let fall down through the grinders a stream of what the rats would call a dream banquet of flavorsome smoothies whose irresistible odor drew these hardy survivalists into bolder and bolder adventures in upward mobility.

Soon the rats realized it was only a frolic and a detour to enter the sewer pipe to the toilet bowl. This would have been an easy connection to make by The Exterminators if only they had been told the real story, which was that the rats were treating the toilets as their private oases.

7 · Rumblings

"WHAT TO DO? WHAT TO DO?" whispered The Speaker to himself, as he was busy over stacks of paperwork or conducting short meetings with legislative assistants and colleagues.

Before leaving for home, he called Regina and asked if he could have a big bowl of boiled prunes with a little ice cream for dessert.

His wife understood and replied, "Why, of course, dear."

Later, at the dinner table, The Speaker consumed every last prune, washing them down with warm water to achieve the desired combination for an early morning bowel movement to be consummated in his home john. Alas, it was not to be. He left home the next morning still filled. However, by the time his limousine reached the House Office Building, he was feeling a rumble — the deferred prune effect — that reached an intolerable level, nearly overcoming his suppressive mind control. He raced past a startled Sarah into his restroom and, taking no chances, unloaded directly into his bathtub.

"How long can this go on?" he asked himself while breathing a sigh of sublime relief.

Meanwhile, a few miles away at NSA Headquarters, a three-person surveillance team, specializing on Congress, was connecting certain strange dots. Their sensors had picked up the bellows, screams, conversations, and even mutterings of The Speaker and The Minority Leader. At first, they suspected the rats were the products of animal-directed sabotage by terrorists. After all, the CIA, going back decades, had been expertly training ravens, dolphins, cats, and other animals to be carriers for espionage activities. After spending several days sifting and arranging the metadata, the team concluded that the precipitating events were just what they were: *ferae naturae* doing its instinctual thing. Not of concern. However, they parked the information in a specially encrypted electronic file titled, "To be *seeded* if necessary."

Two days later, The Reporter was sitting in The Minority Leader's office, having been given a rain ticket by staffer Joanna Swift, who had had to cancel the prior appointment. Ms. Swift gave as her reason an emergency call that came in from a group of constituents in her boss's district. But the real cause of cancellation was that Ms. Swift was not fully prepared for the questions that this legendary lone wolf reporter could be expected to ask. (She hated to lie, but there was no choice.)

At 11:00 a.m. sharp, Ms. Swift bounded from her small office to cheerfully greet The Reporter and usher him to a chair by her desk.

"Sorry about last time," she said.

"Forget it. Things happen," replied The Reporter.

He adjusted his tape recorder and launched immediately into a touchy subject.

"Before I get into my investigation of what your leadership is doing about timed insider stock trading, revealed recently, as you know, by a freelance author, to be widespread in the House, I'm curious about something else. In the anteroom, I saw two large boxes labeled 'portable toilets'. Is there something seriously wrong with the plumbing?"

The Reporter looked casual, in a "by-the-way" manner.

Ms. Swift blushed, but, suspicious of his uncharacteristic casualness, felt it was better to reveal some of the truth, and so blurted out, "There's been a rodent problem we're having attended to by the House Exterminators."

"Oh?" said The Reporter. "That's not so infrequent. But in the toilets?"

"Well ... yes, it actually has been quite frightening," she responded.

This is where experience comes in. The savvy Reporter skipped the usual follow-up inquiry — "What do you mean?" — and probed, "So, that's what the screams were about from The Minority Leader's suite when I was here waiting the other day."

Ms. Swift felt a trap was about to be sprung. She wasn't supposed to know what only The Minority Leader and Velvet knew, but "mum's the word" has a notoriously short life in Congressional offices. Now she was facing double jeopardy: letting a reporter, no less, know what she wasn't supposed to know herself.

"I really don't know what you're talking about. Screams? I didn't hear any screams."

Her office was on the side of the suite where the staffers did hear the screams. (She hated to lie, but there was no choice.)

"Can we get back to your interest in what The Minority Leader is doing about the report of insider trading among some of her fellow Democrats?"

"Yes, yes, by all means," rasped The Reporter, who knew he was on to what his colleagues would call a very high-rated story. But he decided it was best not to press any further with this inadvertent informer.

8 · Out of the Bag

A COUPLE OF HOURS LATER, The Minority Leader returned to her offices and was pleased with the sight of the portable toilets. It wasn't fun exercising bowel movements in a shower stall. In a moment of collegiality, she called The Speaker and told him of her temporary solution. The Speaker, smiling to himself, told her that "great minds think alike," and that his portable toilets had arrived today as well.

The Minority Leader wondered, "Does the plural mean that the problem has spread to other toilets in your suite?"

"Well, yes, as a matter of fact. How about for you?"

"It has. In another bathroom, my assistant came upon a dead mouse floating in the bowl. It was too much for her, and she had to go home early," averred The Minority Leader, in an upset tone.

"Wow, wow, do you think the *rat* is out of the bag, so to speak?" said The Speaker with high concern.

"Not if I can help it, but I may not be able to help it," worried The Minority Leader.

"You took the words out of my mouth."

Ms. Melosay replied, "We'd better stay in close touch, Mr. Blamer."

Brought together by the common problem, they were already on a last-name basis.

9 · Party Time I

THAT NIGHT, the nocturnal rodents, down deep in the Congressional Catacombs, were having a ball. More than bits of food were everywhere. Whole chunks had been cast aside by the workers who were celebrating the retirement of one of their crew (sadly, he had incurable emphysema). And what chunks: fish, chicken, and steak bones that were easily accessible in overflowing, uncovered trash cans. The rats, with their ever-growing incisors, loved the bones.

At the same time, the regular Thursday evening "small parties of relief," as they were called, were underway upstairs, put together by staffers whose bosses were returning to their districts until the next week's Tuesday-through-Thursday work period came around. The food digesters (i.e., garbage disposals) in The Speaker's and The Minority Leader's offices were kept busy, which, in turn, kept the sewer rats and mice deliciously busy, eating and populating. Well-fed and protected from most predators, the litters poured out of the mothers' wombs in their dark nests.

The staff flushed away quite a few visiting rats in the regular toilet bowls, more with disgust than fear now that they were using portable toilets themselves. They still expected The Exterminators to eventually enforce eradication. The staff members were oblivious to the fact that the rat killers did not know about the toilet bowl visits and so were concentrating their poisons and traps in nooks and crannies away from the main rat pathways.

10 · A Clean Breast

ARRIVING AT HOME FOR DINNER with Regina, The Speaker was unusually troubled, as his wife recognized by noting how he raised his eyebrows in fast succession. His wife rarely saw such signs of deep worry. "Tell me, dear,

what is eating at you these days? There is nothing in the news that could explain your vintage eyebrow flutters."

The Speaker sighed deeply, thinking that if he couldn't divulge what was happening — his private, personal secret — to his beloved wife of 42 years who knew every inch of his body, who else could he reveal it to? The moon? So he began.

"My dear, something is happening in my office. No, it doesn't involve great matters of state or whispers of some forthcoming exposé of corruption in the House of Representatives. To cut to the chase, it involves rats coming up inside my toilet while I am sitting ... yes, sitting answering nature's call. I heard splashes, and a rat brushed against my testicles before I leapt up screaming. When my staff came running, I made up the excuse that it was an old spasm acting up suddenly." He then recounted what had transpired afterward.

Regina was still puzzled. It wasn't her husband's fault in any way.

"Why are you so upset?" she asked.

The Speaker put down his fork and took a deep breath. "My dear, if this situation reached the media, it would be very serious for your poor husband. Politics is all about deception, distraction, and appearances. Take away the appearance, the decorum, the surface dignity and neatness, and all hell will start to break loose. Once we are mocked, satirized, and laughed at due to a story that is tailor-made for public ridicule by just about every part of the news and entertainment business, we will lose the sheen that glosses over what we're doing and not doing. That varnish is keeping us low in the polls, but not affecting our re-elections. It's about the consequences of the Emperor having no clothes!

"Consider the meticulous attention we give to appearances, to the protective gloss. We are immaculately dressed. You instinctually grasp this whenever, before I leave for work in the morning, you point out a slight slant to my tie or a wisp of hair sticking out of my coif. Notice that when you see members of Congress head for the floor with their entourage, you can always tell the legislator as the one who is erect, striding forward with confidence. Posture is crucial to an appearance of stature and dignity. It's maintained with aplomb by a legislator even after he's gone through such sordid exposés as being caught frequenting prostitutes, cheating on his wife, or thrashing others in alcoholic fits."

At this point, Regina wasn't sure if her husband was talking to her or giving a speech, but she listened patiently.

"Consider how daily attention by a large cleaning and maintenance staff is given to our offices, our corridors, our hearing rooms, the furniture, the flags, and the plaques. These are all symbols that protect our appearance of dignity. Take that dignity away and then the awe of power, affecting friend and foe, dissolves, and we descend to the level of despised next-door neighbors. Why do you think our concise, level-toned statements to the press are so carefully scripted to prevent any slip of the tongue or eruption of raging emotions signifying lack of control?

"Bring up the subject matter of sexual parts being nearly nibbled — even fondled! — by rats, and the ranting of every two-bit radio or TV commentator, columnist, talk-show host, cartoonist — not to mention every water-cooler conversation across the nation — will go wild with ribald ridicule. And now there is the internet — an endless vacuum for gossip already — and you've got the whole world guffawing and hungry for the latest development. And believe me, this is a story that will keep on giving, because, as of now, I don't see any light at the end of the tunnel if the episodes, which I suspect are also happening to Marcy Melosay, are not suppressed from public view."

"Marcy Melosay?" asked Regina with a wink of jealousy. "How do you know?"

"We've talked, and I learned we've both ordered portable toilets, if you know what I mean," The Speaker confided.

"How many people know the actual, intimate details?" she asked.

"I can't say. My entire office knows about the rats there, but how many know about the rats in the toilet with me sitting there depends on how many can connect my terrifying outcries from fear of the scurrying creatures on the floor to my fear of being emasculated on the throne.

"You know, Regina, if The Exterminators continue to plant their rat poison, and the rats keep coming, who is going to adhere to any oath or secrecy? It is just too good a conversation piece, since everybody fears rodents and loves to talk about that fear. So it is not just a matter of protecting the boss. Sure, the story of rat infestation may be big enough to absorb my personal incident, but not if others are having the same experience when they are on their toilets. Going public will affect both the whole institution and each member, providing the greatest possible ammunition for taunting, jeering, mocking, and the asserting of utter Congressional incompetence.

"I can see the headlines: 'Rats Play Catch with Lawmakers' Balls,' 'They Are Worth Something: Speaker's Balls Attract Rats,' 'Hungry Rats Invade House Toilet Bowls, Spreading Terror Where the Sun Don't Shine,' 'Why is Speaker Blamer Screaming in His Bathroom?' 'Unlike The People, Rats Gain Access to Politicians.' And those, my dear, are just the first-stage headlines, assuming the rat invasion goes no further."

By this time, Regina was convulsed with laughter. For the life of her, she couldn't take the matter as seriously as her husband did. "Don't worry, dear, The Exterminators will take care of the rats. Meanwhile, why don't you wear that heavy jockstrap left over from your football-playing days? It'll protect you from any first swipe and still leave your anus open for discharge. Just kidding. Have some more prunes to get you going early before you leave for work."

11 · To the Next Level

IN THE NEXT SEVERAL DAYS, two developments converged. The Exterminators, who, in their professional zeal, wanted to leave no rat hiding place undisturbed, received permission to descend to the Catacombs to place their rat poison everywhere. They saw lots of food-bits discarded by the workers. Their strategy was to get the rats before the rascals even thought of ascending through the pipes. The food thrown here and there would be the bait and the poison they added to the debris would finish off the pests.

As many humans have done in the past, they underestimated the intelligence of rats, who make connections, learn, and transfer their learning to their close kin. After some casualties, the rats figured the food placed near them was hazardous, and they started going back upstairs, accompanied by mice. They preferred the safety of the pipes going to The Speaker and The Minority Leader's splendid accommodations to the dangers of the tainted food. The rats were aided by another development. The nighttime workers had increased the discarded food sent down the digesters in order to keep down the volume of garbage they left behind, which might indicate the size of their supper and the time they gave to its consumption.

One day, Speaker Blamer entered his bathroom to use his portable toilet only to see a mouse perched on the sink. The next day, he saw a young rat trapped in the bathtub. He bludgeoned the intruder to death with his large hair brush. "Ugh, ugh, ugh!" he exclaimed. "I can't take this anymore!" Whereupon he rushed into his office and dialed his special administrative assistant, Duke.

Duke, an ex-infantry captain, strode in smartly with an urgent message of his own to deliver. But first he had to hear out his boss.

"Duke, the Exterminators cannot do the job by themselves. Get me the most aggressive cat you can find to stay here, 24/7."

"Yes sir, on the double. But I have been instructed to tell you that the House Administrator has been receiving dozens of calls today. It seems that last night there was a mass invasion of rats and mice into the offices of scores of House members. It seems," he said, "that something happened below to drive them en masse from their lairs."

A preliminary inquiry revealed that the workers themselves had brought in several cats to drive away the rats, whose keen sense of smell detected the cats far and near. Thus, the flight northward occurred more quickly. The Exterminators received a rush of calls from Republican and Democratic offices. Some staff went home in fright. The rat killers knew that the density of rats within the Congressional complex of buildings was much higher per person than elsewhere for two reasons. One was the absence of natural predators in so many secluded enclaves. Second was the presence of so many cafeterias, reception areas, vending machines, and exposed garbage disposals. Rat heaven!

12 · Enter the Fourth Estate

THE REPORTER WAS PUTTING the finishing touches on his core story about the rat incursions when he got a call from a tipster over at the House Administration Committee about the rat invasion. It looked like the whole thing was about to come to light. He called his editor to tell him that if he wanted a scoop he had "to move *prontissimo*." The Reporter's crisp, wry, but factual narrative was sent in with the headline:

> RATS, AHOY! SPEAKER BLAMER AND MINORITY LEADER MELOSAY
> RECEIVE TERROR JOLT THAT
> NEARLY TOPPLES THEM FROM THEIR THRONES.

The editor wanted an even more racy title, but The Reporter said no — it was his reputation at stake, not the editor's. He preferred a deadpan style:

House Speaker Reginald Blamer and Minority Leader Marcy Melosay are like ordinary Americans in basic ways. About every day, they have to defecate while at work. Recent days, however, have been a nightmare that few ordinary Americans have had to experience. Black rats have been surfacing in the toilet bowls of both legislators' private bathrooms at the exact moment when Mr. Blamer and Ms. Melosay were dropping their drawers to have a bowel movement. They had no advance warning, so it was terrifying when they heard a rustling below and looked down to catch a horror in the making. Your reporter, by sheer coincidence, happened to be in both offices when the hair-raising screams reverberated from the leaders' suites. Such outcries are not the usual auditory experience for visitors to the offices of Congressional legislators.

Reliable sources said that the purchase of portable toilets — which this visitor saw delivered — was prompted by the invasion of rats apparently rising from the

Catacombs beneath Congress. Sources added that Exterminators were called to position rat poison throughout the office suites. Yesterday's expansion of the rat invasion to other House of Representatives' offices is being attributed to the lack of garbage control and the retention of cats deep under the Congress by the underground workers, who were trying to contain or drive away the infestation of rodents. The rats fled the cats and found their way up the pipes into the lawmakers' bathrooms.

There is no evidence that the rats' incisors made any contact with the underbodies of Speaker Blamer or Minority Leader Melosay. No schedules were disrupted. The House Clinic was not visited on those days by the two solons.

With the spread of the rats to other offices, there are reports of terrified staff rushing home from their jobs out of stark fear. Rats are known to bring a variety of diseases and infectious pathogens. As of this writing, the situation seems to be getting direr and is nowhere near coming under control. The Congressional press corps is requesting a news briefing from both leaders inasmuch as rumors, some lurid, are outrunning the available facts. This is truly a breaking news story. There is much more information that the public has a right and a need to know about. Check our website for up-to-the-minute postings.

The Reporter's story almost blew out the search engines. The visits, hits, clicks — call them what you will — came pouring down like a full-blown avalanche in the Alps. The Reporter had told himself he wasn't going to lose a minute scrolling down to read the comments on his exclusive. This was breaking news, and he had to concentrate every moment on keeping ahead of his colleagues, who were now joining the emerging bedlam.

13 · Will It Never End?

Then what had to happen, happened. Loretta Langone, sitting at her computer working up material to be sent to the *Congressional Record* for her boss, Arkansas Congressman Sebastian Savant, felt something crawling up her ankle. She instinctively pulled back her foot and looked down to see a mouse with a death grip on her sock. What happened next was the sound of "AARGHASYEEEK!" as Ms. Langone fell backward, tipping her chair over as her knees upended her computer.

The mouse dropped the sock, spun away, and disappeared from view. Her co-workers rushed over, but Ms. Langone lunged toward the door, bolted down the wide corridors of the Russell House Office Building, ran down the stairwell and out the door, and hailed a cab to take her home. Sobbing, breathing heavily, and shaking with fear, she allowed her imagination to conjure up what further horrors could have happened if the mouse had had his way with her.

Of course, it was not long before a gaggle of reporters rushed to Congressman Savant's office only to find that their smartphones were ringing with news of other rodent-to-human episodes in other Congressional offices. After a moment of cognitive dissonance, each went to what the newsperson believed to be the most newsworthy destination. To some, that meant dashing to the Senate where all rat hell was breaking loose as the rodents were looking for pipes, apparently happy to be in ones not as crowded with fellow beasts as were those in the House plumbing. Those reporters reasoned that Senators are just bigger news.

14 · Damage Control

SPEAKER BLAMER BEGAN to experience the early stages of panic. He phoned Senate Majority Leader Horatio Clearwater to urge that they join together in closing the Congress for at least a day. Though he could visualize the expected headlines: "Rats Chase Politicians From Capitol Hill," he had to thwart further incidents and real panic. There could be blood on the floor. Senator Clearwater readily concurred but insisted that the Capitol Police stay on the job. "It wouldn't be good for morale and our law-and-order stance were they to be seen as being chased out by rats," he explained.

Since it was a Thursday, early in the Congressional session, there would be no appropriations or other legislative emergencies complicating the need for at least a three-day shutdown. The two also decided to call on President Winston DooLittle to proclaim a Congressional state of emergency — based on health and safety factors — in order to avail the Congress of the expert resources and assistance of the Executive Branch.

Speaker Blamer — the more politically savvy of the two — said that they should immediately request The Centers for Disease Control to dispatch teams that would highlight the diseases and pathogens that could emerge to spread beyond the confines of Congress. At his upcoming news conference, he would also note that rats were the carriers of the deadly bubonic plague, which, as recently as the 14th century, had caused devastation in Europe. "Such menacing references," he asserted, "will direct the public's attention toward possible epidemics instead of allowing them to follow their natural inclination to treat the shutdown as a laugh fest."

Senator Clearwater responded with some skepticism as to whether this maneuver would work, but he concluded it was worth trying, especially if The Speaker had experts to back him up and could exhibit some killer rats at his press conference so that revulsion would replace the fast spreading derision. They both issued the order to evacuate all nonessential personnel until further notice.

Putting down the phone, The Speaker felt wet under his armpits — an unusual sign of stress. He closed his eyes, dreading the media's demand for an immediate press conference. Then he thought of a way to gain more time. He would tell the press (or, rather, his Press Secretary would inform them) that he would go on Sunday's *Meet the Press* and answer any questions.

"He has to fully concentrate right now on defeating the rats," explained his Press Secretary to a crowd of raucous newspeople.

The President quickly obliged the legislators by issuing an emergency proclamation, calling the rats "animal terrorists," which led him to further call up teams of Special Forces, the CIA, and the NSA to focus their talents on this city within a city called Congress and its 33,000 employees.

"You can't negotiate with rats," he declared. "They have to be killed or captured."

Shutting down Congress had the benefit of shutting down the press — at least *in situ*. The reporters had to clear out of their Capitol Hill pressrooms along with the lawmakers and staff. The reporters still tried to find contacts on the Hill, but there was no one around except the Capitol Police, and they were not talking. So they started working their smartphones and, when they occasionally got through to a potential source, they soon found out that there weren't many new details except for stories of fear, dread, and hot-footed escape. How many stories about such matters can you do? Moreover, Congressional staff was instructed to say very little to the media.

15 · The Lay of the Media Land

THE REPORTER WROTE HIS COLORFUL STORIES to keep his website buzzing. But he knew the deeper news was the question of what was being done to the rats and, more importantly, what he saw as the looming political fallout from the masses. He got his answer to the first question when, moving down to the freight entrance, he saw trucks with cages of cats going into the garages. He followed them and saw the cages unloaded and taken by workers to various parts of the Capitol. The cats were not languid pussycat types — they were mean alley cats, and, as one unloader told him, "They are specially suited to pursue rats directly and to leave their urine around, which will scare off the rats they can't catch."

Once again, the rats were underestimated. The urine scent simply drove them back into the Catacombs and into new, unexplored spaces. Sure,

several hundred rats would be killed, along with a few cats, but there were thousands more, not counting the mice.

The Reporter knew the public would be interested in the origins of The Speaker's discovery in his bathroom. But he thought: Now is not the time. Now was the time for him to stay ahead of the developing story so that the insatiable public would see his website as the go-to site for the latest eruptions. First, The Reporter needed to scan the media coverage and the audience feedback. He found it was journalistic bedlam. The rat invasion was such an off-the-charts story, without precedent, that it produced a riot of rumors, sneers, editorializing in news reports, satiric condescension, and wild cartoons. The right-wing radio talk-show hosts went wild even by their brutish standards. All their venom, scarcely suppressed in normal hours, exploded like a volcano. One host, in a tone of savage seriousness, urged an indefinite shutdown of Congress, saying that the rats could run the place better and not cost the taxpayers as much.

The conspiracy boys were having a field day with their callers. Some opined that this was all a plot hatched by pinko lawmakers who wanted to avert an upcoming tax-cut debate favored by all red-blooded Americans. "It's all about distracting us and giving these critters some more vacation time," drawled a Texan caller.

A letter to the editor by a super patriot demanded that all American flags on the Capitol be taken down. "How can our beloved flag fly over buildings dominated by hordes of rats?" she wrote. One news headline, decrying the "mum's the word" posture of the lawmakers, declared, "Congress United Not to Talk: Rats Achieve the Ultimate Filibuster Shutdown."

The Reporter always admired cartoonists as being the least restrained but most imaginative of his journalistic colleagues. He was not disappointed. One after another drew cartoons of the terror-stricken Speaker and Minority Leader in their bathrooms reacting to the officious rodents whose facial expressions conveyed a "What the heck is going on here?" message. A particularly good one showed an armada of weapons moving toward the Congress followed by (in the next panel) a group of rats dining on some spilled food, with one rodent speculating, "Do you think they'll use an F-35?"

The late-night TV shows showcased a range of experts whose attempts at serious commentary produced even greater laughter from the audiences. A medical specialist in infectious diseases pondered the effect of rat bites on different parts of the human anatomy. When a psychologist was asked whether the Congressional buildings could ever be a place where young women would wish to start their careers, he replied, "Why did you single out young women?"

"Well," replied the host, "don't they have the most horrifying eek factor?" The audience groaned and laughed at the same time.

The mainstream press tried to cover the rampage as a serious obstruction of government, a health problem, and a foreign policy setback due to the disrespectful global press treatment. At the White House press briefing, reporters asked with whom The President was meeting. They reasoned emergency declarations are associated with emergency meetings. The Press Secretary said that The President was meeting with leaders of Congress and with his national security and health teams.

"Toward what end?" exclaimed the reporter from the *Washington Toast*.

"Toward developing a rapid response with first responders to overcome the scourge and its contamination," said the Press Secretary.

"Are the State Department and the Department of Defense engaged at all here?" queried the reporter from the *New York Chimes*.

"They are on alert to detect any foreign powers trying to take advantage of our Congressional emergency and are ready to respond to any foreign attempts to turn a serious health problem into an object of caricature or lampooning. After all, there are plenty of rat problems in every country," asserted the insurgent Press Secretary. "Indeed, the French Parliament was overrun by rats in 1952, but nobody talks about that."

(In his mind, the Press Secretary was thinking of the global image problem that the rat invasion was causing. He couldn't say it this way, but the nation's image was taken very seriously by the DooLittle Administration, especially because The President's surname made him the butt of many demeaning jokes.)

The Congressional invasion of the rats was a difficult matter for the media to handle, despite its sensational dynamic. There was really no one to blame, there were no prior pro-rat proclamations by politicians to highlight hypocrisy, and there were no grounds to pit one elected official against another — the rats were bipartisan in their nomadic ventures. There were no laws violated or unenforced and there were no human adversaries or fat-cat funders to produce endless questions.

The Reporter took in all these media forays and spent some hours digesting their aggregate significance as a way to help him to determine where he should go next. He was not the mimicking type, obviously.

16 · The All-Important Sheen

MEANWHILE, SPEAKER BLAMER SAT DOWN to dinner with Regina and started his requested appetizer: stewed prunes in warm water followed by

a dish of raisin bran soaked in warm milk with maple syrup. An ordinary dinner of flounder with pears, carrots, and mashed potatoes was the next course. While he was slowly consuming his meal, The Speaker wanted to talk, to say things that were on his mind that no one but Regina was allowed to hear.

"My dear, Regina, let me unburden myself further about my deep concerns over what is happening. As I mentioned, superficial appearances and images are extremely important to preserve, even though no one wants to admit or talk about this truism publicly. One reason for escalating this rodent mess to a Presidential emergency is to take away the laser of journalist attention that was fated to fall on me and The Minority Leader. Our strategic moves have taken the rat problem to a different, complex level of overall seriousness. This seems to be working so far, but it is fraught with the peril of boomeranging if and when the media start looking into the origins of this unforeseeable tumult.

"Look at the crucial psychological function of the sheen, the cover. No one ever visualizes George Washington on a toilet or Thomas Jefferson urinating or making love on top of a black slave. The masses learn from elementary school to see General George Washington on his white horse followed by the regulars of the Continental Army or to think of Thomas Jefferson posing with others signing the *Declaration of Independence* in 1776. When you think of the Crusaders to the humming of 'Onward Christian Soldiers,' you see them in proper regalia, not in a blood fest, beheading thousands of Saracens in the aftermath of one victorious battle. When brutal, bloodthirsty, sadistic police for a murderous dictatorship show up for work each day, they are checked for clean, pressed uniforms and polished boots.

"Even to see us — members of Congress — in the gym or vigorously dancing perturbs this essential imagery of steadfast command, upstanding resolve, and serious demeanor, regardless of what we are doing against people's interests and needs day by day. So when I see where the media are going, I'm deeply disturbed. Why, one fellow brashly asked a urologist on television, 'How serious would it have been had the black rat bitten off my balls, given that my wife and I are through having children?' You see where this whole thing is going. The reporters are taking us into a chasm of tastelessness, and that sick pit is bottomless."

"Did you say 'bottomless,' dear?" winked the irreverent Regina. "Never mind. I interrupted you. Keep going."

"Well, to finish, I see an emerging national mindset arising from the Presidential emergency that can grow and will end up undermining our essential personal vanities that, so effectively, shield us from the masses.

By playing this so big, I may have created a monster, a Frankenstein. *Meet the Press* is coming up Sunday, and I have to go to my study and think long and hard about my presentation."

"Any dessert, dear?" Regina asked.

"Yes, sweetheart, bring me a bowl of those freshly picked figs with coffee," he said.

17 · The Experts Weigh In

AT AN UNDISCLOSED LOCATION around a large conference table sat the nation's top-level military, national security, and infectious disease officials. The President had ordered them *not* to leave the premises without an immediate, comprehensive action plan. He added that they already had the resources, the knowledge, and the authority; they just needed a plan that had better work — and work fast! "This is not foreign policy!" he had snapped knowingly.

The Anti-terrorism Chief opened the deliberations with a digital slide presentation that included real-time video. Using the buildings' security cameras, he showed them the entire Capitol Hill complex. Room by room, one could see the little mammals scurrying around or leaping from place to place or gnawing on hard and soft objects. Some appeared motionless, seeming to sense danger. They were right. The savage cats on patrol were making their presence known and had already crushed the bones of rodents they'd caught.

In contrast to the active felines, the Capitol Police all seemed to be languidly looking at their smartphones, oblivious to any need to be alert now that the legislators and their staff had fled.

"As you can see, my colleagues, the scene is an unusual one, to put it mildly. The rats have now occupied all spaces and then some. Meanwhile, the mice sense opportunity as well as peril and are increasing in numbers. But there is so much food that they're not fighting each other.

"As the presentation suggests, we should not overreact. Overreaction plays into the hands of these little terrorists — and that's why they are attacking the space of innocent civilians with their many pathogens. It is equally imperative not to underreact, given the time pressure we're operating under.

"Next, let us get an up-to-date report from the Catman as to how the cats are doing."

He turned to the feline specialist, who said, "Thank you, boss. First, there are not enough cats, and they are starting to fight each other. They have mean genes.

"Second, after they kill and chew on two or three rats, they get lazy and lay down to sleep. Apparently, there is only so much action they can take."

("Like male lions," mumbled one attendee to herself.)

"My judgment is they're not the solution to the dilution of the rodents."

"Most interesting, Catman," noted the Anti-terrorism Chief. "We'll accept your candid conclusion and move to the higher plane of technological response. Let us hear from Chemical Warfare Man."

"Thank you, Chief," said this specialist, who had a gas mask dangling casually around his neck. "I believe the only way to exterminate and make their successors unable to return is with our new gas, Rod Blot. Rod Blot is harmless to humans after a 48-hour interval — once the polluted air in a sprayed space is flushed out — its manufacturer claims. But rodents' genes are extremely sensitive to Rod Blot. Specifically, rodents of the rat and mouse gene type.

"So the plan is that we advance on the Congress with giant hoses, spraying Rod Blot into every square inch and crevice and pipe of that exalted architecture right down to the Catacombs. The gas expands very quickly," he added.

"Where else has it been used?" demanded the Infectious Disease Man across the table.

"This will be its premiere real-world application, the company told us," responded Chemical Warfare Man proudly. "These rats will be just as good as lab mice for our purposes."

"What? What?" shouted the Infectious Disease Man, pounding his fist on the table for emphasis. "You are planning to use 535 of the most important people in our country, and their staff, as guinea pigs?"

"Of course not," replied a second, red-faced, Chemical Warfare Man. "Rod Blot has been tested on guinea pigs, as well as assorted reptiles and mammals, including one great ape. The short-term findings on its killing power were reassuring, says the manufacturer."

The Chief interjected testily: "Chemical Warfare Man II, your 'short-term' Rod Blot is utterly too risky as a response to what should be a modest challenge. That is, if my associate, Infectious Disease Woman, agrees that the pathogens can readily be brought under control."

He glanced down the table to one of his disease experts, "What say you?"

Infectious Disease Woman had the confidence that did not suffer fools gladly. She was glaring at the brash Chemical Warfare Man II but quickly composed herself to say that pathogens on rats can thrive only on contact, except for bubonic plague fleas, which were not operative there. So long as there was no touching of fluids, no bites, and no contamination of anything edible, the situation should be amenable to normal control. "So I must say," she added, "I approve the evacuation. We can wipe them out handily because, so long as the rats are not exceedingly hungry, they will not behave in an unusually aggressive manner or take risks about where they roam."

The Chief was relieved and said so. He then asked, "What do the professional rat exterminators think about the scale of this challenge?"

The Liaison Woman answered that they were recommending deploying large numbers of rat traps and poison as well as sealing any holes, crevices, or cracks. It's what they had always done, with satisfactory results, although they did feel a little bit overwhelmed, and, certainly, the company that had been retained felt it lacked sufficient personnel for the task ahead. The company had said it would take a thousand workers — frontline and back-up — to do the job in about 20 days.

"Twenty days!" exclaimed the Congressional Rep, throwing up his hands. "That would wreck us! Don't you realize that our standing in the polls is plummeting by the hour from this media frenzy? As one libertarian wag put it, 'the flight of the rats from the rats' is dominating the small talk of the people, folks who never knew the names of their own Senators until now. Even before this, there was a historic plunge in esteem and respect for the Congress as an institution. Now its members, not just the institution, are being held in low regard. Why, already there are rumors afoot of marches on Congress to throw dead rats at our edifices. Each marcher, it is said, will have a sign around his or her neck signifying anger over some supposed bad deal or sellout by their representatives. Who knows what other clownishness and high-visibility farces are on the horizon? Twenty days are an eternity and — if I may continue to mix metaphors — one with a long tail."

"He's also throwing in god-awful puns," Liaison Woman muttered.

"You've got to do better!" wailed the Rep, sounding almost pathetic.

The Chief felt baffled but didn't show it. He had never encountered such foes in his career. He looked at the CIA Man and asked if he had a solution.

"No, sir, this problem is above all our pay grades and outside all the specialties at the agency. All we have found is that it doesn't seem to be a conspiracy, either domestic or from North Korea, China, Cuba, or the Russians. And our top men say rodents don't have the intelligence to hatch a plot to bring down our government."

The Chief looked further down the table. "How about you, NSA Man? You got any ideas?"

"Well, sir, though we have the classified, 'throne room' conversations — and exclamations — arising from the first discovery of the rats in the toilet, I am afraid the rats have bested us by using their natural-born encryption," he reported, smiling wanly and, to the Chief's mind, inappropriately, given the gravity of the situation.

The DC Police Chief and Fire Chief, along with DC's Rodent and Vector Control Division Director, were listening to these exchanges with quiet astonishment. Their thoughts ran along similar lines, amounting to: "So this is what the 'best and brightest' can come up with. Nothing! We might as well let the traditional exterminating firms be given the funding and support to go after these rats the old-fashioned way. We can brook no further delays unless some unknown genius comes up with a better way."

The Fire Chief voiced the opinion of all three: "Given the difficulties that all of you are expressing, why not try crowdsourcing to get the best possible recommendations quickly? Just lay out the problem and ask people to come up with ideas. The internet is the world's greatest suggestion box."

The Fire Chief's suggestion was a nonstarter all around. Publicizing the problem and the experts' problem in finding a solution would be an admission that the government, with all its resources, had laid an egg. It was bad enough that Congress was taking all the abuse while the Executive Branch was unscathed.

Not even considering the Fire Chief's suggestion, the Anti-Terrorism Chief asked for a show of hands of those who wanted to go with the expanded extermination attack on three shifts daily. All hands went up, except for that of the Infectious Disease Woman, who abstained.

The Task Force had gotten its marching orders and transmitted them to The President who, nonplussed over the absence of any high-tech remedies, nevertheless initiated the procurement of 1,000 Exterminators who would start immediately. This meant signing contracts with a dozen firms who were told to work together, carve out their territories inside the Congress, and coordinate daily.

18 · The People's Wrath

NOT A MOMENT TOO SOON, for the rumors mentioned in the war council were not far from the truth. The country's people were arousing like never before.

A contingent from New York and New England, led by nurses and students, delivered a truckload of "Wall Street Rats" with a sign explaining that the Congress that had refused to pass a Wall Street speculation tax would obviously welcome them. Such a sales tax would have provided $300 billion a year that might have been utilized to provide healthcare and reduce the student loan burdens. Millions of postcards were being sent showing one giant black rat on the Capitol Dome with a sign saying, "You Didn't Listen to Them — The People — But Now You're Going To Listen To Us."

That was only a sliver of the corrosively critical anthropomorphism attributed to the rats and their imagined political agenda. They had become the voice of the public! Little statuettes of Blamer, Melosay, and Clearwater wearing crowns upon which lolled a pompous rat, were selling like hot-cakes. Poster art rose to new heights of imaginative, symbolic, and real-life portrayals of what was increasingly being called the perfidious "Withering Heights" of Washington, DC.

The calendar was filled with nonstop street action: rallies, soapbox speeches, marches, and sit-ins at zoos where the protesters said the rats should be given luxury cages as reward for their heroic takeover. The media couldn't get enough of it. Ratings soared, and increasing print, radio, and TV time was being devoted to what was making a very deep impression everywhere. Protests across the country — red state, blue state, north, south, east, and west — were moving into mobilization stages with overdue specific demands for justice, fairness, and participation *qua* citizens replacing control *qua* wealth as the *sine qua non* of government functioning. And, the most ominous sign of all for incumbents: there were early indications of candidates, holding the same beliefs as the protesters, readying challenges to the lawmakers in the upcoming primaries.

Petitions were circulating on the internet demanding that the members go back to their jobs regardless of the rat infestation. Millions of workers show up every day at jobs far more dangerous. They don't cower in fear. If they did, they would have their pay cut or be fired by their bosses. The petition pointed out that Members of Congress were getting paid while they stayed home in bed. Outrageous! These petitions contained common left/right demands — the kind that really scare politicians.

19 · Speaker Blamer Searches His Soul in Public

SUNDAY MORNING, Speaker Blamer's driver arrived to pick him up for the 9:00 a.m. TV taping for *Meet the Press*, which would be played nationwide at 10:30 a.m. Woodcock Toad, the legendary interrogator, had been prepping for this hour nonstop since Speaker Blamer had agreed to come on. For the full hour, the usual format was to be tossed aside. There was no time for the insipid commentator panel of cautious but very vocal reporters and syndicated columnists.

Speaker Blamer arrived at the entrance to the spacious NBC headquarters on Nebraska Avenue only to encounter a gaggle of reporters outside who began throwing questions at him while he hastened to the studio door. "No comment, have to go," he told them. "Watch the show."

He kept his head up, his posture erect, and his visage confident, using his most impressive baritone voice to brush them off. "Dignity, Bearing, Image," he silently repeated to himself.

Once inside, he was ushered into the Green Room, which was replete with fruits, drinks, and bakery delights. From there, he was taken next door to makeup where a true artist of the form made him look almost regal. Back in the Green Room, he was greeted by Woodcock Toad (nicknamed Woody) and told that the whole hour was being devoted to the Congressional rat invasion and how the government and the American people were reacting to this unprecedented Congressional Emergency. There were a small number of people comprising a studio audience, Blamer was informed, but all the questions would come from Woody.

Mr. Toad began the show with a three-minute introduction, discussing the shutdown of Congress due to the rats, and spicing his comments with suitable clips of the evacuation scene and statements by some Senators and Representatives. Mr. Toad ended with a picture of a dozen rats scurrying merrily in various directions in a Congressional office.

Turning to The Speaker, the host launched his first question: "Speaker Blamer, the reliable dispatches of The Reporter tell us that the first rat intrusion was in your own personal bathroom and that you let out a screeching bellow when you saw a big black rat in your toilet just as you sat down to use it. Could you describe for our audience your first reaction, how this came to be, and what you have tried to do about it?"

Speaker Blamer: "Mr. Toad, I never was one to look backward. All I wish to say is that the rat invasion became Congresswide and created this most unfortunate shutdown, which was necessary to allow the Exterminators to go to work. This is not about me."

Mr. Toad wouldn't be distracted.

"But there are conspiracy theories being woven about why it started with your bathroom and why the first rat picked on your — err — you? Could you put these rumors to rest?"

Speaker Blamer said, stiffening ever so slightly, "Mr. Toad, I can't deal with rumors and the crazed delusions of plot spinners. As far as I can see, it was just a random occurrence, the entrance into the plumbing of a fleeing rodent seeking food. Can't we talk about the larger picture here? For heaven's sake, the country is aroused over this shutdown as never before."

Mr. Toad was not to be tamed.

"Very well, Mr. Speaker, but is 'aroused' the right word here? That might suggest you are garnering the public's pity. Let me show you some of the

clips from the demonstrators and a reading of the polls. Instead of sympathy from back home, you're getting an eruption of anger over the long-standing performance of Congress on behalf of the wealthy against the people. Look at these spontaneous rallies everywhere: Dayton, Austin, Miami, Providence, New York, Los Angeles, Denver, Peoria, Knoxville. They are even erupting in your home state of Indiana. And look at the polls, which show Congress's approval rating plummeting to single digits in red and blue states. What do you choose to say about all this?"

Blamer tried to turn the tables.

"Mr. Toad, putting on my amateur psychologist's hat, I suspect the masses are vicariously identifying with the rats who, unlike them, have achieved an undreamed access to Congress and its members and have upset the place as never before. No foreign enemy or invader has come close, not even the British in 1812. So in their frustration, people are getting some glee and taking the opportunity to send all of us in Washington a message."

Mr. Toad shot back, "A message, Mr. Speaker? That's interesting."

Mr. Toad scented news was about to be made.

"Just what would that message be?"

Unbeknownst to the media, Blamer was anticipating a strong candidate emerging as a possible opponent in his next election, so he had decided to do what he could, though it would shock some of his fellow representatives, to steal this guy's thunder.

"Mr. Toad, to put it simply, the people are telling us to do in Congress what they sent us there to do — represent them — and stop this mad rush to raise money from commercial interests, which ends up making many legislators stand for these interests against the people. The public found a very effective way to send that message — and they are filling in the details by the day — and that is through mockery, derision, lampooning, satire, all with the abetting of a media climate that is very attentive to anything sensational. I don't need to tell you in the media — because you are the transmitters — that turning us all into a laughingstock is a devastatingly effective way to get our attention. It takes away our dignity, our presentation of self. So that's my two-minute psychological sermon. Next question."

Mr. Toad couldn't help but show surprise in his voice.

"Mr. Speaker, you're flooring me. It is one thing for you to describe this mass arousal that is growing by the hour, but you, a conservative, seem to be acceding to its message. It's as if you are egging these malcontents on. Or am I getting something wrong here?"

Blamer was thinking that as he had started on this route he might as well go all the way, harking back to the teachings of his youth, which still had a faint resonance in the depths of his consciousness.

"Mr. Toad, I've been around a long time. And I've seen and sometimes participated in, I say to my shame, a lot of sleazy deals. For me, very frankly, it is by the grace of God that I still have my testicles, in both senses of the phrase.

"I feel this dispensation to be a salvation of sorts, almost a divine intervention, which is telling me to heed my maker and to begin applying the teachings of Jesus, the Son of God. You know, most of my colleagues go to their places of worship and leave their scriptural values there when they leave. I've decided that I must now take seriously the Ten Commandments, not as something we demand be placed in secular public places for ornamentation, but as words to live by. They don't know it, of course, but if I'm right and other of my fellow legislators are feeling this same change of heart or, better said, are getting a heart, the way I am, then in their coming massacre by the Exterminators, these little animals are dying for our souls. And if it took the rats to do this instead of our own consciences, our pretensions, our own knowledge of the awful deprivation, exclusion, devaluing, and disrespect of our people back home, so be it!"

Whereupon The Speaker bit his lip a bit for emphasis.

Back in The Speaker's home, Regina sucked air spasmodically — in delight. Years ago, she had given up hoping for this moment of epiphany to come, one she knew lay latent for so long in Reginald's inner self. This was the first time in memory she could recall watching him on TV when she actually waited for more of his words with pleasure.

But a thousand reporters and commentators weren't waiting — they were filing their stories, gulping their drinks, and trying to clear their heads, hardly believing what they had just heard.

Their instant reports reflected their political inclinations. "Speaker Blamer Capitulates to Rats" headlined a reporter for Faux News. "House Speaker Glows in Epiphany Moment" wrote a freelancer for a religious magazine. They had only time to quote his words verbatim. The commentary would come later after the conclusion of the program.

Mr. Toad announced a commercial, adding needlessly, "Stay with us!"

The Nielsen was registering an increase of 150,000 viewers per minute!

20 · Blamer Still Telling It Like It Is

AFTER THE BREAK, Mr. Toad, who had thrown out all his notes, resumed, "Mr. Speaker, I have to be blunt. How do you square your declared religious principles with your steadfast, long-standing opposition to raising — or what some call restoring — the federal minimum wage, a move which is supported by about 80 percent of the American people?"

"Mr. Toad, let me play amateur psychologist again," The Speaker began. "Humans are very often of two workings, having an inner and an outer person. Now you and the nation's public are seeing my authentic inner person. I am in the process of casting off my parasitic external self, maintaining only the few positive qualities linked to that self, and merging it with my true inner self. Put that all together, and you see a humble servant of the Lord.

"Perhaps you are used to hearing empty words from me. No more. On the reopening of the House of Representatives, I will put forward a bill to take the frozen minimum wage, this cruel and unnecessary chokehold on 30 million of my fellow human beings, to $15 an hour. This will almost reflect a 46-year inflation adjustment and a doubled productivity rate. Think about this. The latter means that, due to automation and streamlining of the company's operations, one Walmart worker today does the work accomplished by two Walmart workers in 1968. I think the CEO of Walmart can tolerate such a raise, much of which will be spent in Walmarts anyway, inasmuch as he makes $12,000 an hour, along with getting extraordinary benefits and company-paid luxuries."

At that moment, the watching media went into high gear, collectively screeching out or trumpeting, depending on political stripe, The Speaker's message, which was, as one put it crisply in a message headline: "Speaker Tosses the Bosses to Make Up the Workers' Losses." Inside the Beltway, commentators speculated that his fellow Republican Party members would be tossing The Speaker upon their return. But outside the Beltway — in America's cities, towns, and rural centers — those commentators who had a feeling for the popular pulse said the grassroots' *will of the people* was responding to Blamer's remarks with a roar, shaking both the leader and the rank-and-file of Congress to their boots.

Much as he liked The Speaker's chutzpah, Mr. Toad was skeptical about Blamer's claim that he could really accomplish much by taking a hard charge at Congress.

He prodded, "This is remarkable, Mr. Speaker. Do you believe you can bring along your Party which has been opposed to any minimum wage increase for years?"

Speaker Blamer waxed lyrical: "Yes, I do. You know a famous poet — I think it was Shakespeare — said, 'The times they are a-changing.' Many of my fellow representatives tell me they have been feeling the heat from back home for over a year. As one gentleman told me, 'Walmart workers who call themselves conservatives are not so bamboozled by their ideology that they would *refuse* to take the dollars long overdue them to put food on the table for their families.' You know, Mr. Toad, I'm coming to feel the wealth of Wall Street is no match for the will of the people once it's

expressed vigorously. The few can only rule the many when the many are asleep without an alarm clock. Well, the rats have given them the alarm clock. Talk about a Black Swan event!"

Mr. Toad was still trying to get on handle on Speaker Blamer's shocking turnabout.

"Mr. Speaker," he said, "let's explore the political fallout that will result from your stand this morning. Can you give us some idea of what you see as happening in the coming weeks, with the extermination period and the resumption of Congress?"

Blamer didn't see himself as a prophet, as he told Mr. Toad. "I am not prone to speculation. One reason I wear a vest is to keep myself close to it. All I can tell you is: Keep an eye on the many-faceted upheavals and outcries that are occurring around the country. That's where I think a new chapter is being written. This may be a period of American history where the people *lead*, and the leaders *follow*. It won't be the first time. That's what occurred in the first intense American Revolution against King George III and his edicts. It began nonviolently in 1774 with the farmers in central and western Massachusetts, who were starting mass protests before Boston, Lexington, and Concord got into the act and seized the credit. I would guess that so many outbursts and creative pushes, Mr. Toad, are going to come out from the people — who have for so long given up their sovereignty in a kind of prolonged American serfdom — that those of you in the media, even working around the clock, won't be able to keep up."

21 · Keeping It Clean, for the Moment

MR. TOAD RESUMED with a neutral question, "Mr. Speaker, what do you think of these demonstrators who are seeking a mass resignation of Congress and new elections?"

"Well, I think that is quite premature. They might wait to see if it is at all necessary when the Congress returns from its enforced vacation and takes up the new agenda I'm considering."

"What do you mean, Mr. Speaker?" Mr. Toad probed.

"When we return, my first order of business will be to meet with my Caucus *in public* and call on them to join me in ending all doubletalk.

"Most will know what I mean, but just in case some are ignorant, I'll offer them a few examples. Some supported the oddly named 'The Water Rights Protection Act,' which would end federal authority to maintain minimum stream flows for fish and wildlife and give skiing companies more control over their use of water on public lands. How's that for protection?

" Or how about the 'Restoring Healthy Forests Act,' which would allow more cutting in our national forests by companies that would be able to chop away without public input or environmental review? Then there's the 'Reducing Regulatory Burdens Act' that would let agribusiness dump regulated pesticides into navigable waterways without having to get a permit.

"Or take this doubletalk gem: the 'Ensuring Public Involvement in the Creation of National Monuments Act,' which would hamstring The President's century-old authority to help protect millions of acres of public land. All these fabricated bills actually passed the House of Representatives but were blocked in the Senate. God help us if they ever come up with the 'Human Protection Act.'"

"And you know, Woody," Blamer said, getting a little avuncular, "doubletalk always goes hand in hand with double-dealing and hypocrisy. If you want to see hypocrisy practiced as a fine art, look to the deficit-reduction crowd. We — and, to my shame, I have to include the old me in that number — are always demanding that the federal deficit be slashed. Yet while Congress uses chainsaws to cut welfare benefits, it uses a toenail clipper on the Pentagon's budget, even refusing to drop projects and domestic bases that the Pentagon itself wants eliminated.

"We keep cutting the IRS's modest budget to the bone so that it doesn't have the personnel to find and collect the $300 *billion* a year — one year — in unpaid evaded taxes. Is that counterintuitive or what? It's certainly a dumb way to swell the deficit. If the boys and girls want more examples of unneeded bloat that can be unfunded and necessary services that benefit the people, that need more money, my staff will flood them with examples. That's something that will be done in full public view in front of the Capitol Hill Press Corps."

Mr. Toad asked, "Mr. Speaker, many of your colleagues are watching you say all this *live on national television*. What do you think they are thinking about doing?"

"Mr. Toad, right now, while some may be thinking about the reactions of their deep-pocketed supporters, I'll wager most're thinking about what the common people watching this program are thinking about them. Then they'll start rethinking. Maybe, as an aid to their musings, I can suggest they also get a copy of 'the golden rule' and text it to The Chairman of the House Rules Committee with the words: 'This is the way to simplify your daily work.'"

Mr. Toad interrupted The Speaker's flow of words. "But why are you singling out The Chairman in particular?"

"Because, as you know, this 'Chairman Nyet,' as some critics call him, is considered the hardest of the hardliners."

"Mr. Speaker, you seem to be fully at ease with what I will call your new worldview, but I've never heard you express even a trace of this before. Don't you think this is too sudden? That you might have discussed this at least with the inner circles of the Republican Party, giving them a heads-up, so to speak."

The Speaker's exuberance seemed to know no bounds.

"Woody, when the time comes for an out-of-date totem pole of political structures to fall, it falls fast, just like the Soviet Union fell. To let the debris flake and then slide off at an increasing rate, bringing the structure to a slow collapse, is destabilizing to our national security. There is the need for a clean break to see if redemption is possible."

As the show was almost over time, Mr. Toad came up with a tremendous finish, which might even allow him to go into overtime.

"Mr. Speaker, I've just been informed that a small crowd of Washingtonians is gathering in front of our gated NBC Building, including numerous members of the media eager to ask you questions. You can see them on the monitor. What do you say we go out to greet them and take questions? Don't worry. NBC's security team will keep some semblance of order and quiet. If things get overwhelming, we'll just come back into the studio."

The Speaker nodded his head, indicating the move outside was agreeable to him.

Mr. Toad added, "We'll keep showing what's going on around the country and some cartoons for our viewing audience as we move outside."

"OK by me, Mr. Toad. Just keep the din down so we can hear."

22 · Taking It to the Streets

AS THEY LEFT THEIR SEATS and moved down the corridors of the NBC offices, camera operators and assistants moved with Mr. Toad and The Speaker to the front entrance.

Once outside, Mr. Toad changed hats from being an interviewer to being a stage manager. He looked out at the crowd pressing toward them. "Hello everyone. Let's first hear from members of the media and then our reporters will take some questions from other audience members. Please, make your questions crisp as there is not much time left."

The first questioner was a female TV journalist: "Mr. Speaker, people always say, 'it takes two to tango.' My question is: What about the Senate — a notoriously independent body? Will they get behind your plan?"

The Speaker replied, "The rats will take care of them, too. I expect smooth relations in our rapid response to the folks out there in the country."

That seemed overly optimistic to many of the listeners, but rather than argue that point with him, the next journalist, a male radio reporter, asked for details. "Mr. Speaker, can you come up with an agenda as comprehensive, as varied and as straightforward as the people are insisting on in their mounting sense of liberated power?"

This radio guy had been reporting on the protests around the country, which inspired his query.

"Rest assured," The Speaker explained, "the agenda I'm proposing has been around for a long time. It could be called 'Catching up with Canada or Western Europe,' or with going back to the Populist Party Platform of 1912 or parts of the 2002 Texas Republican Party Platform or, to move even further back, to some writings of Adam Smith or, to move back millenniums, the scriptures of the great religions."

The Speaker saw a sly grin on the reporter's face.

"I'm not being facetious," he told him. "The modern forms are on paper, written by some of our enlightened legislators here, and at the state level. They are in neglected GAO Reports and in the studies by the Congressional Research Service and our universities and citizen groups. Also you can find them among existing best practices of local, state, and federal governments or in the better corporations like the Interface Company in Atlanta, Georgia or Patagonia in Ventura, California. The challenge of finding a viable agenda is the least of my worries."

At this point, Mr. Toad decided to mix things up a bit by allowing a citizen to ask a question.

The man queried, "Mr. Speaker, what then are your bigger worries?"

Now it was the turn of The Speaker to wear a wry smile.

"Whether we can move fast enough before the Congress is torn down, as was the Bastille in 1789."

Mr. Toad was shaken by this allusion and jumped in.

"The Bastille? Surely, Mr. Speaker, you're not anticipating violence, are you?

The Speaker was quick to backpedal.

"No, of course not. I was being metaphorical. After all, the Bastille wasn't literally torn down on the spot. I was referring to an old saying about archaic, ossified institutions — whether public or private — 'If they don't bend, they are going to break.' I assure you, Congress will bend, or it is history."

The Speaker paused then, as an afterthought, added, "This is an election year, you know."

Mr. Toad identified the next questioner, a black woman standing with her assembled family of husband and little children. "Our race knows about revivals — like Reconstruction — and what can come after, groups such as the triple-K Southern Redeemers who were depicted so lovingly in the racist film *The Birth of a Nation*. Have you thought about any backlash and who would make up its adherents?"

Mr. Toad was disappointed to learn, via a text, that the network would not extend his program any longer. "Wow, that's a heavy good one. Unfortunately, Mr. Speaker, although it would be great if you could speak at length on this topic, you've got two minutes left for your reply."

"A profound issue, Madam," The Speaker began, then admitted, "I haven't really given it much thought, except to believe that everybody wins when America catches up with Justice. Sure, those shortsighted barons of Wall Street and Houston will have to give up significant power, but isn't it possible they will be smart enough to know that, in the long run, they'll be better off? The change will make them better behaved, too.

"You don't have to read Aristotle's *Politics* to see that democracies are always more prosperous for everybody than plutocracies in part because of the people having more spending power from higher incomes and everyone being willing to invest more due to the society's greater stability. Some of the rich may grasp this, but the ruling one percent usually includes some really rich, really greedy people who don't consider society's overall prosperity but act to worsen inequalities and divide the people into warring factions.

"Maybe my confidence is misplaced. But I'm foreseeing the Congress, prompted by the rat onslaught, will awaken as I have. I imagine this awakened Congress will not try to divide and rule and generate class warfare, and work for everybody except, in the short run, the global corporations who will have to toe the new line of fair play. After all, they are supposed to have been chartered into existence by governments to be the servants of the people, not their masters. My key message goes out to the common woman and man, not to my colleagues in Congress. It is: keep building reasoned, serious pressure on all legislators. Then you can direct your representatives from a position of knowledge and power. After all, aren't we supposed to be your ultimate public servants? So, shouldn't you, the people, be setting the agenda?"

Mr. Toad had the last word.

"Mr. Speaker, this has been an outstanding *Meet the Press* thanks to you and people out there. We hope to have you back very soon. And, for now, on behalf of NBC and my colleagues, if it's Sunday, it's *Meet the Press*."

Roars erupted in neighborhoods around the country. The thousand reporters and commentators rushed to write their stories and opinions. The headline experts smacked their lips as they unloaded some doozies for the morning papers and the weekly magazines. The sensationalist media got its sensations.

23 · The Story Behind the Story I: Workers Do Their Utmost

ON THE FOLLOWING MONDAY MORNING, The Reporter was not where all the others were: ditto-heading and rehashing their accounts of the Big Sunday Story. He was assembling a groundbreaking batch of fresh revelations into a dispatch that would show the story behind the story and, incidentally, prove once and for all that he was and would remain *numero uno!*

Spending day and night around the congressional complex — he had no trouble seeing what was going on at night as there were Kleig lights everywhere — The Reporter mixed with the workers who were coming in and out or sitting in trucks waiting in line to deliver or take away equipment and materials. He also casually approached them as they sat in nearby fast-food eateries. Here is what he put in his latest dispatch:

> Reliable sources at the rat extermination sites say that the number of rats and mice is increasing. This appeared hard to explain until this reporter learned that rats communicate to one another over wide ranges. Faraway rats were told there was plenty of food and spaces to hide in the Congressional complex. It also turns out that these rats have discovered and gnawed through emergency stores of food hidden all over the Congress, put there in the old Cold War Days of civil defense. The word spread, and the rats started coming over from Executive Departments in the vicinity, then further away from the slums of Anacostia and the underground tunnels of Washington, DC's aging water/sewage systems, subways, and other infrastructure.
>
> To be sure, the rat slaughter has commenced in earnest. But rats are accustomed to seeing dead rats, eliminated by predators, diseases, and man-made disasters such as fires and storm damages. Rats also cannibalize themselves, especially as they need much nourishment growing up from infancy to adulthood in just a few weeks. Moreover, rats always come back — sooner or later.
>
> Other developments are causing new worry among the extermination teams and their health/safety overseers. One rat bite — of a worker who had carelessly stuck his hand into a crevice — turned out to test positive for rabies. Two other workers have come down with a cough that may be associated with rat fleas. The health specialists are taking no chances. They ordered cessation of the work until all laborers were outfitted with hazmat suits. This order, which will be announced tomorrow according to spokespeople for the cleanup, will delay the job for at least three days. In addition, to get a fix on possible health hazards, bottles holding sample rat fleas have been flown under super secure conditions to the Centers for Disease Control in Atlanta, Georgia.

Despite these problems, the morale of the Exterminators is quite high, according to interviews by this reporter, in part because they feel excited to be part and parcel of the biggest news story in the country. This is a marked contrast to their normal situation where they work in the shadows, unheralded and unknown. They are not used to being described in the same glowing terms used, for instance, for courageous firefighters. Second, they, too, heard the jokes. The cartoons and late-night TV skits are circulating on their smartphones as well. One late night comedian, Wally Wholebear, went viral with this offering — "Well it took the Rats to make the pompous politicians in Congress have some skin in the game." So, they can appreciate the rats are, in their unknowing way, doing a patriotic service by getting the public aroused. Of course, this hardly stops the workers from doing their utmost to eliminate the rodent scourge. From my contact with them, I can say the American people can rest assured that these men and women are skilled and dedicated to delivering a rat-free U.S. Congress on time!

The Reporter filed his dispatch and told his editor that he was leaving town because that is where the next Big Story was Developing! The Editor smacked his lips in anticipation as he opened The Reporter's FYEO file.

24 · The Story Behind the Story II: Congress on the March

THE REPORTER HAD ACTUALLY turned in two stories. The other one answered the question: "Where did all the Congressional lawmakers go when Congress was rat-closed?" He found, through his many calls, leads, and informants that about a third of them went out of their home districts, usually out of their state, for vacations in the Caribbean and sunny spots elsewhere. A few dozen accepted invitations to attend business conventions or golf tournaments at resorts. About 60 of the lawmakers went on taxpayer-paid junkets to study parliamentary systems abroad with Europe being the prime destination, particularly going to countries that had fine restaurants. The rest went home to do politicking. The headline read: "Congressional lawmakers vamoose for watering holes of the rich, famous, and powerful during Rat Recess."

The Reporter winced a little at such titular sensationalism, but he understood the news business. He also guessed that he would be the leader of the pack. As soon as his story was available, the rest of the press picked up and ran with the disclosures. The opinion makers were not far behind. The bellowing radio talk show hosts were in high gallop, led by the growling,

Tush Limba. The websites of the lawmakers had long since broken down, and their phones were not answering, which further outraged the citizenry who were already aroused by angered radio hosts and the innumerable blogs. New domain names were registered, which were too inflammatory for the more discreet press to mention, except for the more reserved ones such as "Make Congress Collapse," "Clearwater Crap-out," and "Congressional Medal of Honor for the Rats."

Tush Limba summed up the citizens' responses: "Say it to Melosay and Blamer and all of them: Get out."

25 · A Movement Is Born From Stony Beginnings

PROTESTS RISE AND FALL in the ether for the most part. They generally don't ripple out from the core group of concerned people who originate them. Experts on crowds attribute this to little planning, minuscule budgets, poor leadership, and the lack of focus that induces protest fatigue among the core before they make an impact. The core never convincingly answers the questions, "Just How Far Do The Majority of Our Fellow Citizens Want To Go, and How Do They Expect to Get There?"

Another explanation for the lackluster showing of protest movements in this country is that American politicians, over the past 25 years, have learned to quietly dismiss big rallies, demonstrations, and even temporary "occupations," because they have gone nowhere. The lawmakers never consider them when making decisions. Remember, too, that in Washington, giant rallies, such as those against the Iraq War, for the environment, or for a jobs program were traditionally held on weekends when neither the members of Congress nor the journalists are around. These crowds are lucky to get a picture in the Sunday newspapers. The lack of publicity curtails any impact they might have had. The smaller gatherings, including even those by Veterans for Peace, get zeroed out completely, rating, at best, a paragraph squib deep in the paper.

One small interconnecting group that was gathering might have seemed destined to the same fading-away fate. Called "Summon Our Lawmakers To Us," (SOLTS), it was well-nigh invisible at first. Its quietude was not due to an inability to make an impact, but due to its concentration, from the first, on planning intensity. This group was not into venting, but engaged in laser-like, *in personam* lobbying. The members had seen that the most powerful, most successful lobbies on Congress — the ones that twist the lawmakers like putty pretzels — did not bother with demonstrations or marches. Corporate lobbies and organizations such as the NRA and AIPAC (American Israel Public Affairs Committee) have most of the 535 men and women doing their business, right on Capitol Hill.

The Summons Group — probably not yet more than 250 varied citizens scattered throughout the country, including some, but not many, who were well-to-do — were not experienced lobbyists. They just were serious, calm, informed, and competent. You know the type when you see it.

What caught the attention of many watching *Meet the Press* on that fateful Sunday was The Speaker's allusion to the first American Revolution of 1774 and its inception in the farmlands of Massachusetts. Promptly circulated by the more scholarly of their group was the book *The First American Revolution: Before Lexington and Concord* by Ray Raphael. This enlightening volume, based on many primary sources from those heady days, told the amazing narrative of determination, presence, self-restraint, and focus displayed by thousands of farmers who played a large part in getting the revolt going. What organized them was the sudden, monarchical displacement of their local governments and courts by King George III and his Tory henchmen, their power grab backed by a sizable garrison of Redcoats billeted in Boston.

The networker who initiated this Summons Group, mostly via the internet, was Doug Colebrook, a recently retired stonemason whose ancient craft he had mastered and practiced over 40 years. Methodical to an extreme, he started as a quarryman splitting sheets of rock, moved on to becoming a sawyer cutting rough blocks into cuboids, and then learned how to be a banker mason in the workshops that shaped the various kinds of stones into those right for a specific building's design. Doug was a serious history buff in relation to stone craft. His reading took him back thousands of years to all the famous works of stonemasonry, including the Egyptian Pyramids, the Parthenon, Angkor Wat, the Taj Mahal, Cusco's Incan Wall, the mysterious Easter Island and Stonehenge statues, and Chartres Cathedral. His respect for markers and context led him into studying the cultural and political history at the times of these ancient constructions.

When Doug read the first article by The Reporter, one about the stirrings of protest around the nation, he sensed an historic opportunity flowing from the existence of so many kinds of vast and vivid reactions from the populace. Up to this time, he had despaired of anything being done to radically reform the country, especially through the existing system, given the deservedly low regard in which the public held Congress and the way that towering institution had walled itself off from the very people who sent its members there.

26 · Learning From Our History

DOUG COLEBROOK OBTAINED *The First American Revolution* and read it in one sitting. What struck him was the way the farmers — often 500 to 1,000 of them — would quietly surround the home of the resident Tory — who was their neighbor — and ask to see him. Then three or four of the assemblage would step forward and ask the Tory to renounce his assignment as a local implementer of the King's usurpations.

There was no threat of violence. The farmers were very careful not to give the King's men any excuse to label them a "riotous mob," inviting an assault from the disciplined Redcoats. There was, however, a promise that if the Tory did not sign a recantation then and there, his independent neighbors would shun him, the farmers not sell him any of their products. And — note this — they would not even use the Tory-appointed court judges or their sheriffs to present their regular claims or grievances, thus making these new, captive institutions a dead letter.

The Tory really only had two choices in these towns and villages of central and western Massachusetts — either to recant or leave for Boston and its protective Redcoats. Hanging around was just not a comfortable option, though some Tories would sporadically come back to spend time on their property and then go back to Boston if things got too hot.

The stonemason was impressed with the ability of the farmers to turn out in such large numbers during a time when the population of Massachusetts was about two percent of what it is in the present-day census. The peer group's mutual understanding that they were all in the struggle together and that they all had to pick up the oars in the lifeboat instilled awe in Doug. And this was underlined for him as he thought about how hard it is today to get voters to the polls or citizens to town meetings or rallies.

27 · A Plan Gels

AS A STONEMASON, Doug Colebrook was used to reflecting while working. Unlike the more finely detailed tasks of plumbers, electricians, and roofers, stonemasons can concentrate on their craft while also thinking of other things. For Doug, these other things had come to be sequentially thinking through a problem or a challenge. That is, he became adept at mental concentration.

When he was younger, the necessity for this trait as part of an effective person's skill set was brought home to him when he heard a lecturer recount Isaac Newton's response to a guest who asked why he was so much more brilliant than his scientific peers. Newton denied his superior acumen, noting only that he could hold a problem in his mind longer than most.

So after hours of concentrated reflection, Doug came to the conclusion that it only took a small number of determined people — backed by geographically widespread voiced public opinion and wielding sound tactics and strategies — to make history; that is, to make significant changes in the body politic. After all, he told himself, there were only 535 of them in Congress, and they had the immense authority and power to steer the country one way or the other.

Doug began putting out, in both the real world and in virtual reality — and in a very conversational manner — his thoughts on the traits, skills, and experience that would be needed by those who would set out to bring together a tightly knit, purpose-driven association of latter-day patriots. He carefully followed up any responses via the internet with lengthy personal phone calls, letters, or personal one-on-one discussions with those who were nearby. Carefully matching policy agreements with the requisite personality and character strengths, he came up with about 350 persons whom he believed concurred with him and each other on a list of long overdue redirections and reforms.

It was after just completing his list that he read the latest investigation of The Reporter. The findings were exciting. After a careful survey of all Congressional primaries, The Reporter listed the names of 310 registered primary challengers in the House of Representatives and 28 in the Senate. These were serious challengers from the same Party as the incumbent, presenting a very rare and serious situation for incumbents accustomed to easy victories from their safely gerrymandered districts. Immediate media devolution followed The Reporter's scoop as hundreds of follow-up stories by state and local reporters appeared, ones that meshed powerfully with the ever-mounting popular outbursts, demands, and corrosive humor transfixing the land.

To the rat-evicted members of Congress, the near future was truly getting out of hand, out of their control, and unpredictable. Perhaps, they worried, their temporary displacement from Congress by the pesky rats would become permanent once November rolled around.

Suggestions from the circle that Doug was assembling included one by a self-described "very rich old guy," printed in Tudor English on a scroll. The elder proposed the issuance of a formal summons by the voters to the two senators and representatives of each of their states, who would be asked to come to open town meetings, chaired by the people, who would directly present their agenda, sent earlier to the lawmakers to be studied, for discussion and response. Thus the website, summonourlawmakerstous.org.

Now Doug followed up by preparing summonses to the both incumbents and their primary challengers at other town meetings to review their capabilities and receptivity for the august offices in the Congress. Delighted, the "very rich old guy" called Doug up and said he would pay the travel expenses for all the circle's members to gather at Chicago's O'Hare airport to take matters to a new level of range and intensity. Doug scheduled the meeting at a large hotel for ten days hence.

28 · The Country on Fire

MEANWHILE, THE REPORTER was filing his daily, ground-based reports on the variety of condemnations and demands proliferating throughout the country, going, in his words, "creatively and effusively open source. It's America 2.0!"

The Reporter continued in one of his more comprehensive stories:

> What is transpiring is a multilayered rising — a controlled civic riot producing seismic jolts at a rapid rate, fueled by the energy of millions of unemployed, underemployed, and retired people, and supplied by an expanding mainstream market for material, such as rat figurines, posters, DVDs, balloons, pennants, banners, fireworks that explode to form the shape of the rat, brand new rat merry-go-rounds at theme parks that sell 'ratburgers' (made of beef), and fantasy videogames where the player becomes a rat hot on the heels of a pants-less politician. Add the constant booming tunes for every taste, making fun of the members by name in rap, rock, and — note this — waltzes. Not to mention the new trend for people to dine in *Ratskellers.*
>
> In the smaller towns, parade permits are setting all-time records, and protests are bringing people in record numbers to business-hungry storefront merchants.
>
> To this reporter, it seems everybody has a favorite gripe or pet peeve against these politicians, whether it be an irritating phrase that a solon uses, an unanswered communication, a perceived air of remote arrogance, a lack of caring for any non-elite person's plight, or the legislators' cavorting with the Wall Street or Hollywood crowd. It's very trans-partisan, almost a global repudiation.

Covering several locations a day in his red, white, and blue minivan, The Reporter filled his columns with local color and depictions of vociferous characters with their outsized props. There was theater to be sure, including marches with pitchforks, tar, and feathers, but The Reporter didn't describe these scenes as particularly festive. There was anger and disgust aplenty, rather than playfulness. People were picking up on each other's good ideas. The grim *rumble* from the people — the last thing politicians wanted to hear — was growing daily.

Moreover, for the politicians, these rumblings seemed highly ominous. In East St. Louis, Missouri, a turnout of low-income workers held posters saying, "We Need a Living Wage … or Else!" The "or Else" tagline went viral and began to bookend dozens of demands for a responsive Congress. "Repair Our Schools … or Else!" "Close Down The Nukes … or Else!" "We Want Our Homes Back … or Else!" "End Hunger and Homelessness … or Else!" "Tax Wall Street and End Student Debt … or Else." "We Want Simple Medicare For Everybody … or Else." "Regulate the Big Boys … Not Us … or Else!" "Bring Our Troops Home … or Else!" And of course, "Pro-Life … or Else!" and "Pro-Choice … or Else!"

29 · Politicians for Change Face Usurpers

THE FIRST WEEK OF RAT EXTERMINATION having just passed, Speaker Blamer, Minority Leader Melosay, and Senate Majority Leader Clearwater met at Blamer's home at 10:00 p.m. This was being done on the QT, off the radar, and undercover.

In something of a generational turnabout, these older leaders were trying to get out in front of a movement for fundamental change, but they had found — and this was why they were meeting — that a group of younger heads was seeking to bring them down. The three had sensed the early signs of a palace revolt.

At this point, it was evident mostly in the House, but it was quite capable of spreading to the other body. A clutch of Young Turks was starting the blame game. They were saying that if Blamer and Melosay had not been so secretive about their own asses and the toilets visited by rats, the rodent infiltration could have been nipped in the bud before the creatures went wild, swarming upstairs from the Catacombs. The Young Turks stoked each other's fires, talking each other into heaving expressions of outrage. They saw their careers, so carefully cultivated with sycophancy toward their bosses and donors, going down — not in flames over some principle or ideology or campaign contribution — but in the face of public derision. How ignoble! This infuriated them!

As the trio sitting at Blamer's house had learned, the Turks had started discussing how they could separate themselves from their erstwhile leaders and save themselves from what they had come to believe was an approaching from-the-ground-up tsunami, which would soon sweep away the ruling leaders of the Congress.

It wasn't easy for the Turks to figure out what to do. Not easy at all! So they kept meeting — all 33 of them — nervously absorbing each day's developments around the country and searching for a way out that would promote, not deep-six, them. For added secrecy, the Young Turks had taken to meeting away from the Congress, but even so, the elder trio had become privy to their younger cohorts' plans.

Regina poured wine, setting the bottle down next to a neat display of well-regarded cheeses and nuts she had laid out for her husband's colleagues. She then sat with them in The Speaker's comfortable, electronically swept den/study.

Blamer opened the proceedings. "Welcome all. Please do not hesitate to indulge in Regina's repast. You know why I called this meeting. As if the rat invasion and the emerging revolt of the masses are not enough to preoccupy our days and nights, now we have a sprouting of Young Turks thinking about breaking the venerable rules of succession. I tell you, this whole situation is wearing me out. What about you guys? Are you feeling some fatigue?"

Minority Leader Melosay was having none of that gloom.

"I'm not tired, my friend. I'm invigorated by all this conflict. You know, Reginald, I'm of the school that if you can't stand the heat, get out of the kitchen."

("Or off the toilet," Regina told herself.)

"We have to create a luminous arc of immediate, substantive possibilities that takes away the spotlight on everything that is worrying us," Melosay said rather eloquently. "We have to put forward a vision of what we wish to implement for our beloved country, taking things progressively ahead in many directions, but ones that fall well within our Constitutional authority."

Senator Clearwater, who had not achieved his rank by eschewing caution, threw in: "Do you think we have to go all the way at this early date? I mean, straight to the last resort, so to speak?"

To Clearwater's ears, Minority Leader Melosay was getting as testy as Blamer. She said, "If we wait, we lose. If we don't seize the moment, the moment will seize us personally, and … it won't be good for the country."

Regina thought Melosay's pause made it seem like the country was an afterthought.

The Speaker, for his part, cast a quick glance at the rare-book Family Bible open on the side table, perhaps as a bracer to stiffen his resolve as he expressed his next thought. "You know, Marcy, I don't need any convincing that we need to take the country in a new direction. Ever since my Sunday appearance on *Meet the Press*, I am a different man. When you speak of how we must make fundamental alterations in the polity, you are speaking to a new choir or, rather, a liberated choir. But right now, I am a choir of one in my Party. I don't see anyone seconding my recently voiced opinion. My partisans have been totally mum for the past 60 hours since I downloaded my conscience and made Regina proud."

Regina smiled with a slight nod.

Speaker Blamer turned to Clearwater. "Senator, I also believe this rat uproar has unleashed irreversible forces around the country. It is early springtime, universally recognized as the season for protests, and I've heard that there are numerous 'cause' marches — students, minorities, wounded veterans, impoverished workers, foreclosed homeowners, concussed athletes, and other affinity groups — set to go as the weather gets warmer. I'm not talking about a single, one-time-only demonstration on the Mall, but a separate march daily, picking up adherents mile after mile, with excited media in tow as the protesters head for the day's named legislators on Capitol Hill. The demonstrators are making it very, very personal.

"And to top it all — something none of us would have expected — there are some billionaires ready and eager to fund, and speed up, the whole avalanche heading for our heads! I see not one but many 'perfect storms' of completely unforeseen dimensions that our years of political savvy have never had to visualize, contemplate, much less learn to confront. To add gasoline to the fire, your Socialist Senator Ernie Banders is quoted in *New Yak Magazine* as saying he favors such singular marches on Washington and is looking forward, with gusto, to speaking before them. He adds that the marchers intend to bring caged, pet rats with them. For heaven's sakes, this dreadful symbol lives on undeterred and seems striving for our internment! If we don't do something, these rats will be carved on our headstones!"

Calming himself after that outburst, The Speaker went on enumerating the components of the rising movement.

"This giant rumble is going open source, and its adherents are coming up with refinements that are like a thousand deadly cuts. Why something called a people's bakery out of Kalamazoo, Michigan, is selling some juicy concoction in the shape of heads and torsos looking exactly like each member of Congress. These tasty tidbits are to be fed to the rats during the course of the marches!!! Egad!"

"I'd rather be burned in effigy," groaned Senator Clearwater, "than be a witness to such lowly indignity — ugh, just *ugh*. And another *ugh*!"

At that moment, Melosay's smartphone, programmed to alert her when breaking news required her immediate attention, rang out. She pardoned herself and read the missive from her confidential assistant, Livinia.

"Ms. Melosay, The Reporter has struck again, exposing the meetings of the Young Turks plotting against The Speaker. It is just now coming across the wires. In some detail, I might add, but nothing we didn't know. Now the world will know."

Ms. Melosay turned and, without comment, read aloud the message. In response, The Speaker blanched, and the Majority Leader of the Senate clenched his jaw.

The Speaker did see this as an opportunity to drive his point home. "This just gives more urgency to our conversation. You both saw my preliminary list of reforms on *Meet the Press*. I know you would approve, Marcy. What about you, Senator? Where do you stand?"

"From what I recall," said Senator Clearwater, "you spoke for the majority of the people. You might call it a big left/right supermajority. Things like union rights, better welfare, and so on are programs the folks in Western Europe would recognize since those amenities have been part of their lives for many years. So, in a phrase, and as I see it, 'No Big Deal.' Not that many of our fellow elite would characterize it like that. Even so, I'm sure you had other items on your mind, maybe even more fundamental changes, which there was no time to talk about."

The Speaker nodded. "You've read my mind on that one. Of course, there are other essential alterations that I have in mind, but some of them are reforms of Congress and the electoral system that don't 'sound bite' and would register in listeners' minds as dull and uninteresting even if I had more time to outline them.

"But we're meeting now because of this Young Turk bubble-up, so let's focus on that for a minute. You know where they are coming from. This is a group of hardcore, conservative-feigning corporatists, elected when voter turnout was at the lowest in the century and people were thoughtlessly biting their own noses to spite their own faces. These extremists are still oblivious to what's been going on in the country in recent days or, if they are paying attention, they think it is just a lot of hot air blowing from the hinterlands, which will cause a momentary temperature ripple and then blow out to sea. Either way, these Turks are a problem inside a puzzle and hard to take apart ... or take down. Any ideas?"

Ms. Melosay speculated, "You could play the victimized statesman role. Make them *look* as if they are ungrateful jackals, viciously snapping at the heels of the man who had conferred innumerable benefits on them, besides their being out of touch with the American people, as the daily polls are demonstrating. This has to be done with finesse. That's why I stressed the word 'look.' Don't put it into words or strip *any* of their Committee posts. Just let the media do the work for you, following your subtle hints. The media's airing of these themes will provoke coarse, extremist comments from the Turks. Meanwhile, Reginald, you maintain your dignity, your impeccable bearing, your sartorial splendor, and your polite demeanor. You will seem above the fray as they destroy themselves."

Regina displayed observable delight at these splendid, savvy suggestions, and she knew Reginald was similarly overcome.

Senator Clearwater wasn't far behind in his own delight. "I heartily concur with this strategy. And may I add that Ms. Melosay is one smart and compassionate lady, Mr. Speaker, to give you such advice when she is the leader of your opposition who would like to replace you some day as Speaker. There is a new kind of political patriotism emerging here."

The Speaker, signaling agreement with Clearwater, but directly addressing The Minority Leader, said, "Well, I really appreciate your words, Marcy. What they point to is a temporary 'Let's wait and see' posture on our part, along with my dropping of pregnant hints to the media about the short-comings of the Turks. We also know that we must stay in close, confidential touch, OK?"

Speaking nearly at the same time, and with the same enthusiasm, Melosay and Senator Clearwater readily agreed.

Regina stood up and asked, "How about some pasta with my special tomato sauce recipe, before you go?"

The trio all gave a smiling, relieved, affirmative nod. It is always easier to decide not to have to make hard decisions.

30 · The Movement Keeps on Snowballing

WHILE SPEAKER BLAMER, Minority Leader Melosay, and Senate Majority Leader Clearwater were meeting, and long into the night afterward, The Reporter was burning the midnight oil, deep in reams of data. The reason why even his associates call him The Reporter, rather than using his name, was because of his penchant for not just for reviewing seemingly nonrelevant databases but being able to put together information from those sources in unique, fresh reports.

At this all-nighter, he had come up with three new polls that showed a sharp increase in the number of eligible voters who knew the names of their members of Congress. Another item he linked to that finding, which he found while scrutinizing pictures of the marches and parades that came over his computer screen, was that the protesters were increasingly carrying

signs picturing the faces of senators and congresspersons — a grim portrait, name and date of birth — as if they were mug shots on the police blotter. Only the word "Wanted" was absent.

In addition, he counted many primary challengers parading along with the marchers, joining as participants. They were not featured as leaders or otherwise identified, but The Reporter recognized them because he had studied their pictures earlier. The intrepid newshound blended all these separate findings into a story. His editor composed a telling headline for the piece: "Loaded for Bear: The People Know Who They're Coming For."

31 · The Summons Group Caucuses

A NUMBER OF MOTIVATED CITIZENS that Doug Colebrook called "The Small Community" (named after that 75-year-old book by Arthur Morgan extolling how little groups have a unique ability to spur change) started flying into O'Hare Airport for their initial person-to-person strategy gathering. One of the billionaires that Speaker Blamer was so worried about had reserved four floors of a large hotel and separate conference facilities. Obviously, privacy was a priority.

Doug, who set the agenda, was well prepared to have the group focus on two key questions. First, given the historic groundswell heading its way, what kind of short- and long-term changes did Congress need to make in order to refashion American democracy? And second, who needed to be enlisted to move these well-conceived changes through Congress and over to The President with deliberate speed? Speed was of the essence as the more time passed, the more the public would begin to fatigue — and the powerbrokers would have a chance to mount a counterattack.

As Doug met many of the associates for the first time in person, he was reassured that his careful selection, based on what they did, said, and wrote, was valid. The people were very different from one another: anti-war veterans, shop stewards, engineers, farmers, social studies teachers, emergency medics, members from the repair trades, immigrant and native-born small business people, caregivers, street lawyers, factory supervisors, retired investment and economic specialists, physical therapists, sports coaches, and others. It wasn't that they were chosen for their experience or knowledge — though that was a positive — it was that Doug had gauged each of them to have the right character and personality. He loved to read and was struck by the validity of what the ancient philosopher Heraclitus said, "Character is destiny." From his own study of life, Doug added his own aphorism, "Personality is decisive."

He'd done his homework on these arrivals the best he could, but he now found that some had gotten through the screen — people he would not have chosen if he knew them better. They exhibited social justice concerns but were troubled personally. That's OK, though, he thought. Their presence will help etch the contrasts, highlighting the strengths of the majority.

For a three-day weekend, which was preceded by weeks of thought, they worked through the highest quality proposals, ones that had long been placed on the public table by the thinkers and doers of America. These included all areas concerning the establishment of a basic standard of living for everyone, the role of our country in the world — peace replacing war — and civic globalization as the measure of other interactions. In addition, the ideas of nurturing respect for global ecologies, the fostering of community, and the fulfillment of human possibilities, coupled with distinctive cultural tolerance, were deliberated.

The assemblage of people worked over these proposals so as to situate them in ways that made them more responsive to on-the-ground dynamics as well as to make them able to correct misperceptions that might arise. An expanded brain bank of specialists was put together for the time when they would be needed to contend with the obstruction of purported technicalities and procedures.

The participants also took turns relating the tumult in their regions, and all agreed that speed was critical to press forward at each inflection point in order to keep the offensive momentum going and to deny the establishment any time to regroup and defeat the progressives' aims. One coach put it well: "We're here to plan for the end game or, at least, the fourth quarter. All those good people who get us there deserve decisive reinforcements. And we must also remember to watch the terrain of the playing field as the nature of the game changes when we move from the streets to the suites."

"No, no, no," responded a sunburnt farmer from New England. "I object to your last few words, 'the game changes when we move from the streets to the suites.' I'm from the land of town-meeting forms of local government, and that's where that distinction you are making is not very apropos. Where I hail from, *we* are the legislature, taking over if our town selectmen do not do what we want. If that town meeting level doesn't work, we go to referendum. Our practice is about as close to having the streets *being* the suites as you can imagine. As I see it, taking our fight to the Congressional level is just a matter of scale, a difference in degree, not in kind. We must think about the coming weeks in that way, or the big boys will make sure that the chasm between the streets and the gated suites becomes unbridgeable."

For Doug, the farmer's words were like a flash of brilliant light, a bolt from the blue that showed the necessary way to a seamless path to victory.

It answered in a significant way the questions before this congregation that would emerge more fully as their movement went ahead. They didn't yet have all the details, but they had a strategy.

On the last day, each participant chose his/her assignments to return home and their Congressional District. Each would be acting so as to increase their quality numbers (but still keeping the core to the size of small community) and to move with the much larger numbers of engaged residents who were moving the country, in baseball terms, toward Third Base.

32 · The Reporter Follows the Rat Trail

THE REPORTER CURSED HIMSELF for not being in on the O'Hare meeting. He found out about it way too late to make it out to Chicago, being clued in at midnight via text just as he was going down to see how the night shift Exterminators were doing.

The workers were having a tougher time than they had anticipated. They told The Reporter that they were working under strict orders not to over-apply the chemicals since the Congress would be coming back as quickly as possible, leaving little time to air out the place. Having gotten rid of the cats, which, after being satiated with tasty rats, had turned into self-indulgent nuisances, the managers discovered that the rats were not going quietly to their extermination. They were learning how to withdraw by day when most of the Exterminators were prowling around, and to race around by night to forage.

Moreover, in another adaptive strategy, acting like trapped rats (or at least very harried ones), the rodents had found their ways into areas of the Congress upon which no four-leg had ever trod. These spaces included bookcases, sofas, liquor cupboards, closets, and all kinds of secret enclaves that senior lawmakers used as privileged sanctuaries. The Exterminators were instructed to be very careful not to become bulls-in-the-china-shops on entering such sacred spaces. Having to be extra careful meant the job took more time.

But progress was being made. As The Reporter learned, the nightly body count of slaughtered rats kept rising until it plateaued, which meant that, with a little luck, the dead rat catch would start to decline because there were fewer rats left to deep-six.

Ordinary reporters were satisfied to learn the chemicals used were called "rat point." The Reporter wanted to know the trade and scientific names of all the chemicals, which he checked out on the EPA website and other databases.

That tedious labor produced a significant exposé headlined: "Exterminators Using Chemicals Deployed in Vietnam and Iraq Wars."

As The Reporter noted, some of the chemicals were not licensed for use on civilian sites, let alone the hallowed halls of Congress.

The rest of the media ran with The Reporter's initial scoop, adding many more interviews of dissenting experts condemning the chemicals and demanding a response from the pertinent federal regulatory agencies. By the time the furor subsided with the withdrawal of the offending chemicals, the work had been shut down for five days. The rats had a reprieve, which they took advantage of by recovering lost ground.

33 · Rat Revelry, Exterminators' Finishing Touches, and the People's Wrath

THE RATS CELEBRATED this temporary respite with a rat orgy in The Speaker's private bathroom, relieving themselves everywhere. Meanwhile, to replenish their ranks, pregnant mother rats kept giving birth to litter after litter deep in remote dark places.

The eradication period was now nearing a full month. For the homeless legislators, this was an intolerable delay, especially with some of the citizenry challenging why the legislators were continuing to receive their paychecks. They were loudly asserting that nothing in the law provided for "paid rat leave." In reaction to this, by remote, a near unanimous and frightened Congress passed a resolution naming March 31st as the last day for The Exterminators. The workers were told that if they meet that deadline, they would get a fifteen percent bonus on their contracts.

Sure enough, money talks in the rat death business, too. The Extermination Teams declared victory, on time, with the dead rat countdown to under 50 — a normal level — and prepared to evacuate the sprawling premises after a modest "job well done" ceremony proudly conducted by their trade association: The Unbreakable Fraternity of Rat Removers. As you can see, the fraternity had a keen sense of public relations.

But the American people had another ceremony in mind for that same evening. They sought to keep in the public eye the galvanizing symbolism of rats taking over Congress, especially at the very moment when the solons were attempting to re-establish BS politics as usual. Activists felt they needed the rats around until the people arrived to establish their own sovereignty. The rats were, so to speak, irreplaceable "placeholders."

The first act of these public-spirited citizens was to clamber up to the roof of the Teamster's building, which enabled them to project a Giant Rat on the nearby Capitol Dome — a rat showing its teeth as if it were about to devour that building. The media photographers then sent the picture all over the country for millions to view on TV, their computer screens, smart phones, and in newspapers. Another raft of satiric and crude commentary ensued. The cartoonists and the widely syndicated *Doomsbury* had a field day, giving the electronic rat many anthropomorphic views and intents.

A second maneuver that took some attention away from the Rat Fraternity's pending celebration was the arrival of two 18-wheelers containing dainty little cages with a pet mouse for each member of Congress. On the cage was a picture of each lawmaker with the caption: "A pet mouse for your house" and, in small print, "Certified by Mice For Medical Research Labs, Inc."

The Team accompanying the trucks, which went to the rear of the Rayburn Office Building's loading dock, negotiated a deal whereby, in return for the trucks 'going away,' the Exterminators would deliver each mouse cage to the reception desk of each member of Congress. It was done efficiently and quickly enough so that the 18-wheelers were gone before the commencement of the ceremony.

34 · An Old Rat Sounds Off

THE NEXT MORNING in the *Washington Toast*, there appeared a column by the newspaper's famous humorist Lean Beergarten titled,

FROM INVASION TO EXTERMINATION — THE VIEW FROM A GREAT, GREAT, GREAT GRANDDADDY RAT.

I am an old Rat, and I have seen just about everything in my travels. I've gotten into many fights with other Rats, which I didn't start, and I have the scars and wounds to prove it. Probably sired 3,000 little Rats from dozens of mothers. That's what male Rats do: they eat, fight competitors, and hump lady Rats. It's a good life, and we, as a species, have survived everything humans have thrown at us: poisons, chemicals, mashing machines, drownings, sudden suffocating confinements with no exits, feral cats, hungry dogs, even snakes that can get into our crevices and nests. Once I just got away — though my then-family didn't — from sonic raticide — a high-pitched blast that drove us mad. You sure have the killing tools. And, of course, your medical scientists vivisect us and our little mice relatives — by the millions — every year.

But in my long life, I've never seen humans behave so stupidly as they have in this Congressional war against our frolics through their offices. Why stupid? Because it was an invasion of their own making. First, the casual scattering of much food and the conditions in the Catacombs brought us into your domain. Then, the bringing in of the cats disrupted our normal, cautious comings and goings through our escape routes. What did you expect us to do?

Think about it. We're the ultimate survivors of the fittest, on our merits, battling our way through life's dangers — unlike Congressional big shots, who rig their long careers so that they have little competition to contend with. And lack of competition stalls evolution of their species.

The whole ridiculous scene could have been prevented if humans were intelligent enough to apply Russian scientist Pavlov's approach, what's called "Conditioned Response." You could have stopped distributing crumbs and food wrappers all over the grounds. If we found nothing to eat after a few forays, we would have learned not to disturb your "nests."

Instead, the Congress overreacted, paid for our annihilation, poisoned their own nests and corridors — you humans call it "blowback" — and provoked a people's rebellion that at this point knows no limits.

In fact, for us, this uprising is an added plus. As more people come to town and march around and camp out, they tend to eat out and scatter food and packaging everywhere, giving us free provisions so that we can thrive and multiply. Just as often happens with your blundering militaristic overkill policies abroad, what has happened is that you've done it *to yourselves.*

However, our centuries-long study of humans means that your shortsighted actions are no surprise. Our sages tell us that Rat lives are all about sacrifices. We're used to a culture of suffering and death. That's why we're so tough.

As our philosophers also remark, you humans, especially lawmakers, are the opposite. You're bullies until you're put into a corner, then you become criers, whiners, and whimperers. Combine that with the tendency of your plans to backfire, and I can see the future. You think you've driven us from your premises. Let's say you have returned us to a normal level of what you sneeringly call 'infestation.' But now, due to your own increasingly noticed shortcomings, you may soon be evacuated by the very people who sent you here. Then we'll really hear some crybaby bawling.

We Rats have never been much concerned with human history, though, as our Rat chroniclers tell us, we've often had a paw in shaping it. We've had a big influence in the past, as when our fleas took out nearly half of you in Europe during the 14th century 'bubonic plague.'

I can't credit that all to our and the fleas' ingenuity. It was really due, again, to the stupidity of your rulers and clerics, who assassinated almost all the cats: our eternal enemies.

But the historical role you've given us now is different. During the plague years, we were death-dealing, but in this instance our influence may be life-liberating for millions of human beings, who may be freed from the yoke of your Congress and the marauding corporations that call its tune. You've outsmarted yourselves. Thinking you were too smart for the Rats, you ended up out of your comfort zone. All Ratdom nearby will be watching what happens next, as we never seem to get tired of viewing the heights and depths of human folly.

Survivingly yours,
A Very Old Rat

35 · Young Turks Take the Offensive, Meeting Captains of Industry

EVEN IF THE "YOUNG TURKS" had read Beergarten's animal fantasy, and they probably hadn't, not one of them would have creased a smile or been prompted to snicker. They were perennially angry, self-righteous characters, always preaching to the persuaded, wrapping religion around their promotion of "free market" greed, and seemingly devoid of any sense of secular community.

They were also quite fact-deprived, relying on slogans, their chosen authority figures, and the elections they had just won handily, brazenly not even hiding their agenda, which catered to the desires of the rich and powerful or, as they called them, "the Job Creators." It was the latter "legitimacy" — the skewed sense that the people voted for the corporate welfare agenda (which was packaged as a way to provide jobs and economic benefits to all) — that fortified their determination to tip the balance of power held by The (now ideologically questionable) Speaker in their favor on bill after bill, on budget after budget.

What had the whole country up in arms: the invasion of the rats; the vociferous and widespread reaction of the people, both left and right; and the hammering of Congress by the media. None of those pressures bothered the Young Turks. They still looked back complacently on their easy last election; saw that The (wobbly, now repulsively leftish turncoat) Speaker would have few deep-walleted allies; and looked forward to a future where, even if everything went wrong and they lost the next election, a one-million-dollar a year position awaited them in the offices of the plutocracy they had so vigorously served. How could anything or anybody, even their plummeting public approval ratings, change their minds?

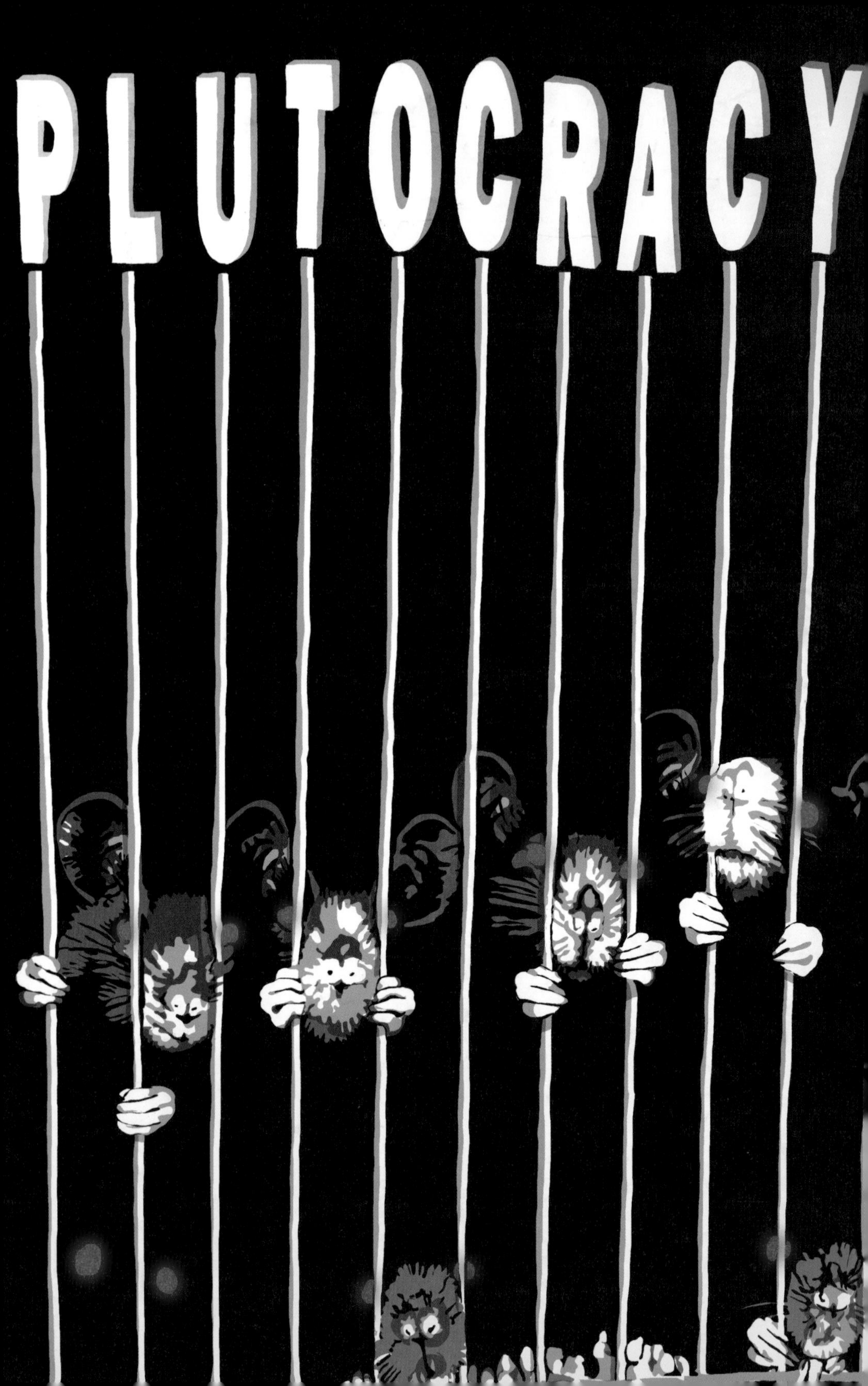
PLUTOCRACY

Rather than reflect on the public's rejection of their type of politics, they would act — do the exact thing the public was condemning them for — except in a bigger way.

The Turks decided to go to New York for a meeting with The Chairman and his core cohort (to what they believed was the real seat of the government, Wall Street) to tell them what they wanted to do, get their advice and support (read: money), secure endorsements from the fawning business press, and gain access to the high rollers' Rolodexes.

The Chairman was happy to see them, opening the get-together with: "Welcome to all of you whose sterling voting records speak to your being our staunchest allies, except that, if you will permit me to say, none of us appreciate your recent bandying about of that awful phrase 'crony capitalism.' I realize this is just your way of playing to the public, and you don't intend to have anything you say about these business buccaneers reflected in legislation, but I also think you should understand that the so-called 'excesses' of 'crony capitalism' are just our efforts to take back what was taken from us in the first place by the thinly veiled socialists down there in Washington.

"Forgive me. I just had to get that off my chest. In any event, I don't want to get into this argument with you. There's more urgent business that I gather you wish to run by us."

A Young Turk, well turned out in one of Armani's finest, spoke first.

"Mr. Chairman, let us get right to the point — and thank you, by the way, for having us here. None of what is bursting out around the country frightens us. We've seen these summer squalls come and go before. As they say, the only poll that counts is on Election Day, and a glance backward shows that that was a sweeping victory for our party, even with all the pro-corporation bills — which some rabble rousers are now questioning — that we got through the House on the open public record. So there was no deceptive advertising that our adversaries so often accuse us of buying. What the public saw they must have liked, as they gave us a thumping success. And, by the way, Alf Radar and all the other nutjobs running for independent tickets were laughed out of the race.

"We're not here to worry about this momentary outcry against us, but we are here today because we want to replace The Speaker and his cronies, who can't seem to get with the program. If there was any doubt about the need to do this, his appearance on Mr. Toad's *Meet the Press* should have convinced any timorous doubters on our side. I presume you saw his conversion on live television — hopefully before you had your breakfast, because otherwise you would have downloaded what you ate into the sink after hearing his disgusting remarks."

Since the first meeting, a number of foreign members had joined the business leaders' group. Now, one with streaked gray/black hair and a high-end Wolfgang Joop suit joined the conversation. "I'm from Germany, but I have been on the Board of the New York Stock Exchange for ten years. May I ask just what you found so objectionable to what The Speaker said?"

This mild-mannered remark set off another of the Turks, this one well served by a pricey Hugo Boss suit. He lashed out: "Mr. Chairman, are we to be judged by the twisted standards of this German fellow or by tried-and-true U.S.A. free market principles? Cutting the budget of our national defense, collecting more taxes, calling our environmental bills 'doubletalk' and the laws' titles hypocritical while actually having named several himself and, adding insult to injury, slandering our revered Chairman of the House Rules Committee by calling him 'Chairman Nyet.' And then to top off this crazed interview, The Speaker talked about a Bastille moment if the Congress doesn't bend, predicting it would end up, otherwise, in the dustbins of history. Isn't that enough? And who knows what else he would have said to feed the appetites of our Marxist press had he had more time on the program."

The Chairman, making a gesture as if he were throwing a friendly arm on the Boss-clad Turk, tried to calm him: "I don't think you fellows in Washington are getting the big picture. Frankly, your views are just a little too parochial for any of our tastes here. What I mean is, from a broader perspective, there is nothing very revolutionary about what The Speaker said or on what or whom he based his opinions in discussing our hallowed past and present. We are in an expanding global economy, and we have to keep abreast of what is going on in those nations that we defeated in World War II and left utterly destitute. Now, like phoenixes, they have risen from the ashes and become sharp global competitors.

"This is not to say that I don't also realize where you folks are coming from. You have philosophical convictions, not business strategies. You have donors who insist you maintain those convictions to contrast with your political opponents, and you have core supporters — less savvy business-people — who fear that what they see as their heritage and their traditions will be taken away from them by a very rapidly changing world.

"Again, if you'd adopt a wider view, you'd correctly identify that the Main Street vs. Wall Street slogan is not just a neat politically combative rallying cry. It is recognition that the Wall Streeters are far more able to transfer their costs — of regulation, of paperwork, or of taxes — to others than can a small Main Street business. And, if that doesn't work, our attorneys can always take advantage of numerous waivers in rigid existing laws that are difficult and expensive for smaller businesses to use. But keep in mind, a huge percentage of what are called small businesses are franchisees who, I must admit, are entitled to greater support from the giant chain franchisors in order to level the playing field a bit. The point being: this conflict is not simply ideological, though that's how you Washingtonians seem to interpret it, but involves dollar-and-cents issues."

Another, slightly older Young Turk took the floor. Being more mature than the others, he favored a conservative herringbone suit by Tom Ford. He spoke in measured tones: "Mr. Chairman, what you've just said raises so many questions to digest that, if you don't mind, I would like to consult in private with my colleagues for a few minutes."

The Chairman, who was bending over backward to accommodate these (as he privately called them) "nincompoops," said, "No problem. Jeeves, will you please guide these good friends to Conference Room #4 down the hall?"

36 • Young Turks Need to Reboot

INSIDE CONFERENCE ROOM #4, the Turks, who were much more nonplussed with their reception than they had let show on their faces when they were in the presence of the corporate bigwigs were doing some quick reassessing.

The older Turk was quick to spell out what all his younger, less well-dressed colleagues, were sensing."We have to face facts. The Chairman is really with The Speaker. Maybe The Speaker knew this before going on *Meet the Press.* We are in less of a comfortable position than we thought. Say what you will about our Main Street support, made up of many small business people, without Wall Street we are substantially isolated because Wall Street has so many hooks, so many controls, over Main Street that they can work around us if they so wish.

"You'd think it would be enough, that through their influence on the Federal Reserve, the Big Bankers get their way with interest rates, credit, and so much else. And, on top of that, Wall Street is the Empire of crony capitalism, meaning most of the goodies are reserved for the inner circle. You heard what The Chairman said about not wanting to get into an argument with us on crony capitalism. It is pretty hard for honest small businesses to compete with crony capitalism and a servile Congress. However, to return to my opening point, we can't frighten these moguls by saying we have Main Street at our backs. They have their ways of controlling Main Street and ousting us from our cozy relationship with the voters if they decide that it is in their interest."

One Turk, dressed in a blue Prada, hadn't been able to get in a word yet. He was a pragmatist who could turn on a dime. Having already digested the veiled rejection of their position by the moguls, he quickly went for a new tack. "It looks grim. We can't afford a blow-up, a heated argument when we get back to The Chairman and his buddies. My instinct tells me that we should soft-pedal our views here and concentrate our fire on undermining Speaker Blamer in Congress where we'll be on our own turf. The Speaker cannot get much through if the House Rules Committee Chair doesn't allow the bill to come up for a vote, hardly an unusual practice for the House leader that The Speaker has labeled Chairman Nyet!"

Another hotheaded member of their group, clad in Dolce & Gabbana, was thinking even further ahead.

"What if The Speaker is no longer The Speaker? What if he just goes poof? Can't we all put together a majority of the GOP caucus to run him out? Or do you all think his control's too deep and too connected for that to happen?" The Dolce wearer was a Southerner.

Many liked what they heard and murmured affirmatively as they considered this route.

Of all of them, the next Young Turk to speak kept his mind most focused on their present situation. After all, they had come here to talk with these moneybags, not argue about legislative strategy. He brought his fellow lawmakers back to the present. "I think we've all heard enough from The Chairman to grasp that we're not going to get what we came for.

"I say we face it and move on. We need to let these rich guys know that they *need us*. Don't they get it? We're like a dike standing between them and the public. We muscled through the Trade Agreement's Fast Track. We starve corporate crime enforcement budgets. We keep the capital gains and dividend tax rate lower than the regular income tax. We preserve the 'carried interest' charade for the Hedge Funds. We stopped a Wall Street transaction tax from being imposed. And we oppose any breakup of the Big Banks which, we claim, are too big to fail. Just about 90 percent of the people want that last one.

"That ought to be a long enough laundry list of good turns and giveaways that we have delivered to make them realize how valuable we are. From our side, I bid you to remember we need to keep our lines open to *them* and retain their financial support for our campaigns. So let's do nothing more to antagonize them. I really believe they don't want a division to occur that forces them to have to choose between us and The Speaker's much larger camp. In short, let's cool it and show that *they need us*. We'll have our say, have a drink and leave on good terms."

And that is just what happened to the mutual relief of all concerned, at least on the surface. As the Tom Ford dresser remarked on the trip back to Washington, "When you don't have the cards, don't try to force the play."

37 · Dissident Billionaires Get Into the Act

AT ABOUT THE SAME TIME that this was transpiring in New York City, three multibillionaires gathered at the Washington, DC, home of one of them — a happy-go-lucky fellow who always seemed to be at the right place at the right time as an early investor. Most of the start-ups that he put money into turned out to be blockbusters. Maybe it was intuition, but he made it big by pouring money into several small internet firms just before their shares went through the roof.

As part of his strategy for finding promising ventures, he felt he had to have wide knowledge, not only of the business climate but of the general social environment. He spent lots of time reading, looking at documentaries, and knowing a lot about what was going on in the enveloping worlds of politics, business, and popular culture.

The second very rich person, who was from the West Coast, called himself a progressive libertarian. That meant that he didn't take narcissism — the freedom to do what you will — so far that it boomeranged, hurting yourself and other people.

His views had made a splash recently when he had revealed them in a lengthy article he'd written for *Politico* arguing for a $15-an-hour minimum wage as being good for everyone, from the bottom all the way up to those like himself perched near the top of the economic pyramid. What caught the Big Boys' attention in their executive suites was his remark: "While pundits look into their crystal ball and worry about interest rates going up; deflation coming; or more job-displacing, efficient automation if this minimum wage increase is instituted; what I see, if it is not instituted, are pitchforks."

"Pitchforks!" cried one famous boss, while he scooped lobster meat from the shells with one of those little forks as he sat in a well-appointed millionaires' club.

While the third super-affluent one inherited and invested so well that he could devote himself to his two other great loves: board games and free soup. He divided his time between playing advanced chess in Chicago and responding to hundreds of soup kitchen appeals so as to pay for ten million nutritious meals a year around the country.

All three men, who knew each other from their years at Princeton, had watched closely the Congressional rat invasion and the exploding public reaction, including all its nuances. That's why they got together just about the time the Congress was reconvening with the successful and

expensive — $100 million — completion of the Extermination Program. The billionaires got to chatting on the phone about developments and decided it would be worthwhile to have a meeting.

Over mint juleps, Happy Go led off their talk, mincing no words. "You know, all this hustle and bustle around the country — really very impressive and creative and deeply felt — seems to be without an organizational form. No one is harnessing this political energy busting out. I know enough about street movements — it's one of the things I've kept tabs on over the years — to comprehend that people's energy unharnessed and without full-time organizers helping to shape it, can peter out, even if it doesn't encounter formidable police and other opposition. I suggest we appoint ourselves funders of the harnessing stage, helping to bankroll the movement straight through the working-out of viable agendas to their enactment by our sweetly shaken Capitol Hill."

Our libertarian was pleasantly shocked, because he had come prepared to propose the same game plan. "Perfecto, Happy! Just what I had on my mind.

"Let's not complicate what needs to be done. It's been in the air a long time, and now it's finally coming into view. The trains are on the track. They are being refueled by the hour. The destination is known. The product delivered is overdue justice for the people."

He had a laptop open in front of him and now he turned it so his friends could see the colorful rats on parade, driving out tuxedoed legislators. "Just look at those compelling posters."

He set aside his computer and spoke earnestly. "Here's my take. Let's make the changes, the faster the better. Momentum is not only for competitive sports. Moreover, some of the tactics we hit them with have to be ones that the politicians have *not* had to confront before. The unknown breeds indecision, conflict over how to respond, delays, recriminations. Happy, as you know from your study of history, such inept reactions to the unexpected are themselves beautifully predictable. Look how a battalion of black rats paralyzed them. Those guys from Vancouver who put out the magazine *Badbusters* sense this, as evidenced by their comment on the rodent revolution where they push for 'culture jamming' — the disruption of media images and messages. But the pressure has to be polite, urgent, relentless, and *in personam*, to use the legal term. That is, each media disruption has to laser-target one single legislator and his or her immediate circle of handlers, advisors, and mentors. But always first and last on the singular lawmaker. That will get maximum results."

The chess-playing billionaire also felt they were all of the same mind. Of course, this had already been established in their numerous phone conversations, but it made more impact when they conversed face to face. He opened his heart to his friends. "I like what both of you are saying. You know, from my previous conversations, about the Summons Group that Doug Colebrook is stitching together very tightly out of Chicago. I've recently been helping him with some expenses to fly his network to a meeting. His focus is exactly *in personam*, and the summons-from-the-voters idea is the personal carrier of agendas right back to the Congress. Zoom, zoom, dead on target, no zigzag!

"As I see it, the Summons Group wants an understandable, unified agenda setting out items that repeated opinion polls show already have majoritarian support. The agenda items are not talking points, but rather carefully drafted legislation, vetted by leading law and other experts. Having the demands in this finished form not only reduces the risks of continual bickering but meshes well with the essential approach that our libertarian friend outlined, which was 'the faster the better' as far as being the way to increase the likelihood of enactment. If the Summons people keep up a quick tempo, the powerful, corporate members of the political and business elite, so used to being on top and getting their way, will have no time to mount an effective opposition. Sure, they will have time for mass propaganda, but no time to engage in their historic practice of dividing and ruling. That's why I just love your 'pitchforks' metaphor in that it evokes the image of resolute unity, each prong being a different focused group, all linked together at the base."

"Well," began Happy, "what you have told us about the Summons Group has brought me to look into and reflect upon one aspect of social movements that has sometimes been an Achilles heel for them: leadership. Harnessing the energy has generally involved leaders — mostly meritorious or charismatic leaders.

"But at this point in the trajectory of the rat-inspired uprising, I sense that selecting leaders will create dissension, delay, and vulnerability to expected opposition strategies. You know the saying, 'You go up with the leaders and you go down with the leaders.' That means if a leader is discredited or is corrupt, it can take down the movement.

"I know you guys sometimes rib me for all the time I spend with my head stuck in history books, but to go to my favorite source for relevant examples, let me recall for you some things about The American Revolution against Great Britain. Many of those social movement pioneers made the distinction in organizations between leaders — top-down stuff — and leadership — people who know how to get things done in their area of competence. I like the style adopted by the farmers in Massachusetts in 1774. No pronounced leaders. Just rotating leadership tasks. They combined that with clear goals and the use of pivotal locations as they confronted the Tory stooges of King George III who were trying to enforce the monarch's commands.

"To forestall your objections, because I think you might say, with truth, that we're in a far more complex society, I would underline that, no matter the different circumstances, human personalities, characters, and the steady virtues, frailties, and vices are still the same. Otherwise, why do people today still flock to Shakespearean plays and ancient Greek theater?

"Here," he went on, facing his laptop in their direction, "I taped a sequence on We-Span TV, which illustrates how the new people in the struggle are handling the leadership dilemma." Happy had archived an interview by the well-known host Ryan Mutton, sporting his trademark muttonchops, of the early-bird activists who had already arrived in Washington, DC, to keep pressing for the reforms the rat invasion had gotten people to think about.

"Who are your leaders?" asked Mutton. The three viewers knew that the corporate news media had to have a leader to fix upon whenever there was any kind of demand for change.

Almost as if she had been reading the same books as Happy, the first person to speak said, "Everyone is a leader for whatever job needs to be done."

A couple of others chimed in, "We speak for ourselves," almost talking over each other, laughing at the confusion.

Mutton didn't lose any of his aplomb and went on blandly, "OK, then I'll ask some questions and any of you can answer. Whoever sees it as his/her job."

Happy switched off the television, over his chess-playing friend's objections.

"Hey, I was getting into that!"

Happy grinned — nothing fazed him — and said, "I'll send you the whole tape. Right now, I want to segue to a related point. When the agendas have to be conveyed to Congress to enact, a number of spokespeople will have to stand forth as representatives of the whole. What I want to emphasize to the movement people is that they have to hold tight reins on the people's spokespeople as they engage with the legislative branch. That is why the very natures of the mandates must be unique. They must know they are not there to seek compromises and negotiated, watered-down settlements. These spokespeople are coming with completely drafted legislation, driven by irresistible rhetoric rooted in irrebuttable evidence, filed by so many members of both parties as to approach unanimity: a consensus that totally overrides the insidious procedural traps that have marked the Hill's culture and the reign of Chairman Nyet."

The Libertarian, always concerned with what role he could play, as opposed to worrying about what others were doing, struck in, "Let's back up a bit. How are we going to fuel this emerging wonder of American history? What I'm thinking is that we should have in our minds a minimum of money, split three ways, which can be drawn down expeditiously and accountably. In that way, we will not be bothered to pay expenses pouring in, coming in dribs and drabs. That could test our tolerances.

"I suggest $250 million each, and, if things are going swimmingly in the next few weeks before the competitive primaries start, we can quietly agree to add more. Remember Ben Franklin saying to a woman outside that small Philadelphia building in 1787 on the completion of the draft of the Constitution, though without yet the Bill of Rights, when she asked, 'What have you made, Mr. Franklin?' He replied, 'A Republic, if you can keep it'."

He nodded to Happy. "I threw that in to show you that you're not the only one who has spent many a night with a history book in one hand and a notebook in the other.

"Let me return to Franklin's thought, and build on it, perhaps a bit melodramatically. Perhaps if someone were to ask us what we were doing, we might say: We're keeping a failing ship of state from capsizing so we can bring it to a new and long-dreamed-of destination."

And, recalling the speaker's noteworthy pitchfork reference in his essay, the chess player said, "We are all ready to *pitch* in."

While Happy, having his mind on The Libertarian's apropos reference to old Franklin, added, "I'm ready right now to *fork* over the Benjamins."

Whereupon they began taking assignments to assure that the most efficacious and sober modes of this democracy-rising renaissance could focus on its goals without constantly worrying about the bills.

38 • A Pay-for-Play Congress on the Ropes

STILL FAVORING THE OSTRICH OPTION, once the cleaners' ceremony was over, the chambers properly fumigated, and the new rules about not leaving crumbs around the suites were in place, the lawmakers spent very little time ruminating about the Rat Invasion which, if it was up to them, would be erased from the national memory as thoroughly as the rats seem to have been from the buildings' pipes.

Reporters who reminded them of what had just passed were told either "What's past is past" or "That's ancient history."

That reaction wasn't a manifestation of post-traumatic stress, but rather a hidden avowal that they were suffering *current*-traumatic stress in the form of a swarm of candidates challenging them in the primaries. Little else mattered, though they, of course, didn't say so publicly. Almost in panic, they ramped up their clamor for campaign cash, carried out particularly in icky meetings with Political Action Committees (PACs) in restaurants and hotel suites in Washington.

They universally thought of them as "icky," because, accomplished as some of the lawmakers were in this practiced Kabuki Dance that took place on the line between legalized bribery and shakedown, no one relished playing the role of asking for cash for promises or financial rewards for past legislative sales.

Seasoned analyst Ron McFain put it succinctly during the Republican presidential primary in New Hampshire back in 2000. He described, "a campaign finance system [that was] nothing less than an elaborate peddling scheme in which both parties conspire to stay in office by selling the country to the highest bidder." But few put it more succinctly and blatantly than Pennsylvania Republican Senator Boies Pemrose. Over a century ago, he explained to a gathering of his business supporters, "I believe in a division of labor. You send us to Congress; we pass laws under ... which you make money ... and out of your profits, you further contribute to our campaign funds to send us back again to pass more laws to enable you to make more money."

Odorous as this ritualized auction is to all lawmakers — for it's annoying and degrading to put oneself up like a Victorian lampshade to be bought by the highest bidder — they constantly decline to act together to put an end to it. The repeated pathetic excuse by those who, at least, have the courage to even allude to the matter: "I will not unilaterally disarm before my opponents." Not the most cogent response, in that reform would come if the lawmakers all dropped their ties to their cash providers at the same time.

It was this refusal to act on the impulses of their inner woman or man (in the way that Speaker Blamer had) that meant that the stench of stasis grew worse from election cycle to election cycle. Plunging into this ignoble cash-register politics, the lawmakers incurred even more denunciations. Even the usually indifferent-to-elite-wrongdoing mass media reported the campaign contributions of the moneybags, and fuller public reporting of it was easily accessible to those interested on websites. And for a public fed up with the antics of what more people were calling the "Senatorial Rat Riders" or "the Representative Rat Fleers," new reports and rumors of the payola-seeking taking place as the legislators returned to business-as-usual mode started a whole new round of public attack and ridicule.

Ironically enough, while the current lawmakers were begging for more contributions, almost licking the shoes of the well-heeled, in order to help them overcome their newly appearing opponents, the primary challengers rode on this wave of revulsion against this pay-for-play culture and punctuated it mercilessly during their speeches and debates with the incumbents.

To say that the polls were dropping like thermometers during a sudden freeze for the Congress (as a whole and, unusually, even for individual members in their home districts) is to understate what was really a plummet — like the drop of a roller coaster — to single digits. The people wanted them OUT, OUT, OUT.

The challengers weren't the only ones holding get-togethers to denounce the ongoing corruption. The people's movement was meeting publicly constantly. The first daily rallies — which grew larger each day — took place in front of the expansive back lawn of the U.S. Capitol. The message was devastating in its simplicity. The demands were specific on the placards and banners.

But more broad-gauged was the human-voiced callout, over and over again, enhanced by the hypnotic, low drum beat, the same used by the ancient Roman Army on the march: BOOM, BOOM, slowly; BOOM, BOOM, BOOM, BOOM quickly.

That underlay the callout of: "RESIGN, RESIGN, [slowly, then] RESIGN-RE-SIGN-RESIGN-RESIGN [quickly]. ALL OF YOU. YOU ARE COLLECTIVELY GUILTY OF HIGH CRIMES AND INJUSTICES. WE THE PEOPLE GAVE YOU THE AUTHORITY, AND THEN WE GAVE YOU THE POWER OF ELECTIVE OFFICE. YOU TURNED THAT POWER AGAINST US. WE WANT IT BACK. WE WANT IT BACK. RESIGN, RESIGN — RESIGN-RESIGN-RESIGN-RESIGN!"

Something of a mouthful, but repeated and repeated, it became a mantra that strengthened resolve and focused purpose.

Seeing this on TV, agreeing with every word, and wanting to be part of it, the people started coming by car, train, bus, and airplane to join the daily callout before Congress. Once there, they found other tasks to accomplish along with chanting, as different manifestations of the democracy surge began to take shape.

39 · Summoned to Washington

DOUG COLEBROOK AND HIS COOPERATORS decided it was time to expand operations to Washington, DC. The preliminary work and agendas were ripe for a deeper engagement, which would swing into the *in personam* focus that the Summons Group's presence in the nation's capital would facilitate.

The adequate funding, which was given at just the right time by the billionaire trio, relieved the group of restraints and restrictions that were dollar-based. The fact that they chose not to work in the media spotlight was extremely useful in keeping them away from distractions so they could sort out the talents, tasks, and co-ordinations of this band of brothers and sisters. They knew that the tranquility would soon end as they entered the fray more directly, and they were preparing for a transition that they would shape. As they conceived it, moving to Washington was but an extension of the steadfast Summons-driven activity being carried on back in the districts. The circuits had been carefully organized back home so that the plug, once put in the socket in Washington, would flow with energy and light up the arena where Congressional voting takes place.

The Cooperators, as they now called themselves, arrived ready to initiate an ingenious approach. They would tap into the expertise of the appropriate think tanks and citizen groups but steer clear of the occupational hazards of those organizations, which included bickering, intrigue, and overblown claims of influence on their members around the country.

To accomplish their purposes, the Cooperators located advocates for very well-thought-out legislation for reforming the campaign finance system, for progressive taxation that would give the country needed revenues to fund progressive policy goals, for providing facilities that enable focused organized civic cooperation associations where people would have the space to voluntarily band together to redress imbalances of power and foster community self-reliance.

Besides drawing from the think tanks and already organized citizen groups, the Cooperators knew they could get help from those who had impressive expertise, however subdued, among retired dissenting military, security, and diplomatic persons. These experienced Americans could inform them regarding military/security budgets as well as on foreign policies that prevent wars and enhance standards of living, health, and safety.

Once in Washington, they soon learned of other groups that had developed budgets that represented the values of justice and compassion with attention to workers, children, and posterity. They found seasoned, articulate promoters of energy conversions away from fossil fuels and nuclear energy and toward renewables. The Cooperators had hardly anticipated that so much data-driven common sense and experience would so quickly flow into their modest offices. As Doug Colebrook remarked eloquently, "The traditional virtues have a way of simplifying the common good. Invidious motivations complicate to hide. They build in cancers against public interest. They twist, turn, obfuscate and commercialize in order to subordinate civic values to short-term commercialism."

The Cooperators didn't have to prove themselves to gain entry to the varied progressive organization they found in Washington. They drew on their support back home to earn the respect of these organizations and readily accepted cross-monitoring and checking by other specialists of their submissions. The spreading impression that the Cooperators had large financial resources at their beck and call did not harm the alacrity with which their calls were returned.

They learned that many of the honest experts tapped by them were frustrated, daunted, and discouraged after witnessing years of the crude monetization of the nation's public institutions. But their spreading sadness had not dented their work ethic, because they remained committed to the belief that someday the situation would change so they had better be ready. Their files were gold mines. The Cooperators were enthused to discover in the archives scores of enlightened bills filed over the past century by senators and representatives of both parties but never passed, sometimes never even heard, but kept as a record of what our country could become. Publicizing and taking inspiration from these bills showed that the Cooperators were moving with the rhythms of the best of the past as formulated by legislators of conscience from all parts of the country, and this strengthened the standing of the Cooperators' missions.

Other citizen groups provided the Cooperators with excellent comparative material showing that in Western countries from Australia and New Zealand and Canada to Western Europe, for a long time people had enjoyed the fruits of social justice movements and multiparty vigor, giving them more vibrant polities and more citizen rights, although recently the virus of corporate financial globalization was destabilizing their political economies and fraying the edges of their productive and distributional practices.

These materials provided quite a lesson for the public, showing that people in nations not aggregately wealthier than ours have obtained higher wages, stronger unions, universal health care, good pensions, highly used, modern public transit, one month or more of paid annual vacation, free university education, well-maintained parks and support for the arts, paid maternity leave, daycare, family sick leave, and more humane criminal justice and prison policies. This fortified the Cooperators' position beyond their expectations, as they were astounded by the wealth of material.

As each new bit of information was gleaned, these studied "assets" were conveyed to the Cooperators' fast expanding constituencies and informal alliances, given out both person-to-person and over the internet, even reaching the world of teenagers who were starting to understand the stakes they had in what was transpiring.

Doug and his civic kin particularly wanted expertise in simplification. While most experts are trained to dote on complexity, the ones the Cooperators were searching for would be able to simplify laws, regulations, forms, red tape, and those uncompetitive sign-on-the-dotted-line fine print contracts. They also needed experts who could do *weeding*, ones who could pinpoint outdated, useless laws and laws that shoveled taxpayer monies into crony capitalism, all of which needed to be repealed. This expertise, more often than not, was available at self-described conservative think tanks and related civic organizations.

On this note, someone brought up at a left/right meeting, that the Canadian Medicare Bill, written in the 1960s, which provided full healthcare with free choice of doctors and physicians (i.e., public insurance and private delivery of health services) was all of thirteen pages long. By comparison, the new health insurance legislation in the U.S. ran over 1500 pages with thousands of pages of regulations. The abundance of confusing detail and bureaucratized language confused and froze people in bewildering ways.

The Cooperators task force on this specific issue challenged the rule-writers, who were crafting a new health insurance law, to explain everything in plain English. For they saw that *what* those who had put together the current legislation couldn't explain was the enormous time expended over exemptions, waivers, co-payments, deductibles, and tax consequences that regular citizens were obliged to endure, suffer, or even be brought down by when they fell into innocent violations. The task force well knew that Canada covers all its people at half the average per-capita cost of what the wasteful, corrupt, incomprehensible health care billing industry in the U.S. imposes on American citizens — and still millions of Americans go without insurance.

The Cooperators realized that while the hardline conservatives they worked with understood the corporate control problems, they pigheadedly insisted on free market solutions. They could not, however, provide any very convincing facts or results to testify to real-world cases where their honestly held abstract philosophy actually proved workable or beneficial, especially as they consistently overlooked the perverse incentives and exclusions that reigned in the health insurance fee-for-service business, resulting in avoidable loss of life and other physical and psychological harm to consumers, workers and other citizens.

In working with collaborators of all ideological stripes, the Cooperators tried always to determine and separate expertise from such things as fact-deprived ideology and biased or hidden agendas. Obviously, their own preference was for democratic, open, community action when individuals were unable to cope with the forces arrayed against them or simply unable as individuals to acquire what they needed without engaging in common action. While this suggested an idealism in their preferences, at bottom, the Cooperators were very empirical. They wanted to leave open what scientists called "options for revision." This meant they constantly sought nourishment from their base. They backed a devolution of activities to local levels wherever possible to enrich and advance continual improvements into the future.

40 · A New, Formidable Progressive Alliance Is Formed

WITH CONGRESS BACK IN SESSION, The Reporter was back at his post. It did not take him very long to note a fervent mobilization of progressive, and sometimes libertarian/conservative lawmakers in both Houses. While other reporters were mesmerized by the right-wing revolt against The Speaker, The Reporter kept his eyes on the formation of a real political alignment, being cemented without much ballyhoo, and calling itself the All-American Caucus (AAC). This trans-partisan alliance was not bipartisanship in the old sense. They were not meeting to cut the difference between them so as to locate themselves in the lukewarm middle. They met to see where there was, issue by issue, principled common ground for action. Where there was no agreement, the subject was dropped.

About 105 Representatives and Senators joined AAC. Some were seasoned Congressional veterans. Others made up for their brief experience with hard work and a fresh optimism about making history. They lacked the hard-to-suppress hopelessness of the sensitive old-timers, whose faith in positive change had been dimmed by the erosion of years mired in gridlock.

The ACC's agenda was quite similar to that of the Cooperators, and they promptly reached out to initiate a working relationship with them. Both groups knew that inside and outside pressures were critical to aid them in getting enacted legislation to the White House. Tactically, they decided to lay low and keep their alliance out of the news as they prepared a very solid groundwork of considerable intricacy, fitting their members for action, equipped with carefully written legislation, without having the press on their back and the fulminating talk shows bookers baying at the moon.

One thing the alliance didn't figure on was The Reporter's unparalleled contacts. Tipped off by the adversaries of the AAC inside the hardcore Rules Committee, The Reporter wrote a 1500-word scoop that named names, meetings, and even mentioned some upcoming moves. Given everything going on around the country and in Washington, DC, the scoop did not cause much surprise. It served to intensify the time sensitivity of the AAC, which had one eye on the upcoming primaries as a widely recognized deadline for decisions, and the other eye on the rampant impatience of the rapidly multiplying, enraged public. As one of the Alliance's originators, Representative Christina Eckhardt, said, "The shortness of time is on our side."

Something else was on their side: Rats! Every day, several rats were seen scurrying across the carpets of some Congressional offices, seemingly trying to escape the whole complex, but trapped in it by the closure of every aperture by the Exterminators.

The CIA analysts called it one of their favorite words, "blowback." Exits had been sealed, food was no longer left lying around, and so the rats were hungry, looking for any tiny bit of food and spot of water. And each time a rat emerged, the staff went crazy — some fled to their homes, others started weeping or got furious. "When will it ever end?" seemed to be their common cry.

It didn't help calm things down when many witnessed a designated office rat hunter, left on site by the Exterminator company, bludgeon a cornered rat to a messy death. Nor did it quiet the ravenous reporters looking for a daily rat story for the insatiable masses, who could never get enough of those rodents. For the AAC folks, the perennial rodent stories in the news served to maintain the public ridicule, the hooting and howling that seemed to have instigated the positive transformation of the dignity-obsessed Speaker of the House of Representatives — along with promoting an expanding sense of public engagement.

41· The People's Tide Flows In

MEANWHILE, by car, bus, rail, plane, and even by bicycle and by foot, people of all ages and backgrounds continued to pour into Washington. They filled the restaurants and motels. They needed to find rooms in a city where there were few affordable apartments but many large, under-inhabited houses whose longtime owners wanted to make money to pay for their property taxes and repairs. So they rented to the new arrivals.

The ways these visitors made their voices heard were quite imaginative. There was a cavalcade of horseback riders in a procession down Constitution Avenue resplendent with the signs, "Pass this …" or "Pass that …", always ending with the ominous "or Else!" One horseman was using his trumpet to raise the emotional level of the demonstration, which was fully covered in the press. Others joined the daily "Resign … or Else" rally going on at the backside of the Capitol. Mini-demonstrations were becoming daily events in front of the White House and at other major government buildings containing departments and agencies. Even those agencies in the suburbs, such as the Pentagon, the CIA, the Patent Office, and the Food and Drug Administration, where the employees had thought they would be beyond reach, did not escape their rallying.

As the arriving tenants began to converse with their hosts, they learned about the de facto "colony" of the District of Columbia. Very few visitors knew about DC's absence of voting rights for members of Congress. DC had a delegate who could watch but could not vote. These first timers in the city also learned there was a push for DC statehood. Some became indignant and added this to the grievances that had drawn them to the city. They were riled up enough to make placards calling for the proposed state of Columbia, parading them in front of the White House.

42 · Visiting Your Local Congressperson *In Situ*

NOT SURPRISINGLY there were a lot of freelance, unaffiliated organizers among the popular inflow of citizens, and being self-starters, they took their own initiatives. One of them was to rent space near Congress from which emanated scores of people dropping in on their own member of Congress. The Congressional corridors, until then filled by grasping lobbyists, began to be utilized by common people with uncommon pursuits.

This storefront organizer was no mere dispatcher, though he did handle logistics for the visitors so that they could properly schedule their visits. The fellow once was a staffer for a state senator in Massachusetts, in charge of handling letters from constituents. He was familiar with the granular, easy-to-miss differences in the way letters were written, which determined what got attention and what went straight to the circular file. In the latter group were the "we protest/we demand" ones. The storefront guy offered free 30-minute long orientation classes several times a day in which he explained how to compose these missives and also how to approach their district legislators, giving the benefit of his experience to the human flow in and out of his gathering rooms.

He advised visitors not to do all the talking but make their points and ask the lawmakers or their staff for their reactions orally and in writing for later reference. As Storefront explained, politicians love to have their visitors do the talking so that they can simply smile and make no commitments or judgments. He counseled the visitors to exude some mystery about how large their circle was and who was in it. He said they should have factual questions written that require the staff to get the answers from, for example, the Congressional Research Service. In the process of finding information, the staff would be learning about their concerns. Moreover, he said, in talking to one group, "Don't leave unless you give the staff and the legislator a clear impression that you and your group are only going to get stronger when you meet next time either here or back in their district or state. You may wish," he added, "to ask for a town hall meeting some weeks hence and inquire about how many names on a requesting petition he or she would like to see before coming to your community to talk about your chosen subject. Finally, do your homework on the politician's record and background before you show up."

Storefront wagged his finger and said, with a trace of sadness, "Too many voters are in awe of the aura of power in the Congressional offices and just make nice. That means they leave empty-handed. Politicians know full well how to be very polite and empty. It's practically a job requirement."

Prepared with instructions on how to make the most of their stop-ins, the visitors piled up the meetings with their senators and representatives, who were often unnerved to find how different, how well prepared, how determined their constituents were by comparison with what they were used to. What they were asked about were often things the congresspeople would have preferred not to talk about, and when they left, the visitors impressed them to no end by saying such things as they were now on the way to meet with the lawmaker's primary opponents. The smooth, seldom-seen-through public relations veneer that coated Congressional offices like a fine varnish didn't begin to work with these people whose attitude was simply, and (for the lawmakers) shockingly, "You work for us. We are the people calling for these necessities. You will do what we want … or else."

"Wow" and "Whew," both the legislators and their staff sighed after the visitors departed. Yet, it seemed the minute one contingent left, the congressperson's secretary would be ushering in another bunch. They never seemed to stop coming — hour after hour, their accumulating pressure demanded urgency, action. They would no longer listen to the usual excuses, instead, insisting, if not in these exact words: "No more bullshit or excuses or blaming institutional lethargy."

It didn't help the legislators' peace of mind that while inside talking with the visitors, the incumbents could hear the roars of the rhythmic, "Resign, Resign, Resign, Resign, Resign, Resign," coming from the assembled masses on the back Capitol lawn. For all they knew, their visitors would be going outside to join the shouters as soon as they left the Congressional offices.

43 · The Reporter Keeps Spelunking While the Masses Get Arty

SUCH A TIDAL WAVE OF VISITS, along with all the other new developments, began to have a haunting effect on the solons. The "other developments" included the gentle pressure of the AAC, the rat-crazed media, and the coming-out of The Speaker — who knew he was a "closeted Commie," as Tush Limba, who used our public airwaves for free to make millions of dollars yearly, put it.

There were also the approaching primary battles, the demanding editorials and, especially, the volcanic eruption of the Cooperators' agenda, which was now being widely publicized — its immense popularity measured by incessant polls, e-mails, telephone calls, and letters.

Further, there were demands for meetings from their constituencies, coming from what they would have to call the "unusual suspects," meaning people who had never been heard from before. At this stage, what you had were 535 lawmakers looking for survival, for any way out, and for any stratagem that would turn the popular tide from enmity to admiration.

The Reporter caught these dynamic strains on the members and noted that these were new experiences for them. The old slogans and assurances, the intimidating campaign cash hoards, and the manipulation of patriotic and religious symbols were not only not working, they were backfiring — evoking a blowback of ridicule, not acquiescence.

It was The Reporter who characterized the legislators' new state of mind with such accuracy and trenchancy that the politicians had to be impressed. After reading The Reporter's latest articles, which seemed to peer into their souls, instead of avoiding him as they used to, they were calling him up for interviews. They also wanted to pick his brain as to what he felt was heading their way on the fast track. The Editor provided two interns to help The Reporter handle all the requests. As he saw it, the more the legislators came to depend on The Reporter, the more inside information would come his way.

The most frequent question legislators put to The Reporter was: "What do you think all those corporate lobbying firms, the trade associations and the powerful Chamber of Commerce are going to do about what is happening?"

To his mind, one of the lawmakers' underlying fears was that the spigots of lobbyist-sponsored campaign cash and resources — so-called fact-finding junkets to places with good golf courses — and other perks would be abruptly turned off. Rather than allay that fear, The Reporter merely called it as he saw it. "There's a good chance the lobbyists, trade associations, and other such organizations will lie low so as not to be caught in the Tsunami. Some overdue restored redistribution of wealth they can take in their stride. Some wildly popular law and order motions, especially targeted at egregious corporate wrongdoing, they cannot visibly oppose. Only when they feel their wealth and acquisitions personally are being expropriated or confiscated will they behave like the proverbial cornered rat, stand on their hind legs, and fight.

"Remember, corporations are expedient, opportunistic. When they have to, they'll adjust. That's a lesson from American history. Whenever Congress meant business, business backed off to avoid worse, so as not to let the public think they were as vulnerable as they really were."

For the congresspeople The Reporter spoke with, this message was hardly reassuring, especially as he made no mention of whether this would affect their perks. Personally, The Reporter quite enjoyed watching the way those he was chatting with on the Hill squirmed whenever the back-door protesters got particularly loud.

Truthfully, the hourly, "Resign, Resign, Resign, Resign, Resign, Resign," was becoming a little tedious for the listeners, though individual town criers didn't do this shouting out for hours, but rather took things in turn as the organizers would rotate fresh criers from the large influx of people into their nation's Capital.

They also started to break the monotonous drill by featuring prominent artists singing songs of rebellion, of peace not war, and of unionism. The first celebrity volunteer on stage was Patti Smith who sang, with the crowd joining for every word, not just with the chorus, her famous composition "The People Have the Power" several times in one day. She insisted on inviting any member of Congress or their staff who was listening to join with them. To the astonishment of the assemblage, several dozen lawmakers and assistants came down from their offices to lend their lungs and lock swaying arms. Other singers followed with their own famous renditions.

This addition of famed artists to the lineup attracted a different kind of media: the entertainment and celebrity reporters who reached actual and larger virtual audiences rarely touched by even the most vibrant political demonstrations. Such celebrity performances also attracted fans, some of whom, feeling they couldn't really enjoy the music of their favorite singers and bands unless the experience was "enhanced" with some libations, became unruly when they became tipsy. The police made some arrests.

Other provocations were not so easily explained, leading the organizers to suspect the authorities were using the old technique of infiltrating the crowd with deliberate provocateurs, who would bring the police swarming in when they created a disturbance. So far, organizers had good relationships with the Capital Police, the DC Police, and the Park Service. There seemed to be no evidence of the casually dressed informants and agitators that the FBI had sent to anti-war rallies in years past. Just in case, however, the organizers began "deputizing" young, strong, alert people to be informal sentinels, who would nip brewing trouble in the bud.

Along with talking to those who now held the power, The Reporter, getting antsy, wanted to interview some of the primary challengers who were tearing up the hustings and soon enough might themselves be power brokers. If they were elected in droves, which was not inconceivable, it would represent the second eviction of the current lawmakers from their offices.

He approached some of these new faces, selecting two challengers in a Kansas Congressional District. One was taking on the incumbent, Republican Danforth Dufur, in the primary and the other, as a Democrat, was set to run against Dufur in the November election. Strangely enough, to The Reporter, these erstwhile opponents seemed downright chummy. The Reporter asked how this could be since there were on different sides of the electoral and ideological aisles.

"We have something very important in common," smiled the primary challenger, "and it's not our great hairdos."

"It's a secret society," teased the November challenger, "with tentacles everywhere."

Not sure he was hearing this right, The Reporter took the bait. "What's that?"

The primary fellow answered for both of them "We both belong to a small select organization around the country. It has no staff. All it has is a name and an indomitable spirit."

He bit on this one too. "So, what's its name?"

"It's called Ousters United in Time or, mellifluously enough, OUT," exclaimed the Primary Challenger. "Each of us has agreed that we need a new agenda, something like the one the Cooperators are working on. Our first task is to give permanent layoffs to the entrenched waddling around Congress at the moment."

His Democratic friend continued the discourse, "We can't lose. If my bud doesn't win the primary, he'll have left Dufur in such a weakened condition, that I'll simply be administering the coup de grace at election time."

"It's like tag-team wrestling," the Primary Challenger ended with a flourish.

Although The Reporter would have had to admit, if pressed, that he wasn't all that familiar with the gentle sport of pro wrestling, he found the comparison was quite appropriate.

Everywhere he journeyed, The Reporter witnessed a similar confident élan and a sharing of resources between supposed opponents. Everywhere the tumult of the masses was providing the backdrop for the challenger's brazen boldness. Those running in elections acted audaciously because the public dared them to.

The Reporter's three-part series, in which he detailed the spirit and strategies of the challengers, raised the fright index to stuck-in-a-haunted-house level on Capitol Hill. But the public reaction was almost gleeful, with some comments reflecting the prevailing determination among them, which could have been put into words as: "Whoever wins, they're going to be taking orders from 'we the people'."

44 · The Rats and Their Handlers

AS A SIDEBAR, The Reporter updated the public on what had happened to the white mice in cages that the two 18-wheelers delivered to the Congress for each member's office. They didn't last long in their new digs. Within a day, they were collected by an accommodating chain pet store and put up for sale. However, that was not the end of the white mouse saga.

Daily, visitors to the Congress carried caged white mice, some undercover in large tote bags and others in plain sight, right through the X-ray machine and past the guards. Since pets were allowed into the Capitol, the police did not know how to stop them.

Their Chief went to see the Administration Committee Chairs, who in turn called in the House and Senate Parliamentarians.

"What can we do without arousing the animal rights and welfare lobby?" asked one leading Senator, a guy who was said to leave no interest group without a nod — and a request for a donation.

One of his staff told him, "The House Parliamentarian said that they conceivably get legislation passed that would bar 'mice,' from accompanying visitors. But — and you know these Parliamentarians are all lawyers — they say there would be a problem of definition. You'd logically have to include rats, but how about other rodents such as voles, hamsters, or woodchucks?"

The Congressman at the discussion threw up his hands. "Whatever we did, we'd look like fools as well as anti-pet. There's no label that will destroy your career faster than being called anti-pet, a person who doesn't like cats, dogs, or even guinea pigs is pilloried. It's worse than being labeled a Red."

"And can you imagine," The Senator added, "how this will feed the cartoonists a five-star dinner? Imagine when *Doomsbury* gets ahold of it."

"You're probably right," replied the Senate Parliamentarian, who was, indeed, a lawyer, "too narrow a definition would be an animal bill of attainder, that is, it would deny singled-out species their day in court, and too broad would be inviting charges of animal abuse, especially if the humans claim that the pet rodents perform as 'service' creatures, something like seeing-eye dogs though offering, obviously, more intangible benefits."

The House Parliamentarian paused, holding up a hand to indicate that he still had more to say. Raising an eyebrow, he contemplated something that had just come to him in a 'light bulb' moment. He resumed, "We could, maybe, stop this scandalous rat-toting by having the rodents declared a public health threat. For the Congressional medical clinics to impose a quarantine is well within their discretionary authority."

"Presto!" said the Senator. "That's why I keep saying we need more of these brainstorming sessions to handle the all these new challenges ... and challengers."

"Perfecto," said the relieved Congressman, though, since he was removing a cigar from his vest pocket, it was unclear whether he was referring to the solution or the brand.

Both rushed to the doctors, with their demand that pet rats be declared risk factors. The prudent doctors said they would have to check the science before deciding anything.

And while that checking went on over endless days and delays — the Ides of March had come and gone — there were more visitors, more pet mice, and more consternation among the denizens of Capitol Hill encircled by omnipresent press corps eagerly updating their rat stories. And, without any takers, brazen press photographers asked the congresspeople to pose with the pet rats.

45 · The Cooperators Step Up Their Game

NOT MANY BLOCKS AWAY, as the Capitol-ists endured visits from rat-carrying constituents, Doug Colebrook's group was working furiously as if every day were a deadline. The Cooperators had lined up the most proficient, action-starved citizen groups and think tanks as crews to work on crafting basic legislation covering the necessities of life for the American people. The categories were many: 1) Food, 2) Housing, 3) Energy, 4) Health, 5) Safety, 6) Transportation, 7) Communication, 8) Insurance, 9) Credit, 10) Security, 11) Taxation, 12) Public Works, 13) Children, 14) Retirement/Pensions,

15) Education, 16) Leisure/Play/Art, 17) Work/Wages, 18) Civil Rights/ Civil Liberties, 19) Street and Corporate Crime Prevention/Enforcement, 20) Environment, 21) Clean Public-Funded Elections With Choice, 22) People Empowerment, 23) Community and Self-Reliance, and 24) Corporate Accountability.

All these laws were put forward within a broad frame of political, economic, and social philosophy, one that drew from the best of both left and right traditions. For example, to conservatives who might view the numerous categories as invitations to expansive government, which, they might feel, was meddling in the polity with no limits, they offered a paper by a prominent legal philosopher, in which he described the two pillars of freedom: *Freedom To* fulfill human possibilities and *Freedom From* arbitrary and abusive power whether public or private in its sourcing. Using these as guiding principles, the philosopher explained how the new laws in multiple areas would enhance these two goods.

Meetings between Cooperator personnel and the over 100 sympathetic members of Congress and/or their staff were daily and intense. Everybody knew that time was of the essence. The plutocrats and the oligarchs were caught off guard, but it would not be long before they would develop a multifaceted counterattack. Before they did so, the Cooperators were trying to put those opposing them on the defensive.

In war and in politics, it comes down to who is seen to be on the offensive and who is seen to be on the defensive. Fence sitters decide which side to back according to their understanding of which side is pushing forward and which side is giving ground. This perception of who is advancing and who is retreating is acutely judged on Capitol Hill. Members of Congress shape their behavior, their expectations, their very daily identity according to what they perceive. On any given issue, lawmakers know immediately who is on offense and who is on defense. At this crucial juncture, the people were decidedly on offense. History — and we know Doug and many of the Cooperators were profound students of history — shows the people do not usually get a second-strike opportunity if they muff the first.

A key part of keeping up the pressure and maintaining the offense was keeping the object of struggle in the public eye by putting up posters and carrying placards, physically and on the internet, that contained a set of common-sense, democratic slogans. What the innovators were demanding was not exactly exotic or alien to American capabilities or expectations. The U.S. has a heritage of democratic rebuffs to the fat cats. The visitors roaming Washington, DC, in ever greater numbers, had come up with a particularly juicy poster slogan, referring back to that heritage, though some criticized it as unglamorous and less radical than it might have been, given the scope of change demanded by the general public.

Hundreds of placards were carrying the words: NO BIG DEAL — WE'VE EARNED IT, WE'LL GET IT! It was a phrasing that resonated for anyone with a modest knowledge of American history. This was not Franklin Delano Roosevelt's New Deal, it was not Harry Truman's Fair Deal, nor was it Lyndon B. Johnson's Great Society.

It was, simply, "No Big Deal!," a slogan that summarized their key demands: get it over with; put civic-spirited people in office; and let us live better lives utilizing the resources that we've already produced and earned, resources that have been aggressively taken from us for over half a century.

46 • Hear, Hear

THE ALL-AMERICAN CAUCUS had a seminal meeting, which they all attended with their legislative calendars in hand. Now numbering 110 and all calling themselves "co-chairpersons," the members agreed that the next order of business was to press for prompt Congressional hearings for each item on their tables and the Cooperators' agenda. Fortunately, the logisticians among them had found that there were many under-challenged Committees and Subcommittees with readily available hearing rooms and budgets.

Of course, AAC members realized that stopping a bill in the hearing was a traditional way to block any action since the routine was that no piece of legislation, except for refueling the country's boomeranging wars such as in Iraq and Afghanistan, could go to the Floor without prior hearings. With this in mind, the AAC wanted hearings for reasons of professionalism and to take away the excuses of obstructionists and their lobbying friends, who, if the AAC had tried to put a bill on the floor before it had been vetted in hearings, would have cried foul, labeling the process unfair, precipitous, and authoritarian.

Although as Committee Chairs, conservative legislators were reluctant to hold hearings, they were swayed not only by the clamoring inside the buildings of the AAC caucus but by the clamor arising outside when the "Resign, Resign" crowds started chanting, "Hearings, Hearings." Their voices reverberated and were repeated throughout the congresspeople's districts back home. The chairs of the committees, no matter their positions, felt they had no choice but to schedule hearings for ten straight days, allowing only one-week advance notice for preparations and witnesses. Obviously, weekends were cancelled, and all hands were on deck.

The media were relieved. Reporters did not like how demonstrators and many in the public had taken to calling them "Rat Reporters" or "journalists on the Rat Beat."

It demeaned them even though all this political discontent and protesting sold papers and got high TV/radio ratings. They were sick of being assigned to reporting on these tedious government news conferences, in which they were asked to be no more than conduits, presenting the official view to the public. They were ready for substance and the clash of interest groups.

Their editors, seeing the public was hungry for this news, reassigned reporters and columnists from the business, style, and sports pages to join their colleagues on Capitol Hill and bolster coverage of the hearings. These men and women, having become bored feeding the masses' once-insatiable desire for gossip and sports stats, were more than glad to be freed from their daily drudgery to join in conveying to the American people, and the world, what was going on during these historic days of action, drama, of serious purpose.

As would happen with most anyone, the prospect of significance — that is, the fact that what they did might make some valuable imprint on the world — elevated their feelings of professional self-regard and competence. Before this historic opening, the newspeople's marketing of trivia, repetition and other dreary formulaic routines was feeding a work attitude of just "put in your time," then retire.

Once Committee hearings were scheduled and their times posted, long lines, starting at dawn, formed outside the House and Senate Office Buildings as the common people sought entrance into the limited seats of the hearing rooms. This was not going to be the usual fill-'em-up with lobbyists unless, that is, the lobbyists themselves — no paid stand-ins — were willing to line up in the cold at 5:00 a.m. and wait for four hours till the doors opened.

The Reporter, who was covering the hearings and the lines, noticed that the lobbyists' customary ploy — hiring young men and woman at $20 an hour to stand in line for them until the hearing room opens at which time the lobbyists sauntered in to take their place in line — was not working. The street ralliers had warned the lines against such usurpations, so that now crowds identified such substitutes and politely ushered them away.

Once inside, and after the committee and subcommittee chairs had gaveled open the hearings, The Reporter found another departure from business as usual. The witnesses were distinctly unrepresentative of the tight circle of professional testifiers from corporatist think tanks, trade groups, and compensated "experts," who usually dominated the witness stand.

The average people spoke during these sessions, put forth by populist politics back home. They related the experience, expectations, and demands of usually forgotten, excluded, disrespected, and overcharged people. It was a veritable citizens' army of the harmed, underpaid, uninsured, pension-stripped, job-insecure, workers. Those chosen to represent were unbowed — they were the thinkers and doers unbound and free to speak truth.

The chairs, forced to accommodate such plain speakers, were happy when, having given them a fair say, they were able to call on the characters they were more accustomed to listening to: the well-heeled "suits," with well-oiled tongues.

Yet the chairs and The Reporter each saw that something was wrong. The lobbyists and corporate flaks presented their views, but the calm exhibition of command was not there. The overall climate in the country seemed to have discouraged them from coming out so complacently with their usual warnings that if anything was touched in the business world there would be massive layoffs, and companies would move abroad or lose the incentive to produce.

Yet even with largely toned-down presentations of their business-first views, which called for standing pat on all the current, cozy arrangements, there was a clear contrast between what they claimed and what the rest of the population challenged and knew. It was really no contest.

Everybody — those inside the hearing rooms and the vast streaming audience outside — recognized the change. Whether they were elated or they were biting their tongues, no one could assert that there was a lack of information, public records, or working models, as AAC staffers supplied the facts pertinent to each subject area.

Throughout the hearings, there was a wealth of on-the-record cross-examinations, exhibits, and filings for public discussion in all media.

47 • They Keep on Ticking

AS THE HEARINGS CONTINUED, The Reporter became intensely curious about the stamina of the people clamoring daily everywhere.

So many pundits had predicted that the public's burnout was just around the corner that he wondered what kept them going on, seemingly on an upward curve by which it seemed their involvement was continually expanding, not flagging as so often has happened to other movements over the decades.

Since the hearings and the background stories were being covered by hundreds of reporters, and, as we know, The Reporter didn't like to hunt with the pack, he asked his editor to send him around the country for a whirlwind week so he could try to fathom this remarkable civic constancy.

The Reporter's first stops were the bus lines. He Greyhounded it across the land, listening in to the small talk of the passengers. People were talking about how the demonstrations for this and that change were going to make their personal families lives better. Others were on their way in clusters to marches and rallies and city council hearings.

Even high school students were looking at each other (instead of their iPhones) as they talked over the rising possibility of their getting free college educations and high minimum wages for their part-time jobs.

The Reporter filed his first story, giving it the title: "Small Talk Down, Big Talk Rises." It was chocked with quotes he had overheard from his fellow bus riders. He captured the spontaneity and emotion of the common folk in a far better way than had ever been done in a stilted "man in the street" interview.

Next stop on his explorations were the diners and crowded fast food eateries. In them, he heard arguments about substantive proposals before Congress. He was surprised to hear that the speakers often evinced considerable knowledge of the subjects, more, perhaps, than that possessed by Congress members.

It persuaded The Reporter, as he wrote in a second article, that when people give themselves a chance to read, talk, and think, they can, even in this flashy, sound-bite media age, rise to the occasion. He included in his story a quote from a 20th century organizer who, when asked why she fought so hard for democracy, had replied, "Because it brings the best out of people."

His next dispatch was based on his visits to the teeming student populations, heavily minority, whom he found attending California's large community colleges. He quickly learned that students were cutting their vocational classes so they could hear open-air speakers discussing the current democratic revival or to attend workshops for pending actions demanding big changes in how the country was run.

Previously, for a piece he'd done on that level of education, The Reporter had noticed that community college students, mostly from low-income families, were all about the business of enhancing their employment prospects. Apart from some charitable activity, there seemed to be little civic awareness or activity on campus, at least when he'd filed his story two years ago. That seemed long ago, for there had been a sea change in campus opinion.

The new dispensation was striking. It was as if the new political discourse had allowed students to articulate a sense of injustice in relation to their families' plights in the inequitable economy, which then galvanized them, finally putting some muscle into the "community" designation of their schools.

As The Reporter made his rounds, he noticed, further, that student involvement in civic actions was having a psychological effect. Activism and showing up for gatherings, rallies, and meetings was the thing to do, and, as this continued, the experiences had become internalized so that everyone counted on everybody to pull together as part of the local culture. Not turning out for a demonstration was frowned upon. The "mavericks" were the people who were apathetic.

In his fourth article, The Reporter alluded to the ancient city of Athens where the word "idiot" referred to residents of that remarkable town who did not engage in Athenian democracy. They shirked their citizen duties, and so were labeled ignorant, self-isolated, and not public citizens.

Idealists throughout the centuries have looked back to those ancient Athenians (although they restricted women and other subdued groups from full participation) as ideal insofar as it was a city state where peer group pressure bent toward public, civic engagement and reproached people who withdrew into their individual selfishness. They saw voluntary, self-motivated engagement as a collective survival practice.

The Reporter had a talent for weaving in such historic references to older state forms into his daily narratives, giving them context and gravity.

In his final wrap-up article on visiting engaged people across the nation, he described the emerging culture of civic-ism finding roots in the psyche, the status, the self-actualization of many people. He noted that people such as these, who were making history often did not realize it, and, if they did, they would push forward with even more force and profundity.

Common people reading his now-celebrated reports felt pride. Uncommon people, namely the oligarchs, felt dread. They gritted their teeth and hunkered down with the belief that corporate stamina would eventually outlast these public outrages. They had to be careful not to overplay their hands. Refusing to bend, they could indeed be broken. Bending became their present tactical mantra.

Little things began to worry the ruling cliques. An exchange of words from several high-schoolers waiting for their bus went viral. Three students were overheard chatting about some politicians' voting records. A couple of students, laughing, told them they "were not turned on to politics," and urged them to come to a dance that night.

One of the serious students replied, "Don't you remember your history courses? Whenever people anywhere in the world were not turned on to politics, politics turned on them. Viciously."

"Activism by the young has become 'cool'," concluded The Reporter.

48 • People's Democracy, Could It Be Good for Business?

BACK AT THE CONGRESSIONAL HEARINGS, the chairs had to frequently admonish witnesses to offer their specific opinions on the pending legislation and not grandstand. The major bills that called for big changes were, not surprisingly, those supported by the grassroots, the Cooperators and the AAC. The designated numbers of the bills — "H.R. This" and "S. That" — were already all over social media and on posters and placards carried by the marchers and held aloft at the rallies. Constituents brought copies of the bills on their visits to Congress, perhaps stuffed in a pocket on the side of their pet rat cages.

The AAC didn't object to the filing of other bills related to each subject — nefarious bills expertly contrived by corporate law firms to negate or weaken the AAC's agenda. While the AAC would fight tooth and nail against these bits of legislation, it was part of the AAC's design to take away all possible excuses from their opponents by giving them full right to introduce any noxious legislation they wanted.

A pleasant surprise for the AAC and a source of groans for the hardliners were the testimonies of enlightened, recently formed, ad hoc business organizations whose corporate executives took offense at the U.S. Chamber of Commerce presuming to speak for them as if all of business was of one mind against introducing major changes.

These witnesses attracted media attention as they came out in favor of equitable taxation; a leaner, more efficient defense; and public-spirited environmental, consumer and labor positions. As a whole, they were arguing that the evidence overwhelmingly proved that the stronger a democracy is, the more prosperous and productive it is. As one executive put it, "To have a robust economy, it's a simple matter of higher wages, larger consumer demand, better public services, superior business ideas, and the security and fairness of the law."

While these testimonies were irking to the corporate boosters, they were gratifying to the three billionaires since they indicated that fellow businessmen and women were hearing the message of reform that the trio had harkened to early on. The three of them were forthright in urging forward and facilitating the presence of these good business groups.

One evening, gathered in Happy's Washington penthouse over drinks, the start-up backer read to his chums a passage from one of his favorite thinkers, the British philosopher/mathematician of the early 20th century, Alfred North Whitehead, to wit: "The behavior of the community is largely dominated by the business mind. A great society is a society in which its men of business think greatly of their functions. Low thoughts mean low behavior, and after a brief orgy of exploitation low behavior means a descending standard of life."

"Very impressive," responded The Libertarian.

"Very motivational," declared the chess player, "especially for us who are thinking 'greatly of our functions,' which boil down to fighting to give the people a deciding vote in how business and politics are conducted."

It had come to this. They, behind-the-scenes players, were ready to step into the limelight alongside these other progressive business people. Duly instructed, their "action man" made it happen. It turned out not to be that difficult. They were ready to make their voices heard on prime time.

The entrance of alternative business advocacy groups upset the equations of power in Washington. Over the years, the mainline, old trade lobbies had succeeded in forging a remarkably unity. They almost always did speak with one voice, even turning the large National Federation of Independent Business into a dependency, who slavishly followed the big business line. Whistleblowers, players who got sick of the fixed game and spoke out, were few and subject to a dedicated retaliation of discrediting and blacklisting.

Now, to the consternation of conservative trade agencies, along came the various issue-oriented business groups speaking their own minds, writing op-eds, giving national television interviews, and applying their great expertise with social media — greater than that possessed by the old-line groups due to their mostly younger leaders.

With business unity so broken, "Would Humpty Dumpty," as one pundit put it, "ever be put back together again?" Or, in the whining words of Tush Limba, "Did even Hercules have to deal with such a Hydra?"

49 • Washington and Wall Street Face Off

THE ENTRENCHED BUSINESS LOBBIES were perplexed and did not know what they could counter with other than mere repetition of their arguments. Never before had they faced such treachery in their own camp. There were no ideologically alien "isms" to taint their rising corporate tormentors with nor could they accuse them of not meeting payrolls or not being innovative or profitable or of acting to undermine capitalism. How could these business lobbies cast aspersions on their fellow businessmen when they themselves were vulnerable to attack for demanding subsidies and being

instrumental in creating the crony capitalism so hated by both left and right? Who were they to be righteous? Meanwhile, in a maddening way, the upstart business groups set up shop in Washington for the long term as if they had no plans of going away.

It was high time for one more confidential strategy session. The Washington lobbyists went to New York to size up the situation with what they pejoratively called the "Wall Street Crowd." The Washington trade lobbies felt that if they were culpable in small ways, such as asking for handouts, the very nature of Wall Street business — making big profits from pensions, mutual funds, and small investor money in ever-more destabilizing and speculative ways — was much more objectionable. Wall Street made more profits by such rampant speculation than the people who made real products and provided real services could ever hope to see. And the indiscriminate American public, sickened by Wall Street shenanigans, tended to taint all business with a broad brush.

The chronic tension between the two business blocs was not widely known because of the way the well-oiled public relations firms had effectively contained it. Since Wall Street had collapsed on the entire economy in the great recession in 2008–2009, the resentment had worsened. The Washington trade groups and their members back home rightfully feared that the "too big to fail" banks were still with us and still addicted to playing dangerous games with the public's money. According to the trade groups, these goliath banks and their reckless financial circles had not learned their lesson. They were continuing their risky speculations, especially with multi-tiered derivatives (bets on bets on bets) that could, once again, sink all businesses and bring on Uncle Sam's overzealous bailouts. Still, as they filed into the great conference room with its majestic mahogany table, the Washington lobbies had to put their best face on the situation and swallow their antagonisms to concentrate. It's no time to quibble when you are facing a tidal wave.

The rarely agitated Chairman seemed agitated now, greeting the arrivals as colleagues in distress. "Ladies and gentlemen, pardon the strict security procedures and the frisking of all cellphones and other metallic and plastic objects on your person. It was done for the good and safety of all of us.

"Now let's get down to business and hear first from our guests. Please proceed."

Rising to speak was a middle-aged gentleman, sporting a large U.S. flag button, known to them all as the leading spokesman for the U.S. Chamber of Commerce.

"The situation is clear. We're facing from the people alone a triumvirate in this onslaught. The three elements of protest are: first, those demonstrating *en masse* day after day back home; second, the huge influx of people pouring into Washington, organized and funded for an array of tactical show-ups and showdowns, most prominently the RESIGN, RESIGN, RESIGN bellowers at the rear of the Capital; and, third, rich people who have come from out of nowhere to provide an endless source of funding to keep this hubbub going.

"What has really got us worried is that these carryings-on are not confined to energetic protests but have been turned into a cluster of bills finely drafted and filed, ones which, if passed, would upend our whole cozy little system. And does anyone think they can't be passed? The hearings underway are convincing the public of these measures' value, and the fear of a primary challenger has weakened the position of many of our most ardent champions. And then there is the time factor. Our opponents have squeezed us so that anything we decide to do will have to be initiated and carried through in an incredibly short time span — no more than a month, we estimate. We are unable to either mount a television campaign — for the public is on to us — or counter the momentum that has our allies, if not on the run, then on the defensive or fighting against themselves.

"The train has left the station. The numbers have been counted. All we have been able to come up with are salvage operations like trying to put a short-term leash on the bills, or trying to reduce the budgets for enforcing or implementing these bills if they do get enacted, or deleting some of the criminal penalties these hotheads want to fix on them. Even these last-gasp measures are not likely to be adopted. It's like trying to stop a stampede of bulls with cocker spaniels. Sorry not to be more optimistic, but we have to face facts."

He fingered his patriotic button as if that talisman would give him some strength.

"We're up against, first and foremost, the immediate primary season, and that gives us some spirit as we draw on the survival instincts of the lawmakers. Even so, we know the pitchforks are not coming; they are already here. Crazed rats with pitchforks!"

The Chamber of Commerce speaker mopped his brow and sat down.

The Chairman, who seemed to have lost his agitation — he was a can-do type who loved handling a crisis (the direr, the better) — now had his work cut out for him.

He said to the flag-lapelled previous speaker, "I must say, you are not exaggerating the looming situation confronting us. And it affects us corporate types as deeply as it threatens you, even though you are facing a more immediate catastrophe of being literally unseated from the height of power.

"We are equally affected in that we have long known, have we not, that the strongest source of our global power as businesses has been the Congress?

It is through that foremost of the three branches of government — staffed with our people who are hired by our noble solons — that we secure the lenient laws that allow us to make more of our money. This is just one factor that helps cement together the invincible, synergistic duality of business and government wedded together by the majorities of only 535 people down there.

"Consider it an all-powerful kind of Khyber Pass. I know that those of you who work on global business are aware that the mountain pass between Afghanistan and Pakistan was the historic gateway for all invaders who wanted to grab the booty from the region. Alexander the Great went through there, as did Genghis Khan. Whoever held the pass held the region. So, for business to reign in a nation, it has to occupy the metaphoric Khyber Pass between the people and the laws governing the society. That Khyber Pass is our august Congress.

"You know what? Just as we have dominated this Khyber Pass to get our way, we can fall if the Khyber Pass is taken over as a channel by which the multitudes get their way. Their activists are beginning to realize what we all have privately known, that one percent or less of real active citizens is all they need, *provided* public opinion is behind them, to overcome our one percent."

On his scratch pad, the Chamber of Commerce man wrote, "Live by the Khyber Pass, die by the Khyber Pass."

"Now, to get to the quick," continued The Chairman, "and take a brutal assessment of the situation, which presently is so much in our opponents' favor. To put that in plain terms, just how much do we lose over the longer run if the other side triumphs in Congress?"

All around the room, notepads were being filled at a rapid pace.

The Chairman continued, "Much of what makes up the Cooperators' agenda already exists in Western Europe and Canada. We make plenty of money in those countries. Other sets of bills want to simplify the laws and repeal laws that are purposeless but nagging at us. While yet other legislation gives some balance to labor and consumers to head off the kind of frauds and other violations that give all business a bad name. As far as civil rights and civil liberties, passage of better laws in that sector helps widen markets and enhances predictability and stability. We have learned that lesson, I hope. Main Street must like the emphasis on community business and self-reliance. Don't we want to be self-reliant in energy? How can we oppose clean elections and civic education? For sure, the overall package forces us to share more, but by so doing, we make more. My thought here is maybe we should let the people have the money to spend that they deserve and give them the public services that private capital doesn't want to invest in, though it benefits enormously from them every day. Let's acknowledge those benefits and let them increase while keeping in mind that money in the common people's pockets eventually ends up in our pockets as soon as they consume. And Americans love to consume, piggybanks be damned."

Heads nodded in agreement over that bon mot.

"That's the national field. But what about foreign policy?" The Chairman continued. "Lots of us are sick and tired of all these wars that the politicians are getting us into around the world. They stir up ever more violence against our presence all over. And I'm going to let you in on a little secret. People that hate America don't buy our products.

"My sum-up is their slogan, 'No Big Deal.' It is time to take the longer look."

The Washingtonians blanched and then sucked air.

The Chamber's speaker blurted, "Did I hear what I've just heard?!"

"You damn well did," said The Chairman, who didn't like this fellow's tone.

"I can't believe you're serious. Your speech was nothing short of traitorous. This is Benedict Arnold to the tenth power. This is complete surrender, unconditional surrender, even though you started by inferring it was a hypothetical, and, even now, I dearly hope it was. I can't imagine your distinguished colleagues around the table support you in even raising such a possibility?"

The Chairman smiled expansively. Here was just the sort of challenge he liked. "I don't want to make this a duel between the honorable member of the U.S. Chamber and myself. Let's open things up a little. "Feel free, everybody around the table, to say your piece. After all, that is what a discussion is about."

A New York banking magnate with a dollar sign, in quadruple-plated solid gold, on his lapel, jumped in. "I didn't want to get to where our Chairman went so quickly. But now that we've gone through the Khyber Pass into candor-land, I must share my inner thoughts about our big banks, which have gone right back to speculation and derivatives after nearly destroying the world economy by their let-the-buyer-beware practices in 2008 and 2009. They are still counting on getting off the hook from the next disaster by becoming even more too big to fail.

"Speaking as one who knows, let me say that we bankers can't resist temptation. If we are not saved from ourselves, next time the collapse will find a fed-up, angry electorate that will call for and get nationalization of the banks, regardless of who is in Congress or the White House. You don't need a crystal ball to see that if that happens, it will be followed by turmoil here and overseas, followed by other takeover demands on other industries tethered to our financial networks. Pitchforks? Hell. This time the rats will be driving bulldozers and pelting us with napalm!"

A New York insurance executive, less personally wealthy, spoke next: "As we all know, when the banks speak, insurance listens. Like younger brothers, we walk in the footsteps of those we consider elder siblings. Bank redlining leads to insurance redlining. We follow the credit and then make the bets. The feds are targeting some of our larger insurance companies as 'too big to fail' and, therefore, subject to more regulation and capital reserve requirements.

"To get to the point, if my friend from a big bank sees that now is the right time for radical reform, I can't help but say the insurance companies are more than willing to follow in the tracks of our financial brothers."

All the Washington spokespersons and their adjuncts were taken aback. This was not what they had expected to hear. The scene was getting out of hand. And while they were breaking out in sweats and fingering their lapel buttons, The Chairman's group was not noticeably upset, at least outwardly.

What they personally hated, almost above all, was the confession of weakness on the part of one of the business community. One attending began, "Are we from two different worlds, here? I can't believe I'm hearing such concessions coming from the very business community that screwed up in 2008 and brought down the economy. Now you're saying you can't help yourself, as if you were chronic drunks or cocaine addicts, and you are asking the government to detoxify you as if you wanted to go into some kind of dirty-profit addiction rehab.

"And just to touch on the question of image, I must say that's something you can never say in public, so how are you going to explain your surrender in front of the baying pack of media hounds?"

A New York corporate attorney, who was known as cooler than cool, said, "Let's calm down. I don't think we're anywhere near the point of talking to the public about these views. It's just a discussion, after all.

"The business people here are acting as if all is lost. Let me call up another scenario, one you are all familiar with. Just imagine a dire event occurring, one far worse than a handful of rats eating the legislators' lunches. I'm thinking, for example, of a terrorist attack larger than 9/11 or a sudden collapse of a major corporation with far-reaching tentacles like AIG, or a major earthquake, or infectious epidemic megadisaster.

"Now what if we got credible scientists and national security officials to start predicting such likelihoods? You know there are plenty of doomsayers around, many of them backed by facts. They just need a megaphone. Ones we can provide. The distractions they provide can help divert the people's attention. Break their momentum, to give us time."

A New York securities ratings magnate couldn't let that pass. "Counsel, methinks you are a bit too sanguine in thinking such a complex and exposable plan could be worked. I don't even want to question how you would go about getting this accomplished — whatever the legality — without any footprints. Besides, Armageddon-type warnings are a dime a dozen. Until it happens, people don't give it a thought. They have their daily burdens to worry about. Look at the Bay Area in California and the certain likelihood of 'The Big One,' the doozy of a quake that has been predicted for years if you want to know what I mean."

"Just a thought," meekly replied the corporate counsel. "I was just running it up the flagpole to see who would salute. Maybe you're right — we shouldn't over-imagine."

He was getting dirty looks.

Despite that fact that no one welcomed the lawyer's comments, his let-it-all-hang-out attitude seemed to have an open-sesame effect on the assemblage. Questions and answers darted back and forth like balls in a ping pong game, often not directed at the whole gathering but between adjacently seated business people versus Wall Street types.

Here are some of the quick dialogues.

"You're not ready to oppose higher taxes?" from one unbelieving trade representative.

An adjacent Wall Streeter shot back, "They're not my taxes; they're company taxes or my descendant's taxes. It depends if the money is used wisely for such ends as repairing or building better public facilities, doesn't it?"

Another Chamber of Commerce minion talked about what she thought would be a weak point, "But the corporations will never be persons anymore!"

"So? They never were. The whole idea is sacrilegious." The replying executive was a deeply religious Baptist.

A small business representative raised what he took to be another chink in business people's armor: "You guys will be over-regulated to death."

The answer he got: "Not if we emulate best practices in our respective industries. We'll be ahead of any regulations. Some companies have already followed this line. Look at the Interface Corporation, for example, or the Patagonia Corporation or The Body Shop."

This tit-for-tat exchange went on for 20 minutes between the two groups. Finally, another Washington trade association spokesman stood up and asked for a half-hour recess in an adjoining conference room.

Sensing that this break would be welcomed by everyone, The Chairman sweetly replied, "By all means, friends. Take longer if you wish. But as you talk things over among yourselves, keep in mind the differences between our two groups. You are responding to your dues-paying members who expect you to constantly warn and constantly fight what you have told them is detrimental to their interests. We are responsible to our shareholders who have no power and seemingly no interest in our lobbying positions as such. You may wish to separate this behavioral difference or motivation, realizing we are given much more leeway by the people who are invested in us than you may be your clients. Frankly, I think that may give us a little more objectivity. Think about that when you repair to your deliberations down the hallway."

50 • Breakout Session

AN AGRIBUSINESS CEO: "I think, given the primaries' threat, it is too late to 'nip' anything in the bud or even appear to beat back this tsunami. Just trying will further discredit and disable us, weakening our future influence. Let's admit this is historic in its way and history has not been kind to Tories or southern plantation owners. We would most certainly lose, in any event, and probably help them recruit more activists and more funding and more media for their causes. Our behind-the-scenes activity on Capitol Hill — using arguments like 'Isn't this going a bit extreme?' to win the amendments mentioned by our sagacious counsel — may be the best we can do."

An executive mining magnate was a hardliner. "Am I in the minority in experiencing disbelief over what I've been hearing earlier and just now? Has the fight gone out of us? I hope I'm not speaking only for myself when I say I don't want to have the 1872 Mining Act repealed, making it so our companies have to start paying royalties to the government from our mines on public lands. This affects us all. Can you imagine the environmental mandates, the increase in lawsuits blocking extraction, and the growth of substitute materials that can start putting us out of business?"

"Jack," said a midsize generic drug company chieftain, "much of what you are declaiming against is happening anyway. You're already in the courts, where you win some and lose some. Trends toward more efficient and renewable materials are not going to be stopped. For heaven's sake, the business magazines where you advertise are trumpeting this 'new industrial wave' repeatedly.

"To be perfectly honest, in my business, we have to sell anti-delusionary medicines to unfortunate patients estranged from reality. Not to push this analogy too far, institutions are also susceptible to delusionary behavior. Even our pharmaceutical companies are regularly accused of being unreal in our pricing, in our aggressive promotions, in our incessant discoveries of new ailments requiring medicine. Haven't you heard of shaking leg syn-drome, which some medical researchers claim is an invention of drug sellers?

"Here in our private inner sanctum, I can admit the people's revolt is drawing us closer to reality and away from our risky delusions or, for the matter, our illusions. I guess you could say I am echoing some of The Chairman's views, but couldn't we look at this rat-sparked rebellion and the movement it spawned as a unique time, the compressed eruption being a giant *reset* of our economy. It's one that, if we handle it right, will keep us still operational within a regulated, competitive market economy or, more precisely, an economy of markets for many more decades.

"I guess one manifestation of this *reset* is that we have to internalize and pay for some of the costs we inflict on our customers, our workers, and our environment — a responsibility that should lead to more prevention and more innovation. This is a *reset* of the people's livelihoods in a way that is in accordance with some of our most cherished, long-held values, religious, secular, or otherwise. Sorry for the sermon. End of speech. Hail to the rats!"

While some of the attendees were muttering that they had found another traitor in their midst, a leader from the machine tools industry was willing to see some light in this tunnel. She openly addressed the hardliner Jack. "The 1872 Mining Act, which even lets foreign companies find and extract hard rock minerals for free — well, almost, they pay five dollars per acre — is the ultimate example of crony capitalism. Letting a Canadian company get ownership of NINE BILLION DOLLARS of our gold on public lands in Nevada for less than $30,000 is downright crazeee! What business can be run like that? Only the U.S.A. out of all the countries in the world has laws like this that make it such a sucker. You couldn't get ten percent of the American people behind you on that one, Jack."

Magnate Jack came back at her strongly. "I beg your pardon. Do you want me to start a list of the crony capitalist arrangements each of you benefits from? We're not here to make a donnybrook and insult each other. I'm sorry I even mentioned the 1872 Act. Let's get back to why we've got a recess. What are we going to say to the Wall Streeters?"

A hospital chain CEO declared, "I keep thinking about The Chairman's parting comments. We do have different constituencies. If we consider the profiles of our organization's members, we see that they pay dues and have influence in their own right. Walls Streeters speculate much, invest less. Our members are concerned with the common people in that we meet their real needs and wants.

"Putting all that together, I don't see any reconciliation toward a united front with the Wall Street types, but I also don't see us going into flat-out public opposition. We can go back to them down the hall and tell them that.

"As for us, I suggest each trade association do their own thing, as they see fit. Our most immediate concern now has to be keeping friendly legislators in office. Based on their own needs, let each of us speak to legislators that our trades are associated with and agree to work with them on election plans in their congressional districts. That way, each concerned industry can take responsibility for obtaining the best electoral results in specific states. You know what they say. 'All politics is local,' and it happens to be very true here.

"Telling our incumbents that local companies can help them stave off the primary challengers is probably the best leverage we have right now. While we can help raise campaign money for our local members, the muscle has to be applied where they live and work. Can we agree on his minimal agenda?"

A movie mogul: "I can't remember ever being so frustrated. Every road seems to come up against boulders that cut us off from both advance and retreat. We're trying to fast-fight the good guys without being bad guys. In my business that's a nonstarter, at least from any saleable standpoint. Try imagining Batman killing Superman and then pretending he was a nice guy.

"On the other hand, a popular revolt started by rats. Now that's a great plot and screenwriters are already at work on it, but they can't figure out how the story ends. So, it's hung up in project development hell. Not to complain about my own problems …"

A construction magnate trade representative was furious.

"What? You are complaining about your problems. You are causing us problems. You are seriously telling us a movie is going to be made about the rats, with us as villains, no doubt. I'm torn up … But come to think of it, how can I blame you? This is how you make a buck, just business as usual for Hollywood. Maybe there's even a silver lining here. Could your writers give us some believable scenarios of how this all ends? And I don't mean one of those sappy-happy endings that even my teenage daughter hates by now."

The hospital chain CEO tried to get his fellow whiners back to the point he had made earlier.

"Now we're drifting, really drifting. Let's get back on track. Our fulcrum is the primary. If we can credibly convince our supporters in Congress that we can defeat their primary challengers, we'll at least get a respite, at least more months to stretch out in whereby we can have more time to put forth well-planned tactics.

"Such tactics cannot be developed on the fly. As I see it, we need to come out with some big exposé — an attention-getter that scares people into questioning what is about to happen. The Cooperators have cleverly shielded themselves from any 'isms.' Worse yet, they have lots of veterans in their midst, including some with Congressional Medals of Honor, and lots of social gospel religious leaders. Their wall is high, broad, and has few crevices that I can see. That's why we have to buy some time to figure out how to scale it."

"I have an idea," interjected the hoary trade association head for the giant chemical/pesticide corporations. "This might seem a little crazy, at least till you think it over. Why not return Congress to where it was when it had to be evacuated and could not function? Why not arrange for another massive invasion of rats?"

Some of the folks around the table were shaking their heads in disbelief, but he pressed on, "Why not arrange for the militant animal welfare groups — they're already furious over what they call 'the massacre of the rodent innocents' by the Exterminators — to repopulate the offices and corridors, the cafeterias and the hearing rooms with those randomly behaving furry little creatures? This will suspend Congressional operations again and bring back the mockery, ridicule, and pillorying which launched this nightmare. By winding back the course of Father Time, we may see a wave of public distaste replacing the current wave of fevered reform. People will again get bored, not aroused by Washington dramas."

The Hollywood mogul said to himself, "He should be one of my screenwriters."

He turned to the Washington counsel and asked, "Before you pass judgment on whether such a plan is sensible, can you talk about it from a legal perspective?"

The counsel said, "Clearly, anybody who floods the Congress with rats would be prosecuted, if caught, for criminal trespass and creating a public nuisance. Unless I am mistaken, however, these transgressions would be misdemeanors, not felonies."

The chemical/pesticide organization head was all business in terms of working out whether it could be put to the test. "If you are not mistaken," he said to the counsel, "that means we could always pay someone — say via a charitable contribution — to take the rap, serve out a short sentence, and live happily ever after. Is that correct?"

The counsel, though no enthusiast for this scheme, could divorce himself from his feelings and look at it from an objective legal standpoint. He spoke thoughtfully. "As the law now stands, you are correct. But if the solons get any wind of this, they'll turn this act into a first-class felony in a New York legislative minute."

A media mega-mogul was a bit flabbergasted by the absurd direction the discussion was taking. "What I'm hearing just doesn't pass the smell test. Even if you can figure out the logistics, fill the trucks, get past the guards without incurring mayhem and so on and so forth, it won't work. Also,

I think counsel is wrong. The prosecutors would call this breaking and entering — a felonious act if ever there was one. Candidly, I think our brains have dried up from our unusual experience of powerlessness, so unless anyone has any better ideas, I say we stick with our esteemed hospital chain representative's suggestion, which boils down to: every mogul for himself.

"I move to adjourn and return to the large conference room."

No one spoke, but everyone eyed each other a trifle suspiciously.

The media mogul reiterated the consensus: "OK, it's every trade group for itself. Devolution, here we come! Importantly nitpicking the bills as suggested by clever counsel, here we come!"

"Second the motion," cried several trade magnates in unison.

"So moved. All in favor, say aye."

After hearing a chorus of ayes, the media mogul said, "The ayes have it overwhelmingly."

✳ ✳ ✳

The Wall Streeters received the business representatives' conclusions with little surprise. The Chairman had said the two sides worked from slightly different rationales. He advised the lawyers in the room to return to their "exquisite skills of monkey wrenching," urged everyone to keep in touch, especially if they came up with new ideas and, with a wink, declared it still the better part of valor to "keep writing those checks to our supporters on Capitol Hill."

Whereupon, after some drinks and a nice repast, the weary Washingtonians returned to home base to be greeted by the Million Americans March — a rally that was coming together on the historic mall as the conference attendees landed in the airport.

51 · The Million Americans March

THERE NEVER WAS A RALLY like this giant aggregation of an informed, motivated, and widely representative populace who were staying for the duration, staying until the job was done. No weekend demonstrators here, leaving behind cups, cans, paper, and other debris as they exited town.

All had post-rally assignments, including very respectful vigils in front of every house and condo harboring a member of Congress, including an ever-larger ring around the Congress and the White House, their exploits carried out with the guidance of smart lawyers and logistic specialists and via the internet with very smart media relations colleagues.

The Reporter was everywhere, observing, interviewing, noticing the nuances of the assemblage's remarkable organization and division of labor. To give everyone additional ownership of this event — and to make sure the growing movement was funded as much by the grassroots as by the sturdy oaks (the three billionaires) — 18-inch buckets were passed to collect cash contributions. The money that would be used to set up even more visible storefronts around the country and in the general Washington environs. There were thousands of empty storefronts in America ready to be rented cheaply and used as a clearing house/info shop/community activist center as a place to go about uniting neighborhoods and publicizing, in a hands-on manner, the grand drive for this supremacy of popular sovereignty. The organizers of the bucket brigades, backed by occasional exhortations from the large stage of speakers, estimated they had made a collection of some $20 million, or an average of $20 per person. Additional sums were coming in from smartphone donations.

The Reporter located and interviewed the people in charge of chanting the rolling rhythms that so enchanted the huge television and radio audiences, who were watching the rally. These chants had been crafted to display musical excellence, being led by expert chanters positioned throughout the crowd, thus keeping the tones at professionally consistent levels. The words of the chants were on point.

One chant went like this:

"Of, by, and for the people,
the government will become.
Not should, *not* must, but *will* become
or our society is really done."

Another:

"Justice, peace, and happiness
will mark our time on Earth.
To make this happen more and more,
we must be good stewards as never before."

Having interviewed people at the rally and soaked up the atmosphere, The Reporter raced back to his office to compose his analysis.

He began by playing off the words of one of the chants:

Today was a day like never before. A million Americans who knew who they were, where they were going, and how they were going to get there filled the Mall.

In each of their hands was not a flag. In their hands was their agenda: the promise of America that would make our flag sing the words that climax our Pledge of Allegiance: "with liberty and justice for all."

This was a grand audience, ready for a long haul, not drifting away as happened so often to the sporadic uprisings in the decades before. The people at the rally have assignments they will return to after the day's excitement. These are tasks so specific that their reverberations are penetrating into the nation's Congress and White House. It's as if many years of frustration were being concentrated into days of demands, into a sense of self-discipline that throws in the toilet the myth that the common people can't take control of their own affairs, which has been promulgated through years of public manipulation and control of the many by the few. These are the few who pretend they are running things for everyone's benefit, but are, in fact, doing so out of infinite greed and the lust for domination, passing on their techniques to daughters and sons so as to assure its perpetuation from one avaricious generation to another. And, folks, this is not me editorializing. I'm repeating the words I heard both from the grandstand and in the crowd at this mammoth rally.

"No more!" cried this assembly, whose members, judging from my spot checks, were intelligent and well informed about our nation's needs — the antithesis of a typical mob's attention deficit disorder. Prepared and seasoned before they arrived and ready for interconnected assignments during their stay, this rally was no mere *tour de force*, nor mere civic show of force. This was the serious vanguard, a million strong, fighting for that once distant ideal captured in President Lincoln's felicitous words — "a government of, by, and for the people" — rooted in the permanent presence of a new and renewable civic/political, American culture worthy of Lincoln's legendary words.

Working my way through the citizenry, I overheard what they were saying to one another in between the speeches, in which the speakers elaborated details of the 24 bills that were headed for enactment. In interpersonal talk that took place in this dense togetherness, the rally attendees discussed these bills and their own prospects in the future, a future of livelihoods that mattered, that were secure materially, where people cared for one another's work, leisure, family time, and for looking out for their descendants. The words of the people in the crowd were not pompous and belabored — they were pictorial, describing a landscape where what Jefferson called "the pursuit of happiness," enabled by justice and confident freedoms, were the enabling conditions. Everyone I overheard tended to end their sentences with a smiling, "No Big Deal, We Earned It."

All this may sound pie-in-the-sky, naïve, distanced from the raw realities. Whether it is a dream or an unconquerable movement, the next few months will tell. This time, these people believe, time is on *their* side.

52 · Counterrevolution on the Ropes

IN RECORD TIME, the Congressional hearings and their reports were largely completed. The votes to send the bills to the floor and, in the House, on the discharge petition procedure to circumvent the still obdurate Rules Committee, were underway. There were unusually large numbers of abstentions by Committee members opposed to everything, but not willing to put this opinion on record so as to make them an easy target for their primary opponents. Their explanations for not voting, when asked, revolved around words like, "too precipitous" or "freighted with good intentions but bad unintended consequences."

Quickly composed were three kinds of opposition. First, many of the trade groups warned about "economic collapse," "a freefall for the bond market," "mass layoffs," "an investment boycott," "a lowering of the government's credit rating," "corporate flight overseas," and other sundry, dismal predictions. When the press asked them to be specific, rather cuttingly, with such questions as: "How are improved public works, better housing, safer food, sustainable energy independence, fairer taxation, assistance to deprived children, overdue wage increases, cleaner air, water and soil, law and order for corporate violations, and more honest elections with greater choices on the ballot going to lead to such calamities?" The questioned press offices were nonplussed. They didn't want to sound foolish, so they fudged, saying something about "the evils of bigger government" and, even more pusillanimously, said they would get back to the inquiring reporters, who themselves had to undergo some transformation and reinvention, for being a ditto head no longer cut it.

The second counterattack, if that word can be used, was undertaken by front groups paid to say and do what the corporate funders could not. It was too strong to describe the thugs they hired as "brown shirts," but these groups of young toughs rallying, demonstrating, picketing, and taunting the massed activities of the people's revolt showed no restraint either in their words, placards, bullhorns, or threatening — but not fulfilled — demeanor. They tried to tar members of the social movement with words such as: "Communists," "Freeloaders," "Traitors to the American Way," and labeled the progressive movement as pushing for: "More Big Government," "More Regulation," and "Civil Rights for Rats," to mention only some of the more staid vituperatives found in their mouths and on their posters.

Were these front groups effective? Well, they did get on the media. But they were so extreme as to be a caricature that even a fence sitter was more likely to label them as loonies than to take them seriously. Moreover, when interviewed, they could provide few details behind their slogans. Worse for them were the probes by reporters that uncovered their being well paid, by the hour, by commercial interests opposed to the pending legislation. Still, the cameras couldn't resist showing them on the evening news as "balance."

The third approach was to marshal the business-funded think tanks, which were, by virtue of their regular work, able to be quick studies of what was going on so that they could handily churn out rebuttals of the AAC's bills and rationales. However, here the tanks and their commercial sponsors had to confront a problem: There were left/right concurrences of varying degrees on many of the proposals. While the corporate think tanks had learned how to run with their business grants, making sure their clients got their money's worth, they also tried to evince integrity by issuing occasional reports about "crony capitalism" and the wasteful spending on contractors, though these discussions were one-shot deals with little obvious follow-up.

A private meeting was arranged between the payers and the payees to iron out the dilemma or, as one staffer called it, "a sticky situation." The resolution they eventually came up with was quite forthright. The corporate foundations would provide grants to those who could provide the strongest arguments against such-and-such proposed AAC reform or change. The grants would be openly announced in the interest of vigorous debate and discussion. Since the freedom train was already speeding on the tracks toward its destination, it was stipulated the work for which the grants were paying had to be finished in a very short duration, ten to fifteen workdays. The think tanks had most of the ideas — which would rationalize the status quo — already on tap, and it would not take long for them to assign specific rebuttals to specific bills and their itemized provisions.

Of course, there were other pressure points besides the big three prongs of the counterattack where the reactionaries could bring influence to bear. To keep weak-kneed legislators in line, there were the specially placed campaign contributions, honorary dinners for supportive politicians, and post-Congressional employment hints. Also in the arsenal were the not-so-reliable leaks designed to hurt the AAC, such as supposedly "discovered" internal memos by giant multinationals, which "revealed" that if this or that part of the agenda passes, the firms would have no choice but to shut down named plants and offices in named congressional districts and move their operations abroad where there was a "better business climate."

As far as swaying the minds of legislators, however, all these combined efforts only made a small dent on Capitol Hill in terms of changing minds or solidifying the backbones of waverers, for they were nowhere near as effective as the *in personam* lobbying or the imminence of the primary challenges or the workings of The Speaker and his allies. As the leaders of the counterreaction were learning, these corporate resistances worked best on persuading the persuaded, hardcore supporters in Congress and around the country. But that wasn't nearly enough to begin to change the momentum or to shift the game from who was on the offense and who was holding down an anemic defense.

Of course, to go deeper into the underground that supported the status quo, there were always the privately retained, shadowy private detectives looking for dirt, contemplating entrapments in compromising situations, or nailing down bribes. But this type of skullduggery takes time to develop and involves the possibility of boomeranging risks. Besides, it is power that corrupts, and the people's revolt was not yet in power, so its members were relatively unsusceptible to blackmail.

With one month to go before the first primaries, pervasive gloom and doom permeated the realms of corporate-dom. It was not as if their inner selves, which most had ignored for years, were upset. Those inner selves could see that if the reformers' bills were enacted, there would be a better country ahead, less risk of street chaos, and a more prosperous middle class. But their outer selves — the positions and activism they were paid handsomely to maintain every day — were in full control of their possessors' personalities; and those shallow egos were wallowing in doubt, pessimism, and wit's-end frustration. They weren't used to losing, and this contest promised to end in a gigantic beating for them. They weren't used to thinking creatively when they were stuck on defense. So they hung their feeble hopes on the above-mentioned "counterattacks," knowing they were not even up to the Hail-Mary, last-minute-save kind of scoring.

53 · Ancillary Groups Push the Progressive Project Further

AT ABOUT THIS TIME, four of the numerous ancillary street theater groups — which had sprung up in the movement and whose performances, displaying telling events and socially relevant artistries, had frequently gone viral on social media — asked for a meeting with the Cooperators and the AAC. Once inside a bugproof room, they put an exciting proposal on the table.

Why not schedule a day for passage of each bill in both House and Senate, at which time the theater specialists would orchestrate massive demonstrations encircling the Capitol building? The demonstrators would take up peaceable chants like, "Pass Them, Oh Patriots" or "Vote for the Jeffersonian Revolution — No Big Deal" or "Give Us Your Better Angels, Congress."

"You know," one guerilla theater actress said, "we'd be using real positive language but an unmistakable, unspoken 'Or Else' as the subtext."

"It's the Skinnerian approach," added another organizer who was a Harvard grad and mime. "Positive reinforcement."

One of AAC's brightest lights, Representative Ivan Incisor, who had quickly grasped the value and the possible weak points in the plan, said, "There are 24 major pieces of legislation scheduled. Are you sure you can sustain such intensity outside in all kinds of weather and with the danger of possible provocations that would invite a police crackdown?"

Zono, a world-famous musician and promoter of fundraising events for progressive causes, replied, "To take your last point first, we are exceedingly aware of outside provocateurs who try to start fights or worse. That's one reason we have worked to establish close relations with the police and why we have carefully placed our own armband-recognizable sentinels throughout the ralliers. We've even composed songs like 'Ballad of the Lonesome Provocateurs.' We've discovered that the more we talk about troublemakers, the more the public expects that they will find them trying to infiltrate us and the less likely they will be to associate such disruptors with our side."

Zono readjusted his bandana and continued, "As far as being able to sustain the outside, dense presence daily, we have relays of backup brigades, as we call them. For sure, the same ralliers cannot keep the intensity up for 24 days. So we will put people in rotation. You may know, by the way, that we have mobile medical and legal clinics, kiosks distributing free food donated by Busboys and Poets and other avant-garde restaurants as well as other kiosks that can help attendees with referrals to hostels or rooms available for modest rents for those who would otherwise be homeless or have to go back to their homes."

"You guys are more impressive than I thought," observed Senator Earl Morningside. He had been asked to attend this session although he was a fence sitter at this point. He was needed because he was such an expert on Congressional rules that he regularly impressed the scholarly Senate and House parliamentarians whose job it was to authoritatively interpret the rules. He gave them his take on the situation.

"To begin, let me address the artists and others coordinating the outdoor actions. I understand, from my reading in history, how important an air of expectant success is for the progress of a social movement, and that's something that your street presence conveys around the country. But to turn to those working inside the Capitol, I wonder how you are going to handle procedural points of order and privilege inside the Congress. I believe these will be thrown up like roadblocks and could stretch the time beyond the single day you have allotted for passage."

At this point, Doug Colebrook called on the AAC's own expert on Congressional procedure. The venerable scholar suggested, "the AAC may have the votes to change the procedures generically. The Constitution specifically declares that the Congress sets its own rules, and, in my judgment, no more than a majority vote is needed to alter those rules."

"I guess you asked me here to get my opinion on that issue of Congressional rules, and I must say I concur," remarked Senator Morningside. "Though others may well challenge the majority vote point, it is my understanding that they will lose before the Parliamentarians who will agree with the professor."

On that point, the meetings with the ancillary groups were concluded and the deliberations resumed between the inside and outside forces around the table. The first thing mentioned by a latecomer to the meeting was a news report just off the wires. He read it out, as it was brief:

"The public health experts and veterinarians retained by the House and Senate Administrators to study the safety of allowing the continued admission of caged pet mice to the Congress have issued their report. So long as the pet mice are certified as healthy by a licensed animal lab, there is no basis to ban such mice brought as gifts to members of Congress or their staff or carried as pets."

Chalk up another victory for the rodents.

54 · Sweet Home, Alabama

ABOUT THE SAME TIME as the progressives were cheering the report of the victory for the mice, a quite different reaction was heard from another part of the country when the news was broadcast.

Deep in the heart of conservatism in rural Alabama, during a night when the air was filled with the musical renderings of a cacophony of crickets, a dozen males, who were seated in a dim saloon, known for inviting outspoken views, heard the news about the pet white mice.

"What kind of horseshit is this?" exclaimed one drinker, Billy Phil.

"Liberal horseshit," replied another, Billy Frank.

Billy Joe chimed in, "These traitors are trying to cut down our military that protects our freedoms. That's what they're really up to." This was Billy Joe's favorite topic, and it didn't take much to get him to talk about it. So while the rats were not actually involved in fighting our boys in uniform, the mention of Liberals had gotten him riled.

"You don't really believe that bullshit. Do you think a bunch of ragheads over there, fighting to get us and the Brits the hell out of their backyard

PATRIOTISM   PATRIOTISM   PATRIOTISM

so they can kick out their dictators, are losing sleep angry about our freedoms?" retorted a drinker wearing long hair and a surplus army jacket from the Iraq War.

This fellow was not just imaging what a great soldier he would be if he had ever been in the military, as Billy Joe was. This new speaker had been there, done that.

He continued provocatively, "You go in both directions, Billy J. First, you tell us how much you hate the Feds here at home, and then you hoist the Red, White, and Blue, backing anything the Feds do to brown people overseas. You're even willing to go to kill or die for the politicians and the Big Oil Companies that bankroll them. I mean, if you hadn't lost those fingers at the mill, you'd go and enlist. C'mon, just because you're a redneck like me doesn't have to mean you're stupid."

"Billy Link, if I didn't know your mom and dad, I'd be tempted to deck you here and now. And don't think I couldn't do it, missing fingers and all. Did you forget that we were attacked on 9/11?"

"Billy J, I'm not forgetting. I think I proved my patriotism in my military service. But I'm asking you to contemplate how all this started in the Middle East back at the beginning."

Billy Joe scratched his head. "You mean cavemen throwing dinosaur bones at each other?"

"I don't think we have to go that far back," the veteran said. "Just go back to right after World War I. There were no states as we know them in the Middle East at that time. So who carved up those territories, splitting up ancient tribes, and making them separate states? And then who then backed their dictators, who have been killing and starving them from their palaces with F-15s?

"When I was overseas, I read *War is a Racket*. You won't believe who wrote it, a double Congressional Medal of Honor Winner, Marine General Smedley Butler. He tells you how he went to war for National City Bank in Cuba and the U.S. oil companies in China. It's a short book with grisly pictures of dead soldiers lying on the ground. For who? For what? If you want to unlearn your ignorance, pick it up."

"OK, OK, Billy Link, y'all cut it out," interjected Billy Phil. "I think your mentioning reading is confusing Billy Joe. I don't think he does too much of that. No, just joking man. What I'm saying is, Billy Joe got us off the original topic of the rats in Congress. I mean the four-legged specimens.

"I know a rich guy. Don't worry, he's a good old boy, like us, he just happened to make it big in real estate. He's got an idea of how to play a big ratty prank on the politicians. He wants to load up five 18-wheelers with tens of thousands of hungry rats and, in the middle of the night, unload them around — and, if possible — inside the buildings of Congress and throw food around to keep them there. He'll pay his deliverers $200 an hour to get them up there. Any takers?"

"First, where's he getting all those rats?" asked fussy Billy Frank.

Billy Phil told him, "Brother, rats are not that hard to come by. My rich acquaintance knows someone who can just suck them out from the underground of big cities — you know, from the pipes, the sewers, the tunnels. He said the whole operation could be done smooth and fast. It's just mostly a matter of moolah, and he's got plenty. He wants to see what he calls 'the Greatest Show on Earth' on TV when the hundreds of rats are unleashed on the whole damn crowd of pompous asses."

"Other than a long-distance joy ride, what's this rich buddy of yours trying to make happen?" questioned Steve the bartender as he replenished some beers and wiped the counter. (He was a transplanted Northerner, so he didn't have the name Billy.)

"Beats me," Billy Phil confessed. "You know those loaded million-aires — they don't believe they have to explain anything to folks like us. He wants to hire us as truck drivers to just get the job done. I'll bet he has other motives — no doubt."

He threw in, as an afterthought, "But can't you guys use the green stuff? I sure can."

55 · The Beginning of the End for the Old Order

BACK IN WASHINGTON, the pace became ever more muscular and assured. The people were feeling their strength by the day. Reporters conceded as much in their daily filings, noticing in particular the swelling ranks of the "joiners," who were utilizing their capabilities to aid the movement in just about every task, with a panoply of skills and knowledge. Far from having to beg people to come to demonstrations, rallies, and planning sessions, the organizers had layers of reserves to enlarge the turnouts at events and to carry out the needed services at demonstrations, such as putting out the materials, helping with details, and spelling those citizens who had joined and committed their energies earlier but were now tired and needed a break.

At a heavily attended news conference, the AAC and the Committee Chairs released the legislative schedule — one day for one bill — 24 days in total with only Sundays off. Spring recess was cancelled. The first bill up was to be one that put forward a serious tax reform.

The day chosen for its passage was symbolic, April 15th — taxpayer deadline day.

As the first B-Day approached, there was a press event to announce the full schedule of the bills. At the event, an AAC spokeswoman talked up how carefully things had been prepared and orchestrated, praised the committee chairs and the diligent work of the committee members from both the majority and minority side.

She made sure the media were reminded of how thorough the committees and subcommittees were in their deliberations and markups, and how receptive the majority was to having the minority file their dissents. She threw in that most of the 24 bills concerned subjects and recommendations, which, if never passed before, had been publicly discussed, debated, and reported on at length over the years and decades. No surprises, no trap doors, no legislative tricks.

When it came to their turn to speak, the committee chairs did not dispute anything she said. They limited their remarks to procedures and scheduling for the floor debates and named the Floor Managers for each bill.

And on April 15, the remarkable historic process commenced. The joyous citizen assemblies, as expected, surrounded the Congressional buildings peaceably and at regular intervals changed, following their rotation plan.

Looking out the tall windows of the Congressional offices and corridors, the lawmakers, their staffs, lobbyists, the guards, janitors, and food servers could see nothing but orderly people with signs, balloons, and broad banners — night and day, regardless of the weather. Cocking their ears they could hear, "Pass It! Pass It! No Big Deal! We Earned It!"

Never had this happened before. In 1932 the "bonus army" of many thousands of World War I veterans had walked or traveled in other ways to Congress and set up camp. They were acting out of despair over not receiving the bonus money owed to them for their service in that miserable, avoidable war. They didn't have time to fully impact Congress, as the U.S. Army, commanded by Douglas McArthur, violently dispersed their gathering.

Nothing remotely like this dispersal was in the cards for this people's revolt. The Washington Police, the Park Service, and the standby National Guard were on strict orders to avoid all provocations and maintain close communications with the organizers to head off or minimize any trouble.

Inside the Congress, the corporate attorneys were preparing last-ditch efforts to insert those amendments spoken about during the private meeting with the Wall Streeters. Neatly drafted and explained both technically and in plain English, they sought sponsors, working the room in search of bendable ears.

They were successful in finding a few lawmakers who were willing to offer these amendments on the floor, doing so, embarrassingly, when everybody was looking. It took some real arm-twisting to get a few sponsors. Not only were these legislators less than enthusiastic at being identified with a visibly losing cause, but they knew such amendments — dealing with lower budgets, weaker enforcement, and set expiration dates — were usually inserted during more secretive committee drafts via the offices of friendly staffers. In those cases there was no necessity of explaining the meaning of highly technical legalese. That flimflamming doesn't pass so easily during open floor debates. Still, the few suborned lawmakers went ahead with the requests because they were beholden and dependent on the customary political donations and tit-for-tat political friendships.

And so, day after day, with only a little slippage, the bills became the presumptive laws of the land. The President had already signaled his desire to sign them in a series of White House people's ceremonies. Even if he had opposed the bills, it would not have mattered, because the insurgents had passed them with a veto-proof majority. DooLittle, being a very political animal, understood how to count votes.

56 · The Quick Passage of Earthshaking Legislation Even Shocks the Movement

AFTER THE TAX BILL, in rapid succession, came the food, housing, energy, health, and safety legislation. Each day's bill passage expanded the popular mobilization and excited expectations. Day by day, the naysayers, the negatives, the pessimists that one encounters in every community, shrank in numbers. Cynicism melted into skepticism, which soon melded into affirmative thinking. The hardcore ideologues, who believe democracy is mob rule — the masses running amuck — remained rigid in their views, faithful inheritors of the thought of the early Tories at the founding of our Republic who called the people "rabble." One modern-day Tory, in a West Texas restaurant, was heard to say, "Well, it's their time — let them have it. They're sure to screw things up, and then it'll be our time once again."

After passage of the transportation, communication, insurance, and credit bills, a quizzical Doug Colebrook, lunching with his allies in the Senate dining room, asked his Senatorial collaborators how they could explain this unprecedented, phenomenal cave-in of the opposing members in both houses of Congress.

White-haired Senator Harrison Updike responded, "Doug, I heartily agree with your sentiment that what is going on is phenomenal, amazing beyond belief. Like you, I've been trying to understand what broke the dam and why all the dam keepers seemed to have abandoned their posts. Never seen anything remotely like this in my 44 years here.

"I'd have to say it's a combination of factors that created a perfect storm — a storm on the lake which fronts the dam, as it were — against them and their interest group backers.

"First, above everything, is the timing. Everything in this agenda is long overdue, and our opponents knew it. How many stories have you read, even in our usually compliant press, about twisted, corrupted budgets; unnecessary wars; Wall Street excesses; CEOs paying themselves huge bonuses approved by a rubber-stamp board of directors; and greed draining other people's money? Haven't we read books — going back to Upton Sinclair and Lincoln Steffens — which expose the domination of people by the moneyed interests and describe how tens of millions slave away while financially losing ground?

"Tell you the honest truth, if this upheaval had happened 20 years ago, it wouldn't have been too soon. Not to pun, but at this moment, the congressional bills are almost the same as unpaid debtors' bills, ones marked long overdue. That means it feels like a perfect climate for an 'enough is enough' rebellion.

"Why didn't it happen 20 years back? That's the second factor, the human element. You, Doug, and the Cooperators put it together, quietly, insistently, and knowledgeably. You didn't do much vilifying, leaving it up to their primary opponents to wallow in the mudslinging. I can see why they scooped up the mud so fast. Those old farts weren't used to such challenges, and they scared easily.

"Then there were the unstoppable marches, rallies, and demonstrations that wouldn't go away and never stopped getting larger and more confident. If the fat cats and their legislative adjuncts were waiting for any petering out of the rallies and anti-establishment organizing, the type of gradual waning they had come to expect from past weekend demonstrations, they were sorely disappointed and shaken. Add the conversion of The Speaker and the knowledge that the White House was on the people's side — not surprising, since its current occupant is a past master of repositioning himself the minute the wind shifts — and you could see the collapse coming.

"When the lobbyists read the tea leaves on the streets, and in the restrained quality of the legislative efforts and in the momentum on Capitol Hill, they couldn't present a united front, and all their money couldn't guarantee wins in the primaries. Most of these corporate boys said to each other, 'Not enough time, we're not going to get in front of that train.' What's the phrase — *critical mass* — that's it. I guess in this instance a more appropriate term would be the critical *masses*, for once they joined their effort, with all the preparation so carefully done by you guys, they became what someone, I think it was The Reporter, labeled 'a vanguard of a million people.' At that point, what was considered impossible became a lot easier than anybody, anywhere, thought or dreamed."

Other Senators around the small dining table, with their mouths full, nodded in agreement.

Doug knew that when the lawmaking was over, the reporters were sure to descend on him with questions about the triumphs. That's why he particularly appreciated how Updike had mentioned all the people individually and collectively involved and needed for this victory. When the news people came calling, he wanted to respond so that the credit was not focused on him or even his core cooperators around the states. Journalists, even as they were leaving their ditto-head style behind, still had been trained to see everything being done in the world as the result of some great man or woman. Old press habits die hard. Doug wanted to fight against such pigeonholing of this story. It was his modesty, certainly, but it was more than that. He wanted the responsibility for making the whole effort work to be on the shoulders of all the people collectively.

He remembered jotting down in his journal, based on thinking about his readings of the history of the major revolutions and their destructive aftermaths of the past 300 years: "The only revolution that counts is the revolution that works."

57 · Another Week, Another Revolution in Lawmaking

THE NEXT WEEKS' MENUS contained such mouthwatering items as reforms in national security, public works, facilities for children, retirement/pensions, education, and civil rights/civil liberties. All sailed through Congress. These attracted even larger turnouts in the country's streets, squares, and ballfields. More women, minorities, and children were present. The following week more blue-collar workers, artists, entertainers, nature lovers, and teenagers were in evidence in the inspired throngs that circled the Capitol and almost repopulated the city during the passage of the labor/ work/wages, the leisure play/art, the crime prevention and enforcement, and the environment bills.

Musicians and artists were no slouches as the avalanche of progressive bills were passed. They burst into the current news cycle when, for example, a country-western singer released a new ditty, one that shot straight to the top of the charts, with its signature lines, "Oh, what a beautiful country. Oh, what a beautiful Congress. Oh, what a beautiful country, everything's going people's way," sung to a tune taken from the famous Rodgers and Hammerstein musical. Lovers of *Oklahoma* were flabbergasted upon hearing "Congress" getting such an honor.

The final week of legislation was not without its perilous moments. It was in the face of the bills proposing clean elections with choice, the empowerment of the people, community self-reliance, and corporate accountability under Constitutional subordination that the entrenched corporate interests thought they had to draw a last-ditch line in the sand. They were smart enough to know that if these bills passed, heavyweight shifts in power would make any future corporatist comeback difficult to achieve. The bills would remove the corporate domination of elections via their two-party toadies and would fortify the people's continuing stamina by providing many more full-time advocacy institutions. They would undermine global corporate power over local community economies and — the biggie of them all — strip the corporate entity of its personhood equivalence to real human beings, so as to subordinate the corporate system to the supremacy of our Constitution's increasingly atrophied but now reborn "We the People."

58 · A Line in the Sand at the Last Ditch

THE WALL STREET CHAIRMAN, who seemed dismayingly reasonable, wise, and accommodating to the demands of the progressive insurgency during his meetings with the Washingtonians, now protruded his fangs. It had been mentioned that he liked a good fight because that was time when, his back to the wall, his aggressive instincts could get full play. Those who had seen him act in such circumstances dubbed him, out of his hearing, 'the werewolf.'

If there was a method to his usual mildness, it was to bide his time and then, at just the right moment, launch out with the same sudden blitzkrieg approach that the insurgency was using: fast, furious, and targeted at the key nerve centers.

Before these last key laws came to a vote — ones that would break corporate power once and for all — The Chairman had arranged for a marathon session in Washington, DC. Much as he hated leaving his New York City prowling grounds, he jetted down for a weekend meet-up with nine

super-fighters for corporate hegemony. He had calculated that between them they had a total of 460 years of ferocious experience.

Not known for their overt fulminations — each having self-control that rivaled the werewolf's — eight of these persons were brilliant implementers of orders given by their business's bosses. Their skills were testified to by the ample fortunes each had accrued. One was a masterful personal persuader in tone, logic, reason, and reassurance. Another was known as "carrot man," a guy who could make tough political decisions by the solons — ones that might undermine their standing with any voters who might be paying attention — go down more easily because of the goodies attached to the lawmakers doing the "right thing." A third was a smooth media man whom no one had ever ruffled while he was getting his message across. (He was dubbed "the Buddha.")

A fourth was known as "Mr. Stealth," the kind of person who negotiates in the dark recesses of the legislative process, with a makeshift office down at the Congressional print shops where he was something of an "invisible man," even to the printers working there.

A fifth and a sixth were exquisite legislation-drafting experts who were intricacy nerds, unfazed by arcane cross-references to different statutes of multi-hundred-page bills. These were the masters of puzzle palaces for whom the most difficult chess games and crossword puzzles were "no problem."

A seventh was a "Jim Farley" type (FDR's exuberant Postmaster General), a gladhander who knew every lawmaker, the staffers, the families, the children, and the birthdays and made his rounds on Capitol Hill in order to prove it.

An eighth was a CPA budget expert who worked for years in the White House office of Management and Budget, then did a stint at the Congressional Government Accountability Office (GAO), and then became the Chief of Staff for the powerful Congressional Budget Office. He knew all there was to know about adding and subtracting monies from programs his paymasters favored or disfavored.

The ninth was a woman, an African American lesbian, a well-paid token whose role was to help The Chairman discount any accusations of his ad hoc group being nothing but an extremely super-rich white men's club that had no concern for the common people. Even bringing her on board had caused some grumbling among his associates. After all, when these males had started, there were no women allowed to make the power climb. It was a time when some states prohibited women from serving on juries, a time when "Negros" could not drink at certain water fountains, and cruel homophobia was publicly unquestioned.

In her own right, this woman, a product of the poor education in people's rights offered at Harvard, believed that corporations should direct the nation's future because, unlike politicians, corporate types felt that if they were not successful, they should be held accountable, just as business executives were answerable to their shareholders. And she was not only a token, but she displayed an awesome ability to argue this corporate "philosophy" when accompanying the others to selected Congressional offices.

The Chairman's *aide de camp*, who had found this triple demonstration of diversity in one woman — a woman who was willing to follow orders as long as the price was right — received a large bonus. How absurdly out of touch they still were.

Once assembled, The Chairman called on the hoariest of the attorneys among his "brain trust," who had seen and survived many a pressure cooker in his day, though perhaps never one quite like this.

"First off," The Chairman counseled, "I don't have to remind anyone how serious this crisis is, so let's think hard and act fast. Now, Jasper, please prioritize these four remaining megabills. Then, when you are done, we'll open up to everyone here for concurrence or critique and an action plan."

"Agreed, sir," replied the courtly lawyer with the penetrating eyes. Some, out of his hearing, said he had the eyes of a cobra.

"It is my judgment, given the pressure of time and the political climate, that we can ignore the 'people empowerment legislation' with one exception. Let me quickly run down the reasons we can neglect it.

"It calls for a national referendum. We know how to deal with state referenda — look at California. We can live with that. It calls for easier access to the courts — which brings us back to the 1960s pre-tort reform — we can live with that. So will others," he added with a chuckle. "It calls for taxpayer 'standing to sue,' which, I believe, cannot be done by statute but only by Constitutional amendment, so the federal courts will throw that out.

"Now there is one part of the bill that is novel and dangerous, and this is where I'm going to propose an exception to my policy of ignoring these irritants. The provision requires companies to include invitations in their billing statements to their customers — for example, owners of motor vehicles or consumers of services such as banking, insurance, and utilities — to band together in non-profit advocacy groups. These consumer associations would then act to counter our power by employing consumer lawyers, economists, scientists, accountants, public relations experts, and organizers.

"Membership in these groups would be voluntary, and they would be funded mostly by their members and private grants, thus making them harder to attack. This idea represents a real power shift, but it would be very hard for us to assail, since corporations have so many industry associations and lobbying arms themselves. So critics will be quick to ask how we can object to equivalent organizations working for consumers' interests when we have our own business organizations working for our interests.

"To internally sabotage this bill, I would say we should get our legislative worker bees to add one amendment: make these groups wildly democratic in the elections of their boards. That way they'll be likely to rip each other apart internally, as if they had an out-of-control defibrillator shocking their hearts. That's what's been happening with the board elections of the anti-capitalistic Pacifica radio stations, ruining their functioning. The more democratic the procedures, the more internally divided are leftist organizations and parties. We are drafting, shall we say, a counterintuitive pro-democracy amendment that is sure to get through. History is made by decisive leaders with authority, not by ultra-democracy. That's why airline passengers don't get a vote in the air as to how to fly the plane.

"The other bill that doesn't seem to bring much trouble is the advancing of community self-reliance. First, it is non-ideological and invincible to amendments. Who can object, even indirectly through monkey-wrenching, to the general idea of self-reliance? It goes to our most fundamental values and origins as a nation. For god sake's, I know you aren't literary buffs here, but Emerson even penned a famous essay with that title. Also, who can be against farmers' markets or local solar power or producing locally more of what we consume or community health clinics or credit unions or community banks? I urge that we don't touch this one. I'm well aware in making this recommendation that our global corporate clients can see economic displacement on the horizon. Solar displaces the coal and oil companies, for example, or local food displaces the food giants or participatory sports replacing — well, not to be cynical — the expenditures for being out of shape and overweight, which include Weight Watchers, slimming drinks, and gym memberships. But I say, let's not get too frightened over that prospect. Some of it we all want and is already happening. And please note there are 80 million members of credit unions whose net assets together don't equal that of one of the biggest Wall Street banks. Somehow, us biggies have managed to adjust and profit even with the increased presence of the little guys in business.

"That leaves two bills which are the most serious threats to the way business operates today, or — to adopt the Occupy Wall Street people's phrase — to the 'one percent' and its purported privileges and pleasures.

"One is the bill that would give us clean elections with choice legislation that could seriously undermine business's influence over government. I don't have to remind you that the government we have worked so hard to mold to our interests is in many ways an accounts receivable department for us, an immense honeypot of contracts, leaseholds, grants, tax escapes, and a dazzling array of subsidies that keeps many corporate law firms buzzing with lucrative retainers. Take away government-as-usual and its welfare state, and we'd see consumer demand shrink and our business deals, from the military to public construction to extractions of minerals, far less robust. So let's look closely at the key provisions of this bill.

"First is exclusive public financing of campaigns. This has to be a Constitutional amendment in order to override several Supreme Court decisions concluding that money is speech. Our opponents know the Constitution is involved and are using this chance to start the amendment process. Like us, they realize this is only the start of a long haul to get three-quarters of the states to ratify. So we have plenty of time down the road to block this one, even given the current tumult of the masses. We all know about powerful Speakers of State Houses and Presidents of State Senates who rule with iron hands and have proven themselves in our cause repeatedly.

"The second provision relates to federalizing ballot access for federal elective offices, taking the power away from a mélange of state laws, most of which are real hurdles for competitive third parties or independent candidates. If this were put into effect, there would be tons of viable candidates who were not sponsored by our two understanding parties. This would cause us headaches, give voters a new place to go, and increase the pressure on the two parties to adopt measures for the people's — not our — benefit. In short, a competitive electoral system is not to our advantage. Right now, we are quite happy with the two parties we have, ones that are constantly on their cellphones with us, dialing for our dollars.

"The third provision establishes voting as a legal duty with a $50 fine if a citizen doesn't vote and has no medical or other valid excuse. If this imposition were passed, it would make all the clever ways that have been devised to confuse or obstruct people of certain classes and races from voting both an obstruction of justice and a crime. So voting turnout will rise sharply here — as it did in Australia when similar laws were adopted there — to over 90 percent from the present 30-to-60 percent in Congressional and Presidential elections respectively. Those tens of millions of American who will be forced into voting are largely not our supporters.

"The fourth provision establishes a binding none-of-the-above — NOTA — line on every ballot to give voters a chance to say 'no' to all the candidates, a vote of no confidence. If NOTA wins the most votes, that ballot line is cancelled and a new election with new candidates will be scheduled in 60 days. Voters would love NOTA, but candidates don't like it one bit. Imagine how humiliating it would be to lose to NOTA. This one I'm unclear on. With mandatory voting anyway, it's hard to see how it really disadvantages us."

"The fifth and last major provision ends gerrymandering by the states. Electoral districts will be demarcated by nonpartisan commissions, as in Iowa and a few other states. There is a constitutional issue here for the federal government requiring this, but it is muted with grant incentives to the states. However, I don't think this is enough to clear the constitutional question for objecting states.

"My take is that this law is so toxic we have to oppose it in its entirety. The argument we can go with is that it's an example of government coercion when people are penalized for not voting. The NOTA provision weakens this argument, but we do not have to mention that in our campaign. Coercion is coercion. Just hit that note, hard and often, in our propaganda.

"Finally, the last bill, which is the biggest prize for these lunatics: dehumanizing the corporation by stripping it of its personhood and, therefore, its constitutional rights. That is what our opponents mean by 'Constitutional subordination.' If we lose this fight, then mark my words — the next thing you'll see is legislation prohibiting corporations as corporations from lobbying, testifying, and making campaign contributions. Our effective use of the civil rights and civil liberties laws and the equal protection clause of the Constitution would be eliminated. You would see state laws banning corporate ownership of lands — as if, perish the thought, only individuals could own land. You would see laws requiring all radio and television broadcast licenses to be held by individuals, not by corporations of any kind. The entire set of shields that immunize corporations or allow them to act with impunity will be jettisoned. I'm just giving a few examples of the domino effect.

"So, here I say we have to go all-out to defeat it because if we do not succeed, it is all over for the corporate world as we have known it. This is the bill that would spell the doom of everything for which we stand. The inclusive statutory wording even includes limited partnerships under the bans. These fanatics hold nothing sacred.

"Finally, as with the other legislation, these last bills have been expertly drafted by very skilled counselors. I am forced to say that they are breathtaking in their tight defense against advantageous ambiguity, waivers, exceptions, procrastination, and such. What they cannot control is the year-in and year-out budgeting decisions. Once this hullabaloo is over, that is where we can inflict some useful starvation with our friends on Capitol Hill. So, even if they pass everything, all is not lost. I've said my piece. Thank you for your patience."

The Chairman, with obvious delight, said, "Thank you, Jasper! That was a virtuoso performance. You have shown us exactly where and how battle must be joined."

The Chairman turned to the whole table with his next remark, "So, let's get down to strategies. And I'm expecting intensive, no-holds-barred exchanges among all of you. Act as if your life is on the line, for maybe it is."

Whereupon, for over three hours, The Chairman got what he asked for as the other eight plunged into the details, the tactics, and the strategies. What emerged was a general agreement with Jasper's putting the focus against the two bills. There were a few minor disagreements. The "Jim Farley" type cringed when he heard the phrase they were going to use in their communiqués, "dehumanizing the corporation," which might strike some of their adherents as a trifle absurd. He was seconded by the smooth media man, and they won a replacement phrase, "degrading the corporation." The "carrot man" advised that by openly conceding all the other bills, thus testifying to their willingness to compromise, they added credibility to their cause as they took on the ones so close to the bone. Every agreed that the "going too far" lament was a good psychological approach.

The Chairman was pleased with how the worthiness of each person displayed itself seamlessly in the intense discussion. He had never put these allies together in one room and hadn't been sure if things would click so well. The only exception was the "sleuth" whose talents were drained by the openness of everything. He was ready to make any effort to help the team prevail, but no one called upon him — yet!

Once in agreement on what to oppose, the talk bore down on the nature of the campaign. They boiled down their approach to a conventional, all-points counterattack that would touch all the bases: mass media, personal contact, well-placed campaign contributions, and unleashing small businesses back home. One key part of the plan would be setting up lurid local news conferences of "ordinary citizens" where would be exhibited "minutemen" images of just plain folks challenging big government's compulsory voting demand. These common folk, presumably, would prepare huge petitions saying: "Hell, no, we don't have to vote." These would be brandished in parades with ostentatious veterans wearing their old military uniforms marching smartly in front. Having given the "people's revolt" activities full play, the media, they believed, would have to report on any corporate backlash."

❄ ❄ ❄

The Cooperators' millions were not taken by surprise by the strenuous attack fielded against these last bastions of the economic royalists. The people's champions had advance warning and prepared all their demonstrators with bumper stickers, buttons, posters, and banners emphasizing the importance of these two bills, which were based on the undergirding principle: the absolute necessity of the supremacy of popular sovereignty over corporate entities. They encouraged debates at the community level to arouse a populace almost daffy with the previous successes.

Much of this clash of "who rules" occurred in about ten days of recess, which the corporate lobbyists succeeded in obtaining in order to give the campaign breathing space. Congressional leaders were so exhausted by then that it did not take any arm-twisting to get them to announce the recess.

What a ten days! Broadcast and cable channels, social media, and blogs lit up with what more and more Americans were persuaded was a titanic struggle between real people and artificial entities that don't bleed, don't die for their country, don't love or have children, and don't revere their ancestors.

Poets, novelists, and musicians all found different ways of conveying the difference between a human and a business entity, emphasizing again and again how absurd it was for an advanced society to be run by what law professors called "legal fictions" — corporations that could create their own parents called "holding companies," create their own decoys called, "shell companies," in tax havens. And many of them made sewers themselves out of our world's waterways air and land, where they could dispose of their toxic defecations.

Over and over again, artists and activists lambasted the double standards privileging corporations, beings which were ever more absentee, ever more removed from any sense of patriotism or loyalty to community, ever more demanding of government guarantees. The movement's diatribes, satires, and reasoned arguments sank deeply into the souls of the masses who were mobilizing to rip off the anchor that hung around their necks.

59 · Nuke 'Em

ON THE THIRD DAY of the recess, The Chairman and his tight circle of nine decided it was time for the "nuclear option." They were going to plunge the economy into a downward spiral in order to scare the country into second thoughts on degrading the corporations' powerful status.

One advantage of plutocracy for the royalists, was that when a group wanted to get something done, they didn't have to reach many of the plutocrats to get the desired action underway. After tightly encrypted messages and personal meetings over one day, the bond and stock markets started to shudder and crash. Within 48 hours, trillions of dollars of pension fund and mutual fund paper assets were shrinking. Credit started drying up. Banks moved to increase their foreclosure actions. The dollar began a free fall. Contracts and construction projects were put on hold. Workers started getting pink slips or were furloughed. It was an amazing display of leverage by a tiny number of power brokers, giving veracity to long-time corporate critics, so long ridiculed.

The downward drift of the economy hit Congress like a lightning bolt. Members knew it was planned, so obvious was the timing of this last-ditch attempt. It was even easily discernible to the oligarchs' leading cheerleader — *The Stall Street Journal* — whose editorials couldn't hide but could justify such deliberate scheming as necessary to "save the Republic and the free enterprise system." The legislators looked apprehensively to the response by the multitudes behind the Cooperators.

Speculation was rampant. Would the people panic and run for cover for fear of losing what little they had? Would they say, OK, we got plenty with the other bills that have passed Congress, so let the fat cats have those two before these big boys flee the country with their riches and bring the whole economy down on our heads? Unfortunately for the self-styled "masters of the universe," the vanguard in Washington, DC, and their stalwart allies back home didn't budge. In fact, they called out the Wall Streeters as "unpatriotic saboteurs of the American dream," "21st century traitor Tories," "speculators selling America short in the stock market," and "bluffers who will blink first because they've got the most to lose."

The last pejorative was prophetically chosen, as it did become a bluffing game played out over ten frightening days. The Wall Streeters knew they were playing with a fire that if it got out of control, could consume them. They were gambling that they would get what they want and then everything would rebound in the economy and the stock markets would re-ascend to where they were a couple of weeks ago. And The Chairman and his crew were not wrong in thinking this tactic would put heavy pressure on the Cooperators and their followers, who began to worry that as workers lost their jobs and savers started losing their money, enough of the popular rumble would begin turning against them that the momentum would be broken, taking the pressure off the opportunistic politicians in Congress.

On day four of The Chairman's "D-Day" counterattack, the negotiators on both sides met in the elaborate offices of the House leadership. Like two giant bulls with entangled horns, they pushed and shoved. The AAC emphasized that the two priorities that were scaring the hell out of the Wall Streeters — total public financing of electoral campaigns and the end of corporate personhood under constitutional subordination — were proposed constitutional amendments, rather than enacted legislation.

AAC stalwart Senator Horace Mills tried to calm the cornered Wall Streeters, "Remember, these two proposals still have to be ratified by three-quarters of the states. Our bills are just starting the process of possible Constitutional amendment. You'll have plenty of time and opportunity to argue your case state by state.

"That's the sweetener. But our group also has a contingency plan, which you may interpret as a threat if you wish. If you do not back up, we have a plan to nationalize the banks, start ten new banks — each with $30 billion in capital, giving them over $350 billion each in loan capacity — and to require the Federal Reserve and the Treasury to use the fuller authority we will provide them to reverse the downward spiral of the economy, which appears to be the final twist of your extortion game.

"I think those measures should allow you to understand that we have in our circle experienced people of your ilk. They know the games you play in 'disaster capitalism,' and how to defuse them. Remember, government created you through state charters, and we can re-create you in the way we like through federal charters. Your call."

Jasper Arrington, the hoary lawyer, also known as snake eyes, took the field for the Wall Street team.

"Clearly you all believe you are holding all the cards, given the tightness of time before the primaries. Your surmise is probably correct for the short run. But beware of pushing us too hard and gaining a Pyrrhic victory. You will have won the first round, but bear in mind what has happened to societies that deeply alienate and dispossess their business community, losing its irreplaceable skills and operational knowhow, which are essential in making the economy run smoothly.

"I know you folks say we can learn from looking back at the lessons of history so let me draw something out of the past. About 70 years ago, a prominent judge, Learned Hand, gave an address on liberty. He said, among other things, that liberty contains the sense that you may not be right all the time.

"In this spirit, our proposal is that, in case your two constitutional amendments turn out to be truly harmful to our country, you would agree to an expiration date after which the country can decide whether to renew, refine, or let the amendments expire in the light of their past experience. Add a six-year sunset provision for both, and we'll call off the dogs and go back to our business. We can't vouch for all the business lobbies concurring, but our forces represent most of the immediately deployable influence. We will, should you agree, hold a joint news conference to eliminate any ambiguity or any normal public doubt."

AAC Coordinator, Representative Ray Bray, looking around the room at his colleagues, absorbed enough silent language vibes to see that they needed to discuss this, so he declared a three-hour recess.

60 · Weighing the Wall Streeters' Proposal

ONCE INSIDE A SECURED ROOM, everyone started talking at the same time until their chair, Senator Elizabeth Dimasio, quieted them down. But before they could get down to business, there was a shocking interruption. Everyone's smartphones were ringing off the hook, to speak metaphorically. It was with news that three suicide bombers had attacked the U.S. embassy in Asfurastan, killing 35 Americans and native staff.

"One of our worst nightmares," exclaimed Senator Russell Swift. He was always quick to see the implications of unfolding events. "Here comes, along with the necessary responses, a lot of distraction and demagogy. However, we can face that situation later. We have to come to a quick decision on the Wall Streeter's new *quid pro quo*. I say, give them the expiration date clause. It will expire after the next presidential election, which they hope will bring a hardliner into office. I firmly believe in the people's strength, magnified in the new playing field created by these new laws we have already passed. When it comes time to renew the Constitutional Amendments, the people will be solidly behind it. I'm not concerned about them. What is worrying is the Wall Street crowd and their adjuncts. I sense the awakening of a sleeping giant, caught unawares by our precipitous assault on the system, which is now beginning to find its legs and its language of fear. We partly can stall this development by a timely compromise.

"Moreover, with a sunset provision, we're more likely to get the states to ratify, in that they realize this Constitutional amendment is temporary, subject to reversal if it proves problematic. Also, our passing the final bills will not have to overcome misleading ads and publicity with the Big Boys calling off the dogs here. Though I have no expectation that their baying packs won't resume at the state level, trying to hinder state passage of the amendments. That's what happened with the ERA."

He ended by calling for further input, beginning with, "So, what say the Cooperators?"

The group saw the wisdom of his words, and after some further debate and analysis, went back to the Wall Street gang with a statement. It was not that they agreed with the insertion of the sunset clause, but that they were willing to bring the proposal to their adherents and see how they reacted. If they were favorably disposed, then the Wall Streeters would get their clause.

Harmony had reigned among the assembled Cooperator representatives, but the next 24 hours were something again. First the proposal was floated over the mass media with the affirmation and explanations of the Cooperators and the AAC. It was going to be put to a vote.

"It is now up to you working on the state legislatures," the two groups averred in a joint statement. "If you don't like this six-year sunset provision, you can defeat it. It is fitting that the last judgment will be in your hands, state by state. You have been deliberating in small study groups on the importance of public campaign financing and Constitutional subordination of corporations to your rule. Our independent poll will commence immediately, as undoubtedly will those of the commercial pollsters. We urge a *yes* response. *Yes* will call the bluff of the Wall Streeters who think their deal will split our consensus and, given the economic turmoil, break up our phalanx into warring sides. We all — you and us — need to decide quickly. We await your wisdom."

The polls came back between two-to-one, and three-to-one in favor of the compromise, with ten percent undecided or having no opinion.

61 · A People's Celebration of a Job Well Done

THE BILLS WERE PASSED one day after another amidst a record outpouring of public demand, joy, and demonstrations. Even the inclusion of the sunset clause, which was an unexpected setback, hardly dampened the enthusiasm of the celebrants. One million people massed on the Mall to roar their support for what the large majority of Congress was passing on those especially historic last days. *In personam*, fact-based, and righteous lobbying had proven itself *unstoppable*, working all the way from inside Congress to the U.S.'s farthest reaches in Hawaii and Alaska. With so much left/right convergence back home, the losers in the Senate and House took it quite well, due in no small part to their relief over their sense that their willingness to compromise and the extraordinary amount of work accomplished in the last few weeks would improve their prospects in the upcoming primaries. For Congress could not be called out for inaction, gridlock, or being in thrall to the corporations anymore.

The President joined in the praise of the Senators and Representatives, their staff, and all the citizens who organized and pressed their national legislature into such long overdue enactments. He promised the "largest collective bill signing ceremony at the White House and its sprawling lawn in American history — right on Memorial Day." He added that that day was fitting, inasmuch as, with the passage of these game-changing bills, "the

elected representatives paid full tribute to the memories of our founders and the promise they held forth for these United States."

With unsurprising dispatch, the stock markets started to recover, and the economic projects, investments, and credit, so many of which were put on hold, were back in gear.

62 · Re-Girding Their Loins

THE WEARY WALL STREETERS and the Washingtonian lobbyists went on their vacations to rest and recover before initiating long-range strategic planning for the new era and the battles at the state level over the proposed Constitutional amendments that, let it be said, had received well over the required two-thirds vote in the Senate and the House of Representatives.

As for *The Stall Street Journal*, its lead editorial was titled, "Lo, the poor American people," and what followed was a list of premonitions featuring one forthcoming disaster after another and ending with the sentence, "Closing down the Republic and bringing on the chaos and instability of extremist democracy is no cause of celebration by any cerebral citizens."

With almost all the media attention on the winners, The Reporter, a contrarian as ever, wrote article after article on the losers. His commentary, along with his report, gauged the bitterness, backlash, and second-strike capabilities of those who might want to roll back the legislation in whole or in part. To his surprise, he found an eerie acceptance of their losses among the business class and its government associates. After all, The Reporter reflected, the people's victory did occur fair and square, without dirty tricks, or any autocratic blockage of their dissenting voices or the customary vituperatives that winners often hurled at the losers before their victory. The Reporter ended his observations with the question, "Can the overwhelming sense that the people collectively have spoken be ushering in a new tone and a new kind of belonging by Washington's politicians?"

Doug Colebrook and his colleagues were bone tired even as they knew their work was just the end of the beginning. Implementation was the challenge in the coming months as, if things went as they expected, citizen turnout would dwindle as people inevitably drifted away, and the normal rhythms of social life resumed. For the new democratic turn to take hold, it would be necessary for many new civic watchdog groups to engage. Fortunately, the new laws foresaw that, and the formation of such groups was facilitated under the People Empowerment Act. Although knowing they would have to come back soon enough, the modest Cooperators returned to their homes and to many deserved public recognitions.

63 · Rats Romp Again

DURING THE TEN-DAY RECESS, right after the bills were passed but well before the White House signing ceremonies, five 18-wheelers left their respective southeastern cities at midnight. They had previously rendez-voused in cities along the way, starting in New Orleans, to pick up their cargo: tens of thousands of hungry rats, male and female. After three nights of surreptitious travel, parking during the days at prearranged out-of-the-way farm driveways, they arrived at their destination — the Congressional complex of buildings.

Having trained and rehearsed rigorously, the drivers — Steve and the four Billys (Joe, Link, Phil, and Frank) — took up their positions, confident in their success and unafraid of being busted along the way. After all, they had each been advanced several thousand dollars, been provided with free attorneys in case they needed them, and had souped-up getaway cars ready for quick escape after they stranded the trucks at different points of entry to the Congress and its massive office buildings.

Their trucks were no ordinary vehicles. They were equipped with advanced telecommunications, radar — and catapults that would oper-ate silently to safely hurl the rats right next to the buildings in record time. Other long vehicles, loaded with fine bits of delicious rat snacks and water, would use mechanical apparati to spray the areas near the buildings, entrances, sewers, and other apertures with the tasty morsels to guide and entice the rodents into heading toward the Congressional underworlds. Another truck sprayed cat urine on the outside streets around the perimeter to discourage any rodents from roaming away from the building complexes.

All of this amazingly was accomplished between 3:00 a.m. and 3:30 a.m. The bare bones Capitol Police, relaxing after nightmarish weeks of overtime, were, shall we say, inattentive if not downright nodding off or snoozing. In case any of them became alert and started rushing toward the trucks, naked women and men were standing in convenient shadows, ready to walk out and be arrested for indecent exposure as totally shameless faux prostitutes, who would serve as useful decoys for the few minutes required to distribute the rats and their bait.

The infrared-videotaped operation came off smoothly. As soon as they hit ground, the rats were clambering over everything: stairs, chutes, grat-ings, and garbage containers, munching happily on the provided food. As the truckers and their assistants were getting into their cars and speeding away, the police started to appear. Their first actions were to accost the naked decoys, searchlights came on, sirens sounded. Meanwhile, the rats were momentarily granted free passage, the noise and disturbance extra incentives for them to jump down the nearest grating or other opening. By the time the cops paid attention to them, it was too late.

The venomous, big, pissed-off rich guy — who was watching from hundreds of miles away on his satellite TV — couldn't have been more pleased. Until, that is, in the morning, when he learned that an entirely different interpretation was being given by the media to the spectacle of returning rats, which he had taken care to videotape for further use. It wasn't long before he turned away with disgust over how his plans, so carefully implemented, had boomeranged.

It so happened that The Reporter, sound asleep at 4:30 a.m., heard his phone ringing insistently. Picking it up, he heard a low, mature voice tipping him off to what just occurred: "Rats everywhere around the Capitol. Friend, if you want a scoop, better get over here."

From long experience, The Reporter could usually tell whether calls like these were from cranks or reliable tips. This call sounded legit. Fortunately his apartment was three blocks from the Rayburn House Office Building. He leaped out of bed and was at the wild rat invasion scene in fifteen minutes. It was a wild scene. Police cars, fire trucks, ambulances, floodlights, blocked roads, and the first responders, all of whom, in The Reporter's view, were trying not to smile, laugh, or joke at the absurdity of it all.

He learned that other police cars were trying vainly to chase down the getaway cars, which seemed to have been driven by Indy 500 racers. Other cops were snooping for clues in the abandoned rented 18-wheelers. He also saw that the assembled crews were not making any effort to catch or kill the swarming, darting, disappearing rats. They were taking their stations, a couple kicking at the rodents, and waiting for the convoy of Exterminators to show why they were so named. Since neither lives nor property were at risk, and since they knew it was not part of their job description to go rat hunting, there was almost a festive air. The last few weeks had been pressured, what with the people's revolt and the nightmarish security demands they entailed. The Reporter sensed all this and approached some of the police and firefighters with questions:

"How's this compare to the first rat invasion earlier this year?"

The officer he'd approached, a burly fellow with a cruller in hand, was glad to answer him, "Well, it's a mystery how they got here. The earlier rats seemed homegrown, having been born underneath the buildings. These fellows seem to be immigrants. Could be someone with a nutty sense of humor dropped them off here?"

A firefighter, hooking a small axe to his belt, joined the conversation. "I wouldn't be surprised if someone's been spending a lot of money to get this far just to land a big joke. People will do anything for a laugh these days."

Another officer strolled over and spoke. "The way I see it, it's not aimed at the legislators. No one is in the Congress 'cause it is an official recess, so everyone went home for some R&R. That means whoever cooked up this crazy rat invasion didn't have any political objective. Or, if he did, he never consulted the Congressional calendar. Pretty bad timing, I'd say. The train has left the station."

A sergeant joined the group around The Reporter. He began with a literary reference. "As a reader of novels, my guess is that this is someone's idea of irony. A lot of novels end with the hero or the situation having come full circle. The originator of this new rat incursion could be thinking he was closing the book on this wild spring, the way it opened in the winter: rats out, rats in."

Eureka! The Reporter had his lead sentence. He took the sergeant's name so he could credit him, took some pictures of mice and men, and rushed back to his apartment to start writing.

> I've just returned from Capitol Hill where, around 3:00 this morning, a massive rat celebration took hold of the grounds. The rodents must have come from the grassroots of America: tens of thousands of them had been jammed into five 18-wheelers and then, arriving in our city, were catapulted to the earth and cement in and around all the buildings. Other trucks used high-pressure hoses to spread all kinds of food that rats love in the same area, which got them to openings that lead inside the buildings and their underground rat alleys. Needing no other prompting, the rats dived right in to their new home.
>
> All the trucks, after offloading, were abandoned by their drivers who took off in other cars and have not been located.
>
> Obviously, the staging of this entire rodent theater piece took lots of preparation, lots of successful secrecy, and gobs of money. For what?
>
> Well, after interviewing some of the police and firefighters on the scene, I've come to share their opinions that it's someone's idea of a celebration of rats to commemorate what their earlier cousins accomplished in jolting the Congress to stand up for the people. That someone wanted you, the people, to recognize that both 'we the rats' and 'we the people' did this all by ourselves.
>
> Of course, I can't prove my interpretation is correct, and the rats aren't talking. But what's just as remarkable are the streams of people who have been heading down to the Capitol grounds since dawn. They are coming, it seems, from every direction: Maryland, Virginia, even the District of Columbia, which is not known for joining in national events organized by outsiders. From what I saw, they are coming in ever-increasing numbers, people from all backgrounds and all ages wanting to join in the celebration of the rats who are finally getting their overdue recognition. It looks like the public plans on being there for a while. The food

carts and trucks are setting up shop in anticipation of a whole day of a dancing, singing, and speaking-to-each-other festival.

Stay tuned, your Reporter is racing back to the Capitol for more close contact, more eyewitness accounts …

64 · Party Time II

THE FAST-FORMING GRAND SCENE stumped all the reporters similarly arriving at the first branch of government and its spacious surroundings. None of them could identify what was behind it. Thousands of woman, men, and children were coming by the half hour. Who planned this turnout? Who had the credibility to make so many people believe that they had to be part of this historic celebration of the return of the rats!? A half dozen reporters huddled together to exchange speculations.

"Some super-rich guys probably set this up this shindig," said a guy from the *Daily Barnacle*.

"The same ones who delivered the rats after midnight," said another, the crack reporter from the *Washington Toast*.

"That's not credible," said the more skeptical fellow from the *Lie Busters Journal*. "We know it is very hard to get people out into the streets under any conditions and timetables. And this eruption of so many diverse, unconnected folks had no planning time at all."

"You old-timers have to get hip to the new social media," said an online journalist from *Media Hype*. "My guess is that a bunch of social media bloggers, who have been on this whole story for months, had an instant sense of what good theater and copy this would be. So they collaborated on announcing a full day of wild celebration. You know how fast these guys think and form meet-ups."

Whatever the ruminations of the media, the massing throngs were sprawling all over the grass and cement with uninhibited, happy spontaneity. They hardly cared who prompted the event. They were dancing with rats, between rats, and over rats. The rats themselves, zeroing in on the newly appearing food and water — had they entered paradise? — at first scurried this way and that way, avoiding the people while snatching at fallen food on the run. But it wasn't long before they realized that these were different kinds of humans than those they were used to. These folks were friendly and had no intention of chasing and hunting them down. Rats are fast learners and pick up cues very quickly. So, like pigeons, they flitted in between the people snatching food and drink here and there, and from the human viewpoint, seemingly having a great time. The photographers

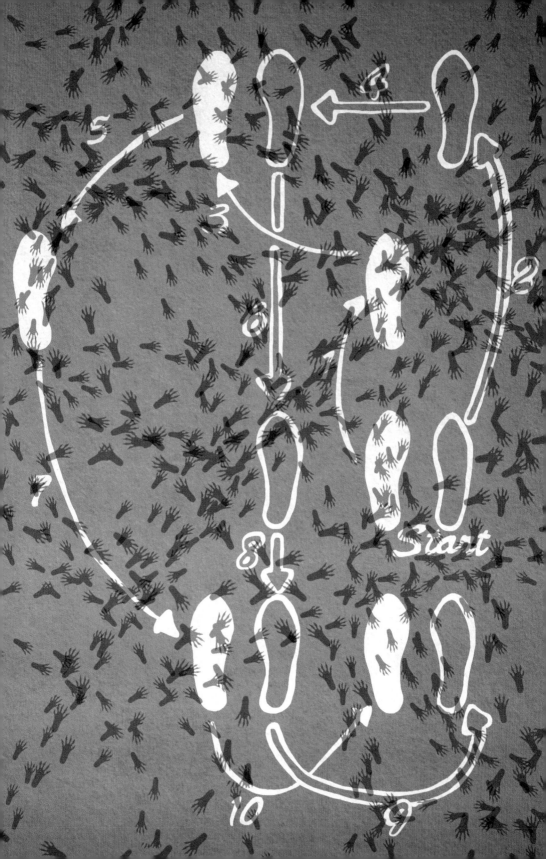

and video guys were having a field day catching some of the most amazing juxtapositions in modern visual history of humans and rodents.

Predictably, spontaneous speakers on soapboxes began popping up. A duet belted out something they called the "Rat Serenade," complete with guitar and drum. A more somber lady was carrying a basket of $2 bills, which she handed out while exclaiming: "Are you glad they showed up on July 4, 1776, to sign the *Declaration of Independence* from their cruel rulers? Now it's our turn to show up to control our rulers." (The $2 bill has Thomas Jefferson on one side and a picture of the founders on the other.)

Hundreds of dancing revelers plucked the $2 bills and held them aloft as they pranced in all directions. Others wore masks to allow fewer inhibitions, as had European medieval persons from all classes during the annual Feast of Fools. Possibly, some legislators or money men were concealed behind these disguises, people who didn't dare reveal to their colleagues that they were rather pleased at the people's (and rats') victories.

Even some of the police dove in, dancing away, and, when faced with slightly shocked glances from passersby, shouted, "Hey this is what community policing looks like!"

As the day wore on, soapbox orators focused more on the overall invasion of the rats. Animal rights advocates were quick to take advantage of a once-in-a-lifetime opportunity — the attention of a huge audience who were primed to recognize the amazing value of a hitherto despised species. Both past and present were evoked in the encomiums. One orator listed the legislative achievements of the rats, which were about to be signed into law by The President. While another provided an anthropological perspective, namely, that long ago on Easter Island in the Pacific, the natives considered rats a delicacy as well as a luxury, which evolved into rats becoming a means of mediation or barter between different clans. The speaker cited Canadian master media analyst Marshall McLuhan as the source of this information. Many people were fascinated, but the vegetarians drifted away the moment they heard the culinary part of the narrative.

All this activity was streamed or went viral and so the crowd swelled and spilled over from the immediate grounds and streets to the larger park-like areas next to the Senate Office Buildings, then onto the large Mall. Helicopters hovering above estimated the numbers heading toward two million, noting that they would present a huge security problem if they got out of control.

Not much chance of that. Too many troubadours, poets, and artists were doing their thing everywhere. As the day entered the afternoon, Doug Colebrook and his Cooperators came back to DC and spread out into the crowd. They soon learned that many of the people who were part of this massive turnout had participated in the events inside and outside of Congress following the rat invasions.

Meanwhile, the rat density was decreasing even as the human density was increasing. Fed and watered, the rats had reached satiety and were looking for quiet dark corners and subterranean sanctuaries where they could sleep or engage in intercourse with each other. As the rats diminished their numbers, some among the multitudes began heeding the appeal of several "soapbox" speakers, only, in this case, the "soapbox" was on the back of pickup trucks equipped with loudspeakers. They were calling on people to sign regally designed petitions. The lines to do so grew longer and longer. These scenes went viral and the electronic signatures from millions of watching citizens around the country poured into the collectors' computers.

65 · Tribute From a Grateful Nation

WHAT WERE THEY DEMANDING through those petitions?

That "A giant bronze statue of a rat in defiant, ferocious pose be erected on the capitol grounds, to be maintained in tiptop condition in perpetuity. The inscription on the base of the sculpture is to read: 'IN GRATEFUL MEMORY OF THE INTREPID RATS THAT FOLLOWED ONE ANOTHER INTO THE PRIVATE PLACES OF OUR LAWMAKERS AND LAUNCHED THE AMERICAN REVOLUTION 2.0!'"

And so it was duly built and dedicated on Thanksgiving of that year by The President and Congressional leaders before a large admiring crowd of grateful Americans who had already begun to benefit by the improvements in their livelihoods, their quality of life, and their prospects for a better future.

It was nearly midnight on that Thanksgiving eve, after the public had scattered, when a shadowy figure approached the statute and gave it a long, silent salute. It was Speaker Blamer.

And as he walked off, he could be heard whistling "The Times They Are A-Changin'."